INDIAN HISTORY CONGRESS MONOGRAPH SERIES

ESSAYS IN MEDIEVAL INDIAN ECONOMIC HISTORY

INDIAN HISTORY CONGRESS MONOGRAPH SERIES

ESSAYS IN MEDIEVAL INDIAN ECONOMIC HISTORY

Second Edition

Edited with an Introduction by
SATISH CHANDRA

INDIAN HISTORY CONGRESS
in association with

PRIMUS BOOKS
An imprint of Ratna Sagar P. Ltd.
Virat Bhavan
Mukherjee Nagar Commercial Complex
Delhi 110 009

Offices at
CHENNAI   LUCKNOW
AGRA AHMEDABAD BANGALORE COIMBATORE DEHRADUN GUWAHATI HYDERABAD
JAIPUR KANPUR KOCHI KOLKATA MADURAI MUMBAI PATNA RANCHI VARANASI

First published 1987
Second edition 2014

ISBN: 978-93-80607-58-0

Published by Primus Books

Laser typeset by Digigrafics
Gulmohar Park, New Delhi 110 049

Printed and bound in India by Replika Press Pvt. Ltd.

Contents

PART 1
Agriculture and Revenue

PART 2
Trade, Market And Currency

Preface to the Second Edition

The Indian History Congress has emerged as a representative organization for a large section of historians in India, providing its members with a forum to present their unpublished research work, using data from across the country. The annual sessions of the Indian History Congress are invariably attended by senior historians, who provide guidance to young researchers in their endeavours. In its multi-pronged activities, the Congress is perhaps one of the few organizations in India to provide a research and publication forum. To this end, it brings out an edited volume containing a selection of the research articles presented at various sessions. In fact, it is the meticulous selection of essays and rigorous editing of the volumes that has given cause for the University Grants Commission to recognize these proceedings to the level of a referred journal for the purposes of granting promotion to college and university teachers under the Career Advancement Scheme.

During its Golden Jubilee Celebrations in 1987, the Indian History Congress decided to publish three thematic volumes focusing on the Economic History of India. This three-volume set, entitled *Indian History Congress Golden Jubilee Year Publication Series* together contained over a hundred essays, with an introduction by eminent historians. The series met with much success, as it provided a panoramic view of 50 years of changing focuses and emphases of scholars on art, religion, and society and issues related to the historical roots of economic backwardness and the resultant economic under-development in India's colonial past.

These volumes on economic history were also important from another perspective. While inaugurating the first session of the Indian History Congress in 1935, Sir Shafa'at Ahmad Khan remarked that, 'economic history is almost a virgin field'. In the years following 1935, research in this area gathered depth and pace. In the subsequent decade and, in particular after Independence, considerable literature too was produced on the various aspects of the economic history of India. A nationalistic critique of colonialism during the process of decolonization was a major factor in developing interest in this topic. Meanwhile, since the mid-1950s the Marxist approach too gathered acceptance in the academic world of historians as an important factor in the explication of historical development. Together, the twin discourses of nationalist critique and Marxist approach became important contributory factors for a heightened interest in the economic aspects of India's historical past.

In challenging the imperialist historiography, Indian historians evolved considerable interest in studying society, religion, and art. They posited that Indian cultural past was essentially composite in nature and different communities lived side by side in a spirit of syncretism. In doing so, historians also examined the nature of religious identities and their role in shaping the contours of societal developments in our past.

Prints of the 1987 three-volume set were soon exhausted. Keeping in view their usefulness and steady demand among scholars as well as students, the Executive Committee of the 71st Session of the Indian History Congress, at University of Gour Banga, Malda, West Bengal, decided to reprint the three volumes, possibly with a new introduction by their respective editors.

To this end, I am grateful to Professor Satish Chandra, Professor Sabyasachi Bhattacharya, and Professor B.D. Chattopadhyaya for contributing substantial pieces for the new editions. And, it is indeed a pleasure to have these volumes released as a part of the preparations for the celebrations of the Platinum Jubilee Session of the Congress.

5 December 2013

SAIYID ZAHEER HUSAIN JAFRI
Secretary
Indian History Congress
Department of History
University of Delhi

Preface to the First Edition

THE EXECUTIVE Committee of the Indian History Congress at its meeting in Srinagar in 1986 had constituted the Golden Jubilee Celebrations Committee, which decided, amongst other things, to bring out a few thematic volumes containing articles published in the Proceedings of the Congress since its inception. Four volumes that are being brought out as part of the Golden Jubilee Celebrations deal with Indian art, religion, society and economy through the ages.

It may not be out of place to recall here the expectations of the founding fathers of Congress, Sir Shafa'at Ahmad Khan, the President of the first session in 1935, said: 'I have no doubt whatsoever that this body . . . is destined to play a momentous part in the building up of a vigorous school of Indian historians. . . . It knows no politics, it will not serve the interest either of our national life and thought propagandists who paint the glories of their country's past in a flamboyant language . . . nor will it support writers who are obsessed with prejudice and racial pride, have completely ignored those features which have maintained and preserved the continuity of our cultural life . . . I dread the prospect of long line of histories of India written by Muslims, Mahrattas, Sikhs, Bengalis and Pathans, each from their own point of view. . . . Should history be tied to the chariot wheels of perverted sectionalism which is now acting as a most serious obstacle to the growing nationalism of India on a whole?'

To what extent has the Congress, which has truly grown into an All-India body and is the largest organization of professional historians in the country, lived up to these expectations? The readers could perhaps look for an answer in the collections being presented here.

Each of these four volumes is preceded by short introduction from the editor, who has already provided the rationale of the concerned anthology. It is hoped that the series will reflect the commitment of the Indian History Congress to scientific and secular history and prove useful to all students of history.

I take this opportunity to thank Professor Satish Chandra of the Centre of Historical Studies, Jawaharlal Nehru University for taking up the responsibility of editing the present volume at a very short notice. On behalf of the editor as well as on my personal behalf, Dr. Muzaffar Alam, Associate Professor, Centre for Historical Studies, Jawaharlal Nehru University, is also to be thanked profusely for very significant help rendered by him. Dr. Bhairabi Prasad Sahu's unflinching help in proofreading is also gratefully acknowledged.

We are grateful to the Indian Council of Historical Research for making a handsome grant which has enabled us to meet partially the cost of publishing these volumes.

New Delhi
15 October 1987

D.N. JHA
Secretary
Indian History Congress

Introduction to the Second Edition

THIS COLLECTION of articles on economic history during the Medieval period from the thirteenth century to the middle of the eighteenth century, extracted from the articles printed in the *Proceedings of the Indian History Congress*, between 1935 and 1986, was prepared more than a quarter century ago. These articles still remain relevant, but are not easily accessible to serious students of history. Hence this present edition. However in the Introduction I have tried to highlight the main trends of economic history of Medieval India during the period, that is from 1986 to date.

It is evident that during the period the study of economic history has broadened and deepened. Papers, articles and books carry forward some of the earlier assumptions or postulates on economic development, but also question some of them. Also, they are often posed in the context of social structures. Cultural developments have also been studied in an economic context. . . . Thus, a holistic picture has begun to emerge.

In the field of agrarian history of India, focus has shifted from the study of administrative methods adopted by the central government for assessing and collecting land revenue, to how these measures operated at the local level, and their impact on different segments of village society. This has led to a deeper study of the structure of village societies, and the economic and social position and role of different sections there. Segmentation of village society has been worked out in some areas such as east Rajasthan. It has also been postulated that the economically stronger sections in village society—the zamindars and *khud-kasht*, played a definite role in expanding and improving cultivation. The richer section of the *khud-kasht*, were actively engaged in expanding cash crops and superior crops (*jins-i-kāmil*) and introducing new crops. However, these sections also largely appropriated the fruits of development in the area.

In this context, it has been noted that the sharecroppers (*muzāriān*) and the landless that formed together the majority of village population lived at the marginal or subsistence level. Among them, there was a process of rural migrations in search for better prospects. Some of these *pāhis* or landless which specially included the scheduled castes, did manage to get land in some areas, such as south Rajasthan. Elsewhere, when the state undertook bringing new land under cultivation, some of it was sometimes given to scheduled castes as a reward for their labour Thus, rural society was not totally unchanging.

Study on the role of towns, including small towns (*qasbas*) has shown that in many of the *qasbas*, specially those on or near major roads, artisans and traders formed a considerable section. Growth of *qasbas* reflected growth of rural society because some of the richer peasants also lived there.

Both Indian and foreign scholars have engaged themselves in the study of the structure of the state, and its role in the national economy. While the earlier assumption that the Medieval Indian state was inhibitive of economic development was discarded quite sometime back, according to some scholars it still remained a major obstacle to economic development. According to them, the state demand of revenue was so heavy, and its appropriation among the stakeholders was so lopsided, that it left little room for economic expansion. This view has been countered by another group of scholars. They consider the Medieval state, particularly the Mughal state, as being basically mercantilist in nature, with the feudal bureaucracy and the royal elements being commerce minded. Hence a fairly close nexus existed between them and the rising class of wholesale traders and financiers (*shroffs*). According to them, this was reflected in the large-scale use of the *hundi*—not only for trade but for financial transactions of the state, including land revenue collection.

This debate is carried forward to the eighteenth century: whether the economy continued to grow during the period, following the decline and fall of the Mughal Empire, or there was a setback in the process of developments, specially during the second half of the century? One view was that, development received a big set back with the East India Company's domination of Bengal and south India. Another view has been that despite some set backs the economic growth continued, largely till the early part of the nineteenth century. Apart from this controversy, study of economic developments of specific regions, such as Awadh and Bengal, Poona, etc., has been carried forward.

The discussion on the nature of the state and its role in economy has led to a study of (a) prices during the seventeenth century (sharp rise or stable?); (b) role of the rupee nationally and internationally; and (c) mints and their role in the growth of trade and economy.

Discussion about the role and character of the Mughal state—patrimonial bureaucratic or feudal bureaucratic, and the function and role has also raised questions about the nature and consequences of the concept of an agrarian crisis in the Mughal empire. It has been shown that agricultural production, or the extent of land under cultivation, did not decline. Nor was there any mass migration of peasants. Hence, the agrarian crisis been seen in the context of a developing social crisis whereby the rising class of zamindars and the *khud-kasht* tried to assert themselves, and sharply opposed Mughal revenue and administrative measures, leading to revolt against it in some areas. It has, however, been noted that while these revolts put pressure on the Mughal state, they were not able to open any new avenues of growth or change the existing system.

There has been emphasis on the study of the artisans—both those engaged in quality and export production, and those working at the local and village levels.

A new aspect which has opened up is women's studies. While a major focus of women's studies has been on their social position, and their cultural role, the position of women artisans, and women workers among the weaker section has received some attention. The position of better off women with respect to their property rights—housing, shops, land, etc., has also received some notice.

Another new field of study which has opened up is the study of mentalities. Such studies go forward from subaltern studies to a deeper study of the position and role of marginal sections, including tribals. Recent studies on mentalities have largely concentrated on the attitude and perceptions of the Mughal ruling class towards religious values, the ruler, and the lower classes.

Study on trade and economy has been furthered by the study of the role, structure and composition of the Indian trading classes: overland up to south Russia, and the sea up to Levant. The domination of the sea by foreign traders—Portuguese, French, Dutch, and their role in the economic, social and cultural developments of the country including boat-building has received attention. However, it has been noted that Indian traders remained active, either individually or in partnership of the Europeans. There were shipowners and large merchants among them. Hence they cannot be called peddlers.

Large-scale study of documents in various libraries is still a lacuna which, when made good, would further deepen and broaden the study of economic history of Medieval India.

5 December 2013   SATISH CHANDRA

Introduction to the First Edition

THIS COLLECTION of articles on economic history during the medieval period of Indian history, i.e. roughly from the thirteenth to the middle of the eighteenth century, has been made from the papers presented to the Indian History Congress in its annual conferences, and printed in its proceedings. The selections cover a period of 50 years, from the inception of the Indian History Congress in 1935. This *festschrift* which marks the Golden Jubilee of the Indian History Congress in a way highlights the growth of historiography in the country during the last 50 years for the Congress has undoubtedly been the most representative gathering of Indian historians during the period.

While historiography in India has developed largely on account of its inner dynamics and the situation within the country, it has never been isolated from the main currents of the development of historiography in the world. Thus, after World War I, it was deeply influenced by German historiography which was then strongly entrenched in the academia of western universities. Indirectly, German historicism strengthened the Indian tendency towards exceptionalism because it was deeply suspicious of theory and lacked a world view. Nevertheless, the methodology of critically sifting facts developed in the west, helped Indian historians in establishing a fairly reliable chronology on the basis of a critical study of contemporary texts. While political history remained the primary focus of study, some valuable work was done in understanding the working of administrative institutions, and of the state. Land revenue administration was obviously a primary focus of study. A few excerpts from these are represented in the present collection.

The end of World War II which was marked by a visible decline in the power and influence of the imperialist states; the end of colonialism and the emergence of a series of independent states in Asia, Africa, the Caribbean, etc., the victory of the Soviet Union and the rise of a number of socialist states in the world saw the rise of radically new trends of historiography in the West. Since these new trends have been pinpointed in Barraclough's masterly study for Unesco, I need not dwell upon them here. However, the changes in outlook and approach are, perhaps, not as radical as might have been postulated. While political history no longer enjoys the primacy it did earlier, and an interdisciplinary approach considered normative, the deep-seated Eurocentric bias has remained. In fact, it has been replaced by a new syndrome—the centre-periphery syndrome, with the western world at the centre, and the rest of the world doomed to remaining the periphery.

While quantitative methods, micro-studies based on socio-anthropological methodology, total history including influence of climate, geography, demography, etc., have been popularized during the period, the influence of Marxist historiography has steadily grown. In the process, Marxist historiography itself has been developed and refined, in relation both to Europe and the non-European world. The attempt to apply the Marxist methodology by Indian historians to the Indian situation is a part of this broader process.

It was in response to these worldwide factors, as also developments within India, that there was a steady growth in the number of papers on economic history presented to the Indian History Conferences during the late fifties, and the sixties. These increased further in the 70s, as also the range of the topics. This new change was also reflected in the establishment of the journal, *Indian Economic and Social History Review* in 1964. It is necessary to underline this because some of the papers on economic history, marking a new break which were first presented at the annual conferences of the Indian History Congress were, on many occasions, first printed in the *Indian Economic and Social History Review,* and only reported in the *Proceedings of the Indian History Congress.* The starting of the *Indian Historical Review* by the Indian Council of Historical Research in 1974, the publication of *Medieval India Miscelleny* by the Aligarh Muslim University, to name only a few, served a similar purpose. Such papers have not been included in the present collection.

The shift towards economic and social history was accompanied by a trend towards regional history. For the purpose, local material including literary and epigraphical sources, were sought to be utilized. In a few cases quantitative methods were also sought to be applied. This also marked a definite shift from the study of policies to the working of the revenue system, and its impact on the lives of the people and on the developmental processes in specified regions of the country. Hence, there is a shift from a study of revenue system to pattern and trends of agricultural production, the role of local elements including *madad-i-ma'ash* holders, and institutions in agricultural expansion and improvement, incidence of rural taxes, etc. This is reflected in the articles on agriculture and revenue presented to the History Congress from the mid-1960s and in the present selection. In this connection, it may be noted that the article 'The Jagirdari System of Maharaja Ranjit Singh in the Light of His Orders' does not strictly fall within the scope of the medieval period as defined. However, it has been included in the medieval section as it shows continuity with the system introduced by the Mughals, and practised in different parts of the country before the introduction of a new system developed under British aegis.

The papers under the heading 'Trade, Market and Currency' further the trend towards detailed regional or local study. It also marks growing interest in urban studies, and in the structure and role of the business community in India, in relation to the growth of the economy, especially the growth of money economy in India, and its relationship to the State. A number of articles deal with coinage and mints which represent a new field of study. A number of papers reflect the growing interest in the study of the Asian trade network, and the role played in it by traders of different regions. Behind all these is the assumption that India was by no means a static society. The processes and direction of change, as also the precise nature of the European impact on this developing economy, and the interplay of the forces which led to its incorporation into the emerging capitalist world system are, however, subjects of study, research and controversy. The development of credit and currency including the mints is another field of study. A number of papers deal with the international debate on the impact of the European trading companies and their system of armed trade and monopoly on the Indian economy and the Indian business community.

Before I close, I apologize for any omissions or commissions that may be found in the list of the articles presented here. As I have explained above, the selection has been made only out of the articles printed in full in the Proceedings. Effort has been made to make the articles as representative as possible, covering both the 50 years of development as also history writing in different regions of India. No effort has been made to tamper with the spelling of place names, persons or technical terms adopted at different times. Printing mistakes, or obvious slip-ups have, however, been silently corrected.

Satish Chandra

PART 1

Agriculture and Revenue

1

Sources of Revenue
Under Firoz Shah Tughluq

Riazul Islam

THE LEIT-MOTIF of Firoz Shah's administration was religious. It was his earnest desire to conduct the government of the realm in accordance with the principle of Shariat. *Futuhat-i-Firoz Shahi* which is the best guide to the working of the mind of Firoz Shah bears ample testimony to his religious zeal.

In the sphere of taxation, Firoz Shah abolished all taxes that were not permitted by the Shariat. *Sirat-i-Firoz Shahi*,[1] *Futuhat-i-Firoz Shahi*[2] and *Tabqat-i-Akbari*[3] give somewhat similar lists of the taxes that were so abolished. A few not mentioned in the above books are given by Afif[4] and Ainul-Mulk Mahru.[5] The details of taxes that were abolished are not of interest to us here. Two points, however, demand enquiry, first as to when the abolition was affected and second how far it was effective.

The date of the completion of *Sirat* is 712,[6] though an incident of the year 776 is recorded therein on pp. 39–40. So the abolition would have taken place at the latest by 772 (or 776). Afif gives the date of the abolition as 777, after a deep change had come over Firoz and he had got himself shaved. Mahru says that certain taxes were abolished by Mohd. B. Tughluq and the abolition was endorsed by Firoz. So we cannot arrive at any definite conclusion though we may just hazard the conclusion that the abolition may have been in 772 and 777. A cryptic reference in Barni[7] suggests that the policy may have been initiated in the early years of the reign. I am personally of the opinion that the taxes were abolished early in the reign to reconcile public opinion and restore confidence among the people.

There is not much to help us to determine how far the abolition was effective. Most of the abolished taxes are urban and it is probable that their abolition would have been effective in provincial capitals. In other terms it would have been a mixed success. All that we get in contemporary literature is a reference to a complaint against the local officials collecting an unauthorised cess.[8]

*7th Session at Madras, 1944.

Kharaj: It occurs in *Futuhat* (p. 6) as *Kharaj Araaz Ushur* and Dr. I.H. Qureshi has rendered it as the Kharaj from tithe-paying lands. My own reading of the phrase is *Kharaj Araazi wa Ushur.* It has to be kept in mind that Firoz Shah is here enumerating the Shari taxes of which Kharaj and Ushur are distinct units. The matter is set at rest by *Sirat*, p. 124 where the parallel passage runs as 'Kharaj of land, Jezia, Zakal' Ainul-Mulk also speaks of Kharaj and Ushur as alternatives.[9]

Now Kharaj is the revenue-demand levied by the state from the peasants directly or through the muqaddams and the rais. Barni (p. 554), uses the word in the general sense of a tax, but the technical sense is the same as explained above. The demand was settled by 'the rule of the produce' according to Barni (p. 574). According to Afif, however, as interpreted by Moreland[10] it was settled by the rule of inspection. The phrase (Hukm-i-Mushahida) may be taken to mean something different, when it is read with the reference to the context. The whole sentence may be translated as 'Khwaja Hisamuddin Junaid toured the territories of the realm for 6 years and settled the demand by personal inspection or observation'.

The reverened Khwaja determined the valuation (the entire revenue demand) at 6 3/4 crore tankas. Firoz forbade the officials to trouble his subjects with extra demands (Muhaddas) and enforcement of demand in case of crop failure (Nabudha) and the like.[11]

The rate of assessment is nowhere mentioned. We can only conjecture that the rate would have been equitable under a benevolent monarch like Firoz. Dr. I.H. Qureshi's contention that the rate was 20% seems to be unconvincing as it is based on the disputed phrase *Kharaj Araazi Ushur.* Probably the rate would not have been so low.

Ushur: No records exist to show the existence of Ushur or tithe-paying land in India at this period. Mention of Ushur occurs, however, in *Futuhat,* Afif and *Munshat-i-Mahru.*[12] Firoz Shah may have referred to it, like Aurangzeb,[13] simply because it was so important an item of Islamic fiscal system even though it had no practical application in India. Afif's reference to it occurs in a strange context which gives it an entirely different meaning. He says that Firoz Shah ordered a certain indigent person to be given one tanka daily from the 'Ushur and Zakat of the City (Delhi)'. This would suggest that Ushur was some urban or octroi impost, though the possibility remains that there were tithe-paying lands in the vicinity of Delhi. Ainul-Mulk's reference to it is simply theoretical and leads us nowhere. He simply says, 'the Wazifa-land is either Kharaj-paying or tithe-paying.'

Zakat: The context in which it is mentioned in *Futuhat* and *Sirat* would lead one to believe that it was the Zakat of Muslim law, i.e. 1/40 of the income which every Muslim has to part with annually. But actually by this time Zakat has already assumed an entirely different import. It had come to mean the import and octroi duties and it is always in this sense that this term is used in contemporary and later literature.

Ainul-Mulk and Afif's[14] reference to Zakat are very clear. In a letter to Jalaluddin (Sadri-Jahan of Firoz Shah's reign) he says that out of regard for him he had not levied Zakat on the horses which were brought for him.

Afif says that goods of merchants were brought to the Sarai adl and Zakat was levied there on them. At another place (p. 449) Afif speaks of the Zakat of the City which obviously means the octroi duties of Delhi.

Jezia-i-Hunud: By Jezia here is obviously meant the tax taken from non-Muslims or Zimmis.[15] The authorities of Firoz's reign, however, differ as to the mode of its collection. But the differences are adjustable. Afif (p. 383) speaks of it as poll-tax and says that there were three grades of Jezia in Delhi—40, 20 and 10 tankas per head. It is, however, just possible that Jezia was levied as a poll-tax only in Delhi or urban areas. For Barni (p. 574) speaks of Jezia (as well as Kharaj) being levied according to 'the rule of the produce' thus giving it the character of a tax on produce and not per capital. This is partially corroborated by Ainul-Mulk who in a letter of Firoz's reign speaks of Jezia and the agricultural revenue of a village being assigned to a soldier who had accompanied Firoz on the Lakhauti campaign.

It can therefore be inferred with considerable probability that Jezia was levied as a poll-tax in the urban areas and on produce (Hukm-i-Hasil) in the rural areas. I need not narrate here the story[16] of Firoz having imposed Jezia on the religious classes, 'the key to the chamber of infidelity', for it is well known.

Tarakat: Tarakat means the property left by a person without any heir and without any will to determine its distribution. Such property was attached by the state. But as Aghnides remarks, it is 'a source of negligible importance'.[17]

The case of the riches left by Imadul-Mulk Bashir may be noted here, although it does not come under this heading for he left a son. This Imadul-Mulk had amassed a huge wealth, by means, which, from Afifs and Mahru's[18] references, do not appear to be praiseworthy. He left thirteen crores of hard cash after him. Firoz took 9 crores out of this to himself, saying 'what is Bashir's is mine'. The argument, however, had no legal force because Bashsir had got himself manumitted when 'he grew old and infirmity set in his bones' (Afif, 444).

Khams-i-ghanaim: It is the fifth of the spoils. 'The Shariat requires that 1/5 should be appropriated by the state and 4/5 distributed amongst the warriors; in this matter the injuction had been completely reversed.'[19] Firoz restored the Shari proportion. It may be pointed out that very few wars were waged in the long reign of Firoz. Of these few the two expeditions to Lakhnauti ended in compromise. The Thata campaign brought tremendous loss and suffering. The Jajnagar hunting expedition would not have brought much booty as Firoz lost his way on return march. So the change of proportion would not have mattered much for the Divan, though it may have in some measure augmented the soldiers' propensity for loot.

Khams-i-Maadin: It is the state's share of the mines. The word Khams (one-fifth) is probably attached to Maadin as well as spoils, for according to the Hanafites the mines are to be treated as spoils and the state's share of both is one-fifth. The other schools of theology treat the state's share as a kind of a Zakat and accordingly put it at one-fortieth.[20] But these schools had never a large following in India.

Mines, however, find mention only in *Futuhat, Sirat* does not include it in the list of legal taxes. *Sirat,* on the other hand, has 'Luqtat' which is not mentioned by *Futuhat.* Luqtat may be a plural of Luqta which means any thing that is picked up from the street. Such things if unclaimed were, it appears, given over to state-treasury. In any case it would not have been an important source of income. Luqtat is not mentioned by Aghnides.

The above are the taxes which are permitted by the Shariat and which according to Firoz's claims in *Futuhat,* were the only sources of state's income. *Presents,* which were a considerable source of income in previous reigns, lost that character. For the value of presents brought or sent annually by the Governors was deducted from the demand of the revenue ministry against them.[21]

Haqq-i-Shirb or 'Water-perquisite': Technically this need not be discussed here, for the income under this head did not occur to the state-coffers but was given over to the Privy Purse of Firoz. But it is an allied topic and a few words be said about it.

When the question was put before the assembly of Ulema and Mashaikh regarding Haqq-i-shirb, they said 'The man who takes pains and makes effort (to dig canals) is entitled to 10 per cent.'[22] There is no reference as to what this 10 per cent constituted. Dr. I.H. Qureshi's conjecture, (pp. 225–27), that the 10 per cent was levied on the gross produce and the remainder distributed between the suite and the peasant is the only sound interpretation. It need be added that even if the 10% was levied on the gross produce, the state and the peasant would yet be not losers. Rather both would be getting a share, even though small, out of the additional produce due to irrigation. A simple calculation would confirm this.

A disputed point in the fiscal system of Firoz is Mahsul-i-Muamlati.[23] Moreland treats it as a tax and says that he did not find any parallel passage to indicate its meaning. I.H. Qureshi also says that the phrase is unique in Barni's writings. But he interprets it otherwise. He breaks up the phrase, interprets Muamlat as transaction and translates the sentences. 'In the matter of revenue they were content to adopt an assessment, so that the peasant...' I support the interpretation of Dr. Qureshi, adding only this much that Muamlat occurs quite frequently in Afif and Barni.[24] A comparision of the various contexts would give its meaning as demand, Kharaj. Its dictionary meaning also is Kharaj, tax.

The question whether the revenue from these limited number of sources was sufficient for the running of administration is an interesting one. But it does not come under the purview of this article.

Notes

1. *Sirat-i-Firoz Shahi*, Aligarh copy, p. 124.
2. *Futuhat-i-Firoz Shahi*, Aligarh edn. p. 6.
3. *Tabaqat-i-Akbari* of Khwajah Nizamuddin Bakhshi, p. 240.
4. Afif, Tarikh-i-Firoz Shahi, *pp. 74–79*.
5. *Munshat-i-Mahru* of Ainul-Mulk Mahru, Aligarh copy, p. 97.
6. *Sirat*, last but one page.
7. Barni, *Tarikh-i-Firoz Shahi*, p. 554. "The merchant is the master of his merchandise and buys and sells as he likes and does not pay any Kharaj. The merchants earn 100 and 200 tankas daily and do not pay a single tanka as tax."
8. This occurs in a letter of Ainul-Mulk, p. 60 written in the time of either Mohd. Tughluq or Firoz Shah. In any case it is significant.
9. "This Wazifa land is either Kharaj-paying or tithe-paying", *Munshat*, p.77.
10. Moreland, *Agrarian System of Muslim India*, p. 232; Afif, p. 94.
11. *Sirat*, p. 124. Bami, 574, Muhaddas means "taxes over and above the stipulated taxes".
12. *Futuhat*, p. 6. Afif p. 449. *Munshat-i-Mahru*, p. 77.
13. Moreland, pp. 139–40, "We are given detailed rules which were almost irrelevant in India . . . . the firman stresses the distinction between tithe-land and tribute-land, but I have failed so far to find a single case of tithe-land existing in India."
14. *Munshat*, p. 73; Afif, p. 375.
15. Firoz Shah also speaks of Jezia as *Zar-i-Zimma, i.e.* money levied from Zimmis. *Futuhat*, p. 11.
16. Afif, pp. 382–84.
17. Aghnides, *Mohommadan Theories of Finance*, p. 422.
18. Afif, pp. 441, 445, Mahru, pp. 96–97, attributes the ruin of Multan's prosperity to Imadul-Mulk.
19. *Futuhat, p.* 6. The reversion of proportion took place probably in Alauddin's time. The step, however, was not totally unjustified. See *Fuluhal-i-Firoz Shahi*, trans, and notes, p. 33.
20. Aghnides, pp. 413–14.
21. Afif, pp. 268–69.
22. Ibid., p. 130.
23. Barni.p. 574. Moreland has translated it as "And a reduction was made in the Mahsul- i-Muamlati..."
24. Afif, pp. 432, 442, 472, 579.

2

Revenue System of Sher Shah

Satish Chandra Misra

'THE LAND revenue system of Upper India', writes Moreland, 'presents a fundamental continuity from the period when the sacred law of Hinduism was formulated, down to the changes introduced in the nineteenth century.'[1] A critical appraisal of the present available data shows that this tradition continued unbroken through the Sur period, and though he modified it in some respects, Sher Shah made no attempt to alter basically, the method of assessment, the mode of payment and the share that the state took from the cultivator's produce.

It has been generally stated that Sher Shah adopted the method of measurement as the basis of his assessment and enforced it throughout his dominions in suppression of the other existing systems.[2] If by the word 'Jarib' which has been commonly used by the chroniclers, and which has been translated as 'Measurement' by the modern writers, it is meant that Sher Shah ordered a general mensuration and on this basis assessed land revenue, the statement can be accepted. If, however, the word 'Jarib' is translated to prove that the entire system of revenue administration was radically changed to supplant systems other than 'Measurement' and the method of payment changed from kind to cash, then the observation is hardly tenable.

First, Sher Shah did not and had he wished it even, could not abolish old existing systems of revenue administration. It was a task beyond the five-year rule granted to him. Akbar waited, and gathered experience for nineteen years before he could reorganise his revenue system on a fresh basis. Till that time he adopted the prevalent schedules of Sher Shah, only demanding cash in place of kind[3] which incidentally proves that the basis of payment till then was kind.

Hasan Khan mentions three systems of revenue administration prevalent in the country.[4] He furnishes details of only one, according to which a person called 'Malguzar' was held responsible for an allotted area from which he collected land revenue, paying a fixed sum in lieu thereof to the state. Due care was taken by the state to prevent over-charging and oppression.[5] This system

*15th Session at Gwalior, 1952.

bears a close resemblance to the 'Zemindari' and 'Malguzari' systems till recently prevalent in Uttar Pradesh and Madhya Pradesh. Obviously in such areas, where this system was prevalent, 'Jarib' or 'Measurement' was not enforced in its sense of cash payments directly realised from individual cultivators by the state. The two other systems, which go by default in Hasan Khan's account, were also clearly old-established ones, which were not interfered with by Sher Shah except for regularizing the procedures and mapping out the land and classifying the tenures and ownerships under which a particular piece of land was held.[6]

Lastly, there were exceptional areas where new ideas could not have been and were not introduced. In Multan, for instance, the traditional assessment and administration was allowed to continue.[7] It would have been scarcely possible to realise any revenue from trans-Jhelum area (Ghakkarland) or Rajputana. In Malwa, the zemindari system was allowed, though the land might have been mapped, for Shujaet Khan is reported to have been rebuked by Sher Shah for withholding lands allotted to his lieutenants.[8]

Therefore though Sher Shah might have had a decided preference for the system of measurement, he did not press his choice except in areas where the system could be worked without handicapping the cultivator. The peasant enjoyed the freedom of choosing any of the prevalent method of assessment, though his rights over his land were clarified and the field mapped. He was freed from the vexatious extortions of the muqaddams and other petty functionaries, the Amin contacting him directly to assess his revenue according to the system he preferred.[9]

Sher Shah was no doubt trying to extend the sphere of king's authority and therefore desired a wider application of measurement. Islam Shah continued the work of his father and under him the administration became more centralised than ever.[10] So it seems to have been Islam Shah who was responsible for what Abu'l Fazl calls, freeing Hindustan from the systems of *ghalla-bakshi* and *muqtei*.[11] He had more time than his father, he was more disregardful of the established usages, the nobles as a landowning power collapsed under his rule and their place was taken by the king's bureaucracy.

The above observation also applies to the second problem, namely the mode of payment. The system was based on the produce reaped and the basis of assessment was grain or other produce. The schedule of Sher Shah given in the *A'in* has kind as its basis and not cash as Akbar's later schedules have.[12] The slate's share could be converted into cash by selling it according to market rates or the cultivator if he chose, for the time being, could pay cash in lieu of his share of his produce. This was encouraged by the state.

The third question, *viz.*, the amount of the share which the state took is the most complicated. Dr. Qanungo and Dr. Qureshi believe that Sher Shah took one-fourth of the produce while Dr. Saran and Moreland are of the opinion that the state's share was one-third.

Dr. Qanungo adduces the following arguments for his statement:

(a) *Makhzan-i-Afaghanan* has it that Sher Shah wrote to Haibat Khan to take 1/4th of the produce from Multan.

(b) Abu'l-Fazl writes, 'The revenue levied by Sher Khan which at the present day is represented in all provinces as the lowest rate of assessment'. Later Abu'l-Fazl writes that Akbar raised the land revenue to 1/3rd. Hence in Sher Shah's times, it must have been only 1/4th.[13]

Moreland refutes the arguments given above:

(a) The above passage (*Makhzan* quoted by Dr. Qanungo) is found in page 135 of part I of Dorn, who writes that Sher Shah who was naturally elated at the conquest of that region, 'exempted Multan from all public charges, except a fourth of the produce which was to be levied.' A more literal translation of the Ms. used by him (No. 60 in Morley's Catalogue of the R.A.S.), would be, '(he) ordered that a fourth share should be taken from the country of Multan, it being exempted from all 'takalif.' The last word has a wide range of meaning from troubles to taxes, but in this context it means cesses or miscellaneous imposts. Multan thus received specially favoured treatment and the fact that the revenue demand was there fixed at one-fourth does not justify the inference that the same fraction was taken from the rest of the kingdom.

(b) In the second argument, Dr. Qanungo has relied on Jarrett's version of the *A'in*, but had he referred the original, he would have found that his version is rather loose. The text says, 'In all provinces at the present day less than that is not indicated', the word "that" referring to a Schedule of Sher Shah's assessment rates: in other words, the assessment when the *A'in* was written, were not Sher Shah's; they might have been equal or greater and the passage cannot be used to prove that they were greater. No statement to the effect that they were raised by Akbar to one-third appears on page 66 of Jarrett nor can Moreland find them elsewhere.

Continuing, Moreland uses the words of Abbas as given in Elliot's translation and which are not found in any of the available Mss., and the Schedule of Sher Shah given in the *A'in* to prove that Sher Shah claimed one-third of the gross produce as the king's share and assessed the claim by measurement on the basis of an average yield determined separately for each crop.[14]

Dr. Saran agrees with Moreland in his conclusions and suggests that the text of *A'in* at this passage clearly says that the 'ray" of Sher Shah found acceptance. So whatever rates were prevailing and were approved by the

Emperor were those which had come down from Sher Shah's time. Hence, Akbar's rates at this time were equal to those of Sher Shah. Dr. Saran then discusses the meaning of the word 'ray" and comes to the conclusion, on basis of the Schedule, that Sher Shah claimed one-third of the produce.[15]

Dr. Qureshi gives the following reasons for his opinion that Sher Shah charged one-fourth of the produce as land revenue.

(a) The passage in Elliot (to which Moreland refers) is based on some exceptional Ms. of 'Abbas Sarwani and is not supported by the versions of the available ones.

(b) A critical study of the passage in *A'in* shows that Abu'l-Fazl is referring to Sher Shah's figure of average produce as the lowest available in the kingdom at the time.

(c) The favour to Multan lay in exempting it from a number of taxes and not in the reduction of land revenue.

(d) There is clear evidence to show that it was Akbar who first demanded a third as land revenue. Timur demanded a third in some of his dominions and Babur demanded a hundred and thirty instead of a hundred. Sher Shah's demand was not exceptional and it was raised by Akbar which Abu'l-Fazl seeks to justify by saying that Akbar abolished various other taxes including jiziyah.[16]

There are three passages in the authorities which furnish a clue to the revenue demand of Sher Shah. Hasan Khan writes, 'The principle (regarding revenue assessment) is that the government demand should be less than the income accruing from the land so that they (the cultivators) might not be afraid of government demand and tax if there is scarcity of water or insufficiency of rains. Rather he arranged that everyone of the landholders and payers of revenue should pay 2½ per cent of their tax to the public treasury so that it might be spent in case of accidents or heavenly punishments.'[17]

This is general. It indicates only the principle of revenue assessment and the fact that 2½ per cent of the revenue was held as a reserve for exigencies.

The second passage is the one in Elliot's rendering of *Tarikh-i-Sher Shahi*, to which Moreland refers. It runs as follows, 'having for its context, a discussion of the pargana officials under Sher Shah.'.... and he ordered the governors to measure the land at every harvest and collect revenue according to measurement in proportion to the produce, giving one share to the cultivator and half to the mukkaddams and fixing the assessment with regard to the kind of grain in order that mukkaddams and Chaudharies should not oppress the cultivators who are the support of the prosperity of the kingdom.[18] The word 'governor' and the continuing 'giving one share to the cultivator and half to the mukkaddams' has no equivalence in the available Mss. of *Tarikh-i-Sher Shahi*. It has led

Moreland to label it as an 'incorrect gloss' though he remarks that it accords with the Schedule in the A'in.

The passage is in fact rather confusing. It postulates the universal prevalence of the system of *ghalla-bakhshi* or division of grains as the basis of revenue administration, for such a rule of thumb could not operate under measurement.[19] Though the former system may have extended over considerable areas it could not have been the only one. It is with caution, therefore, that the passage may be used to represent the revenue which the state realised from areas where the malguzari and the *ghalla-bakhshi* systems prevailed.

Therefore, it also does not deserve the scorn with which Dr. Qureshi treats it, for even if it comes from an exceptional Ms, it equates with what Hasan Khan writes regarding malguzari and what Abu'l-Fazl gives with reference to Sher Shah's Schedule.

This Schedule is the third important piece of information. It is reproduced in original below (in the footnote)[20] and Jarrett translates it as follows: "Of the first two kinds of land, there are three classes: good, middling and bad. They add together the produce of each sort and a third of this represents the medium produce, one-third of which is exacted as the royal dues. The revenue levied by Sher Khan, which at the present day is represented in all provinces as the lowest rate of assessment, generally obtained; and for the convenience of the cultivators and the soldiery, the value was taken in ready money."[21]

Dr. Qureshi considers the translation to be incorrect. In the first place, he thinks the stops to have been wrongly read, the passage being read without a stop after *Zaboon*, which translates as: 'Of the first two kinds of land, the good, the middling and bad produce should be added together and a third of this represents the medium produce . . . .'. For the second part, he believes that the translation of the word 'ray' as 'revenue' is wrong since it is only recently that the word has figuratively come to mean this. Its older connotation was that of 'produce' and it is in this sense that it has been used by Abu'l-Fazl. The correct translation of the latter portion therefore is, 'The (figures of mean) produce adopted by Sher Shah, lower than which cannot be found throughout the provinces, were accepted and for the convenience of etc.'[22]

Abu'l-Fazl is refers here of the classification of land by Akbar into polaj, parauti, chachar and banjar. It appears that the first part of Dr. Qureshi's amendation is correct, for as he writes, his interpretation of finding the average produce is more logical. His second verification is doubtful. How is it possible for the figures of 'mean produce' to have been 'lower than which cannot be found throughout the provinces' unless the years concerned had been those of exceptional scarcity? And such does not appear to have been the case in the reign of Sher Shah. It cannot be supposed that the figures had been deliberately altered to provide a lower level than actual. It appears therefore that Abu'l-Fazl is using the word 'ray' in the sense of revenue and means that, "The revenue levied by Sher Khan, lower than which cannot be found throughout the provinces, was accepted and for the convenience of etc., etc."

Abu'l-Fazl goes on to give tables which are apparently those of Sher Shah. These were generally accepted as the basis of land revenue before the 19-Year Settlement. Until then, Akbar's only modification was to demand cash instead of kind. The full and fresh evaluation which resulted in the 19-Year Settlement and for which also Abu'l-Fazl gives figures, changed this state of affairs.

The estimate here clearly is of one-third. It was due to this fact that Akbar did not raise the land demand except in some cases where he imposed extra cesses.[23] It is also obvious that Sher Shah also charged the same fraction (one-third) of the produce as land revenue.

Multan, certainly, was a special case and was treated as such. It cannot be held up as an example for the rest of the kingdom.[24] For here the Langah tradition was ordered to be continued by Sher Shah and the revenue balance was not altered to bring it into line with other provinces. It is difficult, therefore, to accept Dr. Qureshi's statement that the respite granted to Multan consisted only of cesses.

Lastly, as Dr. Qureshi himself states, Sher Shah's demand was not unusual. Babur demanded a hundred and thirty instead of a hundred and as this tradition could hardly have been disturbed by Humayun, it is scarcely possible that Sher Shah would have cut down this most fruitful source of state income. I have failed to discover the statement in the *A'in* to which he refers in saying that Akbar raised a demand to a third;[25] even if such a statement exists, and Akbar did raise the demand, it does not follow that Sher Shah's demand was a fourth which was raised to a third by Akbar. The difference might have been insignificant and what is more likely, the rates might have dropped in the chaos that followed the death of Islam Shah.

Notes

1. W.H. Moreland, 'Sher Shah's Revenue System', *Journal of the Royal Asiatic Society*, 1926, p. 448.
2. The various modes of revenue assessment and the terms as *jarib, muqtei, ghalla-bakhshi,* and *nasq* have not been explained in this paper for they have been adequately discussed and defined by various writers on the subject, namely, *Some Aspects of Muslim Administration* by Dr. R.P. Tripathi, pp. 357–60; *Provincial Government of the Mughals* by Dr. P. Saran. pp. 453–56; 'Sher Shah's Revenue System' by Dr. P. Saran, *Journal of the Bihar and Orissa Research Society*, vol. XVII, I, pp. 137–40; 'Assessment and Collection of Land Revenue under Akbar' by Dr. S.R. Sharma, *Indian Historical Quarterly*, vol. XIV, pp .701–36, 'Farhang-i-Kardani' by Prof. S. A. Rashid, *Proceedings of the Indian Historical Records Commission*, vol. XIX, pp. 71–74; "Sher Shah's Revenue System' by Moreland, op. cit.
3. *Ain-i-Akbari,* trans, by Blochmann, vol. I. p. 294.

4. *Daulat-i-Sher Shahi* by Hasan Khan. Eng. trans, of *Farmans* only by Dr. R. P. Tripahi. Unpublished. Referred hereafter as *Daulat*, Farman X.

5. "The first is that we make one person from the village responsible for the payment of government dues. He is expected to collect the dues from the various pieces of land and farms and to pay a fixed sum. But (in some cases) some power of coercion shall have to be conceded inevitably. Therefore it is necessary that government officials should be instructed to look to the protection and security of the people so that none of the malguzars should stretch out his hands for oppressing the subjets in any place. Both the Hindus and Musalmans should obey these orders". *Daulat*, Farman X.

6. "The tenth Farman was issued regarding the measurement of the cultivated and uncultivated land of the dominion. Ahmad Khan Tangi (or Bangi) who was the soul of this system of management and whose rank commanded a good reputation in administration, accomplished this work with the help of able and learned Brahmins, and prepared a register in which were entered the rights of owners and the measurement of all arable and other pieces of land. The land was divided into several classes and the rate for every one of them was Fixed." *Daulat*, Farman X.

7. *Tarikh-i-Sher Shahi* by Abbas Sarwani, Allahabad University MSS (hereafter referred to as Abbas), p. 191; Dom, *History of the Afghans*, I, p. 135.

8. Abbas, pp. 232–6.

9. Abbas, p. 216; 10Ms. fol. 106a.

10. A'in, I, p. 296, lines 5–6.

11. Ibid.,

12. A'in, I, p. 294; also A'in, XIV and XV for 10-year and 19-year rates.

13. K.R. Qanungo, *Sher Shah*, pp. 373–74; *A'in* trans, by Jarrett, vol. II, pp. 63 and 66.

14. Moreland, op. cit., pp. 452–9.

15. Saran, (cited in fn. 2), p. 147.

16. Qureshi (cited as above), pp. 118–19.

17. *Daulat*, Farman X

18. Elliot, IV, pp. 414–15.

19. Moreland, op cit., p. 449. "Measurement was based on the area sown; a charge of certain weight of each kind of grain or its equivalent in cash was made on each unit of the area sown and the assessment for the area was complete when the crop areas had been measured, though in practice, it was found necessary to make allowances when the crops failed."

20. Blochmann, *A'in*, I, p. 294.

21. A'in, trans. II, p. 63.

22. *A'in-i-Akbari*, Bibliotheca Indica text, edited by Blochmann, vol. I, pp., 294–5; also A'in, XIV and XV for 10-year and 19-year rates.

23. *A'in*, Blochmann text, vol.1 p. 298ff.

24. Abbas, p. 191; Dom, I, p. 135.

25. *A'in*, Blochmann text, pp. 300–1.

3

Some Documents on Revenue Administration During Aurangzeb's Reign

Sheikh Abdur Rashid

SOME VALUABLE documents relating to revenue administration are contained in a lesser known book *Nigar Nama-i-Munshi*, a collection of letters, official correspondence and administration manuals, drafted on behalf of princes or nobles by one Munshi, known among his contemporaries as Malikzada. The work was compiled by the Munshi himself in 1095/1683. Two manuscript copies of the work are preserved in the Library of the Muslim University.[1] My friend Dr. S. Nurul Hasan, has elsewhere described with great ability this extremely interesting and useful book. I have been able to use the information contained therein for the purpose of this paper through his kindness. Limitations of space do not permit me to give detailed information about the duties and functions of the officials of the revenue department or the general principles of revenue administration of the Mughals. I have given here a very brief, and I am afraid disjoined, summary of the chapter relating to the Revenue Department, and I hope it will be useful for students of Mughal History.

Apart from throwing interesting light on the working of the revenue administration, these documents reveal that:

(i) The state demand was fixed at 50 per cent of the produce;

(ii) The Government made every effort to prevent the levying of any unauthorized taxes over and above the state-demand;

(iii) The Government emphazised with all the force the need for increasing the cultivation;

(iv) The office of Amin was frequently combined with that of the Krori, and sometime with the Faujdar.[2]

(v) The system of *ghalla-bakhshi* and *mustajri* continued to exist in many places along with other methods of assessment.[3]

*15th Session at Gwalior, 1952.

(vi) Strenuous attempts were made to check the accounts, to define duties of different officers of the Revenue Department and to punish slack or corrupt officials and to clean up the administration.

The Manual of Diwan[4]

It contains 15 sections:

1. The Diwan should not see or receive in private Amils, Chaudharies, Qanungos, Taluqdars, etc., but should see them in his office and in public. On the other hand the ryots and the poor people coming with complaints may be received in public or in private.

2. The Amils should be given strict orders that the annual revenue statements should be prepared village-wise and field-wise, giving the nature of produce, quality of the land and the area under cultivation. If the peasantry is destitute, he should make arrangements that every peasant makes utmost effort to sow more land as compared with the previous year and more area is brought under cultivation in the current year; further instead of coarse grain, finer variety of grain is sown. His effort should be to see that no arable land is left uncultivated. He should strive to settle more peasants from the neighbouring areas on such lands, so that all possible means are employed to bring more land under cultivation.

3. The Amils of the parganas should be instructed that the annual revenue statements are compiled village-wise with description of the crop, and the name of the cultivator and on the basis of this statement the revenue should be assessed so as to conduce to the prosperity of the ryot and the economy of the state. This revenue return should be sent without delay to the office (of the Diwan).

4. After the revenue has been assessed and determined, the instalments of payment in each pargana should be fixed. The Kroris should be given strict orders that the collection of instalments due at each crop-season should begin in time, and should be completed within the prescribed period. The Diwan should get weekly information about the progress of collection so that no arrears should remain. If some arrears remain in respect of the first instalment due to some unforeseen circumstances, the same should be recovered along with the second instalment. The entire revenue should be collected definitely along with the third instalment.

5. Suitable and convenient instalments should be fixed for the payment of the arrears of the previous years according to the condition and the paying capacity of the ryots. The Kroris should be instructed to

recover these arrears in prescribed instalments in accordance with their province of collection. The Diwan should keep himself informed of the progress of collection, so that the officials do not become slack in collection.

6. If the Diwan visits the villages for inspection and for ascertaining the condition of the peasantry and the area of cultivated land, the gross income as well as the difference may be assessed properly and accounts should be checked (text is defective here). Report should be sent to the Wazir regarding the work of the Amins, as a result of this inspection.

7. The customary Nankar[5] and the Inam according to practice in the *Khalisa* lands of the Emperor should be included in the revenue. And whatever increase in revenue the Amils of the Sarkar (reference is to Prince Muazzam) have succeeded in effecting from the time of the assignment of Jagir, and whatever arrears have been realised, and the decrease that has taken place, on all matters reports should be called. Where the revenues have remained stationary the fact should also be stated.

8. It should be prescribed that the cashiers should receive in revenue the Alamgiri sikka. If that is not readily available, Shah Jahani coins, or those current in market should be taken. In no case underweight coins which are not current in the market should be accepted.

9. Should some unforeseen calamity befall, the Amins and Amils should be instructed to take utmost care of the cultivated areas that have escaped the calamity and they should assess field-wise what remains undamaged. This work should not be left to Chaudharies, Qanungos, Muqaddams and Patwaris, so that the ryot is not unduly exploited.

10. The levying of extra cesses and taxes which hit the ryot hard should be stopped and Amins, Amils, Chaudharies, Qanungos, and Muqaddams should be strictly warned that no unauthorised collections are to be made. The Diwan should keep himself informed whether any of these taxes are collected, and if report is sent that any official has collected extra taxes, he should be dismissed and replaced by other person.

11. For the purpose of checking, the village papers should be compared with the final returns, on the prescribed forms. The regulation for the preparation of the returns is that at the time of translation of the Hindi document into Persian, all the various payments made by each ryot should be recorded village-wise and the accounts of the receipts as well and what has been taken by the Amin, Amil, Zemindar, etc., should be prepared, and the account of each maintained by name. All the papers of the village should be translated, so that due to the

absence of the Patwari or for some other reason the Amils, Chaudharies, etc., do not take for themselves more than what is prescribed, and they should be made to deposit any excess collections in the treasury.

12. If any Amin, Krori, or Fotadar works honestly, efficiently and loyally and in accordance with regulations, or renders any other good service, he should be shown appreciation and favoured, and a report to that effect submitted, so that he is encouraged. If on the other hand he works improperly he should be reported and punished or dismissed as a warning to others.

13. Instructions should be given that all records are prepared in time, when the Diwan himself likes. Daily statements of collection of revenue and other taxes and price chart should be maintained. From different parganas fortnightly reports of collections and the balance in the treasury should be secured. The accounts of the Fotadar should be compared with the crop-wise collection figures of the Amils, and any discrepancies should not be allowed to stand till the next Kharif, or the papers of Kharif till the next Rabi, but should be promptly despatched to the office.

14. If any Amin, Amil or Fotadar is dismissed, his papers and records should be carefully taken over and sent to the office of Prince Muazzam so that his accounts may be examined and settled in the Kachehry.

15. The Diwani reports should be despatched after each crop season to the court (of the Prince).

Letter Written on the Instructions of Prince Mauzzam to
Mirza Badiuzaman Mahabat Khani, Later Entitled
Rashid Khan (Sulaiman, M.S.,f. 72b and 73a)

Since some parganas under the suba of Punjab have been given in Jagir to Sarkar (Shah Alam) in lieu of salary, the administration of this Jagir is entrusted to the addressee. He will have complete authority of management and administration, including the power to confirm or dismiss Amils of the former Jagir. He should strive to enhance the revenue and pacify the peasants. Detailed statements of the crops in each field in each village should be secured and assessment should be made keeping in view the (current) prices. Half of the net produce should remain with the ryot, and the other half, without any deduction of expenditure should be deposited in the Treasury. Excesses committed by unauthorised occupants of land or collectors of revenue should be checked and information collected about the behaviour of Amils. No one should keep more than the authorised wages of collection. Taxes and cesses prohibited by imperial order should not be levied. Detailed reports about condition (of the ryots and crops) should be sent. Copies of imperial *sanads* regarding the parganas given in lieu of salary are enclosed.

Letter Written on the Instructions of Prince Mauzzam to Muhammad Momin (Sulaiman, Ms.f., 88a)

Let it not be concealed that so and so, Muqaddam of such and such village has written that the settlement of that village since ages has been on the basis of *ghalla-bakhshi* (crop sharing). For the satisfaction of the ryots, a royal sanad was required. It is, therefore, decreed that the settlement of *batai*, provided the agreed grain is adequately protected, which is the best form of settlement, may be made on the condition that the ryot carry on the cultivation to the best of their ability and do not wilfully neglect their cultivation, and the assessment is not made in advance. Peasants should be encouraged to work hard for the prosperity of the state and the betterment of the people.

Letter written to an Amin: (Sulaiman Ms.f. 89)

Since in the course of the comparison of the area of cultivated land of the previous year with the current year, it has been noticed that in the mahals of the iqta of Sarkar (Shah Alam) there are vast tracts of cultivable land which have not been brought under cultivation due to the negligence of the Amils, it is ordered that the Amils of these parganas be instructed to make every effort to bring all arable land under cultivation, so that not a *biswa* remains uncultivated.

Letter of Appointment as Amini and Thanadari (f. 97b–98b)

Since the duties of Amini and Thanadari[6] of pargana Shahabad alias Lakhnaur under the subadar of Shahjahanabad have been entrusted to so and so, he should make every effort to have the assessment made in time and collections completed regularly. He should strive to increase the population, to see to its prosperity and to pacify and console the peasantry. At the time of sowing, he should visit the entire area and see that arable land does not remain uncultivated. The excess payments extorted from peasants should be restored to them. He should work in a way that the income of the pargana increases year by year . . . . Peasantry should be protected from the exactions of Kroris and Fotadars, and from the depredations of the soldiery. No unauthorised taxes should be allowed to be levied. The treasury should be carefully guarded under his seal and the seal of the Krori and the lock of the Fotadar. Not one dam should be spent without the *sanad* of the Diwan written under the explicit authority of the Sarkar (Prince Mauzzam). The balance in the Treasury and the accounts of the Fotadar should be carefully checked, so that not one dam is lost. The statement of receipts and other papers prescribed by the regulations under each heading should be prepared according to regulations for such heads and the balance sheet of the Fotadar should be prepared and scrutinised and signed by him (Amin) and should be sent to the office of Sarkar (Prince Mauzzam). Every effort should be made that no disturbance occurs and expenses do not exceed revenue. The welfare of the ryot should be looked after and he should be treated with kindness. The Chaudharies, Zamindars, Muqaddams and peasants are informed that so and so has been made their permanent Amin and Thanadar and they should cooperate with him and obey his instructions.

On Extending Cultivation (if. 93b)

So and so is informed that he should make every effort to extend cultivation so that the entire arable land is brought under cultivation. Where the Amin is a efficient person the duties of Krorbandi should be entrusted to him and security taken according to regulations so that the work may proceed smoothly and (finished) in time. Similarly where the Krori is efficient, honest and capable, he should also be given the office of the Amin. Where both Krori and Amin are honest and efficient, and cooperate with each other and look after the interests of the government as well as the ryot, they should be maintained separately. Where both are incompetent or dishonest, they should be dismissed and replaced.

Re: Farming of Revenue[7]

Since so and so, in such and such pargana, requests that two or three villages be farmed out to him on contract, it is ordered that: if those villages have been rendered desolate or are not prosperous the revenue may be suitably assessed and villages given on contract, so that within two to three years the revenue reaches the normal standard. The cultivated area should be noted, and its yearly extension stipulated according to a pre-determined schedule. After assessment, the agreement (Qubuliyat) and the security should be taken according to regulations. It should be laid down that the contractor (*Mustajir*) shall strive for the extension of cultivation and satisfy and console the ryot. The Amil should realise the revenue in accordance with the terms of contract of the *Mustajir*.

Notes

1. The first manuscript is in Sir Shah Sulaiman collection, no. Farsiya 152, transcribed in 1195H/1780. The other manuscript is in Nawab Abdus Salam collection, no. 362/132, copies in 1227H/1812–13. Both the manuscripts have lacunae, but together they appear to be complete.

2. The provincial Diwan was the chief Amin and many letters of appointment of a Diwan refer to the recipient of that office as being appointed as Diwan and Amin of such and such province.

   An Amin may also hold the office of an Amil, a Faujdar, or Thanadar. For reference see: (1) Jagat Rai's *Farhange Kardani*, pp. 58, 59. (2)*Nirat-e-Ahim*, vol. I, pp. 334, 391. (3) *Nigar Nama-i-Munshi*.

3. (i) Nasaq; (ii) Zabti; (iii) Kankut; (iv) Ghalla-Bakhshi; (v) Lula-bandi; (vi) Deh-bandi.

4. This is the last document of *Dafiar* Safha 3, Bab. V. This document is missing from the Sulaiman manuscript.

5. Assignment of land or revenue for assistance rendered to revenue officers.

6. There are also instances where the posts of Amin and Faujdar were combined to ensure smooth working (f. 97b).

7. This document is given in *Dafiar* I, Safha 3, Bab V of the Abdus Salam MS. It has not been transcribed in the Sulaiman MS.

4

Classification of Agrarian Land Under Akbar

B.R. Grover

THE CLASSIFICATION of land as developed under Akbar was not only a continuation of the Sur regime[1] but with longer period at hand for agrarian experimentation, was evolved on broader lines. It embodied as much the indigenous and the Sur notions as the traditional Timuride ones.[2] The importance of the judicious assessment rates based on different kinds of land is clearly underlined in the *Ain*[3] and other chronicles. This system continued throughout the Mughal age and further modification in the State demand in the reigns of Shah Jahan and Aurangzeb was within the same classification order.[4]

The description of the *Ain* is not so much in accordance with the categorisation of the nature of soil such as clay, loam or sand since soils differ naturally from one another in respect of their minerological and chemical composition and in respect of the mechanical arrangement of their component parts. The *Ain* in its chapter on 'land and its classification and proportionate dues of sovereignty'[5] emphasises the classification of the cultivable land rather than the classification of the soil. It is based on the simple principle of continued or intermittent cultivation, capability of the land for crops, the rate of assessment and state demand to be fixed for each class of land. Thus the land is divided into four classes, *viz.* Polaj, Parauti, Chachar and Banjar.[6] Polaj land is annually cultivated for each crop in succession and is never allowed to lie fallow. It requires less of labour for ploughing. Parauti land is left out of cultivation for some time that it may recover its strength for recultivation.[7] It needs comparatively more of ploughing labour. Chachar land lies fallow for three to four years and requires much labour for ploughing and recultivation. Banjar land remains uncultivated for five or more years. It needs tremendous labour for recultivation. Some of the land is rendered permanently barren and grows only bushes and thorns as if on a desert or hilly tract. For the purposes of assessment, the Polaj and Parauti lands are further divided according to the

*22nd Session at Gauhati, 1959.

fertility of the soil into good, middling and bad whereupon the medium produce and the state demand is fixed.[8]

Apart from the above broad division which is rather insufficient, a detailed classification of land based on adventitious qualities can be done under two main categories, i.e. unirrigated and irrigated. The former comprises the Barani and the Sailabi whereas the latter includes the Abi, Chahi and Nahri lands.

1. Unirrigated

A. *Barani*: dependent on rainfall.[9] Much of the agriculture in India depends on the rainfall and its uneven distribution in different Subahs.[10] *Ain* has given the topographical and climatic conditions of every Subah.[11] In the Barani land, the Kharif crop is always assured after monsoon, whereas, the fate of Rabi crop depends on the scanty and capricious winter rainfall.[12] For example, in the Subah of Ajmer 'The soil is sandy, and water obtainable only at great length, hence the crops are dependent on rain. The spring harvest is inconsiderable. Jowari, Lahdarah and Moth are the most abundant crops. A seventh or an eighth of the produce is paid as revenue, and very little in money.[13] Similarly in the Subah of Gujarat, 'soil is sandy, dependent on rains, and the spring harvest is small. Consequently the staple crops are only Jowari and Bajra, whereas wheat and foodgrains are imported from Malwa and Ajmer, and rice from the Deccan.[14] The Chachar and the Banjar lands described in *Ain* are mostly Barani and the State demand is fixed accordingly.[15]

B. *Sailabi*: flooded or kept permanently moist by rivers is rendered cultivable and fertile due to inundation caused by the rivers. *Ain* mentions specially of such land in the Subhas of Delhi and Oudh. Regarding Delhi, 'the chief rivers are the Ganges and Jumna, and both take their rise in this Subah. Besides there are numerous other streams, amongst them the Ghaghar. Much of the land is subject to inundation and in some places there are three harvests.[16] As to Oudh, 'Agriculture is in a flourishing state, especially the rice of the kinds called Sukhdas, Madhkar, and Jhanwan which for whiteness, delicacy, fragrance and wholesomeness are scarcely to be matched. They sow their rice three months earlier than compared to other parts of Hindustan. When the drought begins, the Sai and the Gogra rise high in flood and before the beginning of the rains, the land is inundated, and as the waters rise, the stalks of rice shoot up to proportionate length: the crop, however, is destroyed if the floods are in full force before the rice is in ears.[17] In Sarkar, Bhakkar, Subah Multan, 'the river Sin (Indus) inclines every few years alternately to its southern and northern banks and the village cultivation follows its course.'[18] Of course, such crops stand in equal danger of being destroyed by excessive river floods. *Ain* puts most of such land dependent only on inundation as the Chachar one and the state demand is fixed accordingly.[19]

2. Irrigated

A. Though the Kharif crop thrives mostly on the rainfall,[20] at places invariably supplemented by artificial means of irrigation, so easily accessible during and after the rainy season, the Rabi crop lives partly on the scanty capricious rainfall in some portions but generally on the artificial means of irrigation developed throughout India.[21] Zainud-din Khawaf states that in practically all the villages in India, regularly settled permanent arrangements exist for the purpose of agriculture.[22] The fruit plants need regular watering for the first two years but thereafter depend only on rainfall.[23] But the vegetables and the 'Jins-i-Kamil,'[24] especially the Rabi crop subsist on irrigation.[25]

(i) Though Babur regrets the absence of 'running waters'[26] and attributes it to the dependence of the crops mainly on the rainfall and some other artificial means of irrigation[27] the presence of rivulets channeled out from the rivers for the purposes of irrigation for many of the towns in India is amply borne out by the historian Zainud-din Khawaf.[28] *Ain* mentions various Mahals and villages located on the streambanks, e.g. Mahal Hapur (Sarkar Delhi, Subah Delhi) on the Kali Nadi between two streams,[29] and in Mahal Jamalpur (Sarkar Hisar Firozah, Subah Delhi) 'Ghaggar flows through several villages here.'[30] Such villages must have been irrigated by water course drawn from the main stream.[31] Both *Tarikh-i-Rashidi*[32] and *Ain*[33] make special references to Abi land in Kashmir with such means of irrigation.

(ii) As regards lakes, tanks and ponds for irrigation, Babur makes various references to this practice in the extremely limited portions of India toured by him.[34] Zainu-din Khawaf mentions large permanent Jalhas, i.e. lakes and ponds, which in some villages extend from one to three Krohs and serve source of irrigation and cultivation of the vegetables and fruits for the surrounding villages and Qasbas inhabited for generations.[35] For irrigation, the Rabi crop rests upon such permanent lakes and tanks stored with water during the rainy season.[36] *Ain* makes incidental references to the existence of reservoirs at some places. At Mahal Mandauthi (Sarkar Delhi, Subah Delhi), 'the autumn harvest (is) abundant: near the town (is) a tank, which is never dry throughout the year.'[37] 'At Unah (Subah Gujarat) there are two reservoirs, one of which is called Jumna, the other Ganga. The water bubbles up and forms a stream.'[38] Such methods of irrigation through water courses from the streams and ponds inherited from ancient times continued to operate throughout the Mughal age and find description in the early British records.[39]

(iii) Where running channelled water is not available, Babur notes that water supply for some crops is rendered through human labour on the part of men and women by carrying water by repeated efforts in pitchers drawn from tanks.[40]

B. *Ghahi*: watered from wells. The irrigation of the land with the well water—the most indigenous and still an extremely efficient instrument of irrigation—has been known to many of the provinces in India since ancient times.[41] Babur notes the prevalence of both the (Persian) wheeled-well in Lahore and Dibalpur and the indigenous Charsa system of well-operation in Agra, Chandwar and Biana.[42] The Charsa system could work both on the well and the river bank.[43] Babur and Zainud-d in Khawaf describe the well irrigation and the way both the systems of wells operate with much curiosity and interest.[44] Though Am makes a special reference to the Subah of Lahore with irrigation chiefly from wells,[45] the Chahi land was known to practically all Subahs in northern India[46] and was assessed separately as against the Barani and Abi lands.[47] The easiness of approach to the well water-table and irrigation would depend mostly on the nearness to the rivers and sufficient rainfall. For the Kharif crop, in areas with secure rainfall, occasional well-irrigation merely supplements the rains for covering larger portions for cultivation resulting in better yields. At some places, wells are operated only for production of 'Jins-i-Kamil'. Where the rainfall is scanty, the land under well irrigation is essentially dependent upon the river floods or inundation canals and water courses for permanent moisture. The Rabi crop is entirely dependent upon the artificial means of irrigation, mostly on the wells—a fact recorded both by Babur and Zainud-din Khawaf.[48] Thus wells exist both in the Barani and Abi lands wherein the well-irrigation assures regular cultivation especially of the high grade crops and good produce both for the Kharif and Rabi crops. With continuous cultivation in the Barani and Abi region, the Chahi land could be put as Polaj with its normal rate of assessment.[49]

C. *Nahri*: irrigated from canals. Though some small-scale pioneering work had been accomplished by Ghyasuddin Tughlak,[50] in reality Firoz Tughlak was the first Muslim Sultan who realised the importance of the canals for the purpose of irrigation.[51] The two canals, Rajiva and Alaghkhani, opened by him in the East Panjab and Doab[52] were permanent inheritance to agrarian development. They helped tremendously in the increase of the produce of the crops, especially the 'Jins-i-kamil,[53] avoided the recurrence of famines and increased the revenues of the State.[54] As with the lapse of time, the East Panjab Canal had fallen into decay, Shaihabu-din Ahmad Khan, the Governor of Subah Delhi and later on Diwan-i-Khalsa in the 13th year of Akbar's reign, got it repaired and flowing to increase the agriculture of his own Jagir land irrigated by the canal, which came to be named as Nahir-i-Shahab.[55] The canal system was later on extended in the reign of Shah Jahan.[56] The Nahari land was not only rendered fertile but was assured of continuous cultivation for both the Kharif and the Rabi crops. It could be reckoned as the Polaj land for the rate of assessment.[57] Apart from the land revenue fixed in accordance with the classification of land, the State demanded extra charges as the water rate for the irrigation through the canals based on proper measurement of the canal-water consumed by the peasant holdings.[58]

Though the *Ain's* main chapter on the classification of land does not take cognizance of the categorisation of the nature of the soil, it can be safely presumed that it is only a general and a broad division. In its chapter on 'Rawai Rodi' (Currency of the means of Subsistence). *Ain* explicitly states," And because the conditions of the royal state and Prerogative vary in different countries, and soils are diverse in character, and some producing abundantly with little labour and others the reverse, and as inequalities exist also, through the remoteness or vicinity of water and cultivated tracts, the administration of each state must take these circumstances into consideration and fix its demand accordingly."[59] The above factors responsible for the diversity in the nature of the soil exist as much within different regions and their tracts in a state as characterising one state from another. In *Ain's* chapter on instructions to the Amal-Guzar, the latter is enjeined to make assessment on each class of land carefully based on keen personal observation of its nature and only after scrutiny having familiarised himself with the quality of the soil.[60] The fields of agriculture vary considerably in different places with regard to the nature of their soils and certain soils are adapted to certain crops.[61] He should deal differently, therefore, with each agriculturist and take his case into consideration.[62] Thus both the factors, the nature of the soil and the intermittency of cultivation influenced by the means of artificial irrigation, if any, would accumulatively determine the nature and value of the agricultural land which is the real basis of assessment. *Ain*, of course, makes some references to the nature of the soil in the description of the Provinces. Ajmer and Gujarat are stated to be with sandy soils.[63] Kashmir has three kinds of land, Abi, i.e. watered through channels, Lalmi, i.e. Barani—dependent on rainfall, Chalkhai, i.e. stony, rough and bushy.[64] Moreover, the natural qualities of the soil and also the fact that the above-mentioned methods of irrigation did create local conditions for the nature of the soil shows that the latter must have been taken into consideration locally at the time of assessment. Though the main divisions of the agrarian land in its classification as explained hitherto, are the same throughout Northern India in the Mughal age, in their detailed subdivisions and the local terminology applied to them, the practice varied from region to region even within one province. This is confirmed by the later provincial and local records illustrating the indigenous methods with traditional notions of the classification of land.[65] The *Ain's* description is partial as well in the sense that it emphasises the gradual conversion of every class of land to Polaj, for an assessment under the normal Polaj state demand, even though the villages and parganas in every province are always marked by more or less permanent local categorisation of the soil and classification of land for the purpose of assessment.

Notes

1. *Tawarikh-E-Daulat-Sher Shahi* by Hasan Ali Khan, trans, by Dr. R.P. Tripathi in *Medieval India Quarterly*, vol. I, July 1950, no. I, p. 62. Hasan states that the land was divided into several classes and the rate of assessment determined on that basis. He, however, has not explained the way in which the land was classified.

2. *Mulfuzat-i-Timuri*: Ms. Or. Fol 287 Berlin fols 76b–77a. Timur mentions two classes of cultivable land, irrigated and Barani. The former is irrigated through lakes and watercourses and the latter is dependent on rainfall.

3. *Ain*, Br. M. Add. 7652, fols 148b–151b: Blochmann, vol. I, pp. 297–303; Jarrett tr. II, pp. 68, 75.

4. For Shah Jahan's reign, see *Maktubat-i-Khan-Jahan-i-Muzaffar Khan-wa-Gwaliar Nama*, Br. M. Add Rieu, III, 837, Add 16,859 fols 107a–109b; for early Aurangzeb's reign of the various uncatalogued pargana documents in Rajasthan Archives, Jaipur confirm it. For example *Yaddasht-i-Haqiqat-i-Arazi-muzruaat wa Uftada muwazih Pargana Riwari* (Sar- kar Riwari, Subah Delhi) *Fasl-i-Kharif*, dated AM 1073 fols 1a to 16b; 'Bal-wa-Jhat-i- Pargana Riwari Kharif wa Rabi', dated AH 1073 fols 1a to 9b. Such documents are in series with those of the last years of Shah Jahan's reign. For the Subah of Shahjahanabad, ' *Khulastau-i-twarikh*' Sujjan Rai Bhandari, Printed Pers. Text (edited by Maulvi Zafar Hussain, Assistant Superintendent, Archaeological Department Government of India) p. 39, mentions three main classes of cultivable land. Barani (Dependent on rainfall), Sailabi (flooded), and Chahi (well-irrigated).

5. *Ain*, fol. 149b; Blochmann, p. 297, Jarrett, II, p. 68.

6. Ibid., fol, 148b, ibid.

7. Ibid., also *Diwan-i-Pasand*, Ms. 537, Insha, Asafia-Library, Hyderabad, fol. 5a.

8. Ibid., fol. 149a; ibid., such land which is cultivated for both the Kharif and Rabi crops in succession is also termed as Dofasli. "The term does not imply that the land yields every year two crops or cane, which occupies the ground for ten or eleven months and may be considered equal to two ordinary crops; it merely indicates that it often bears two crops in a single agricultural year (Kharif–Rabi)." In contrast, to this, "Ekfasli was used to describe land tilled according to the familiar rotation under which a spring crop in one agricultural year is followed immediately by an autumn crop, and the land then lies fallow for a twelve month." (Doule, *Punjab Settlement Manual*, p. 127). As distinct from Dofasli being under Polaj, Ekfasli would be put in the next category and the rates of assessment for either of them would be different.

Todar Mal's instructions to the state land revenue officials issued in the 27th year of Akbar's reign emphasise that at the time of measurement and inspection of the standing crops, a special note be taken of the Eakfasli and Dofasli lands in the villages under survey. After having recorded their areas, assessment would be done accordingly at their respective schedule rates (A.N. Br. M. Add. OR 27, fol. 3322). This reference to the Ekfasli and Dofasli lands cannot be traced in other versions oi *Akbar Nama* texts, Br. M. Add. 26. 207 fol. 161B, Mr. Or. Quart, 1822 Berlin fol. 2592 and the printed Pers. Text *Bib. Indica*. All these texts' refer only to the agricultural condition of the land for the purposes of survey and assessment. Beveridge's translation, III (P- 563) also follows the later version.

9. Ibid., Blochmann, H, P- 362; Jarrett, II, p. 352; also *Tuzuk-i-Baburi*, tr. Beveridge, III, fn.l, p. 488 have used the term 'Lalmi' but the revenue literature of the 17th century puts it as 'Barani'.

10. Both Babur and his courtier Zain-ud-din Khawaf bear it out for their times in *Tuzuk- i-Baburi*, Beveridge, III, P- 486 and *Tarikh-i-Baburi* Ms. Rampur, p. 149 respectively.

11. *Ain*, fols. 174a.–296a, Blochmann, II, pp. 386–599; Jarrett, II, pp. 129–417.

12. *Tuzuk-i-Baburi*, Beveridge, tr. III, p. 486; *Tarikh-i-Baburi*, p. 149.

13. *Ain*, fols, 242b–234a; Jarrett, II, p. 273.

14. Ibid., fol, 232a; Jarrett, II, p. 246.

15. Ibid., fols, 151a-151b; Jarrett, II. pp. 73–74.

16. Ibid., fol, 249a; Jarrett, II, p. 283.

17. Ibid., fol. 204a; Jarrett, II, p. 181.

18. Ibid., fols, 266b–267a; Jarrett, II, p. 331.

19. Ibid., 151b; Jarrett, II, p. 73.

20. Shaikh Zain, *Tarikh-i-Baburi*, p. 152.

21. Ibid., p. 153; such is the position even today. This is very well explained in the *Report of the Indian Taxation Enquiry Committee 1925–27*, vol. I, p. 99. "The rainfall (in India) varies from 461 inches to about one-hundredth part of that figure. The results are seen at the one extreme in areas in which a crop can hardly be grown on account of excess of water, at the other in areas in which nothing can be grown without irrigation. Between these two extremes every variety of case is to be found; Swamp land that will grow rice unfailingly without the aid of irrigation at all, rice land where the rainfall requires to be supplemented occasionally, land that will grow wheat without irrigation in a normal year, but requires supplementary irrigation in occasional years, and land which will yield a good crop with regular irrigation and nothing without. These considerations affect the value of the water which in some case can convert an arid desert into a smiling plain, while in others it is really needed only in years of scarcity."

22. Ibid., p. 155.

23. Ibid., p. 153.

24. .'*Jinsi-i-Kamil*', means superiorcrops like sugar-cane, betel, yetches, tobacco,opium, cotton, indigo, kaiser, and fruits like grapes, banannas pomergranate, melons, etc. (An 18th cent dictionary Br. M. Add. 6603 fol. 57a; *Tawarikh-i-Shahjahan* by Mohammad Sadiq, Br. M. OR 174, fol. 186a. Rajasthan Archives, uncatalogued pargana documents, and also *Ain*, Jarrett, II, fn. p. 47).

25. Shaikh Zain, *T. Baburi*, pp. 79, 153.

26. *Babur Noma*, Beveridge, II, p. 487.

27. Ibid.

28. Shaikh Zain, *T. Baburi*, p. 149.

29. *Ain*, Jarrett, II, 293.

30. Ibid., p. 299.

31. Though *Ain* makes only implied references to such an irrigation, the early British settlement reports are full of such instances of long established practice in the regions. For example, the *District Gazetteer of Bhagalpur (Bengal District Gazetteers)*, pp. 78–92 in a note on irrigation remarks, "Artificial irrigation which is indispensable over a large area of South Bhagalpur is generally effected by leading off from a natural stream or from a head of water collected in a bandh of tan. The channels are called Danrhs and their smaller branches are called Singhas." The Danrhs are classified into three classes, (a) those commencing from a river (shallow broad stream), (b) those commencing from a Kharra or Jore (deep channel with high bank), (c) those commencing from a head of water protected by a bandh or from a tank. The methods of lifting water into the three kinds of Danrhs are different although the way in which it is utilised for actual irrigation is the same. All channels commence from the rivers Chandan and Chir, their tributaries and branches. The nature of such an irrigation-canals is described in a report of the Superintending Engineer, dated May, 1864— "As its greatest width the Chandan is about 1,500 feet from bank to bank. From the long-continued practice of embanking, its bed is actually higher than the lands on either side, and more especially than that on the eastern bank. Being a hill stream, it is liable to sudden and violent inundations, but except when in flood, the channel is a dry bed of gritty sand, bounded on either side with artificial embankment pierced through innumerable cuts for irrigation purposes." Bunds are also erected in the bed of the river to raise the level of the water so as to enable it to pass on the Danrhs (channels). During floods, water would naturally flow into the Danrhs without any artificial training devices. But when there is no flood or when there is not sufficient water in the river, devices are adopted to put the water in the Danrh either through a small canal dug in the bed of the river known as Jonghar or by digging pits in the bed of the river and by lifting the water by means of buckets, swing baskets, or spoons worked on lever. This kind of water is commonly called Jharana.

32. *Tarikh-i-Rashidi*, trans, by Elias and Ross, p. 425.

33. *Ain*, Jarrett, II, p. 352, 'Abi signifies in the N.W.P. land watered from ponds, tanks, and water-courses, in contradiction to that watered from wells, and being liable to fail in hot season, is assessed at lower rate.'

34. *Babur Noma*, Beveridge, III, pp. 487, 547, 611–12.

35. Shaikh Zain, *T. Baburi*, p. 79.

36. *Babur Nama*, Beveridge, III, p. 487.

37. *Ain*, Jarrett, II, p. 293.

38. Ibid., p. 253.

39. The provinces of Behar, Bengal and the Punjab afford good examples. For the present district Bhagalpur which formed part of both Subahs Behar and Bengal in Mughal period. *see Bengal District Gazetteers, Bhagalpur* by J. Bryne I.C.S., pp. 78–92; for the Punjab, see *The Punjab of Today* by H. K. Trevaskis, pp. 230–34 for India in general, see *Indian Agriculture* by Albert Howard and Gabrielle, L.C. Howard, pp. 11–12; also *Village Uplift in India* by Branye, p. 50.

40. *Babur Nama,* tr. Beveridge, III, p. 487. Shaikh Zain in *T. Baburi,* p. 152 remarks that the water was carried in Mashkas i.e., leather bags.

41. Baden Powell, *The Indian Village Community,* 94 note; H.K. Trevaskis, *The Punjab of Today,* pp. 231–41, Dr. Tripathi in *Some Aspects of Muslim Administration,* p. 286 remarks: "It is well known that in Hindu India wells, tanks and canals were dug by the Princes on a large scale."

42. *Babur Noma,* tr. Beveridge, III, pp. 486–7.

43. Shaikh Zain, *T. Baburi,* p. 1533.

44. *Babur Noma,* tr. Beveridge, II, pp. 486–7; *T. Baburi,* p. 153.

45. *Ain,* fol 260b; Jarrett, II, p. 3316. Also for the Subah of Lahore, *Khulasatu-t-twarikh.* of Sujjan Rai Bhandari, Printed Pers. Text. p. 67 adds. "Cultivation depends upon well-irrigation; old mechanics make water wheels which require 360 large and small pieces of wood and more than 100 small pots. So skilful is their mechanism that a pair of oxen can turn such a wheel at every resolution of which many hundred maunds of water came out of the well in the pots and benefit cultivation. The autumn crops and the cheapness of grains depend upon rain."

46. *Babur Nama,* Beveridge, II, pp. 486–8; 532–3, Shaikh Zain, *T. Baburi,* p. 153. Aurangzeb's Farman to Rasik Das Karori, Ms. Or. Oct. 113j. Berlin, fol 3b (also quoted in *Nigar Nama Munshi, Bodlein.* Oxford Ms. Pers. e.I. fol 128a) mentions two kinds of land, Chahi and Barani. It also directs that the old wells fallen out of use should be repaired and that the new wells be dug at different places for the extension of agriculture and 'Jins-i-Kamil'. The early British records and the District Gazetteers point out the long established practice of well irrigation in all the portions of Northern India. For example, see *District Gazetteer of Bhagalpur, Bengal District Gazetteers,* p. 78.

47. Rajasthan Archives, (formerly known as *Daftar-i-Diwani wa Hazuri*), Jaipur, (uncatalogued pargana documents) *Mal-i-Jihat wa Sair-i-Jihat* of village Fatehpur, Pargana Riwari (Sarkar Riwari, Subah Delhi) fols, l–9b.

48. See references 42 and 43 also see *Economics of Wells-,* H.K. Trevaskis, *The Punjab Today,* pp. 238–41.

49. *Ain.* fols, 149b–50b; Jarrett, II, pp. 69–71; also R. A. Jaipur, see reference 47.

50. *Tarikh-i-Firoz Shahi,* Ziya'al-din, Barani *Bib. Ind.* Pers. Text, p. 442.

51. Ibid., p. 442. Dr. Tripathi correctly points out that this was a revival of the ancient Hindu practice of digging of canals by the prince on a large scale. (*Some Aspects of Muslim Administration,* p. 286). The official view of *Punjab Administration Report,* 1921–22, p. 302 and that of Trevaskis, *The Punjab of Today,* vol. I, p. 244, that the main object of the work was to convey water to the emperor's hunting lodge at Hissar than to irrigate the intermediate country' and that it was a linked series of drainages rather than of a canal, as the word is understood today' is not justified in view of an evidence from *Ain* (Jarrett, II, p. 285) which states 'Hisar (Hissar) was founded by Sultan Firoz who brought the waters of the Jamna to it by means of a cutting. A holy devotee predicted his accession to his request the canal was made.' Apart from this *Ain s* implied reference to the canal's use for agrarian benefits, both Zia (pp. 569–70) and Afif (p. 295) point out the agricultural development following the digging of the canal. That the canal served Firoz Shah's hunting purposes is equally undeniable.

52. Zia, pp. 567–71. Afif, *Tarikh-i-Firoz Shahi, Bib. Ind.* Pers. Text, p. 127. *Tarikh-i-Mubarak Shahi*, Yahya bin Ahmad bin Abdulla, (a), f. 43rd. Ferishta, I, 146–47. Thomas' *Chronicles*, pp. 294–95; Tripathi, pp. 286–88, Articles of *JASB*, 1833,1840,1846 quoted by Dr. Tripathi in *Some Aspects of Muslim Administration*.

53. Ibid., pp. 569–70; ibid., p. 295; Tripathi, p. 287.

54. Afif, pp. 295–6, Tripathi, pp. 287–8.

55. *Padshah Nama*, Mohammad Warns, Ms. 38, *Tarikh-i-Fatsi*, Rampur, pp. 57–8. Perhaps the same canal is mentioned by Badauni in *Muntkhibul Tawarikh*, III, Printed Pers. Text. p. 198, having been re-excavated by Mullah Nuruddin Mohammad Tarkhan in his Jagir parganas of Safadun, Sarkar Sarhind, (Subah Delhi). This canal emnated from river Jamna and extended for fifty krohs towards Karnal and beyond it. It benefited the agricultural lands of the people tremendously and came to be named as Shakhuni canal after Prince Salim who was called 'Shakhu Baba' by Akbar.

56. *Maktubat-i-Khan Jahan wa Gwaliar Nama*, Br. M. Rieu III, 837, Add 16, 859 fols, 107a-109b gives a detailed report on *Nahr-i-Chitung* i.e., canal irrigating the different parganas of Mustafabad, Indri, Kamal, Thaneser, Pandri, Fatehpur, Kaithal in Chakla Sirhind and the parganas of Khand, Jind, Hansi, Hissar, in Chakla Sirhind (Sirhind), Subah Delhi. For the repairs done on the Delhi canal, see/Padshal Nama, Mohammad Warris, Ms. 38, *Tarikh-i-Farsi*, Rampur, pp. 57–58. For the Lahore Canal of Ali Mardan, see *Padshah Nama* by Lahori Ms. no. 565, Khuda Baksh Library Patna., fol, 207b; *Tawarikh-i-Shahjahani*, Mohammad Sadiq, Ms. no. 2093, *Farsi* Rampur, pp. 64–65; *Lubul Tawarikh-i-Hind* by Rai Bindra Ban, Ms. 954/15 F. Subban Allah Collection, M.U. Aligarh, fols, 49b by Aurangzeb's. Sujjan Rai Bhandari in *Khulasatu-t-twarikh* Printed Pers. Text, p. 74, mentions the existence of five canals in the Subah of Lahore. One canal taken was river Tavi extended to Ibrahimbad, a newly founded town near Sodhra by Ali Mardan Khan in Shah Jahan's reign. Four canals emanated from river Ravi near Shahpur (a dependency of Nurpur) "Near Shahpur have been taken out of this river (Ravi) a royal canal which goes to the garden of Shalamar in Lahore, a second canal which goes to the pargana of Pathankot, a third canal which goes to the pargana of Batala, and a fourth canal which goes to the pargana of Biar Patti Haibapur. These canals do good to the crops of the mahals." Shahpur is situated 32. 23, N. 75 44E. (Atlas, sheet 29), north of Pathankot. The present main Bari Doab issues from Madhupur, um. N.W. of Pathankot. Ali Mardan Khan's canal commenced a little below this point (Imperial Gazetteer, II.153). Also see *The Punjab under the Mughals* by Muhammad Akbar, Appendix, translation of the description of the Punjab in *Khulasatu-t-twarikh*, p. 306.

    Apart from this, every region in every Subah had developed its own indigenous canal system drawn from the streams flowing in the territory. This is sufficiently borne by the early British records noting such long established canal work in vogue in the area. See reference 31.

57. Ibid., 149b–50b; Jarrett, II, pp. 69–71.

58. *Muktubat-i-Khan Jahan* Br. M. Add 16859, fols, 107a–109b clearly mentions the canal water charges assessed on different holdings in the canal irrigated areas of

the Chaklas of Hissar and Sirhind (Subah Delhi) under the supervision of an officer called *Mir-i-Ab.* (the Superintendent of canal-water).

59. *Ain,* fol, 147b; Jarrett, II, pp. 58–9.

60. Ibid., fol, 142a; Jarrett, II. p. 46.

61. Ibid.

62. Ibid.

63. *Ain,* fols, 232a, 242b–243a; Jarrett, II, p. 273 and 246 respectively.

64. Ibid., fol, 274a; Jarrett, II, p. 352. As stated above text, for Sarkar Kashmir (Subah Kabul). *Ain* mentions three kinds of land, 'Abi', 'Lahmi' and 'Jalkhayai' For 'abi', see reference no. 9, for 'Lalmi, see reference 33. *Jalkhayai* is a "parched land that has absorbed its moisture". (Jarrett, II, p. 352) Blochmann's text bears the wording of 'Chalkhai', which he has interpreted as 'stony, rough and bushy.' I would prefer the wording as 'Jalkhayai' to 'Chalkhai', as the latter, if interpreted as 'stony land' would not grow even flowers which find description in the context. All this is equally confirmed in the Turki Text of Mirza Muhammad Haidar's *Tarikh-i-Rashidi* quoted in fn. 1, p. 425 by Elias and Ross. The passage of the main text translated by the latter puts four kinds of land and runs as "In this region all the land is divided into four kinds. The cultivation is (1) irrigation (*abi*) (2) on land not needing artificial irrigation (3) gardens, and (4) level ground, where the river banks abound in violets and many coloured flowers. On (leave) ground, on account of the excessive moisture, the crops do not thrive, and for this reason the soil is not laboured, which constitutes one of the charms". Not relying on the authenticity of this passage, Elias and Ross themselves comment in their footnote remarks "The whole of this passage, regarding the land, is obscure and the translation uncertain. The Turki Ms. is clearer but mentions only three categories of land: "One kind, is land where agriculture is done with river water, another where it is done with rain water. Another is the level ground, where the river banks abound in violets and many coloured flowers this land is too damp to cultivate.'"

65. Ms. Or. Oct. 113j. Berlin fol, 4a, an 18th century Ms. while explaining the colonising reforms of Shah Jahan's reign in Subah Behar gives detailed classification of land *viz.,* Bahi, Kahelfi Kanhel, Jungle, well-irrigated and tank-irrigated. Also the 'Records of the Delhi Residency and Agency' (1807–57) printed by the Punjab Government 1911 AD, pp. 327–32, for many of the parganas, Pulwull Rewari, Bohrah, Sonaii, Shahjahanpur, Noh, Hutheen, Horul, which formed a part of the Sarkars of Delhi and Rewari (Subah Delhi) of the Mughal Empire (*Ain,* Jarrett, II, pp. 291–301) give description of the detailer local categorisation of land, the crops grown on them and the consequent assessment made on them.

I.   (1) The Barani land is divided into (i) Duhur, i.e. low land overflows by rivulets and often under water for 1 or 2 months. This land yields rice, baranee, wheat and barley and is a rich stiff loam. Assessed at Rs. 1–12 As. to Rs. 2–6 per beegha, (ii) Dhur, 2nd kind, called also *Chicknawat,* i.e. land not overflown by rivulets, but surrounded with small field, banks to retain the water, yields cotton, mukee, jowar, churree, grain, barley and gram mixed. This is also a hard soil till wet. Assessed at Rs. 1/4 as. to Rs. 1.6 as. each beegah.

(2) Nurmotah, also called mudah is a soft but not sandy soil, yielding cotton jowar, kukkee, churree, barley and gram mixed. Assessed at Rs. 1/- to 1–2 as. per beegah.

(3) Bhoor, 1st kind i.e. a sandy soil yielding in general only a Khurreef crop. It is best adapted for bajra, mote, jowar. The crops are bad unless it rains about December, and it is therefore dangerous to rate it as Rubee (Rabi) land. Assessed at 11 annas to 14 annas per beegah. Bhoor 2nd kind, i.e. a white sandy soil, yielding only bajrah and mote, provided it be allowed to lie fallow every third or fourth year. Assessed at 5 to 8 annas per beegha.

II.   The Chahee (well-irrigated) is thus divided (a) Chahee Dhur, 2nd kind (there is no Chahee Dhur 1st kind here) and murmotah—yields principally wheat, surson. Assessed at Rs.3–6 as tc Rs. 3–12 as, per beegha. (b) Chahee Bhoor, 1st kind only (there is no Chahet Bhoor of 2nd kind) — yields barley. Assessed at Rs. 3/- to Rs. 3/6. Both descriptions of Chahee land yields tobacco, carrois, and other garden stuffs, but these products depend more on the peculiar properties of the water than on the soil and such details are to be found on the record of this office. Some wells yield from 200 to 400 maunds of com, others are famed for red pepper (*sic*). Some Chahee land produces from 50 to 350 maunds of onions per beegha.

III. Khadir, i.e. low and overflown by the Jamuna, to be found only in pargana Palwal. It may be sub-divided as follows—Khadir (1st kind)—A rich black soil yielding baranee wheat or barley, and when not overflown, mukee (maize), jowar and cotton inferior to the bangur. Assessed at Rs. 1-8 as. per beegha. Khadir (2nd kind)—A light sandy and yielding musoor, barley and peas mixed or peas, kungnee and mukkee of inferior quality. Assessed at 12 Annas for each beegah. Khadir is again sub-divided into Chahee (irrigated) and baranee (not irrigated). Khadir (low land) Chahee is not equal to bangur (upland) Chahee land. This is in general to be attributed to the inferior properties of its well water.

      The two grand classifications of land are bangur (upland) and Khadir (low land) subject to annual overflowing by rivers or rivulets. They are sub-divided as above explained. The bangur villages are in general the happiest and most affluent, the Khadir crops are most uncertain.

IV.   Nahri: The Duhur, Nurmotah and Bhoor, irrigated by canal water could pay nearly the same as Chahee (well-irrigated) land.

      The first kind (Duhur) and (Nurmotah) will yield sugar-cane, rice and indigo, and part of the land two crops, viz. 1st kunguee, early bajra, jowar or Churee—the 2nd may also yield, if well manured, an inferior crop of sugarcane and two crops, viz. kunguee samaih (three monthly) early bajra, jowar, and the Rabi crops as usual.

      Similarly, the early British Settlement reports and the District Gazetteers give names of the local indigenous classifications of the land. For example, the *District Gazetteer of Bhagalpur*, pp. 71–72 mentions three main classes of soils—clays, loams and sandy.

      (1) The first clay soil has four indigenous divisions viz. (a) Kharar or Kaiari, a blockist in colour sticky when wet and difficult to plough when dry. It is best suited for the growth of winter rice. When the rice crop is reaped, peas of various sorts, Khesari dal, gram and linseed are sown, broadcast in the mud before it dries up and luxurious crops are frequently raised in this day (b)

Khewal—This is also blackish colour, but is more friable when dry than Kharar. It is suitable for almost all crops except maize, Khurthi, etc. If it lies very low and goes under water when the Ganges is in flood, the land is called Char. Such soils grow only Rabi crops, (c) Gorimati—This soil is reddish yellow hue, and produces all kinds of crops if irrigated, (d) Harm Chikai and pasooti are whitish in colour and are suitable for winterpaddy.

(2) Loamy soils are known as Doras. If low lying winter rice is grown on them generally; if high, various Bhadoi and Rabi crops do well on them. This sort of soil is found around old village sites where it receives cow-dung and all sorts of household refuse. It is generally called Dih or Goora, and it is sown with potatoes, vegetables, tobacco, chillies etc. In low situations, loamy soils are called tan, and all crops except maize, kurthi, etc., will do well on them.

(3) Balmut is sandy loam that will grow anything. Dhus is the name given to sandy loam in the Gangetic diara. As it is submerged when the river is in flood, it is used for Rabi crops only. These crops thrive in it exceedingly.

Soil that is almost pure sand is called simply balu. When a thin layer of silt deposited on the top of the sand, it is called Patpar. In this state it grows mustard well, but as the layer of slit gets deeper it becomes also fit for the barley, oats etc. Diara lands covered with sand are called *balu burd*. Water-melons do very well in such lands. Excellent crops can be raised from such land but there is no stability nor certainty about diara cultivation.

Soils over which there is a Sabine efflorescence due to the presence of the alkaline salt, etc. are unfertile.

The above-cited documents are intended to show the detailed local classification of the land with different rates of assessment rather than the actual rates which were based on quite different methods of assessment in the Mughal age. But such a classification of land falls exactly in line in the general statement made in the *Ain* in its instruction* to the Amal Guzar; see the text with reference 60–2.

5

Nature of the Sair Jihat Taxes

Noman Ahmad Siddiqi

THE MUGHAL government levied taxes on the cultivated and pasture lands, on the produce of rivers and ponds, on the commodities manufactured by artisans, on the sale and purchase of commodities and taxes to meet the administration charges. These taxes were classified under the heads, *mal, jihat, sair-jihat*, and *sair-ul-wajuh*. However, in the assessment account of a village under *zabt*, it was the *mal, jihat*, and *sair-jihat* which constituted the land revenue or the *jama*.

Any attempt to understand the nature of the land revenue demand under the Mughals and to determine the share of the state in the produce of the land necessitates an investigation into the precise meaning and implications of these terms.

The earliest definitions of these terms are available in the *Ain-i-Akbari*. In short, says Abul Fazl, "Whatever was assessed on the cultivated land in accordance with the *rai*" or croprates was known as *mal*. Whatever was collected from various kinds of arts and crafts was termed as *jihat*, and the rest of the taxes came to be known as *sair jihat*.[1] According to the author of the *Khulasat-us-Siyaq*, an accountancy manual compiled in the reign of Aurangzeb, "the collections made from crops were known as *mal* and a number of taxes which were included, under the administration of certain revenue collectors, in the *jama* were known as *jihat*. Later on *jihat* was included or merged into the *mal* and the complex phrase, *mal-o-jihat*, was used as a single term. On the other hand, the taxes on cloth, skin, oil, grains, articles of food and medicine, horses and camels, collected in the market place and at the *chabutra-i-kotwali*, were known as *sair-i-jihat*."[2]

A comparison of the definitions given in the two sources mentioned above, shows that they agree as to the sense in which the term *mal* was used. However, *the jihat* in the *Ain* signifies a tax on various kinds of arts and crafts, whereas in the *Khulasat-us-Siyaq* it has been defined as an integral part of *mal* shown in *the jama*. Moreover, the *Ain* defines *sair-jihat* as those taxes which were collected over and above the *mal-o-jihat*. The text in the *Khulasat-us-Siyaq*

*27th Session at Allahabad, 1965.

implies that the *sair jihat* included all taxes, over and above the *mal-o-jihat*, which were collected at the *chabutra-i-kotwali*.

An administrative manual of Aurangzeb's reign defines *mal* as the real or original tax and *jihat* as the charges collected to meet the expenses incurred in connection with the assessment of *mal*.[3] Here we may note that *jihat* has been used in the same sense as defined in the *Khulasat-us-Siyaq*. However in the manual, referred to above, the nature of *jihat* has been specified. We may, therefore, infer that by the time of Aurangzeb the term *jihat* had acquired a connotation different from the one in which it was used in the Am. In the same administrative manual the definition of *mal* and *jihat* is followed by a definition of *sair-ul-wajuh* which has been defined as all the taxes collected over and above *mal-o-jihat*.[4] We read in the *Siyaq Nama* that all collections over and above *mal-o-jihat* are shown under the head *sair-ul-wajuh*.[5] But this is precisely the definition of *sair jihat* given in the *Ain* and inferred from the text of the *Khulasat-us-Siyaq* which, however, specifies it as taxes collected in the market place and in the *chabutra-i-kotwali*. If we are led by the definitions alone there appears to be some justification for identifying *sair jihat* with *sair-ul-wajuh*. But what follows the definition of *sair-ul-wajuh*, as given in the above two sources, makes it difficult to identify the two terms with each other and necessitates further investigation on the point.

The *Dastur-ul-Amal-i-Mujmalai*, after defining *sair-ul-wajuh*, gives a detailed list of the articles of taxation[6] classified under certain sub-heads such as *hasil-i-sair baz-yaft*, and *sair jihat*. There is yet another sub-head which is not decipherable.[7] A careful examination of the text and the articles of taxation given in the two sources[8] seems to suggest that *sair-ul-wajuh* in these sources signifies those taxes which were collected over and above the *mal-o-jihat* by the *karori*, and that it has been further classified into certain sub-heads including *sair jihat* or *sair-ul-jihat*. While various articles of taxation under the sub-heads have been specified in the *Dastur-ul-Amal-i-Mujmalai*, the text does not specify the items of taxation under *sair-i-jihat*.[9] However, a brief note says that the items of articles of taxation classified under *sair-ul-jihat* pertain to *mal-o-jihat*. In other words the taxes termed as *sair jihat* were charged in connection with the assessment or collection of *mal-o-jihat*. The inference is directly corroborated by a piece of evidence available in the assessment account of village Ganeshpur, given in *the Siyaq Nama*. The evidence clearly indicates that *sair jihat*, as we shall examine it in some detail, was a tax of rural and agricultural incidence which was closely related to *mal-o-jihat*.[10] Thus we can conclude that whereas in the *Ain* the *sair jihat* signifies all taxes collected over and above *mal-o-jihat* by the time of Aurangzeb, *sair, jihat* or *sair-ul-jihat* is referred to as a tax of agricultural incidence and was closely related to the amount assessed as *mal-o-jihat*. On the other hand *sair-ul-wajuh* signified all the taxes which were collected over and above the *mal-o-jihat*, and *sair jihat* appears to have been a part or sub-head of *sair-ul-wajuh*.

The assessment account of village Ganeshpur not only corroborates our inference about the nature of these taxes but also reveals the relationship that subsisted between the three taxes known as *mal-o-jihat* and *sair jihat*. It also helps to form an idea of the magnitude of the land revenue demand or the total share of the state in the produce of land. An examination of the *khasra-i-zabti*[11] and *jamabandi*[12] of village Ganeshpur for the year 1104 *Fasli* shows that the total area under various crops, including the area of land, which was twice brought under cultivation, amounted to 34 *bighas* and 15th *biswas*. The total assessment of the village, for the whole year, including the Kharif and Rabi assessments, amounted to Rs. 106/9 annas. The break up of the *jama* or the total land revenue demand under *mal, jihat* and *sair jihat* is given as follows:

mal	Rs. 88/2 1/2 annas		Rs. 92/10
Jihat	Rs. 4/7 1/2 annas	*mal-o-jihat*	
sair jihat Rs. 13/15			Rs. 13/15
TOTAL			Rs. 106/9

The account shows that whereas separate cash rates are applied for various crops in order to assess *mal, jihat* assessment was made under two heads, namely *Jaribana* and *deh nimi* at the rate of 5%. Calculating a charge of 5% on the *mal*, given in the account as Rs. 82/2 1/2 annas, we get Rs. 4/7 1/2 annas or so which is exactly the amount given in our account *as jihat* assessment. Thus we have definite evidence to show that *jihat* was a tax calculated on *mal* or the original assessment of the share of the state in the produce. Such an inference about the nature of *jihat* only confirms the definition given in our sources and discussed in the above lines. The assessment figures for *sair jihat*, in our assessment account, are given for Kharif and Rabi separately, and the account shows that they were calculated at the rate of 15%. Calculating a charge of 15% on the aggregate amount of Rs. 92/10 annas given as *mal-o-jihat*, we get Rs. 13/15 annas or so, which is exactly the amount shown as *sair jihat* assessment.[13] Thus we can reasonably infer that *sair jihat* signified certain charges calculated on the amount assessed as *mal-o-jihat* and that it was a tax of rural incidence collected from the agricultural community in the village. Moreover, most probably the charges were made in connection with the collection of *mal-o-jihat* taxes. The account under our examination, however, does not specify the items of taxation which were classified under *sair jihat* and for this we should look elsewhere.

Some evidence about the times of taxations classified under the head *sair-jihat*, is available in another account contained in the *Siyaq Nama*. An account of the collections and disbursement of pargana Fatehpur, throws some light regarding the point under investigation.[14] The collections in the account have been shown under three separate heads including the *sair-ul-wajuh*. Various items of taxation under the latter have been specified and the amount collected under each of the items has been noted. In order to clarify the points involved in the discussion, the *sair-ul-wajuh* collections are reproduced.[15]

sair-ul-wajuh Rs. 697

(The break-up of the account is given as follows):

Items of taxation	Amount
sadir-o-warid[16]	Rs. 300
shanagi[17] and tappadari	Rs. 125 (126)
talbana	Rs. 200
saif-i-sikka	Rs. 71
TOTAL[18]	Rs. 696 (697)

A careful examination of the nature of the taxes, given above, will show that excluding the *sarf-i-sikka,* or a percentage on the rupee if not paid in the established coin, the remaining of the three articles of taxation appear to have been exclusively rural and agricultural in their incidence. It also indicates that some of these fees and perquisites were charged to pay those who were employed to collect the land revenue. Such was the nature of taxes known as *talbana, shanagi* and *tappdari.* The perquisites collected under the head *sadir-o-warid,* elsewhere referred to as *mehmani,*[19] were earmarked to defray the cost of entertaining travellers, pilgrims and strangers.[20]

These inferences are supported by a similar documentary evidence available in the Fifth Report, which reproduces the *tumar-i-jama*[21]: of pargana Akbar Shahi in Bengal for the year 1691. The translation of the note introducing the *tumar-i-jama* or assessment account says that it includes the *mal-o-jihat* and *sair-jihat* assessment. An examination of the account shows that *sair-jihat* signified the collections over and above the original assessment of *mal-o-jihat* and that these taxes were rural and agricultural in their incidence. Moreover, these were calculated on the *mal-o-jihat* at a certain rate of percentage. However, it may be pointed out that the percentage given in the *Siyaq Nama* is a flat rate, whereas, in the document, reproduced in the Fifth Committee Report, variable rates are given for various articles of taxation. The taxes specified in the document are *damee*[22] *fotahdaree*[23] *dehdari,*[24] *tukee,*[25] *beha-i-kaghaz,*[26] *qusur*[27] and *mehmani.*[28] An examination of the nature of these taxes will show that these were the taxes which were collected in order to meet the expenses incurred in connection with the collection of land revenue and to defray such other expenses which were the joint responsibility of the agricultural community.

The evidence available in the revenue records of North-Western Provinces shows that certain charges were made on the cultivated field which amounted in certain districts to one-fourth of the original assessment. The early British administrators did not describe them as *sair-jihat* but classified them in view of their nature under the head village expenses, as they were of rural incidence in their nature. As the passage under reference gives a lucid exposition of these taxes and defines some of the perquisites, referred to in the Persian documents, it deserves to be quoted at length. "Over and above the payments stipulated in the Pattah, the tenant has to answer a demand made on him by the landholder on account of village expenses equal to one-fourth of his stipulated payments; in no instance, does it, I believe, exceed this, and the amount is in general more than sufficient for the purpose required, which include the allowance of Patwaree or village accountant, Batta or percentage in the rupee if not paid in the established coin, expenses of measurements and survey wages of Shahnas or people to watch the crops, Talubana or subsistence money to the persons employed in serving writs for the payment of revenue, charity and diet of indigent travellers, beggars, and Brahmins, presents, which later consist of a few rupees given by the landholder at the period of harvest to the Tehsildar or native collector, under whose immediate authority he is, to his *Amala* and to the police establishment in the *Pargunna*."[29]

The passage, quoted above, in the first place clearly brings out the nature of the taxes such as *talbana, shahnagi* and what in Persian documents has been referred to as *sarf-i-sikka* and *sadir-o-warid*. Second, it corroborates that these were the taxes of the rural and agricultural incidence and were added to the original assessment. It may be, however, pointed out that the passage under examination includes the tax collected to meet the expenses of measurement and survey in the list of village expenses which, as we know, in the Persian document is shown as the first separate charge on the original assessment. Moreover, the evidence contained in the *Revenue Records* refers also to the taxes collected to pay the policing charges, formerly known as Faujdari perquisites, which has not been included in our sources under the head *sair-jihat*. These may be taken to indicate either local variations or the changes which had taken place in the administrative practices with the passage of time.

Notes

1. *Ain-i-Akbari*, I, p. 205.
2. *Khulasat-us-Siyaq*, f. 135b; for the definition of the *sair-i-jihat*; see also *Farhang-i-Kardani*, f. 34b.
3. *Dastur-ul-Amal-i-Mujmalai*, f. 28a.
4. Ibid., f. 28a.
5. *Siyaq Nama*, p. 307.
6. *Dastur-ul-Amal-i-Mujmalai*, f. 28b–29a.
7. *Dastur-ul-Amal-i-Mujmalai*, f. 28a-29a; *cf. Siyaq Nama*, p. 307. The sub-head under *sair-wajun, in the Siyaq Nama,* are given *as peshkash,* hidden treasure, *bait-ul-mal, hasil-i- baghat,* and *baz-yaft.*

8. Some of the items of taxation shown under the head *sair-ul-wajuh*, common in two sources namely the *Dastur-ul-Amal-i-Mujmalai* and the *Siyaq Nama*, are given below:
    (i) *peshkash* collected by the Karori,
    (ii) property found lying on ground or on digging the earth,
    (iii) escheated property belonging to men of position,
    (iv) property for which no lawful heir put forth claim, taxes on,
    (v) pressing mill,
    (vi) groves,
    (vii) shops,
    (viii) market.
9. *Siyaq Nama*, pp. 33–4.
10. Also see the *Revenue Records*, p. 260, *Fifth Committee Report*, II, p. 742.
11. *Siyaq Nama*, pp. 3ff, 33.
12. Ibid., pp. 33–4.
13. A perquisite claimed by the Muqaddam of the village which amounted to 1/10th of the collection (See add. 6603f. 61b).
14. *Siyaq Nama*, pp. 62–4.
15. Ibid., p. 64.
16. *Sadar-o-warid* literally those who visit the village; technically a perquisite collected to entertain those who visit the village as travellers, pilgrims and strangers in general (see *Revenue Records*, p. 260). Most probably it refers to the perquisite elsewhere referred to as *mehmani*, ch. *Siyaq Nama*, p. 79; *Fifth Committee Report*, II, p. 472.
17. *Shahnagi*, a fee or tax collected to pay the wages *of Shahna* who was employed to watch the crops (*Revenue Records*, p. 260).
18. The actual total comes to Rs. 696, whereas the opening account gives the amount as Rs. 697. There appears to be a mistake of one rupee in the details which may be described to a faulty transcription.
19. *Siyaq Nama*, pp. 78–9; *Fifth Report*, II, p. 742.
20. *Fifth Report*, II, 742, ch. *Dastur-ul-Amal-i-Mujmalai*, ff. 46ab–47a.
21. (Appendix to *The Fifth Report* from the Select Committee, II, 742).
22. *Damee*. A perquisite of a *dam* per bigha paid to the Zamindar.
23. Perquisite realised by the office of the Fotadar.
24. An article of the village expenses perquisite or fees received from the ryot and appropriated to particular public officer in the village or other expenses.
25. Perquisite of one rupee in Bengal.
26. Charges for defraying the expenses incurred in the purchase of stationery for offices connected with the village.
27. *Qusur*: deductions.
28. Under the Mughal government a deduction from the revenue allowed Zamindars to defray the cost of entertaining travellers, pilgrims and strangers in general. See *Wilson's Glossary*.
29. *Revenue Records of the North-Western Provinces*, p. 260.

6

The Pattern of Agricultural Production in the Territories of Amber (c. 1650–1750)

S. Nurul Hasan, K.N. Hasan and *S.P. Gupta*

Till now it has not been possible to study the pattern of agricultural production as it existed in the medieval period because of the paucity of data. No definite estimate could be made regarding the percentage of the various crops and consequently no worthwhile study was made about changes in the crop pattern.

Fortunately, the Arhsattas of the territories held by the rulers of Amber enable us to fill partly this gap in our knowledge. The present study is based on the examination of the Arhsattas of the contiguous parganas of Amber, (Sawai Jaipur), Malarna, Bahatri and Chatsu. The period covered in these documents is 1664–1750. However, the continuous series is not available and the gaps are considerable.

The Arhsattas contain information, among other things, on the following points:

Total revenue demand;

Proportion of the demand from kharif and rabi harvests;

Cash demand of areas given in *ijara* (for which no particulars are available). Area under each crop assessed according to the *zabti* system, the rate of payment per bigha and the total revenue assessed per crop;

Total revenue realised in kind according to the *batai jinsi* system and the sale price of the revenue realised in kind per crop. Sometime the total produce is also mentioned along with the share of the produce left with the ryot and the share realised by the State in kind.

Although information contained in the Arhsattas is extremely valuable yet its analysis is fraught with serious difficulties. First of all the size of the parganas does not remain constant. For example, the number of villages in pargana Amber, later designated as Sawai Jaipur, increases from 541 in 1677

*28th Session at Mysore, 1966.

to 611 in 1690, 700 in 1715, 780 in 1723, 874 in 1725, 998 in 1737 and 1140 in 1744. This enormous increase was due to the absorption of many contiguous tracts into the pargana. In pargana Chatsu the number of villages increases from 256 in 1708 to 399 in 1737. In pargana Bahatri the number increases from 261 in 1665 to 339 in 1716. In Malarna, however, the size of the pargana remains on the whole fairly steady.

Apart from the fluctuation in size, another difficulty is that detailed information is available only in respect of the villages held by the ruling family in *khalisa* and excluding those areas of the *khalisa* whose revenue was farmed out for a fixed sum. The territory held in *khalisa* as well as that given in *ijara* increased or decreased from season to season and year to year. However, it may be assumed that the crop pattern in the *khalisa* areas would represent the crop pattern of the territory as a whole.

The most serious difficulty in utilising the statistical information in the Arhsattas is that the figures are given in two distinct sets which are, strictly speaking, not comparable with each other, namely the *jinsi* and the *zabti*. As a general rule the crops which are assessed according to the *batai jinsi* system continue to be assessed in the same system throughout the period under review. Similarly, those assessed according to the *zabti* system continue to be so assessed during the period. The figures for the *zabti* system do not give any indication of either the produce per bigha or the price of the crop or the incidence of taxation. In so far as the crops assessed according to the *batai jinsi* system are concerned occasionally the total produce is given alongside the quantity demanded as revenue, but generally only the quantity demanded as revenue is given alongside the sale price of the portion sold. The area sown and the rate of demand per bigha in kind is not given. Thus it is not easy to make the two sets of figures comparable.

To study the relative position of crops the one obvious common denominator has been used, namely to examine the revenue realised from each crop (Table I). Although this method gives a rough indication, there are too many variable factors involved to permit us to judge the crop pattern exclusively by comparing the revenue derived from different crops. Under the *zabti* assessment different rates per bigha were applicable even in individual villages. And there were changes in the rate of demand from year to year. Apparently, the rate depended on the quality of the produce, the productivity of the soil and prices. However, an examination of the rate of revenue demand per bigha for *zabti* crops shows a remarkable continuity (Table II). Since during the period under review there is apparently a general rise in prices (Table III) the *zabti* system tended to be more advantageous to the ryot than to the State. It was perhaps for this reason that there is a tendency for an increase in the cultivation of *zabti* crops.

For the *jinsi* crops too, the revenue figures do not necessarily provide a safe guide to the crop pattern. The fluctuation in price is of course an obvious difficulty. At the same time we know from these documents that the share of the State in respect of the different crops varied even within each pargana and quite frequently from year to year. However, the average remains fairly steady. The following table gives the average of the share of the total produce for each of the principal crops taken by the State in the four parganas:

State Share of Total Produce (in percentage)

KHARIF

Pargana	Bajra	Jowar	Moth	Urd	Mung	Til	Chola
Jaipur	39.6	46.8	40.0	41.0	39.0	42.0	—
Malama	42.0	44.5	41.0	44.0	43.0	44.0	—
Bahalri (Baswa)*	45.0	46.0	44.0	44.0	43.0	42.0	50.0
Chatsu	35.0	36.0	36.0	38.0	39.0	33.0	—

* This pargana contained the qasba of Baswa, which has now given its name to the whole pargana.

RABI

Pargana	Barely	Wheat	Gram
Jaipur	31.8	32.6	36.1
Malama	34.0	34.6	38.0
Bahatri	33.0	32.0	41.0
Chatsu	32.0	33.0	37.7

A perusal of the above table reveals that the incidence of demand for the principal *jinsi* crops of the rabi harvest was more or less the same as that of the *zabti* crops while for the kharif harvest the incidence of the revenue demand of the *jinsi* crops would tend to be 10 to 15 per cent higher than that of *zabti* crops.

Fortunately, some of the *jinsi* crops were occasionally, in part, assessed according to the *zabti* system and therefore the *zabti* rates as well as the demand in kind and price for the same crop in the same pargana is available. It is consequently possible to convert the cash demand per bigha into kind demand per bigha (on the basis of the prevailing price). It is also possible, by assuming that *zabti* rates were calculated on the basis of one-third of the average produce, to work out the average yield per bigha. By examining the average yield per bigha and the average demand in kind per bigha it is possible to work out the area under each crop where the State demand in kind is given. Although this method is not entirely accurate, and it is based on assumptions which are not always correct, it provides a possible method of estimating the total number of bighas under each crop. Such an estimate has of course to be moderated on the basis of the differences in the weight of the maund (ranging from 28 to 40, and even 42) and the size of the bigha (which was generally a square of 75 *haths* (or cubits).

By this method the proportion of area under different crops has been estimated (Table V). Although the proportion of the different crops estimated according to revenue yield and according to the area (Tables I & V) is different in many respects, the over all picture of the crop pattern as well as of the major changes during the period under review appears to be the same according to both the estimates.

The principal crops were as follows:

Kharif

Bajra, jowar and the pulses *moth, urd* and *mung* were the most important *jinsi* crops while *chola*, sugarcane, cotton and *makka* were the most important *zabti* crops. In Malarna, Bahatri and Chatsu, *kodon* was also a very important crop. The other significant crops were *til (Jinsi)*, vegetables, indigo, *barti, marhwa,* tobacco and paddy *(zabti)*.

Rabi

The most important Rabi crops were assessed according to the *batai jinsi* system and the *zabti* crops were only of marginal significance. The principal *jinsi* crops were barley, wheat and gram with mixed crops such as *baijhri, gojai* and *gochani* occupying a significant place. The other *jinsi* rabi crop was *sarson* but its cultivation appears to have been fairly restricted. Among rabi *zabti* crops mention may be made of vegetables *china*, tobacco and *ajwain*. But none of these occupied a significant place in the scheme of agriculture. In pargana Chatsu however *chomli* was an important crop.

The most important changes in the pattern of agricultural production were an increase in the *zabti* crop of the kharif harvest. These were apparently cash crops. The increase is most marked in the following crops:

Sugarcane — in pargana Jaipur and Bahatri
Cotton — in Malarna and Chatsu
Makka — in Jaipur, Bahatri and Chatsu
Chola and kodon — in all the four parganas.

There is a corresponding decrease in the percentage of the bajra and the pulses. The increase in these cash crops, accompanied as it was with a general rise in prices and a comparatively stable cash demand per bigha, was not without significance for the economic life of the region. It reflects a comparative decrease in local self-sufficiency, a greater use of money economy and commodity production and indicates that at least in this region capital was available to some extent for developing agricultural production. This indication is also available from the fact that the proportion of production during the rabi harvest increases in comparison to kharif harvest. The geographical condition of the region is such that rabi production can only be increased if there is a reasonable investment in agriculture.

TABLE I: Table Showing the Percentage of Revenue Derived from Different Crops

KHARIF

Year	Bajra	Jowar	Moth	Urd	Mung	Chola	Sugarcane	Cotton	Makki
PARGANA JAIPUR (AMBER)									
1666	31.0	17.0	27.0	—	1.0	—	1.0	13.0	—
1677	32.0	3.0	35.0	1.0	1.0	—	3.0	16.0	1.0
1688	18.0	1.8	27.0	1.0	3.0	—	1.3	18.0	—
1689	18.0	—	37.0	—	3.0	—	—	11.0	5.4
1690	11.0	1.4	41.0	1.0	3.0	—	—	24.0	2.5
1712	31.0	1.2	32.0	—	2.5	—	2.7	14.0	5.0
1715	15.0	4.6	18.0	1.0	1.0	—	12.0	19.0	12.0
1716	5.7	25.0	18.0	1.0	1.5	5.0	—	19.0	15.0
1718	30.0	5.0	13.0	—	—	2.5	3.0	15.6	12.6
1720	25.0	1.8	15.4	1.0	1.8	5.6	3.0	16.0	16.0
1723	22.0	3.0	20.0	—	—	6.0	1.4	20.0	12.0
1724	8.0	2.0	27.0	—	2.0	8.0	3.0	15.0	15.0
1725	13.0	1.0	7.0	—	—	8.0	5.6	25.0	20.0
1733	3.6	1.0	10.0	1.0	1.4	1.0	3.0	46.0	12.4
1734	4.3	1.7	26.0	1.9	2.3	9.1	6.0	19.8	16.0
1737	6.3	1.7	23.0	1.9	1.8	11.0	4.0	20.0	18.0
1744	7.7	8.0	20.0	—	1.0	6.0	10.0	9.8	17.0

Year	Bajra	Jowar	Moth	Urd	Kodon	Sugar	Cotton	Makka
PARGANA MALARNA								
1690	13.2	26.8	19.6	—	1.0	23.6	9.0	—
1699	29.0	20.0	6.2	1.5	—	16.0	7.8	—
1711	40.0	26.0	9.8	—	—	10.0	1.5	
1712	32.0	15.0	14.0	—	—	—	—	—
1713	35.6	9.3	26.9	5.0	1.0	5.9	2.0	—
1714	41.8	11.0	6.8	2.7	1.9	15.3	3.9	—
1715	34.0	15.5	14.2	3.7	1.8	14.9	6.2	—
1716	26.0	5.2	17.7	7.7	1.7	14.0	7.4	—
1717	37.3	11.2	14.7	9.2	1.0	7.0	7.5	—
1718	42.6	16.9	6.3	2.0	3.3	9.0	10.0	—
1719	24.9	29.3	18.0	2.2	2.7	8.0	—	—
1720	32.0	29.3	7.3	1.6	1.3	10.6	4.2	—
1722	36.8	26.6	8.0	1.6	—	7.0	4.2	—
1723	34.3	33.8	8.8	1.0	1.0	5.4	5.2	—

(Contd.)

TABLE I (*Contd.*)

Year	Bajra	Jowar	Moth	Urd	Kodon	Sugar	Cotton	Makka
1726	21.6	29.6	3.8	2.3	3.2	20.0	9.7	—
1727	27.0	30.0	6.6	3.0	2.7	10.2	6.9	—
1728	21.8	24.4	11.8	1.9	2.3	4.3	8.8	—
1729	22.8	26.0	9.3	2.6	2.0	9.0	13.7	—
1732	16.5	26.0	3.3	1.0	6.3	12.8	22.2	—
1736	15.0	25.3	5.5	3.9	1.7	20.4	22.0	—
1737	19.5	30.0	9.0	1.5	3.7	11.6	12.3	—
1738	28.0	31.6	14.2	2.3	1.6	3.0	2.5	—
1743	30.3	38.2	3.0	—	—	5.3	5.7	—
1744	21.7	26.5	15.0	—	2.0	14.6	2.0	—
1745	29.2	25.2	10.2	2.0	—	7.0	5.0	—
1748	26.8	27.8	12.6	2.5	—	5.5	4.0	—
1749	19.4	34.8	10.2	2.4	—	6.4	2.8	—

Year	Bajra	Jowar	Moth	Urd	Mung	Sugar cane	Cotton	Makka

PRAGANA BHARATI

Year	Bajra	Jowar	Moth	Urd	Mung	Sugar cane	Cotton	Makka
1665	14.8	15.0	13.7	2.0	1.3	—	17.0	—
1669	16.0	21.4	15.3	4.8	2.5	2.0	27.0	—
1684	11.0	15.0	18.4	8.0	2.0	5.0	30.0	—
1685	11.0	18.0	9.6	4.0	—	7.8	44.0	—
1686	15.0	15.0	15.0	4.0	—	6.0	27.0	1.0
1688	4.7	14.0	13.0	5.0	—	8.0	28.0	2.0
1689	—	17.0	22.0	6.0	—	21.0	16.0	—
1691	4.0	16.0	20.0	5.0	—	9.0	30.0	—
1696	10.0	13.0	2.0	—	—	9.0	33.0	7.0
1706	24.0	23.0	17.0	—	—	5.0	19.0	1.0
1708	27.0	25.0	12.0	1.0	—	5.0	16.0	3.0
1710	12.0	13.0	32.0	7.0	4.0	3.0	18.0	2.0
1716	5.3	10.7	13.8	9.9	11.0	12.8	33.0	2.4
1717	18.4	5.6	3.4	—	—	29.8	29.9	2.8
1718	24.4	18.0	12.7	2.5	—	2.7	17.2	4.6
1720	12.2	6.7	13.0	4.1	2.0	14.4	23.0	9.9
1721	14.6	15.9	15.7	5.8	1.6	8.1	15.3	6.2
1723	17.0	17.6	13.8	27.0	—	5.1	23.0	6.2
1724	10.0	10.0	18.9	4.5	1.2	6.0	13.1	5.6
1725	8.6	5.9	16.4	10.3	1.2	10.5	25.4	6.8

Year	Bajra	Jowar	Moth	Urd	Kodon	Chola	Sugar cane	Cotton	Makka

PARGANA CHATSU

Year	Bajra	Jowar	Moth	Urd	Kodon	Chola	Sugar cane	Cotton	Makka
1664	54.0	8.4	13.0	—	1.6	—	—	7.0	—
1708	55.0	5.0	1.0	1.0	—	—	—	—	—
1710	40.0	7.6	26.0	—	3.0	—	—	5.5	1.2
1711	51.0	3.4	16.0	—	4.3	—	—	10.0	1.8
1712	56.0	3.8	15.0	—	3.0	—	—	10.0	2.3
1713	11.0	12.0	35.0	4.0	—	—	5.2	6.2	4.4
1714	35.0	8.0	28.0	—	9.0	—	—	9.0	4.5

(*Contd.*)

TABLE I (*Contd.*)

Year	Bajra	Jowar	Moth	Urd	Kodon	Chola	Sugar cane	Cotton	Makka
1715	41.0	7.0	26.0	1.9	4.5	—	2.0	7.0	—
1716	24.0	—	22.0	5.2	9.0	—	—	19.0	—
1721	35.0	9.0	21.0	2.0	4.8	1.8	1.8	10.0	5.5
1723	36.0	12.0	10.0	—	4.2	1.2	—	18.0	7.0
1724	15.0	11.0	37.0	1.2	3.7	3.3	1.0	9.0	2.8
1726	11.4	7.8	10.0	2.7	1.7	4.0	6.4	42.0	3.4
1730	10.0	1.8	13.0	3.0	10.0	1.8	6.3	32.0	6.5
1731	5.7	1.8	—	—	—	—	8.3	56.0	14.0
1733	7.8	2.3	19.0	3.4	9.8	2.7	4.2	24.0	8.6
1735	3.3	—	28.0	7.4	6.6	5.2	4.6	19.0	2.2
1736	14.0	7.5	6.8	2.0	5.8	5.5	4.5	31.0	12.0
1737	6.0	4.0	27.0	2.5	7.0	5.0	3.0	28.5	9.5
1740	7.7	4.8	19.0	3.7	9.0	4.0	2.4	20.0	11.0
1741	5.4	1.6	12.4	3.2	9.4	1.9	6.3	29.5	12.2
1742	11.0	10.0	3.2	—	4.7	—	8.9	40.4	11.3
1744	10.3	13.5	25.6	2.4	7.0	2.7	3.4	5.7	3.5
1745	14.1	10.3	16.2	3.0	7.3	2.9	3.0	11.0	12.8
1748	10.0	2.9	13.8	1.4	4.9	2.2	—	21.6	14.7
1749	11.5	4.5	14.4	2.8	5.0	2.1	1.7	18.8	19.2
1750	4.6	3.0	7.4	—	—	—	3.3	28.3	25.6

RABI

Year	Wheat	Barley	Gram	Wheat	Barley	Gram
	PARGANA JAIPUR			PARGANA MALARNA		
1665	—	—	—	39.0	29.0	21.0
1677	5.1	49.6	40.0	—	—	—
1688	15.8	52.9	27.0	—	—	—
1689	10.0	57.0	23.9	—	—	—
1690	7.0	47.5	33.0	39.4	29.0	21.0
1711	—	—	—	11.0	14.0	40.0
1712	21.7	58.0	12.0	—	—	—
1713	—	—	—	13.0	54.7	18.6
1714	—	—	—	19.9	66.0	9.7
1715	23.7	57.0	15.0	14.0	48.0	—
1716	31.4	50.6	17.0	—	53.0	23.0
1717	—	—	—	15.0	71.0	9.0
1718	2.0	—	1.2	17.0	69.0	11.0
1719	—	—	—	17.0	53.0	16.0
1720	17.4	72.0	4.0	25.0	38.0	8.0
1722	—	—	—	15.0	62.0	17.0
1723	16.0	77.8	—	17.0	65.0	10.0
1724	17.0	29.0	9.0	—	—	—
1725	10.5	50.0	29.5	—	—	—
1726	—	—	—	9.7	43.0	27.9
1727	—	—	—	18.6	41.0	28.9

(*Contd.*)

TABLE I (*Contd.*)

Year	Wheat	Barley	Gram	Wheat	Barley	Gram
1728	—	70.0	16.0	21.5	25.0	38.0
1729	12.6	61.5	6.0	13.8	35.6	35.7
1730	—	—	—	10.8	38.0	35.4
1732	—	—	—	8.5	67.0	20.0
1733	9.6	52.3	3.2	—	—	—
1734	15.3	73.4	1.0	—	—	—
1736	—	—	—	1.5	70.0	—
1737	11.7	82.0	1.6	17.9	68.0	7.5
1738	—	—	—	24.8	26.0	21.0
1743	—	—	—	37.6	45.8	8.5
1744	12.8	73.8	5.9	25.7	47.0	17.0
1745	—	—	—	21.8	36.9	19.7
1748	—	—	—	36.4	45.0	12.0
1749	—	—	—	34.5	36.5	25.0
1750	—	—	—	42.6	38.0	13.5

Year	Wheat	Barley	Gram	Wheat	Barley	Gram	Chombli
	PARGANA BHARTI			PARGANA CHATSU			
1665	14.5	61.8	17.0	—	—	—	—
1669	7.7	60.8	21.7	—	—	—	—
1686	11.7	61.5	11.7	—	—	—	—
1688	20.7	48.0	9.5	—	—	—	—
1689	24.4	45.0	8.6	—	—	—	—
1696	13.0	78.6	—	—	—	—	—
1697	14.7	72.4	4.3	—	—	—	—
1706	22.0	60.7	11.6	—	—	—	—
1708	21.0	63.0	7.8	—	—	—	—
1710	24.8	39.0	27.4	10.0	48.0	31.0	2.0
1711	30.0	34.0	28.0	16.0	41.0	—	2.0
1712	—	—	—	15.0	60.0	7.0	9.0
1713	—	—	—	30.0	49.0	14.0	—
1714	—	—	—	14.0	49.0	24.0	8.6
1716	32.0	42.0	18.0	13.0	37.0	27.0	10.0
1717	18.0	73.0	—	10.0	78.0	—6.7	
1718	17.0	70.0	3.0	—	—	—	—
1720	28.0	67.0	—	—	—	—	—
1721	25.0	58.0	9.0	15.0	57.0	18.0	2.8
1723	29.0	79.0	5.0	13.0	75.0	—5.4	
1724	28.0	52.0	11.0	17.0	52.0	14.0	4.0
1725	20.0	47.0	19.0	—	—	—	—
1726	—	—	—	10.0	57.0	9.0	12.5
1730	—	—	—	10.0	59.0	18.0	4.5
1731	—	—	—	8.0	77.0	—	7.9
1733	—	—	—	14.0	60.0	6.0	11.0
1735	—	—	—	15.0	56.0	12.0	3.5

(*Contd.*)

TABLE I (*Contd.*)

Year	Wheat	Barley	Gram	Wheat	Barley	Gram	Chombli
1737	—	—	—	10.0	70.0	7.0	3.4
1738	—	—	—	8.0	63.0	13.0	9.8
1740	—	—	—	12.0	57.0	9.0	5.5
1741	—	—	—	13.0	60.0	13.0	4.7
1742	—	—	—	3.2	79.6	1.4	5.0
1743	—	—	—	8.0	74.0	4.0	6.4
1744	—	—	—	13.0	66.0	5.0	5.0
1745	—	—	—	13.0	63.0	5.0	11.9
1748	—	—	—	17.0	65.0	2.0	9.6
1749	—	—	—	11.0	64.0	7.0	10.0

TABLE II: Rate of Revenue Demand per Bigha (in Rupees)

Year	Cotton	Sugarcane	Kodon	Makka	Chola
PARGANA JAIPUR					
1666	1.28	4.73	1.17	1.87	0.94
1677	1.35	4.64	1.17	1.61	0.63
1688	1.28	3.70	1.14	1.57	0.62
1689	1.33	—	—	—	0.60
1690	1.36	3.75	1.16	1.50	0.61
1712	1.13	2.62	1.08	1.28	0.49
1715	1.23	3.31	1.10	1.42	0.48
1716	1.18	—	1.07	1.34	0.49
1718	1.21	3.19	1.12	1.37	0.49
1720	1.20	3.22	1.03	1.28	0.50
1723	1.23	3.30	1.08	1.31	0.51
1724	—	—	1.08	—	0.50
1725	1.27	3.32	1.09	1.36	0.52
1728	1.23	—	1.00	2.00	0.64
1729	1.16	3.91	1.00	1.69	0.60
1733	1.18	3.74	1.11	1.46	0.57
1734	1.29	3.68	1.12	1.45	0.56
1736	1.29	3.69	1.11	1.42	0.57
1737	1.30	3.77	1.11	1.41	0.55
1744	1.36	3.68	1.11	1.41	0.56

Year	Cotton	Sugarcane	Kodon	Makka
PARGANA MALARNA				
1690	1.24	3.24	0.97	—
1699	1.09	2.69	1.00	0.87
1711	1.22	3.15	0.99	1.00
1713	1.21	3.11	0.96	0.94
1714	1.21	3.06	0.98	0.98
1715	1.15	3.01	0.95	1.00
1716	1.22	2.96	0.98	1.00
1717	1.19	7.89	1.00	—
1718	1.18	3.06	0.93	0.88

(Contd.)

TABLE II (*Contd.*)

Year	Cotton	Sugarcane	Kodon	Makka
1719	1.18	2.86	0.88	0.91
1720	1.19	3.07	0.98	1.00
1721	1.21	3.15	0.97	1.00
1722	1.22	3.13	0.97	1.00
1723	1.20	3.19	0.97	0.97
1726	1.21	3.18	0.99	1.00
1727	1.24	3.24	0.99	1.00
1728	1.22	3.25	0.99	1.00
1729	1.23	3.22	0.99	1.00
1730	1.24	3.16	0.99	1.00
1731	1.23	3.19	1.00	0.97
1732	1.22	3.21	0.96	0.94
1736	1.23	3.18	0.99	0.99
1737	1.23	3.16	0.99	0.98
1738	1.23	3.17	1.00	0.99
1743	1.21	3.02	—	0.98
1744	1.21	3.14	0.99	0.98
1745	1.15	3.09	0.97	0.98
1748	1.17	3.09	0.99	0.98
1749	1.17	3.11	0.96	0.98
1750	1.09	3.97	0.99	0.99

PARGANA BHATRI

Year	Cotton	Sugarcane	Kodon	Makka
1665	1.41	2.00	—	1.74
1669	1.44	2.00	—	1.79
1684	1.45	2.00	—	—
1685	1.40	2.00	1.60	1.60
1686	1.44	2.00	1.40	1.23
1688	1.30	1.80	—	1.25
1689	1.39	2.00	1.50	1.74
1691	1.25	2.00	1.25	1.80
1696	1.25	1.75	1.25	1.33
1706	1.30	1.90	1.40	1.30
1708	1.36	1.83	1.33	1.25
1710	1.34	1.87	1.44	1.25
1716	1.30	2.00	1.50	1.20
1717	1.25	1.91	1.46	1.21
1718	1.37	1.96	1.46	1.19
1720	1.34	2.00	1.40	1.23
1721	1.33	1.94	1.39	1.24
1723	1.35	1.96	1.40	1.24
1724	1.42	1.95	1.47	1.74

PARGANA CHATSU

Year	Cotton	Sugarcane	Kodon	Makka
1664	0.82	2.00	0.83	1.09
1708	1.24	—	1.12	1.36
1709	1.23	—	0.96	1.41
1710	1.12	—	1.03	0.95
1711	1.11	2.02	1.00	1.07

(*Contd.*)

TABLE II (*Contd.*)

Year	Cotton	Sugarcane	Kodon	Makka
1712	1.11	2.30	0.98	1.08
1713	1.54	1.06	1.41	1.24
1714	1.10	2.20	0.95	1.05
1715	1.11	2.45	0.97	1.10
1716	1.11	2.71	0.94	1.08
1717	1.10	2.59	0.90	0.98
1721	1.11	2.75	0.97	1.10
1723	1.08	2.74	0.95	1.08
1724	1.11	2.91	0.98	1.10
1726	1.12	2.97	1.08	1.10
1730	1.10	2.01	0.98	1.08
1731	1.08	2.82	—	1.07
1733	1.11	2.97	0.98	1.09
1735	1.11	2.97	0.98	1.05
1736	1.07	2.92	0.96	1.05
1737	1.09	2.93	0.92	1.06
1740	1.09	2.94	0.95	1.09
1741	1.10	2.88	0.96	1.09
1742	1.10	2.91	0.97	1.09
1744	1.10	2.73	0.97	1.07
1745	1.09	2.86	0.97	1.06
1748	1.07	2.44	0.94	1.04
1749	1.08	2.59	0.%	1.06
1750	1.10	2.91	—	1.07

TABLE III: Average Price of Principal Jinsi Crops (In Maunds per Rupee)

Year	Bajra	Jowar	Moth	Urd	Mung	Chola	Wheat	Barley	Gram
			KHARIF					RABI	
1666	2.25	2.48	2.43	2.26	1.98	2.46	—	—	—
1677	1.41	1.42	1.43	1.21	1.11	1.40	1.02	1.53	—
1688	1.35	1.35	—	1.21	1.31	1.47	1.33	1.71	1.69
1690	1.85	2.23	2.50	1.86	1.77	2.33	1.46	2.11	2.14
1708	1.42	1.59	1.37	0.98	1.02	—	0.85	1.26	1.05
1712	0.65	0.79	0.56	0.44	0.41	0.39	0.41	0.52	1.35
1715	0.78	0.80	0.75	0.69	0.57	0.71	0.83	1.07	1.07
1716	0.88	0.71	0.91	0.73	0.67	0.96	—	1.30	1.34
1718	0.59	0.63	0.55	0.51	0.42	0.53	0.58	0.78	—
1720	1.01	1.14	1.08	0.99	0.86	1.11	0.68	0.88	0.82
1723	0.91	1.00	0.91	0.86	0.79	0.91	0.76	0.94	0.80
1725	1.13	1.41	1.18	0.83	0.80	0.97	0.99	1.42	1.41
1728	1.08	2.24	1.14	1.57	0.24	1.36	1.58	2.04	1.58
1729	0.80	0.96	0.92	0.96	0.85	—	0.75	0.99	0.91
1733	0.99	1.23	0.99	0.87	0.81	0.93	0.76	1.02	0.90
1734	0.83	1.13	0.95	0.92	0.80	1.02	0.74	0.98	0.87
1737	0.59	0.73	0.66	0.77	0.53	0.70	0.56	0.75	0.58
1744	0.88	1.11	0.95	0.75	0.75	0.84	0.91	1.36	1.05
1748	0.68	0.69	0.72	0.65	0.62	—	0.55	0.75	0.62
1750	0.90	0.93	0.84	0.78	0.76	—	0.55	0.75	0.62

TABLE IV: Proportion of Revenue from Kharif and Rabi Harvests

	% of Total Revenue		% of Kharif Revenue		% of Rabi Revenue	
Year	Kharif	Rabi	Zabti	Jinsi	Zabti	Jinsi
PARGANA JAIPUR						
1677	49.0	51.0	24.0	76.0	1.0	99.0
1688	18.0	82.0	41.0	59.0	2.0	98.0
1689	38.0	62.0	32.0	68.0	1.0	99.0
1690	46.0	54.0	37.0	63.0	3.0	97.0
1712	42.0	58.0	29.0	71.0	1.0	99.0
1715	47.0	53.0	58.0	42.0	2.0	98.0
1716	33.0	67.0	62.0	38.0	3.0	97.0
1718	55.0	45.0	49.0	51.0	4.0	96.0
1720	37.0	63.0	55.0	45.0	2.0	98.0
1723	48.0	52.0	50.0	50.0	2.0	98.0
1724	89.0	11.0	60.0	40.0	30.0	70.0
1725	19.0	81.0	76.0	24.0	1.0	99.0
1733	34.0	66.0	72.0	28.0	1.0	99.0
1734	38.0	62.0	58.0	42.0	2.0	98.0
1737	39.0	61.0	57.0	43.0	1.0	99.0
1744	30.0	70.0	63.0	37.0	2.0	98.0
PARGANA MALARNA						
1690	70.0	30.0	29.0	71.0	2.0	98.0
1711	50.0	50.0	50.0	50.0	2.0	98.0
1712	96.0	4.0	92.0	8.0	1.0	99.0
1713	63.0	37.0	11.0	89.0	60.0	40.0
1714	56.0	44.0	23.0	77.0	—	100.0
1715	55.0	45.0	24.0	76.0	—	100.0
1716	83.0	17.0	27.0	73.0	—	100.0
1717	20.0	80.0	15.0	85.0	—	100.0
1718	79.0	21.0	23.0	77.0	—	100.0
1719	30.0	70.0	13.0	87.0	—	100.0
1720	70.0	30.0	17.0	83.0	—	100.0
1722	81.0	19.0	13.0	87.0	—	100.0
1723	86.0	14.0	13.0	87.0	5.0	100.0
1726	72.0	28.0	34.0	66.0	—	95.0
1727	70.0	30.0	22.0	78.0	5.0	100.0
1728	79.0	21.0	18.0	82.0	—	95.0
1729	58.0	42.0	26.0	74.0	5.0	95.0
1732	62.0	38.0	50.0	50.0	5.0	95.0
1736	59.0	41.0	45.0	55.0	—	95.0
1737	52.0	48.0	31.0	69.0	5.0	95.0
1738	33.0	67.0	15.0	85.0	5.0	95.0
1743	36.0	64.0	23.0	87.0	5.0	95.0
1744	31.0	69.0	27.0	73.0	5.0	95.0
1745	61.0	39.0	20.0	80.0	—	100.0

(Contd.)

TABLE IV (*Contd.*)

	% of Total Revenue		% of Kharif Revenue		% of Rabi Revenue	
Year	Kharif	Rabi	Zabti	Jinsi	Zabti	Jinsi
PARGANA BAHATRI						
1665	73.3	26.6	27.8	72.1	3.00	97.0
1669	63.3	36.6	30.0	70.0	2.0	98.0
1684	48.1	51.8	40.0	60.0	2.0	98.0
1685	63.4	36.5	57.0	43.0	—	—
1686	64.8	35.1	47.0	53.0	4.0	96.0
1688	35.8	64.1	56.0	44.0	8.0	94.0
1689	53.9	46.1	60.0	40.0	8.0	92.0
1691	55.2	44.7	52.0	48.0	4.0	96.0
1696	24.1	75.8	73.0	27.0	96.4	4.0
1706	66.3	33.6	32.0	68.0	4.0	96.0
1708	74.0	25.9	31.0	69.0	4.0	96.0
1710	48.0	51.9	28.0	72.0	35.0	65.0
1716	23.7	76.2	58.0	42.0	2.0	98.0
1717	21.3	78.6	73.0	27.0	8.0	92.0
1718	71.5	28.4	39.0	61.0	7.0	93.0
1720	41.1	58.8	59.0	41.0	3.0	97.0
1721	49.0	50.9	42.0	58.0	3.0	97.0
1723	65.7	34.2	45.0	55.0	4.0	96.0
1724	55.1	44.8	36.0	64.0	3.0	97.0
1725	42.2	55.7	54.0	46.0	3.0	97.0
PARGANA CHATSU						
1708	82.0	18.0	66.0	34.0	41.0	59.0
1709	53.0	47.0	19.0	81.0	68.0	32.0
1710	53.0	47.0	13.0	87.0	40.0	60.0
1711	55.0	45.0	20.0	80.0	6.0	94.0
1712	52.0	48.0	19.0	81.0	10.0	90.0
1713	66.0	34.0	27.0	73.0	3.0	97.0
1714	58.0	42.0	33.0	67.0	10.0	90.0
1716	54.0	46.0	42.0	58.0	13.0	87.0
1717	22.0	78.0	27.0	73.0	9.0	91.0
1721	63.0	37.0	26.0	74.0	4.0	96.0
1723	74.0	26.0	37.0	63.0	7.0	93.0
1724	58.0	42.0	26.0	74.0	6.0	94.0
1726	46.0	54.0	61.0	39.0	2.0	98.0
1730	33.0	67.0	66.0	34.0	—	100.0
1731	44.0	56.0	91.0	9.0	11.0	89.0
1733	53.0	47.0	49.0	51.0	13.0	87.0
1735	51.0	49.0	14.0	86.0	4.0	96.0
1737	39.0	61.0	51.0	49.0	4.0	96.0
1744	26.0	74.0	33.0	67.0	7.0	93.0
1748	45.0	55.0	52.0	48.0	12.0	88.0
1749	37.0	63.0	57.0	43.0	11.0	89.0

TABLE V: Table Showing the Percentage of Agra Under Different Crops KHARIF

Year	Bajra	Jowar	Moth	Chola	Sugar-cane	Cotton	Makka
			PARGANA JAIPUR				
1677	25.0	1.5	64.0	0.4	0.3	6.2	0.35
1744	5.0	4.7	41.0	9.1	2.3	4.8	10.7

Year	Bajra	Jowar	Moth	Kodon	Sugar-cane	Cotton	Makka
			PARGANA MALARNA				
1690	12.6	16.6	50.0	—	4.0	4.0	—
1749	19.8	28.0	25.0	0.78	1.8	2.1	1.7

Year	Bajra	Jowar	Moth	Urd	Kodon	Chola	Sugar-cane	Cotton	Makka
				PARGANA BAHATRI					
1665	20.0	14.0	45.0	—	—	—	—	9.0	—
1725	5.7	2.6	36.0	20.0	1.2	1.3	4.0	14.0	5.0

Year	Bajra	Jowar	Moth	Kodon	Chola	Sugar-cane	Cotton	Makka
				PARGANA CHATSU				
1708	55.0	0.5	0.9	—	1.8	—	0.3	—
1710	32.0	3.7	51.0	2.0	0.7	—	3.0	0.9
1749	10.9	2.6	33.0	5.5	4.0	0.7	18.6	19.7

RABI

Year	Wheat	Barley	Gram	Chomli
	PARGANA JAIPUR			
1677	3.0	55.0	40.0	—
1744	6.5	79.0	5.0	—
	PARGANA MALARNA			
1690	32.0	34.0	25.0	—
1749	27.0	42.0	25.0	—
	PARGANA BAHATRI			
1655	9.0	71.0	16.0	—
1725	12.0	52.0	19.0	—
	PARGANA CHATSU			
1708	8.0	35.0	2.0	44.0
1710	8.0	55.0	28.0	2.6
1749	10.0	70.0	6.0	8.0

7

Studies in the Land-Grant Copperplates of the Ahom Kings

J.N. Phukan

NUMEROUS LANDS were granted by the Ahom kings more particularly the kings of the Tungkhungia line to temples, religious and charitable institutions, to priests, Brahmins and other persons for their meritorious and outstanding services to the State. In almost all these cases copperplates were caused to be inscribed and issued to giving full details of the grants. Copies of these documents were preserved in the Royal Archives with great care.

A large number of these plates still exist in different parts of Assam.[1] Some of these are still in the possession of individuals,[2] religious and other institutions,[3] some in the Record Offices of the district headquarters,[4] the State Record Office, Shillong and the Assam State Museum,[5] Gauhati, most of which had been collected during pre-Independence days, while many plates were destroyed by natural calamities like flood, fire, earthquake, etc. and by the foreign invasions like the Burmese invasions in the second quarter of the nineteenth century. In this article only the general characteristics of the plates are discussed.

Size of the Plates

The plates are to be found in various sizes. Some plates are as small as 9 ½" x 4" in size, others are quite big. A plate of King Chandra Kanta Singha granted in Saka 1742 (AD1820) measures 19¾" x 11¾" in size.

Language of Inscriptions

The following languages were used in the inscriptions of the land-grant plates.

*28th Session at Mysore, 1966.

1. Ahom, a Tai language of Assam
2. Sanskrit
3. Assamese

Some plates were inscribed in one language while others in two or more languages. On the basis of the number of languages used in a plate, cooperplates can be grouped into the following categories.[6]

Category	Language used in plates
A	Ahom
B	Sanskrit
C	Assamese
D	Sanskrit and Assamese
E	Sanskrit and Assamese on one side and Ahom on the other
F	Assamese on one side and Ahom on the other

It has been observed that plates of A, B and C categories are not large in number. The majority of plates belong to D, E and F categories. In respect of plates of D category it has been noticed that the first few lines are inscribed in Sanskrit language in which the qualities and virtues of the donor king are eulogised. The eulogy is followed by the details in Assamese. The plates of E category follow the same pattern as in D category so far as inscriptions in Sanskrit and Assamese languages are concerned. In case of F category of plates, the details in Assamese are to be seen without any eulogy. But so far as inscriptions in Ahom language of E and F categories of plates are concerned the details given in Sanskrit and Assamese are repeated with the following differences.[7]

(1) that the eulogy inscribed in Sanskrit is peculiarly absent in Ahom.
(2) that in Ahom so far as possible only Ahom equivalent words are used in respect of name of kings, places, dates, professions, etc. For instance, in Sanskrit and Assamese inscriptions Rudra Singha's name is found as *Sri Sri Swarganarayvande Sri Rudra Singha nripati* but in Ahom his name is found as *Chaao Shu-khrung-pha*. The name of places, villages, towns, rivers, hills are found in Ahom equivalent words. For instance Dergaon (corrupt form of *Devagram* or village of gods) is written as Banphi (ban—village, phi—gods (that is village of gods), Jorhat is written as Song-shu-kat, Rangpur (city of merriment) is written as Chemun (che—town, mum—merriment), Dhekial village as Banphakut, barber as *changtha*, the Brahmaputra as Tilao, etc. The dates are also given in Ahom *laknis*.[8]

Seal on the Plates

On the basis of the royal seal land grant plates can be classified into two groups: (1) plates with the royal seal and (2) plates with the seal.

The seal is consisted of two stamps carved on the plates. Both stamps are placed side by side either horizontally or vertically. One stamp contains the name of the king which is sometimes attached with the name of gods or goddesses. For instance, in a plate, King Rajeswar Singha's name is found as '*Sri Sri Swarganarayandeva Sri Rajeswar Singha nripanang*'[9], in another his name is given as '*Sri Sri Maheswari padaparayana Sri Rajeswar Singha nripasya*.'[10] The other stamp contains the figure of a winged lion or a kind of *dragon*, the symbol of the Ahom kings, facing towards the left. There is no inscription in this stamp. Both the name and the dragon are enclosed by semi-circles as shown in Figure 7.1 or by curved lines as shown in Figure 7.2. The stamps are oval in shape with the two ends being conical.

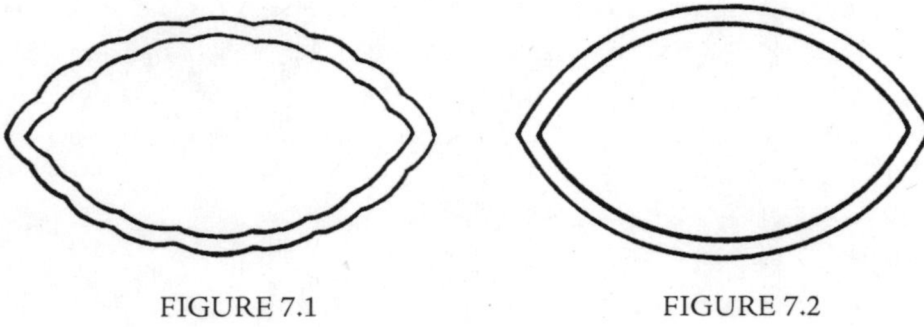

FIGURE 7.1   FIGURE 7.2

Position of the Seals

The two stamps are put side by side either on the right hand top or the right hand side. When placed at the top, the stamp containing the name comes first followed by the stamp containing the winged lion as shown in Figure 7.3. When placed on the right hand side, the name stamp is placed above the lion stamp as shown in Figure 7.4. Only very rarely the royal seal is to be found at a different position.

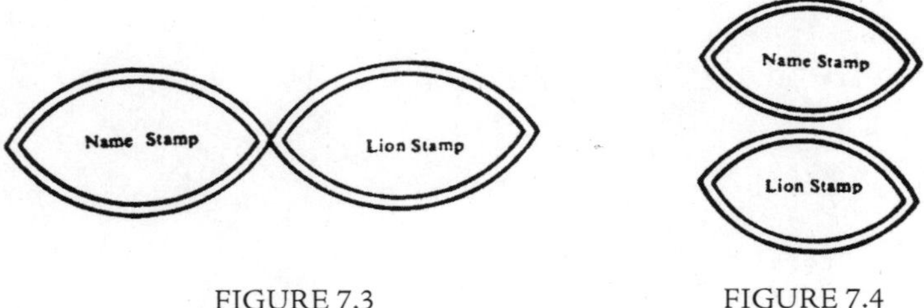

FIGURE 7.3   FIGURE 7.4

It is found that the plates included in A, B and C categories do not contain the royal seal. Most plates of D, E and F categories possess seals. Seals in E and F categories are to be found on the sides written in Assamese or Assamese and Sanskrit languages and not on the side written in Ahom language.

Classification of Grants

The land-grants of the Ahom kings were classified under the following heads:[11] *debottar, dharmottar, brahmottar* and *nankar.*

Lands granted to temples were called *debottar* lands. These lands were again classified under *bhogdhani* and *paikan* lands.[12] Lands exclusively appropriated to Hindu gods and goddesses for the regular supply of ration or *bhog* were called *bhogdhani* lands. The entire produce and income of such lands were to be spent for the management of temples or *devalayas*. A number of persons known as *paiks*[13] were also granted to the temples who were bound to perform menial services and supply all necessary articles strictly in accordance with the arrangements made in the grants. For instance, fishermen were granted to temples whose function was to catch fish in the rivers or bits granted to the temples and supply the necessary quantity of fish, sweeper *paiks* were engaged for cleaning the premises of the temples, drummers for beating drums at appointed hours. These *paiks* were granted separate lands for their personal use which were called *paikan* lands or *ga-mati* (body land).

Lands granted to the spiritual heads of *Satras* or monasteries and other religious institutions were called *dharmottar* lands.

Lands granted to Brahmins were known as *brahmottar* lands. Sometimes *paiks* were also attached to such lands who were required to render services to the Brahmins.

Lands granted to individuals other than Brahmins for their meritorious and outstanding services were called *nankar* lands. *Nankar* lands were granted even to goldsmiths, barbers, drummers, and the like.

Divisions of Land

The following broad divisions of land are to be found in the plates:

1. *Rupit mati* or land suitable for the cultivation of *sail* crop during the rainy season.
2. *Faringati* or highland.
3. *Bari mati* or land fit for house sites.
4. *Baotali* or very lowland fit for cultivation of *bao* crop.
5. *Bori mati* or fallow land.
6. *Doloni* or swamp.
7. *Habi mati* or jungle land.
   Excess land was called *obar mati.*

Unit and Measurement of Land

The highest unit of land was the *pura* which is equal to four standard Bengal *bighas*.[14] *Apura* was subdivided into 4 *bighas* and a *bigha* into 5 *kathas*.

Land was measured by *a nal* or *tar* which was about 12 feet long.[15]

Land Revenue and Other Cess

All lands granted by the Ahom kings were held revenue free which had been expressly declared in the plates. The taxes and other duties as mentioned in the plates are *kar, katal, pada, panchak, beth, be gar, chor, chinala, dhumushi, maresha,jolkar,jawakhar, dan, khut, danda, bandha, chowki, hat, ghat,* and *phat.*

On the basis of contents, the inscriptions on the plates can be divided into several sections.

Section 1. This section is found in plates of B, D and E categories and is inscribed in Sanskrit. It contains the name and the family origin of the donor, his manifold qualities and virtues. He is often compared with the ancient and epic heroes like Bhim and Arjuna. It also contains a short statement of the occasion, the date of the grant and the name of the receiver with his place of residence.

Section 2. This section contains a general proclamation of the King addressing the judicial and revenue officers of the district in which lands were granted. It is to be found in C, D, E and F categories of plates. In case of grant made in Kamrup, the proclamation would run thus: *Let it be known to all the Baruas Barkayasthas, Choudhurys, Patowaris, Talukdars, Thakurias and all others of Kamrup.* In case the grant was made in Darrang, it would run thus: *Let it be known to all the Kings, Princes, Saharias, Hazarikas, Saikias, Boras, Gayrahs of Darrang.*

Section 3. It contains a detailed description of the types of lands granted and the quantity with boundary.

Section 4. The details are followed by the conditions of land holding. In case of *debottar* lands the conditions had been the worship of gods and goddesses and offering of prayer in the name of the donor king. It may be of interest to note that these conditions are observed even today in some temples and prayer is done in the name of the donor kings when they have become the legend of the past.

In case of *dharmottar* lands the conditions of holding were of performing *Name-Kirtan,* reading the *Bhagavat,* burning of oil lamp (*akhanda pradip*) and prayer for the welfare of the king. In *brahmottar* lands, the Brahmins were to ask blessings in favour of the king. In case of *nankar* grants, the grant holder was to wish the welfare of the king.

Section 5. The conditions of land holding are followed by an express exemption of all revenues and duties payable for holding such lands as discussed above.

Section 6. Towards the end in each plate a prohibitory note is inscribed to the effect that no person should violate the conditions laid down in the plate together with a request to the kings in future not to break the agreement. Violation of the conditions by any subject was an offence punishable by law.

Section 7. At the end the date of the grant is found in most plates.

Notes

1. Sir Edward Gait in his *Report on the Progress of Historical Research in Assam,* 1897, gives a list of 48 copperplates of the Ahom kings, pp. 12–15.
2. A land-grant copperplate of King Siva Singha (AD 1714–44) inscribed in Ahom language on both sides was obtained by the writer from a person of Jamugurihat, district Darrang. It is to be published in *Epigraphia Indica.* A few more copperplates of the same king and of other kings were obtained by the writer from different parts of the state.
3. The Sibsagar College Library, Sibsagar possesses two copperplates—one belongs to King Rudra Singha (AD 1696–1714) and the other to King Rajeswar Singha (AD 1751–69).
4. Twenty land-grant plates of the Ahom kings lying in the District Record Office, Gauhati were examined by the writer.
5. About two years ago a copperplate of King Rudra Singha issued to a group of Brahmins was unearthed from a mound in a tea garden near Dibrugarh which has since been deposited in the Assam State Museum, Gauhati.
6. See also Gait's *Report on the Progress of Historical Research,* pp. 13–15.
7. The writer has examined a number of plates inscribed in Ahom language.
8. For details see Dr. S.K. Bhuyan's *Deodhai Assam Buranji,* pp. xxxix-xliv. Also *Assam Buranji* by Kasinath Tamuli Phukan, pp. 122–34.
9. This plate was obtained through the courtesy of Sri Sarbananda Rajkumar while he was Additional District Magistrate at Gauhati. Sri Rajkumar belongs to Ahom royal family.
10. This plate was obtained through Sri Rajkumar.
11. See also Gait's *History of Assam,* p. 255.
12. Ibid., p. 270, *The Assam Land Revenue Manual,* vol. I, p.xxxix.
13. Every able-bodied male person of the Kingdom was enlisted as a *paik.*
14. Gait, *History of Assam,* p. 256.
15. In a copperplate grant the length of *nal* is given as *sat hat ebigat chariangul.* See also *Satsari Assam Buranji,* p. 77, edited by Dr. S.K.Bhuyan.

8

Position of the Patel in Eastern Rajputana During the Eighteenth Century

Dilbagh Singh

IN THE course of my research work I came across a number of documents in the form of letters written to or from the revenue officials which throw a good deal of light on the power, position, functions and the role of the *patel*. While the information corroborates the description of the *patel's* office available elsewhere, in addition it throws some fresh light on the subject. A few instances are given below to highlight some of these features.

The office of the *patel* formed a regular part of the local and land revenue administration. The *patel* is depicted in our documents as the chief village official[1] besides the *patwari*. With regard to study of the development of the office *of patel*, in the majority of the cases, the holders of the office tried to make it hereditary[2] and gradually the *pateli* rights began to be treated as 'property' which could easily be bought, sold or mortgaged.[3] This concept of the office of the *patel* being a property was implicitly recognised by the state.[4]

The number of the *patels* in a village could be more than one at a time.[5] There are instances of as many as seven *patels* at a time.[6] In the villages where the number of *patels* exceeded one, their respective jurisdictions were clearly stated, their shares being shown in *biswas*.[7]

Though hereditary rights to the office of *patels* were entertained,[8] the state reserved the right to appoint a *patel* or remove him from his office at its discretion.[9] The state also exercised its right of appointing *patels* for villages which were newly colonized or were due to be settled; and for those villages where the office fell vacant due to failure of natural heirs or dismissal of the *patels* from the office by the revenue officials.[10]

The *patel* was not merely a government servant, he was normally a peasant himself and usually a *zamindar*.[11] When the office was conferred upon a person, he was required to pay a lumpsum as *peshkash*[12] generally payable in two annual

*32nd Session at Jabalpur, 1970.

instalments. He was confirmed only when the sum due from him had been fully paid. In the newly settled villages the *pateli* was usually entrusted upon the pioneer colonizer of the settlement[13] or upon a person who could settle ruined villages by his personal efforts. There are instances when an original settler of the village had at times combined in himself the offices of the *patel, patwari* and *zamindar*. Thus the offices of the *patel, patwari,* and *zamindar* were simultaneously conferred upon Harbhagat Brahmin, who was the pioneer colonizer of the village of Harbhagatpura in pargana Chatsu.[14]

The *patel* could claim to resume his *pateli* rights to the village which he had previously held but had left for certain reasons such as harassment by the *bhomias*[15] or failure to pay state dues.[16] He was in the former case asked to resume office on the assurance that he would not be harassed in future and in the latter case had to pay the arrears outstanding against him, if he desired to resume his rights. In case of repeated recalcitrance and evasion of the payment of state dues, a *patel* could be ousted from his office and his *pateli* rights could be conferred on another person.[17]

Though the revenue was assessed by the state officials the responsibility for the collection of the *hasil* from the village rested with the *patel*. The *raiyat* of the village normally paid their revenue through the *patel* who was required to deposit it in the pargana *tahvil* or had to entrust it to the assignee in an assigned village.[18] He was the person whom the revenue authorities held responsible for the payment of the assessed revenue of the village. It, therefore, became his responsibility to collect the revenue share of each individual peasant and the performance of this service was regarded as an official service to the state.

In addition to it, the *patel* undertook to collect the legal cesses from the *raiyat* of the village.[19] From many references it would appear that it was not unusual for the weaker peasants being exploited and harassed by the *patels* under the pretext of realizing *malba* or other cesses.[20]

The *patel* performed an important role in the extension of cultivation by bringing cultivable waste land under the plough.[21] The *patel* had full power in the choice of new settlers for it and could bestow the land on whomsoever he liked, this being implicitly recognized by the state.[22] The *patel* was also authorized to settle 'pahi' *kashtakars*[23] to develop the cultivation in the village.[24] Sometimes the *patels* divided the land of the village under their jurisdiction and tried to attract the cultivators to the village by offering them better terms.[25] The *patel,* however, could not interfere with the land already occupied, though we find a *panchayat* consisting of ten *patels* conferring arbitration in a boundary dispute between the two neighbouring *zamindars,* i.e. the *zamindars* of the villages of Kherli and Ram Singhpura Khurd in pargana Bahatri.[26]

It was expected of the *patel* to reclaim the fallow land.[27] In case he failed to discharge this duty, he was required to pay the *hasil* of the fallow land to the state.[28] The *patel* was entrusted with the responsibility of tilling his personal land by himself or get it tilled by the tenants,[29] failing which he could be deprived of the right to allot the land belonging to him and it could be given to any one by the state for cultivation.[30]

It was also his duty to acquaint the revenue officials of the condition of the *raiyat* and their agricultural fields.[31] He could recommend the poor and deserving *raiyat* for the grant of agricultural loan and it was to be distributed among the *raiyat* through him.[32] He could suggest ways and means for the betterment of the condition of cultivators.[33]

Apart from these obligations, at times the *patel* was required to prepare the *jamabandi*[34] and *khasra*[35] papers of the village with the help of the *patwari*. The *malba* cess was also assessed by the *patel* in the *khalsa* villages, but in an assigned village he had to assess the *malba* in the presence of the assignee. The assignees were instructed by the State to realize their legal dues in the presence of the *patels* of their respective villages.

The *patel's* jurisdiction over the village was not only financial. He was also partly responsible for maintaining law and order in the village. He was required to investigate the criminal cases such as theft, fights, murders, etc., within the village boundary. He could seek help from the higher authorities for the purpose of maintaining law and order.[36]

The *raiyat* presented their demands and expressed their grievances to the state through the *patel*.[37] In case of unjust assessment and unauthorized amount realised from *raiyat* by the pargana revenue officials, the former could approach the state authorities through the *patel* of their village.[38] The *patel* could lodge complaints against any oppressive pargana official as well as the *jagirdar* on behalf of the *raiyat*.[39] We find *patel*'s lodging complaint against the Amil of pargana Bahatri, who had exacted unauthorized amount from *khalsa* and *jagir* villages of the above-mentioned pargana.[40] The *patel* of the village of the Mundawari in pargana Malarana lodged a complaint against Fateh Singh Harha, the *jagirdar* of the village, who was extending his aggression over the lands of *jamindars* and the cultivators and against his high handedness on many other matters with the *raiyat*.[41] In the case of over assessment by the revenue officials, the *patel* also represented the matter on behalf of the *raiyat* to the state.[42] Thus the *patel* had a dual authority; first, as a traditional leader of the village society, and second, as the official headman of the village.

The *patel* acted as an arbitrator in those disputes which arose in the rural society. The *patel* also decided the disputes regarding the land. We find *a panchayat* consisting of the *patels* of four neighbouring villages, arbitrating in a dispute between the *jagirdar* and the *patwari* of the village of Kiratpura in pargana Chatsu regarding a cultivated field.[43] In another case we find higher authorities instructing the Amil to settle a dispute regarding the property rights in a field and a well in consultation with the *patel* of five villages.[44] A land dispute between the *zamindar* of the village of Jagner and the *jagirdar* of the village of Sri Raypur in pargana Lalsot was decided by the *patels* of five neighbouring villages.[45] A boundary dispute between the two *zamindars* was settled by a *pane hay at* consisting of the *patels* of ten neighbouring villages.[46] A land dispute between two *jagirdars* was decided by the *patels, chaudharys* and *quanungos* of five villages.[47]

In lieu of his services, the *patel* was entitled to customary privileges. In fact the right to the *pateli,* even though hereditary was conditional upon service to the state. The *patel* was considered an official for the purposes of the realisation of the *hasil* and its regular payment to the pargana *tahvil.* As such his remunerations were equally conditional upon the performance of the service to the state. Though the *patel* was not directly paid from the state exchequer, he was entitled to receive *muqaddami,*[48] out of the *hasil* of the village at the rate of 2%, *bisondh,*[49] twentieth part of the *hasil* of the village and *degali,*[50] a customary dress which the *patels* used to get from the village. Apart from these perquisites he was entitled to charge a share from the amount realized under the head of *malba. Patel's* share was known as *patelai ka malba.*[51] He also received *pateli ka khera ka dhol,* a customary amount paid to the *patel* on the occasion of the departure of a marriage procession from the village.[52] Apart from these usual remunerations and perquisites, the *patel's* personal land was nominally assessed by the state.[53] Thus the office of the *patel* was a profitable one; providing its possessor, admittedly a social and economic superiority over the rest of his co-cultivators in the village.

Notes

1. Adasatta of pargana Chatsu vs 1807/AD 1750, Rajasthan State Archives Bikaner, Mavajana Kalan Pargana Chatsu, *RSAB.*
2. Sanad to the Amil pargana Chatsu, dated Asarh Vadi 11, vs 1812/ AD 1755; ibid., dated Asoj Vadi 12, vs 1810/AD 1753, Chitthi to the Amil pargana Bahatri, dated Asoj Sudi 8, vs 1820/AD 1763, *RSAB.*
3. Chitthi to the Amil, pargana Chatsu, dated Sawan Sudi 6, vs 1810/AD 1753; Chitthi to the Amil, pargana Swai Jaipur dated Jeth Sudi 9, vs. 1810/ AD 1753, *RSAB.*
4. Chitthi to the Amil, pargana Bahatri dated Jeth Sudi, 9, vs 1819/AD 1762; Chitthi to the Amil pargana Chatsu, dated Vaisakh Sudi 11, vs 1808/AD 1751, *RSAB.*
5. Mavajana Kalan pargana Chatsu, *RSAB.*
6. Ibid.
7. Chitthi to the Amil pargana Swai Jaipur, dated Kati Vadi 14, vs 1829/AD 1763, Amber records letter of vs 1824/ AD 1761, *RSAB.*
8. Chitthi to the Amil pargana Chatsu, dated Asarh Vadi 11, vs 1822/AD 1765; ibid., dated Asoj Vadi 12, vs 1810/AD 1763, *RSAB.*
9. Chitthi to the Amils pargana Swai Jaipur, dated Jeth Sudi 12, vs 1816/AD 1759; Chitthi to the Amil pargana Chatsu, dated Asoj Vadi, 12, vs 1810/AD 1753, *RSAB.*
10. Amber Records letter of vs 1824/AD 1767, *RSAB.*

11. Chitthi to the Amils pargana Bahatri, dated Jeth Sudi 14, vs 1819/AD 1762, *RSAB*.

12. Adasatta of pargana Bahatri vs 1813/AD 1756; Chitthi to the Amils pargana Sawai Jaipur, dated Jeth Sudi 9, vs 1810/AD 1763; Chitthi to the Amils pargana Chatsu, dated Asarh Vadi 11, vs 1812/AD 1755, *RSAB*.

13. Mavajana Kalan pargana Chatsu; Chitthi to the Amils pargana Chatsu from Diwan Kanhi Ram Nand Lai, dated Asoj Sudi 5, vs 1819/AD 1762; Chitthi to the Amils pargana Chatsu, dated Asarh Sudi 7, vs 1823/AD 1766, *RSAB*.

14. Chitthi to the Amils pargana Chatsu, dated Asoj Sudi 5, vs 1819/AD 1762; Chitthi to the Amils pargana Bahatri, dated Asoj Sudi 8, vs 1820/AD 1763, *RSAB*.

15. Yaddashti Pradakhti pargana Malarana vs 1783/AD 1726.

16. Sanad to the Amils pargana Sawai Jaipur, dated Jeth Vadi 14, vs 1811/AD 1754, *RSAB*.

17. Chitthi to the Amils pargana Chatsu, dated Jeth Vadi 3 vs 1813/AD 1756, *RSAB*.

18. Chitthi to the Amils pargana Bahatri, dated Karar Miti Jeth Vadi 7, vs 1807/ad 1750; ibid., dated Maha Sudi 12, vs 1818/AD 1761. Chitthi to the Amils pargana Chatsu, dated Bhadon Sudi 7, vs 1810/AD 1753, ibid., dated Vaisakh Snwt. 9, vs 1812/AD 1755, ibid., dated Asoj Vadi 2, vs 1814/AD 1757, *RSAB*.

19. Chitthi to the Amils pargana Lalsot, dated Sawan Vadi 11, vs 1809/AD 1752, *RSAB*.

20. Chitthi to the Amil pargana Malarana, dated Karar Miti Duji Vadi 10, vs 1812/AD 1755; Chitthi to the Amils pargana Lalsot, dated Sawan Vadi 6, vs 1817/AD 1760; Chitthi to the Amils pargana Chatsu, dated Chaitra Sudi 5 vs 1811/AD 1754, *RSAB*.

21. Yaddashti Pradakhti pargana Malarana vs 1753/AD 1726, *RSAB*.

22. Chitthi to the Amils pargana Malarana, dated Karar Miti Duji Vadi 10, vs 1812/AD1755, *RSAB*.

23. Pahi Kashtakar was a peasant proprietor but his holding was in a different village from that of his residence, cf. Irfan Habib, *Agrarian System of Mughal India*, p. 123.

24. Chitthi to the Amils pargana Chatsu, dated Asarh Sudi 7, vs 1823/AD 1766, *RSAB*.

25. Chitthi to the Amil pargana Chatsu, dated Pos Sudi 14, vs 1820/AD 1763 *RSAB*.

26. Chitthi to the Amils pargana Bahatri dated Bhadwa Vadi 12, vs 1819/ad 1762.

27. Chitthi to the Amils pargana Swai Jaipur, dated Jeth Vadi 15, vs 1811/AD 1754, *RSAB*. ibid., dated Kati Vadi 14, vs 1826/AD 1769.

28. Ibid., Amber Records, Likhant dated Sawan Sudi I, vs 1811/AD 1754, *RSAB*.

29. Chitthi to the Amils pargana Lalsot, dated Sawan Vadi 6, vs 1817/AD 1760, *RSAB*.

30. Chitthi to the Amils pargana Chatsu, dated Jeth Sudi 15, vs 1822/AD 1765, *RSAB*.

31. Chitthi to the Amils pargana Chatsu, dated Sawan Sudi 2, vs 1815/AD 1758; ibid., dated Pos Sudi 14, vs 1920/AD 1763; ibid., dated Asarh Vadi 9, vs 1816/AD 1759, *RSAB*.

32. Chitthi to the Amils pargana Dausa, dated Asoj Sudi 3, vs 1816/AD 1759.
33. Chitthi to the Amils pargana Chatsu, dated Asarh Vadi 5, vs 1815/AD 1758, *RSAB*.
34. Chitthi to the Amil pargana Khohari, dated Sawan Vadi 7, vs 1806/AD 1749, *RSAB*.
35. Khasara of Mauza Aniyala pargana Malarana, vs 1824/AD 1767, *RSAB*.
36. Amber Records, Letter from Nawal Rai Mahachand to Dcwan Rai Chand, dated Chaitra Vadi 3, vs 1851/AD 1794, *RSAB*. Amber Records letter dated Maghishri Sudi 14, 1853/1796.
37. Chitthi to the Amils pargana Malarana, dated Asarh Sudi 13, vs 1812/AD 1753; Chitthi to Amils pargana Bahatri, dated Jeth Sudi I,vs 1819/ad 1762; Chitthi to the Amils pargana Dausa, dated Karar Miti Duji, Sawan Vadi, I, vs 1817/AD 1760, *RSAB*.
38. Chitthi to the Amil pargana Chatsu, dated Pose Vadi 14, vs 1816/AD 1759, *RSAB*.
39. Chitthi to the Amil pargana Bahatri, dated Vaisakh Vadi 11, vs 1807/AD 1750; Chitthi to the Amil pargana Chatsu, dated Chaitra Sudi 6, vs 1825/AD 1768, *RSAB*.
40. Chitthi to the Amil pargana Bahatri, dated Vaisakh Vadi 11, vs 1807/AD 1750, *RSAB*.
41. Chitthi to the Amil pargana Malarana, dated Vaisakh Sudi 15, vs 1826/AD 1769, *RSAB*.
42. Chitthi to the Amil pargana Chatsu from Diwan Kanhi Ram Nand Lal, dated Pose Vadi 14, vs 1816/AD 1759; Chitthi to the Amils pargana Bahatri, dated Vaisakh Vadi 11, vs 1807/AD 1750; Chitthi to the Amil pargana Chatsu, dated Chatra Sudi 6, vs 1825/AD 1768.
43. Chitthi to the Amil pargana Chatsu, dated Maghishri Vadi 1, vs 1822/AD 1765, *RSAB*.
44. Chitthi to the Amils pargana Bahatri, dated Maghishri Vadi 10, vs 1820/AD 1763; Chitthi to the Amils pargana Chatsu, dated Kati Vadi 8, vs 1808/AD 1751, *RSAB*.
45. Chitthi to the Amil pargana Lalsot, dated Kati Sudi 8 vs 1815/AD 1758, *RSAB*.
46. Chitthi to the Amils pargana Bahatri, dated Bhadwa Vadi 12, vs 1819/AD 1762, *RSAB*.
47. Chitthi to the Amil pargana Chatsu, dated Bhadwa Sudi 12, vs 1809/AD 1762, *RSAB*.
48. *Dastur-ul-Aml* pargana Niwai, dated Pose Vadi 4 vs 1800/AD 1743, *RSAB*.
49. Chitthi to the Amils pargana Malarana, dated Vaisakh Sudi 2, vs 1810/AD 1753, *RSAB*.
50. Chitthi to the Amils pargana Sawai Jaipur, dated Asarah Vadi 5, vs 1814/AD 1757, *RSAB*.
51. Chitthi to the Amil pargana Malarana, dated Karar Miti Vaisakh Sudi 2, vs 1810/ AD 1753, *RSAB*.
52. Chitthi to Anand Singh, the Fauzdar of pargana Sawai Jaipur, dated Sawan Vadi 9, vs 1816/AD 1759; Chitthi to the Amil pargana Lalsot, dated Chaitra Sudi 3, vs 1823/AD 1766, *RSAB*.

53. *Dastur-ul-Ami* pargana Gijgarh vs 1780/AD 1723, *RSAB*; Chitthi to the Amil pargana Malarana dated Vaisakh Sudi 2, vs 1810/AD 1753; Chitthi to the Amil pargana Malarana, dated Karar Miti Duji Vadi 10, vs 1822/AD 1765, *RSAB*. Amber Records, letter from Diwan Raichand to the *patels* of the village of Parana, dated Sawan Vadi 9, vs 1858/AD 1801.

9

Some Aspects of the Changes in the Position of the Madad-i-Ma'ash Holders in Awadh, 1676–1722

Muzaffar Alam

THIS PAPER makes a brief attempt to discuss the changes in the position of the *madad-i-ma'ash* holders in the late seventeenth and early eighteenth centuries in the Mughal Province of Awadh. It will try to show how these changes were brought about by certain concrete socio-political realities which affected the Mughal system over the period between 1676 and 1722.[1] We are aware of the limitation of our sources and have therefore largely refrained from making categorical generalizations.

This institution of the *madad-i-ma'ash* had an important bearing on the social and political life of the Mughal times. The revenue grantees were not a class of mere parasites. The state had its own interest in maintaining this 'Army of Prayer'. They were state's creatures and therefore its natural propagandists. In principle, persons belonging to four categories were eligible for the grant of the *madad-i-ma'ash*: (i) scholars who were 'seeker after truth and had renounced the world, (ii) persons who 'eschewed the urge for greater gain and chose a life of seclusion and self-abnegation'; (iii) the destitute and the poor 'who were incapacitated to earn their livelihood'; and (iv) persons of noble lineage who 'ignorantly deemed it below their dignity to take to any employment.[2] In the period under review, however, the institution of the *madad-i-maash* did not represent simply the act of charity. In Awadh where the *madad-i-maash* holders constituted a considerably strong social force, there were numerous grants which extended over more than two or three hundred *bighas* of land. The influence and power of the grantees in certain cases encompassed two or three entire parganas. A sale-deed document dated 11 *Ziqada,* 1099 AH August 29,1688 from the *sarkar* of Bahraich shows one Mir Saiy id Muhammad Arif as holding a *madad-i-ma'ash* of over 990 *bighas* in the *sarkar.*[3] In the pargana of Husampur, in the same *sarkar,* one Saiyid Muhammad held over 645 *bighas* as

*35th Session at Jabalpur, 1974.

his *madad-i-ma'ash*.[4] On 9 Shawwal, in the 4th R.Y. of Farrukh Siyar/27 September 1714 two hundred *bighas* of *madad-i-ma'ash* land in the pargana of Sadrapur, *sarkar* Khairabad are recorded to have been confirmed in the name of one Saliha.[5]

Our records further show that those who held large *madad-i-ma'ash* grants, acquired enough wealth and power to purchase *zamindaris*. The acquisition of a number of villages in the parganas of Haveli Bahraich and Husampur in his *zamindari* and *milkiyat* by Mir Saiyid Muhammad Arif clearly bear this out.[6] With the exception of some families who had long enjoyed the privilege of combining a number of imperial offices with those services which were normally remunerated through revenue grants, the acquisition of *zamindaris* by revenue grantees seems to be a late seventeenth century development. By the beginning of the eighteenth century, the process seems to have been intensified.

The *zamindaris* of the *madad-i-ma'ash* holders seem to have received exceptionally generous treatment from the Mughals. Unlike the ordinary *zamindars*, the *madad-i-ma'ash* holders seem to have been exempted from certain levies of their *zamindari* holdings as well. A *parwana* of Namdar Khan, the *diwan* of Awadh, in response to a petition by one Saiyid Ahmad, a *madad-i-ma'ash* holders of pargana Husampur, directs the local official to not that the *taluqa* of Saiyid Ahmad was exempted from *shud-amad* and that its *jagirdar* in the past, unlike the existing one against whom the complaint was lodged, had never levied *sadrana*, etc., on him. The *taluqa* was thus recommended to continue to be exempted from the levy.[7] The newly acquired privileges of the *madad-i-ma'ash* holders seem to have brought the *jagirdars* into direct conflict with the *madad-i-ma'ash* holders. The nature and conflict can be further known from the incident that took place in the pargana of Harha. Aziz Khan, the *jagirdar* of Harha and Unam (Unnao) is reported to have invaded Husain Nagar, a *madad-i-ma'ash* of the Saiyids. Six hundred Muslims and Saiyids were killed or burnt alive, 700 people including the *mahajans* and the artisans were captured and over Rs. 200,000 were misappropriated.[8] In view of the slackening of imperial control over local administration and the imminent danger of and in a number of cases actual occurrence of in subordination of the old *zamindar* families, the Mughals evolved a conscious policy of facilitating the acquisition of *zamindaris* by the revenue grantees. The case of the family of Muhammad Ihsan, the *Qazi* of the pargana of Bilgram in the time of Muhammad Shah, can be presented to illustrate the point. The changes in the position of the *madad-i-ma'ash* holders in Awadh family is known to have been involved in 'this worldliness' to such an extent that, to quote an eighteenth century biographer, the 'virtues that had long distinguished them vanished owing to the wealth they obtained in the time of Bahadur Shah'.[9] Again the temptation to get money to purchase lands encouraged and increased corruption and malpractice in the courts of the *qazis*.[10]

Some of the *madad-i-maash* holders appear to have acted as revenue-farmers and money-lenders. In 1088 AH/AD1677–78, the *jagir* of Namdar Khan in *tappa* Chaurasi, Pargana Husampur was farmed out to Mir Saiyid Ahmad for Rs. 463/8. Hiranand, the *gumashta* of the Mir made the transaction on behalf of the latter.[11] One Bansi, the *gumashta* of Mir Saiyid Muhammad Arif is reported to have held some village on *ijara* for Rs. 330/10 for the year 1097 *fasli*.[12] One record shows Shaikh Nimatullah and Shaikh Pir Muhammad and the others, the *maliks* of the village of Gondvi in the pargana of Husampur as having pawned their village to one Saiyid Habibullah son of Saiyid Taj Muhammad for an amount of Rs. 52. Much later, their descendants repaid the debt to the Saiyid and got the village released from his possession.[13]

As according to the *madad-i-maash* documents, the absence of any other means of income was invariably the sole justification for holding grants, with the acquisition of *zamindaris* and *ijaras* and a capacity to lend money to the *zamindar*, the revenue grantees should have theoretically forfeited their right to retain *madad-i-maash* land. In actual practice, however, they still maintained grants. In 22nd R.Y. of Aurangzeb (1678–79) the *qanungo* of the pargana of Haveli Bahraich realized the *qanungoi* from Mir Saiyid Ahmad and some other grantees of the pargana. However, in response to their petition a *dastak* from Khairandesh Khan soon arrived, directing the *qanungo* to return the collected amount of 'illegal cess' to the grantees.[14] A document dated 1108 *fasil* records *tappa* Mubarkpur in the same pargana as the taluqa of the *madad-i-maash*, the *milkiyat* and the *zamindari* of Mir Saiyid Muhammad Arif.[15]

A separate department to look after the grants was maintained by the Mughals. The department was headed by the *sadr-us-sudur* at the centre. Local *sadrs* and *mutawaliis* worked under him. These departments were under the direct control of the imperial centre. In the appointments, promotions and dismissals of even the pargana *mutawaliis* an imperial farman or *hasb-ul-hukm* seems to have been essential. However, in Awadh, in our period the appointment and security of the job of the pargana *mutawaliis* seems to have depended more on the goodwill of the *aimmadars*. This is borne out by the case of one Shaikh Karm Ali, the *sarristadar* of the *aimma* of the pargana of Barudanja (?) in the *sarkar* of Khairabad. His appointment and service at the office owed to his capacity to keep the local grantees appeases. In contrast to this the appointment of his grandfather and father to the same office is explicitly mentioned to have followed the imperial *farmans*.[16] This clearly shows how the requirements of an efficient and stable administration became subservient to the interests of the grantees. This development may by noted against the background of the fact that the prime responsibility of the *mutawallis* was to keep a watchful check on the grants and the grantees.[17]

A considerable part of the *madad-i-ma'ash* grants was earmarked for the *qazis*, the *sadars* the *mir-adls* and the *muftis*. By the beginning of the eighteenth century almost all these offices had become hereditary. The *farmans* conferring these offices usually followed the actual acquisition of the offices. The role of such *farman* was thus reduced to the status of mere confirmatory directives. In 1718 after the death of Muhammad Nasir, the *qazi* of pargana Bilgram, his son, Muhammad Ihsan, who was barely fifteen years old was proclaimed by 'the people of the town of Belgram' as the successor of the deceased. As he was considered incapable to deal with the responsibilities of the *qaza* independently, one Inayatullah was asked to assist him as his *naib*. Over two years later in AD 1721 the imperial *farman* was issued in the name of Muhammad Ihsan appointing him the *qazi* of the pargana of Belgram.[18] The Abbasis of Kakori in the *sarkar* of Lucknow also acquired hereditary claim to the *qaza* of the pargana, Muhammad Hafiz Abbasi who was a contemporary of Burhan ul-Mulk and Safdar Jang succeeded his father as the *qazi* of the pargana of Kakori. After his son, Muhammad Waiz who was in close contact with Safdar Jang is reported to have taken over the *qaza*.[19]

The principle of heredity does not seem to have remained confined to only those parganas where the office of the *qaza* was held by the relatively powerful families. This is illustrated by an incident of the seventeenth century which also reveals the circumstances in which the convention of heredity began to evolve. One Wali Muhammad, the *qazi* of pargana Husampur, in the *sarkar* of Bahraich, who had been dismissed due to his reported clash with the local *zamindars* and the grantees, is recorded to have refused to give up his claim to the land which he had obtained against the pay claim of his office.[20] Hereditary control over the office would obviously bring to them rich dividends both in terms of land possessions and strong social ties.

The *madad-i-maash* holders did not have any right to interfere with the established *milkiyat* and *zamindari* over land. They did not have any rights which were not previously claimed by the imperial administration.[21] The rule, however, does not seem to have been ordinarily followed in the early years of the eighteenth century. That the grantees, especially those who enjoyed the privileges of holding big *madad-i-maash* grants and the *zamindars* together, often violated the rule can fairly be conjectured. The privileged position of the grantees and their capacity to encroach on the *zamindari* rights seem to have constituted a potential source of tension in the villages. It becomes meaningful in this context to see that in a number of cases now the *zamindars'* hostility became directed against the local *shurafa*, *sadat* and *mashaikh* A campaign against one Lai Sahi, the *zamindar* of Manohargarh in Baiswara is reported to have been undertaken on the petition of the *gumashta* of the *jagirdar* and the *shurafa*. The Chauhan *zamindars* of *mauza* Ganjora, pargana Shahpur are accused of having been especially hostile to the *shurafa*. The harassment of Saiyid is included among the serious irregularities committed by Rajsahi and

Jethi, the *zamindars* of pargana Harha. The *zamindars* of Ghaffaranagar are recorded to have devastated the Saiyid settlements around.[22] The *zamindaris* of Rustam Khan, Nasir Khan, Haisham Khan, Fateh Shah, Man Singh, Nayan Rai and Kharak Rai, residents and *zamindars* of *mauza* Kothi and other villages in pargana Sidhora were conferred upon one Mirza Muhammad Zahir, for they had forced the Saiyids of Zaidpur to pay certain cesses. Later in 1114 AH/ AD 1702–3, the *zamindaris* were restored to them when they took a pledge not to levy any cesses from the *taluqa* of the Saiyids.[23] An analysis of some of the letters which contain information about the malfactor *zamindars'* revolts in Awadh in the last years of Aurangzeb's reign would possibly suggest the *madad-i-maash* grantees to have been a major source of disturbances in the villages. In the month of Jumada II, 1125 AH May–June, 1713 the village of Ahrora in the pargana of Husampur, a *madad-i-ma'ash* of the Saiyids was invaded by a gang of over five hundred Rajputs of Dodh, a neighbouring village. A number of the resident Saiyids of the village were killed and their houses, libraries and other properties were set on fire. Five of their women were burnt to death, and the serving women and children of their community were driven out bare-fotee. Simultaneously, the villages of Badholia, Kamalpur, Kauhatta and Malhari which were in the *milkiyat* and *zamindari* of the Saiyids were completely devastated, and the graveyards of their ancestors, the mosques and the *madrasas* were levelled to ground.[24]

Indeed in the regions where the malfactors had their sway, the *madad-i-maash* holder could hardly afford to stay.[25] Owing to the domination of the Gaur *zamindars*, the *shurafa* and the *sadat* of Khairabad, along with the students of their *madrasas* had to migrate from their home town to the neighbouring territory of the Bangash Afghans of Farrukhabad. For about ten to twelve years, they wandered homeless. Ultimately in the beginning of Safdar Jang's governorship when an arrangement with the Gaurs of Khairabad was finally made, Muhammad Khan Bangash recommended to the governor the restoration to them of their houses and other properties in Khairabad.[26]

These incidents should not be taken as an expression of Hindu-Muslim rupture, as we have seen in the cases of the parganas of Harha, Unam (Unnao) cut across religious identities. Besides *Rajab* 19, in the 35th R.Y. of Aurangzeb (April 9, 1691) Mulla Qutbuddin of Sihali, father of the better known Mulla Nizamuddin, founder of the famous *madrasa* at Firangi Mahal was killed by the Muslim *zamindars* of the parganas of Sihali, Bijnor and Fathpur Dewa.[27] Again, we have evidence for the Rajput *zamindars'* support to the Muslim *madad-i-ma'ash* holders in the latter's venture against the bigger grantees-cum-zammindars. The *qazi* of the pargana of Husampur who seems to have been sacked due to his allegedly improper behaviour with Mir Saiyid Ahmad and Mir Saiyid Muhammad Arif, is recorded to have made encroachments upon the *zamindari* of the Mirs in the village of Katora. For this he was instigated and supported by one Ram Singh, the *zamindar* of Dasmandi who simultaneously plundered and usurped the revenue *oimauza* Sumanpur, which also was in the *zamindari* and *milkiyat* of the Mirs.[28]

Decline of the imperial control over local administration was possibly one of major factors responsible for the changes in the position of the *madad-i-ma'ash* holders. To arrest the growth and expansion of the *zamindars* revolts[29] which posed a threat to the imperial authority seems to have initially been the motive behind the additional privileges that the Mughals extended to the revenue grantees. Aurangzeb's *farman* of 1690 which made the *madad-i-maash* completely hereditary also seems to have been guided, at least partly, by the same factor.[30] The grantees exploited the new situation to their full advantage. They bettered their fortune by purchasing *zamindaris* and accumulating enough wealth and influence for money-lending and *ijara*. At the same time, they managed to retain their earlier facilities and exemption from certain levies to which the *zamindars* were not ordinarily entitled. This obviously violated the established rule and did not accord with the theoretical position of the revenue grantees. Hence, the local official's attempt to impose the regular cesses on certain *Madad-i-ma'ash* holdings in Bahraich. The conflict between the *jagirdars* and the grantees can also be thus explained. It is interesting to note that the *parwanas* of the *Diwan-i-Awadh* which reprimanded the *qanungo* and the *jagirdar* of Husampur for levying the cesses from the grantees show no concern for the difficulties of the latter and the circumstances. This suggests a basic difference between the approach of those who were actually involved in local problems and of those who ruled the country from a safe distance.

The revenue grantees' encroachments on the rights of the old *zamindars* showed the power that came up in the wake of these changes. This expressed itself in their actual clashes with the peasantry. The social tension[31] that these clashes resulted in can again be ascribed to the crippled imperial sway over the villages. As the control of the Mughal State over the villages slackened, the internal contradictions of the medieval Indian society which had so far been kept in check by it came now to the surface.

Notes

1. In regard to the problems we have proposed to discuss, the period is extremely important. In 1676 a new policy of vigorous military operations in the Deccan was opening up. This seems to have considerably conditioned the Mughal Emperor's attitude towards the Muslim orthodoxy which resulted in concessions to the *Madad-i-maash* grantees as well. cf. Satish Chandra, 'Jizya and the State in India During the 17th Century', *Journal of the Economic and Social History of the Orient*, vol. XII, pt. Ill, 1969. Though the later Mughals tried to remove the association of orthodoxy with the state, the *Madad-i-ma'ash* holders, due to various reasons, continued to increase their fortune. In Awadh, however, this process came to an end around 1722 when Burhan-ul-Mulk seems to have begun to make new arrangements with them

by abolishing the revenue grants, cf. Ghulam Ali Azad Bilgrami, *Maasir-ul-Kiram*, I, Hyderabad, 1913, p. 222.

2. *Ain-i-Akbari*, I, p. 198, cf. Irfan Habib, *Agrarian System of Mughal India*, p. 307; N.A. Siddiqi, *Land Revenue Administration Under the Mughals*, pp. 23–24.

3. *Allahabad Documents*, no. 1300.

4. Ibid., no. 196.

5. Ibid., no. 924.

6. Ibid., no. 1284 of *Shawwal* 1088/November 22,1677 records the purchase of one Maha Singh son of Lai Sahi Khatri's share in the *zamindari* and *milkiyat* of Unchhapur, *tappa* Chaurasi, pargana Husampur. No. 1295 dated 11 *Ziqada*, 1092/November 13, 1681 records the purchase of one Tara Chand's share in the *Zamindari* of Debidaspur in the same *tappa*. No. 1298 dated 19 *Rajab* 1098/May 22, 1687 records the purchase of the share of Daya Ram and Kaidhi Brahmans and their mother in the *zamindari* of Bedauri, No. 1300 dated 1099/1687–88 records the purchase of Narain and Puma Brahmans' share in the *zamindari* of Pasnajat, No. 12132, dated 19 *Jumada* 1105/January 8,1694 records the purchase of Nawazi Brahman's share in the *Zamindari* of Pasnajat Banyanhari, a village in *tappa* Mubarakpur, pargana Haveli Bahraich is also recorded to have been in the *zamindari* and *milkiyat* of Mir Saiyid Muhammad Arif, No. 1309. In AH 1701–2/ AD 1113 the Chaudhris of pargana Malanwa, in the Sarkar of Lucknow, are reported to have sold their mango garden which extended over five *bigas* and six *biswas* and comprises 68 trees to the qazi of the pargana, No. 136. Irfan Habib has used these documents for ascertaining the value of the share of the *zamindars* compared with that of the land revenue demand. *Agrarian System of Mughal India*, pp. 152–53, the numbers of the documents given in this paper are according to their re-arranged registers at the UP State Archives, Allahabad.

7. Ibid., no. 1283, dated 20th R.Y. of Aurangzeb (1676–77).

8. *Insha-i-Rashan Kalam of Bhupat Rai, Kanpur,* 1298, AH 1880–1, p. 10.

9. Shaikh Ghulam Husain Siddiqi al-Firshori, Sharaif-I Usmani (a biographical dictionary of the important families of Bilgram compiled in the middle of the eighteenth century), MS Department of History, A.M.U. Aligarh. p. 70.

10. See for instance *Akhbarat-i-Bahadur Shahi*. 5th R.Y. p. 74. Sitamau transcripts which records Saiyid Abdul Karim and about fifty others persons to have lodged a complaint against the *qazi*, stating that the latter accepted bribes (*murtashi*).

11. Allahabad Documents, no. 1285.

12. Ibid., no. 12124, in this document Mir Arif is mentioned as the *malik* and *taluqadar*.

13. Ibid., no. 1317.

14. Ibid., no. 1291, we do not have any evidence for the background of, or for the motive that operated behind, this incident. Can we conjecture that the *qanungo*, having legal expertise regarding the land possessions and the revenue, acted quite expectedly on proclaimed policy of the Mughals. For, he might have thought that the Saiyid after acquiring the *zamindaris*, etc., had forsaken his claim to any exemptions.

15. Ibid., no. 1309.

16. Ibid., no. 11992. Appointments of Shaikh Qutb, his grandfather, and of Shaikh Abdun-Nabi, his father, were made on the *farmans* of Aurangzeb.

17. cf. Irfan Habib, *Agrarian System of Mughal India*, p. 299n.

18. *Sharaif-i-Usmani*, p. 166, Qazi Sariful-Hasan, *Tanqih ul-Kalam Fi-Tarikhi Bilgram* (an Urdu local history of Bilgram based primarily on the two eighteenth century MSS., *Sharaif-i-Usmani* and *Musajjalat Fi-Tarikh al-Quzat* of Qazi Ahmadullah, s/o Qazi Md. Ihsan), pp. 193–4.

19. Muhammed Hasan Abbasi, *Abbasiyan-i-Kakori*, p. 9.

20. *Allahabad Documents*, nos. 882, 934, 1280 of the 19th R.Y. of Aurangzeb

21. cf. Irfan Habib, *Agrarian System*, pp. 299–300.

22. *Insha-i-Roshan Kalam*, pp. 3, 4, 6, 14 and 27.

23. Allahabad Documents, no 1565. The word *taalluqa* in this document (like *taalluqa-i jagir, taalluqa-i jaujdar, taalluqa-i qaza, etc.* and also in some other documents referred to earlier seems to have been used in its literal sense domain.

24. Ibid., no. 1315.

25. On the basis of the sources we have examined, the case of the *Madad-i-maash* grantees of Jais offers the sole exception in this regard. They are said to have fought with Balbhadra Singh, the *zamindar* of Tiloi against the *zamindar* of seventeenth and early eighteenth centuries used to say with pride that his *zamindari* had the backing of the blessings of Shah Ata Ashraf, a descendant of the celebrated saint of the Sultanate period, Shah Jahangir Ashraf. He is also said to have been the first to apply *tika* on Mohan's forehead. "Tarikh-i Jais" (a local history of Jais compiled possibly in the late eighteenth century) MS, Dr. Abdul Ali collection. Nadwat-ul-Ulama, Lucknow, 127b. The friendship between the Saiyids of Jais and the *zamindars* of Tiloi is traced to a credulous story of Saiyid Shah Inayatullah's curse to the *zamindar* in the fifteenth century. Ibid., f.27a.

This is to be noted that Mohan Singh, in resentment to his father's proposition to nominate his other son, Newal to succeed to the *zamindari* after his death, had killed the former and usurped the *zamindari* without seeking formal sanction from Mughal Diwan. W.C. Bennet, *A Report on the Family History of the Chief Clans of the Roy Bareilly District*, Lucknow, 1870, pp. 41–42. In his enterprise, Mohan seems to have been backed by the Saiyids and Shaikhs which neutralized the loss that he was faced with because of the desertion of his own clansmen

26. *Khujista Kalam* of Munshi Sahib Rai, Rolograph, Raghuvir Singh Collection, Sitamau, (a collection of the letters of Nawab Muhammad Khan Bangash), pp. 165–66. "Also see *Shahnama Munawwar Kalam* of Shiv Das Lakhnawi for Singha Gaur, the *zamindar* of Kateskar's atrocities on the revenue grantees of Laharpur and Kheri in *sarkar* Khairabad (ff. 73–74a) Rotograph, Department of History, A.M.U., Aligarh and *Ajaibul-Afaq* (a collection of the letters of Chhabela Ram and Girdhar Bahadur and of some *akhbarat* of Fanukh Siyar's reign) for conflict between the *zamindars* and the *Madad-i-maash* grantees in Daryabad 66 Sitamau Rotograph).

27. Mulla Qutbuddin was a *Madad-i-maash* grantee and ran a well-established *madrasa* in Sihali, in the *sarkar* of Lucknow. Two of his students, Shaikh Ghulam Muhammad, a maternal grandson of the celebrated Shaikh Nizamuddin of Amethi, and Shaikh Izzatullah of Sandila were also killed by the assailants. His son Muhammad said, the *qazi* of the pargana of Sihali and a number of the Mulla's pupils received serious wounds. The women of the mulla's family and his other

relations in the town were humiliated. The library of the madrasa which comprised about 900 books including the copies of the Holy Quran, the Hadis were set on fire. The atrocities on the family and the *madrasa* of the Mulla are said to have been due to his intimate relations with the Emperor. cf. Mufti Muhammad Raza Ansari Firangi Mahali, *Bani-e Dars-i Nizami Mulla Nizammuddin Firangi Mahali,* pp.25–30, Ansari reproduces the *Mahzar* cf Qazi Muhammad Said with its photostat copy and quotes from the contemporary and near contemporary unpublished biographies and family histories.

28. *Allahabad Documents,* no. 934. An old feud seems to have existed between the *qazi* and the Mirs. Even during the tenure of his office, the *qazi* had seized over a thousand *bighas* in pargana of Fathpur, *sarkar* Bahraich, where he held 250 *bighas* as his *Mashrut madad-i-maash.* The land misappropriated was in the *zamindari* of the Mirs. Also one Jafar, a relative of the *qazi,* is reported to have usurped their *zamindari* and *milkiyat in* the villages of Sahya, Karmullahpur and Kantaur in parganas Selak and Husampur. Ibid., no. 1280.

29. We do not have at the moment any statistics of the *zamindar* revolts on the Mughal Suba of Awadh under Aurangzeb. From a cursory survey of the sources of Mughal India, the increase in the magnitude of such revolts both in terms of number and intensity, can fairly be conjectured, cf. Satish Chandra, *Parties and Politics at the Mughal Court,* Introduction, p. xxxi, Irfan Habib, *Agrarian System,* ch. 9; S.N. Sinha, *Subah of Allahabad under the Great Mughal,* pp. 65–82. The *InshaiRoshan Kalam* which records 18 revolts in a single region of Awadh (Baiswara) within the tenure of the favidari of Rad Andaz Khan clearly indicates the nature and extent of the *zamindars* refractoriness in Awadh in the late 17th century. See for instance, pp. 3, 4, 6, 9, 10, 14, 15, 18, 19–20, 22, and 27.

30. cf. Irfan Habib, *Agrarian System,* p. 306.

31. For a different opinion see N.A.Siddiqi's *Land Revenue Administration under the Mughals. pp.* 133–34.

10

New Evidence on Agrarian and Rural Taxation in Eastern Rajasthan, Seventeenth-Eighteenth Centuries

S.P. Gupta

ONSIDERABLE ATTENTION has been paid by scholars to study various aspects of the economy of Eastern Rajasthan from the middle of the seventeenth to the close of eighteenth century. It is well known that much material is available owing to the fortunate survival of the archives of the Jaipur State. Recently, I came across a number of *dastur-ul-amals* and *amal-dasturs*, which are preserved in the Rajasthan State Archives, Bikaner. An attempt has been made in this paper to interpret the data contained in these documents in order to shed light on some aspects of the economy of Eastern Rajasthan during the period indicated above. The evidence contained in these documents either corroborates or supplements certain conclusions already made by me from a detailed analysis of other documents viz., *arhsattas*, *chitthis*, etc.

A word is necessary about the definition of *dastur-ul-amal* and *amal-dastur*. Yasin, the author of the late eighteenth century Persian glossary of revenue terms, defines *dastur-ul-amal* as a *dastur* (schedule of taxes, etc.) which is old and which is applied, as opposed to a *amal-dastur, viz.,* a *dastur* which has been established recently by the revenue authority itself.[1] Yasin does not imply any necessary contradiction between the two sets of rules. The *amal-dastur* could very well simply supplement the *dastur-ul-amal*. Wilson, citing Eliot, however writes as if the *amal-dastur* supersedes the *dastur-ul amal*;[2] but it appears from our East Rajasthan documents that this was not usually the case. The *amal-dastur* here usually provides information or rules for the exactions and levies (particularly regarding local trade and commerce) which is not given by old-established schedule. The *dastur-ul-amal* and *amal-dastur*, in fact comprised together, the entire set of rules and regulation which provides us a comprehensive schedule of the local revenue rates.

Though the *amal-dastur* and *dastur-ul-amal* were framed by the local officials from time to time, they could be superseded by the Mughal court. In

*36th Session at Aligarh, 1975.

pargana Merta in AD 1663 the Maharaja had to grant certain reductions when the ryots petitioned the Mughal court.[3]

Sometimes the word *dastur* has been used in these documents as an abbreviation of *dastur-ul-amal* in the sense made familiar to us by the *Ain-i-Akbari*, representing the incidence of demand on each crop that the peasant had to pay to satisfy the land revenue demand.

The information of different rates of *mal* (land revenue) and *jihat* (other perquisites) is offered under two distinct categories, *viz.*, *zabti* and *jinsi* on the same pattern as given in the *arhsattas*. The rates under the two categories are strictly speaking, not comparable with each other. The crops assessed to *zabti* were assessed in terms of money per *bigha* according to different *dastur-ul-amal* over a number of years. The rates in *zabti* do not give any indication of either the produce per *bigha* or the price of the crop. Under the *batai jinsi* (crop-sharing) the proportionate state share and *ryots* share out of the produce is given along with the share claimed from other sections of cultivators such as *Mahajan*, Brahmans, etc., who were assessed at a concessional rate (see table). Unfortunately, we do not have any statement of area when the crops are assessed on the basis of *jinsi*. We can perhaps establish some correlation between *zabti* and *jinsi* if some of the *jinsi* crops had also been assessed according to the *zabti* system.

Under the *zabti*, the *dastur-ul-amals* give us detailed tables of revenue-rates stated in cash, applicable to different crops in a pargana (see Table I). There were changes in the rate of demand made upon individual crops assessed under *zabti*, apparently due to the quality of soil, *e.g.*, the rates upon the *magro* (hilly) lands were lower as compared to those *of goriwa* (sandy).[4] However, an examination of the rate of revenue demand per *bigha* for *zabti* crops set out in the same table shows a remarkable continuity. The rates of certain crops in pargana Phagi (AD 1601) given in the *dastur-ul-amal*, when compared with the rates in *arhsattas* of the same pargana (AD 1694) correspond with each other, but seem to be a little higher than crop rates of AD 1744.[5] There is, however, no distinct upward or downward trend. Alternative explanation of the low rates in AD 1744 may be furnished partly by the indices of prices.[6] The rates of *vani* (cotton) and opium are very close in pargana Merta[7] (Western Rajasthan).

TABLE I

Crop	Rates		Index (Cotton=100)		Index Ain=100
	A	B	C	D	E
1	2	3	4	5	6
PARGANA PHAGI					
	1691	1595	1691	1595	
Sali	1.00	1.36	100.00	88.89	73.53
Vani (Cotton)	1.00	1.53	100.00	100.00	65.36

(Contd.)

TABLE I (*Contd.*)

Crop	Rates		Index (Cotton=100)		Index Ain=100
	A	B	C	D	E
1	2	3	4	5	6
Madhwal	1.00	0.54	100.00	35.00	185.19
Opium	2.50	2.29	250.00	150.00	109.17
Kodon	1.00	0.42	100.00	27.45	238.09
Vegetables (Kh)	0.50	1.36	50.00	89.00	36.76
Indigo	1.25	3.25	125.00	212.42	30.77
Maka, Jowar	1.50	0.44	150.00	150.00	340.99
Kakri, Kharbooza and Vegetables	1.50	1.36	150.00	150.00	110.29
Cheena (arzan)	0.75	0.52	75.00	34.00	144.23
TAPPA BAWRI					
	1715	1595	1715	1595	
Varh	2.50	3.27	263.16	213.73	76.45
Vani	0.94	1.53	100.00	100.00	61.44
Sinn (sunn)	0.67	2.00	72.63	130.72	35.00
Kodu, Kagni	0.75	0.43	78.95	28.10	174.42
Madhwa	1.75	0.54	184.21	35.29	324.07
Indigo	2.25	3.25	236.84	212.42	69.23
Opium	2.31	2.29	242.11	149.67	100.84
Vegetables, Kharbooza, kakri, lahsun, methi, etc.	1.31	1.67	136.84	109.15	77.84
Zeera	1.50	2.04	157.89	133.33	73.53
Cheena (arzan)	1.50	0.52	157.89	33.99	288.46
PARGANA AMARSAR					
	1726	1595	1726	1595	
Jowar, Maka	2.00	1.19	160.00	46.67	168.07
Varh (sugarcane)	6.25	4.40	500.00	172.55	142.05
Indigo	1.50	5.10	120.00	200.00	29.41
Sunn	1.50	2.04	120.00	80.00	73.53
Vani	1.25	2.55	100.00	100.00	49.02
PARGANA JHAK					
	1715	1595	1715	1595	
Vani	1.00	1.53	100.00	100.0	65.36
Madhwa	1.50	0.54	150.00	35.29	277.78
Indigo	1.00	3.25	100.00	212.42	—
Posta (opium)	2.50	2.29	250.00	149.67	109.17
Baigan, Kada, Lahdari, Methi, Zeera	1.50	0.62	150.00	40.52	241.93
Cheena (arzan)	0.75	0.47	75.00	30.72	159.57
PARGANA MERTA					
	1663	1595	1663	1595	
Vani	1.37	1.53	100.00	100.00	89.34
Vegetables	1.37	1.36	100.00	88.89	100.00

(Contd.)

TABLE I (*Contd.*)

Crop	Rates		Index (Cotton=100)		Index Ain=100
	A	B	C	D	E
1	2	3	4	5	6
Opium	2.50	2.29	183.82	149.67	109.17
Vegetables	1.30	1.36	100.00	88.89	100.00
PARGANA SOJAT					
	1661	1595	1661	1595	
Vani	1.50	1.53	110.29	100.00	100.00
Vegetables (Rabi)	0.50	1.36	36.76	88.89	88.89
PARGANA PHAGI[8]					
	1774	1595	1744	1595	
Vani	0.67	1.53	100.00	100.00	43.79
Maka	1.08	0.44	161.19	28.75	245.45
Kodon	0.61	0.42	91.04	27.45	145.24
Madhwa	0.90	0.54	134.33	35.29	166.67
Indigo	1.00	3.25	149.25	212.42	30.77
Vegetables	1.45	1.36	216.42	88.89	106.62
Opium (aufro)	2.33	2.29	347.18	149.67	101.75
Zeera	1.50	2.04	223.83	133.33	73.53

We can compare the Ain's rate index with the rates of *dastur-ul-amal* of different parganas in Eastern and Western Rajasthan and the *arhsattas*.[9] I Table II shows that the seventeenth-eighteenth century *dastur-ul-amal* rates are not on the whole appreciably higher than *Ain*. Some are indeed lower. The interesting fact which emerges is that the cash-crops seem heavily underrated in comparison with the food crops. Thus whereas the food crops (*kodon* and *madhwa*) show considerable increase over the *Ain*'s rates, cash crops like indigo and cotton show heavy decline. Columns 'C' and 'D' in our table also bring out the relative position of these crops in the *dastur-ul-amal* and the A'in by adjusting the figures to the rate of cotton, as base=100. Does it mean that there was a deliberate attempt on the part of the administration in the seventeenth century to encourage cash crop cultivation in this area by assessing lower revenue rate? It was perhaps for this reason that there is a tendency for an increase in the cultivation of *zabti* crops, which were to a large extent cash crops.[10]

An interesting point is that the pargana officials, *viz.*, *chaudhari* and *qanungo* were charged land revenue at much lower rate than the ryot. Th is concession was granted to them practically in all parganas. The following was the *dastur* in 1715 in pargana Phagi,[11] *sarkar* Ajmer.

Rate of Demand (Rupee per bigha)

Crop	Chaudhari-qanungo	Ryot
Varh (sugarcane)	1.00	2.50
Vani (cotton)	0.25	0.94
Sunn	—	0.67
Sakarkandi	0.25	1.37
Kodu and kagni	0.25	0.75
Madhwa	0.25	1.75

In pargana *Amarsar*,[12] *sarkar* Nagaur, subah Ajmer (AD 1726), the *patti* (cultivator) was charged at the rate of Rs.2/- per *bigha*, for jawar and makka while the *patel*, etc, and *shekawat* Rajputs were charged at Rs. 1.75 and Rs. 1.50 respectively for the same crop.[13] Another privileged class which was assessed more highly consisted of Brahmans, Rajputs and *mahajan* cultivators. There were definite instructions to the collector and assessor (*amil* and *amin*) not to collect from them according to the *dastur-ul-amal* and to issue a separate *patta* (agreement) upon concessional terms.[14] The same concessions were granted to them in Marwar.[15]

We may now pass on to the incidence of taxation under *jinsi*. An examination of the *dastur-ul-amals* of different parganas reveals the fact that the land revenue demand was fixed at one-half of the produce in kharif and rabi.[16] (Table ll). But it would be very unreasonable to generalise from this and consider it a universal or unvariable proportion. Some of the principles which determined the magnitude of land revenue demand in crop-sharing are brought out in our documents. Different rates of land revenue demand were prescribed on the land based on irrigation facilities, *viz. bara*[17] or *von* or *vara kyari* (land of the first quality), *piwal* or *piyal* and well (*dhenkli*) *tal* (tank).[18] A perusal of Table II shows that the incidence of land revenue demand in *batai* or *bhaoli* on the ryots was one-half in respect of all crops except wheat and bajra where it was two-fifths. Other revenue-payers such as Brahmans, Banias (*mahajans*) paid only one-third in Kharif, while the Bhumias were charged only at the rate of one-fourth.[19] In Rabi, too, the Brahmans and Banias were granted at a concessional rate. The rates of bajra were reduced to two-fifths for those cultivators who had brought the cultivation of the land of bajra, etc., in Rabi. The *pahis* (temporary non-resident cultivator) either were exempted from taxation or were asked to pay a very lower rate. The pargana officials were authorised to issue a *patta* separately to such cultivators.[20] The available evidence shows that part of the produce which was appropriated in addition to *mal* under the head *jihat*. The *jihat* were subdivided into two categories namely *dastur chaudhari*, *qanungo* and *farah*. The, rate of perquisites (*dastur-chaudhari qanungo*) was one seer per maund. In *farah* two cesses were levied, *viz. seri*,[21] at 3 *seer* to 4 *seer* per maund and *nirani* (a charge made to the ryot who paid his rent for the carriage of the grain to the place (*qasba*) where it was sold) which

TABLE II: Cropsharing (batal)

Crops	State	Palti and Ryots	Brahmans	Pahi	Rajputs		Patel, etc.	Bania (Mahajan)	Sirdar ketri zamindar, (bhumias) also chaudhari qanungo	Farah (Jihat)	
					Shakhawat	Others				Seri	nirani
Kharif	50%	50%	—	V	1:3	1:3	—	1:3	—	Mahajan exempted *jihat* is exempted from patel *seri* % per mound from *raiti*	Rajputs exempted dastur Chaudhari qanungo @ seer/1/ per md.
Sali (rice) and singhara	2:5	3/5	1:3 *jihat* exempted	Exempted	—	—	2:5	1:3 *jihat* exempted	1:4 *jihat* exempted	—	—
Madhava	2:5	3/5	—	—	—	—	—	—	—		
Rabi											
Gram	50%	50%	—	—	—	—	2+5 (*jihat* exempted)	—	—	—	—
Barley	50%	50%	—	—	—	—	—	—	—	—	—
Wheat	2:5	3/5	1:3	—	—	—	2:5	2:5	1:4	—	—
Bajra	2:5 instead of 50%	3/5	—	—	—	—	—	—	—	—	—

varied from place to place and crop to crop. The latter was fixed @ *taka* 2/6 (approximately 1/8th of rupee) per maund upon moth and mung, etc.[22] The *jihat* imposition was remitted by the order *of diwan* Ali Ahmad Khan in 1113 H. (1702).[23]

Besides *mal-o-jihat* the other resources of the state were exactions made under *sair-jihat*[24] and *siwai-jamabandi*.[25] Under *sair-jihat* several items of taxation are specified. The *gausumri* (cattle tax) was a tax levied on cows, *dhor*, buffaloes, *chaille gader* (goat and sheep) @ Re 1/- per animal.[26] The Rajputs, *mahajans*, Brahmans and Charans (bards) were exempted. *Khunt*[27] (*Khut*) were fixed @ Rs. 2.50 upon each plough drawn by four oxen.[28] The other items of taxation are *charai, dastur chaudhari qanungo* @ *taka* 1 per rupee), *habubati*, etc. (see Appendix). The main items of taxation under *siwai-jamabandi* are the sale of trees (state share 50%) *mapa, halat* (plough),[29] *dastur-chaudhari qanungo* on the villages of *jagirdar* @ Rs. 2.50 per hundred, *aghori, kayali, bagdam* (marriage tax @ Rs. 0.50.), *kiraya* (different rates were fixed on the carriages carrying different articles,), etc.[30]

Our documentary evidence thus leads us to estimate the rough incidence of taxation on the *ryots* in the parganas studied. The land revenue took away a half of the produce of the cultivator on most of the crops. In addition to it a peasant had to pay roughly a tenth of the produce directly or indirectly by way of various exactions, as has already been discussed elsewhere.[31] Thus it seems that the peasant in these areas was under considerable fiscal pressure. On the other hand, the *mahajans*, Bhomias (sardar kotri, etc.), pargana officials (*chaudhari qanungo*), village official (*patel*), certain Rajputs (mainly Shekhawat), belonged to the privileged class within the village.

We now move on to the information provided in the *amal-dastur* documents. An examination of the commodities brought to the towns throws interesting light on the local trade. The raw material supplied consisted of two types: first, the commodities meant for long-distance trade such as indigo, silk, cotton etc., and second, the commodities for local consumption such as *jinsi* (cereals), gur, ghee, salt, etc.

A study *of amal-dastur rahdari*[32] and *amal dastur chabutra kotwali*[33] documents give the impression that a very large number of peasants were not able to reach the open market, and therefore had to sell their goods to the local merchant. On the way to and in the market, the peasant had to pay a variety of dues and perquisites on different items, which are recorded in our documents ('Tables III: 'A, 'B' and 'C').

Different duties were levied upon local merchants who bought commodities from the villages and sold them either in the same village where they had purchased them or in villages around, or upon the *bichhaiti*[34] (petty dealer) who bought the commodities from adjacent places and sold it in the village. The rate of *rahdari* on local merchant dealing in tobacco was fixed at 1 *taka* per rupee *ad valorem* whereas the *bichhaiti* had to pay *taka* 2 per rupee.

Since the peasants had to pay the land revenue in cash, the share in *jinsi* was always commuted into cash on the basis of current prices. In most of the cases he himself carried the commodity on carts to the local market or *qasba*. Different rates were fixed on the carriages of different commodities. (Table III 'A').

Significantly enough, brokers are not mentioned in these documents. Of course, we hear of moneylenders like *mahajans, vohras* and *sahukars* playing an important role in carrying the trade.

Amal-dastur bhomi: also provides us with a detailed account of taxation fixed upon *bhom* land.[35] But their information mainly corroborates the evidence contained in the *arhsattas*, which we have already examined in a separate paper.[36] It leads us to the same conclusion arrived there, that the total *bhomi* levy, relatively to the total land revenue realization, was not very high.

TABLE III

'A'

The Rate of State Charges on Each Carriage (in taka)[37]

Carriages of the Items	Rate
Lun ka gara (a carriage carrying salt)	2
Naj ka gara (grain carriage)	2
Ruee ka gara (cotton)	4
Til ka gara (til)	3
Kapra ka gara (cloth)	4
Gur khand ka gara (sugar)	4
Kirana ka gara	4
Khalra ka gara (?)	4

'B'

Dastur Chowki Kasba Phagi (customs charges from *banjara*)[38]

Carriages (oxen)	Rate (in taka)
Grain and salt	2/25
Gur	6
Cotton	5/25
Ruee aal (raw cotton)	Rs.0/8/0
Camel	0/25
Kafda bringing cloth	5
Indigo	Rs.0/5/0
Glass, sugar and kirana	Rs.0/4/0

'C'

The Rates of Rahdari

Carriage carrying *glass*	Rs. 1/4/0
Carriage carrying *khand* (sugar)	Rs. 1/4/0
Carriage carrying cotton	Rs. 0/8/0
Carriage carrying indigo (*neel*)	Rs. 1/8/0
Carriage carrying *ghee*	Rs. 0/12/0
Carriage carrying *til*	Rs. 0/8/0
Carriage carrying rice, sunn	*taka* 6/0

APPENDIX

Habubati[39] (Muwafiq jamabandi)

Asami	Jumlo (total amount)	Bhent jamabandiki	Kamli	Kagai	Aghori	Halat
Q.Phagi	26.8.0	1.0.0	2.0.0	11.0.0	0	12.8.0
Murhez	5.0.0	1.0.0	1.0.0	1.0.0	1.8.0	1.8.0
Kunwarpur	3.0.0	0.8.0	0.8.0	0.8.0	0.8.0	1.0.0
Kagya	4.8.0	1.0.0	0.8.0	1.8.0	0.8.0	1.8.0
Govindi	2.48.0	1.0.0	1.0.0	14.0.0	ijara	8.8.0
Kishanpur, etc.	3.12.0	1.0.0	0.8.0	0.12.0	0.8.0	1.0.0
Churoo	36.4.0	1.0.0	2.0.0	14.0.0	2.8.0	1.74.0
Chakhara	16.3.0	1.0.0	1.0.0	6.0.0	1.0.0	7.3.0
Jaisingpur	5.4.0	1.0.0	1.0.0	1.0.0	1.4.0	1.4.0
Halro	6.8.0	1.0.0	1.0.0	2.0.0	0.8.0	2.0.0
Datuli	5.8.0	1.0.0	1.0.0	0.8.0	0.8.0	2.8.0
Obarokpur	3.4.0	1.0.0	0.8.0	0.8.0	0.4.0	1.0.0
Ribharo	4.12.0	0	0	0	0	4.12.0
Narhar	25.8.0	1.0.0	1.0.0	1.40.0	1.0.0	8.8.0
Pachalo	6.0.0	1.0.0	0.0.0	2.0.0	0.8.0.	1.8.0
Pandi	1.0.0	0	0	0	0	1.0.0
Biharipur	8.0.0	1.0.0	1.0.0	3.0.0	1.0.0	2.0.0
Mohanpur	6.3.0	1.0.0	1.0.0	2.0.0	0.8.0	1.0.0
Mahavan	3.4.0	1.0.0	0.8.0	0.8.0	0.4.0	1.0.0
Maharajapur	5.12.0	1.0.0	1.0.0	1.0.0	1.0.0.	1.12.0
Mehandwas	8.0.0	1.0.0	2.0.0	2.0.0	1.0.0	2.0.0
Rampur Sahi	8.2.0	1.0.0	1.0.0	2.8.0	1.0.0	3.10.0
Ranipur Shaqi	4.0.0	1.0.0	0.8.0	1.0.0	0.8.0	1.0.0
Raipur G	6.0.0	1.0.0	1.0.0	2.0.0	0.8.0	1.8.0
Rarnpur G.	1.0.0	1.0.0	1.0.0	2.0.0	0.8.0	1.8.0
Lahilagyo	10.0.0	1.0.0	2.0.0	3.0.0	1.0.0	3.0.0
Sakarpur	7.4.0	1.0.0	1.0.0	2.8.0	1.0.0	1.12.0
Sirasyo	8.0.0	1.0.0	1.0.0	2.0.0	1.0.0	3.0.0
Surtajai	1.12.0	0	0	0	0	1.12.0
Habaryo	7.4.0	1.0.0	1.0.0	2.0.0	1.0.0	2.4.0
Gokalpur	4.8.0	1.0.0	0.8.0	1.0.0	0.8.0	1.8.0

Notes

1. Khwajah Yasin's *Glossary*, B.M.Add. 6603 f. 62. cf. Mss, Khudabaksh Library, Patna. The latter defines '*Dastur-ul-amal* as the term for the old rule which the former *amils* had established and the *amal-dastur* for the newly framed rules that comes about when the present *amil* invents a new rule'.
2. Wilson's *Glossary of Judicial and Revenue Terms*, p. 129.
3. Naiusis' *Pargana Ri Vigat*, II, p.93. Also *see dastur-ul-amal pargana Jhak*. Diwan Ali Ahmed Khan of Suba Ajmer exempted the *jihals* in *fasal* Kharif and Rabi in Hijri year 1113 (AD 1702).
4. *Dastur-ul-amal* and *amal-dastur pargana* Bhagi, vs 1748/1691.
5. Ibid. Also see *arhsattas* of pargana Phagi years AD 1695 and AD 1744.

6. S.P. Gupta and Shireen Moosvi 'Weighted Price and Revenue-Rate Indices of Eastern Rajasthan,' (c. 1665–1750), *Indian Economic and Social History Review*, vol. XII, no. 2 (see figure I where the price indices comes low particularly in AD 1744).

7. cf. *dastur-ul-amal* pargana Merta in *Pargana Ri Vigat*, vol. II.

8. *Arhsatta*, pargana Phagi, AD 1744.

9. The *Ain's* rate have been converted into rupees per *bigha-i daftari* which was in use in the area under study. Forty dams went to a rupee and the *bigha-i daftari* was equal to 2/3rd of the *bigha-i Ilahi*.

10. S. Nurul Hasan, Mrs. K.N. Hasan and S.P. Gupta, 'The Pattern of Agriculture Production in the Territories of Amber, c. 1650–1750', *IHC*, Mysore 1966, pp. 244–64.

11. *Dastur-ul-amal, tappa* Bawri, pargana Phagi, vs 1772/1715.

12. *Dastur-ul-amal*, pargana Amarsar, vs 1733/1726.

13. *Dastur-ul-amal*, pargana Amarsar, AD 1726.

14. Ibid., also see *dastur-ul-amal* and *amal-dastur*, pargana Phagi, cf. *arhsattas*.

15. G.D. Sharma's article on 'State Land Revenue Demand in Marwar During the 17th Century', published in Rajasthan History Congress, Pali, 1974. cf. *pargana Ri Vigat*.

16. In pargana Merta the *bhog* (revenue demand in *jinsi*) was one-half of the produce in Kharif, *Pargana Ri Vigat*. cf. *dastur-ul-amal*, Phagi, Amarsar Jhak.

17. *Bara* is land next to or surrounding a village (perhaps from *bar*, an enclosure). Land of the first quality, although containing a portion of sand. Wilson's *Glossary*.

18. *Dastur-ul-amal*, pargana Phagi, Khohri. Jhak, Amarsar.

19. *Dastur-ul-amal* and *amal dastur*, pargana Phagi. AD 1691.

20. Ibid., also see *dastur-ul-amal*, pargana Amarsar, AD 1726.

21. A perquisite of *seer* in the division of crop.

22. *Dastur-ul-amal*, pargana Jhak. *cf. Arhsattas* of different parganas. For the perquisites *jihat* in *zabt* see *lawazim* in 'The System of Rural Taxation in Eastern Rajasthan, c. 1665–1750', *IHC* Muzzaffarpur, 1972.

23. Ibid.

24. A study of the nature of cesses under *sair-jihat* suggests that they were collected from the miscellaneous taxes from a variety of imposts either as prescriptive fees or cesses levied upon the resident of a village. See S.P. Gupta's 'The System of Rural Taxation in Eastern Rajasthan, 1665–1750', published in *IHC*, Muzzaffarpur, 1972.

25. *Siwai-jamabandi* appears to represent additional cess besides the customary revenue. It was an increase in the amount of the revenue or otherwise or new or additional cesses levied upon the entire pargana, including the *mauzas* assigned in *jagir*, (cf. ibid.)

26. *Dastur-ul-amal* and *amal-dastur*, pargana Phagi, 1691.

27. Ibid.

28. Ibid.

29. See Appendix.

30. *Dastur-ul-amal* and *amal-dastur*, pargana Phagi, 1691.

31. 'The System of Rural Taxation . . . .'

32. *Amal dastur hasil rahdari,* vs 1773/1715.

33. *Amal dastur kotwali chowtra qasba,* Phagi, vs 1710/1713.

34. *Bichhail* is defined by Wilson as a petty dealer who does not keep a shop but carries his goods to a fair or market . . . or a mat or cloth spread on ground. *Glossary,* p. 85.

35. *Amal dastur bhomi, qasba* Phagi, vs 1741/1634.

36. See S.P. Gupta and Shireen Moosvi's article, 'Bhomi in the Territories of Amber, *c.* 1650–1750', *1HC,* 1970, Jabalpur.

    The amount of *bhomi* as percentage of the total revenue realization varies from 1 to 3 and 1.25 to 4.25 in parganas Narmina and Malama respectively.

37. *Dastur-ul-amal and amal-dastur,* pargana *Phagi,* 1691. Also see *dastur-ul-amal* and *amal-dastur chowira kotwali, qasba* Phagi.

38. *Yaddashti dastur-ul amal and amal-dastur hasil rahdari,* pargana Phagi. vs 1772/ 1715.

39. *Dastur-ul-amal* and *amal-dastur,* pargana Phagi, AD 1691.

11

The Deshmukhi Watan with Special Reference to Indapur

A.R. Kulkarni

Importance

During the medieval period the village administration in the Maratha country was entrusted to a set of civil servants called the *watandars*. The *deshmukh* was the chief of a pargana comprising a number of villages. The routine administration of the village was conducted by the village headman, the *patil*, but the ultimate responsibility of the village administration rested with the *deshmukh*. *Watan* was a rent-free land grant made to a person in lieu of his services to the village community. The office created by the *watan* was a hereditary one and it continued in a family as long as the office-bearer served the village community loyally. In common parlance, therefore, this grant was callcd *cakari watan*, that is, service tenure.

As the jurisdiction of the *deshmukh* extended to the entire pargana, he had to supervise the work of all the *patils* under his charge. The *deshmukh* also enjoyed the *patilki watan* of some villages of the pargana. In the absence of a permanent *palil* in a village under his charge, the *deshmukh* customarily acted as patil of that village till a permanent arrangement was made.[1]

The *watandars* enjoyed a privileged position in the village administration. The *deshmukh*, being the chief of the pargana, was too powerful and the *de facto* master of his pargana. This was mainly because of the unstable political situation in Maharashtra at the beginning of the seventeenth century. The Maratha country was parcelled out among the Mughals and the Deccani powers like the Nizam Shahis of Ahmadnagar, the Adilshahis of Bijapur and the Qutb Shahis of Golkunda. The alien powers had to depend on the *watandars* for the continuation of their rule in the Deccan. The *deshmukhs* and other *watandars* hardly bothered about the political changes in their areas as long as their *watan* in the pargana was not disturbed by the new power. They did not mind even if their pargana was distributed among two or more powers

*36th Session at Aligarh, 1975.

at the same time. After the extinction of the Nizam Shahis in 1636, for instance, one part of the pargana of Poona was under the Adil Shahis and another part under the Mughals. The *deshmukh* of Poona was partly controlled by the Adil Shahis and partly by the Mughals, but this did not affect his position as pargana official. His authority was respected by both the powers. It means that the authority of the *deshmukh* was permanent, whereas that of the state was temporary, and that the *deshmukh* was primarily the officer of the pargana and only then that of the state. He was thus loyal first to his pargana and then to the state.

The pre-eminent position enjoyed by the *deshmukh* in the pargana has been aptly brought out by Ramachandrapant Amatya in his famous work on Maratha state policy called the *Ajnapatra*. He states:

They (*deshmukhs*) are no doubt small, but independent chiefs of the territories (*deshnayaks*). They are not to be considered as ordinary people. These people are really the sharers of the kingdom (*dayads*)[2]

If the king happened to be the *deshmukh* of a pargana as well, his name was included in the list of *watandars* of that pargana as well as in the *rajmandal* and he had his own seal as a *deshmukh*. For instance, Chhatrapati Shahu's name was included in a decision of a council which included the names of state officials and *watandars*. This again emphasizes the permanence of the village offices as against the state ones.[3]

Origin

The origin of the institution of *deshmukhi* is still shrouded in obscurity. Grant Duff endeavoured to investigate it. The problem before him was whether the *deshmukhi* institution was Hindu in origin, or whether it owed its existence to the Muslims, who occupied the Deccan during the fourteenth century. He entered into a long correspondence on this subject with Captain John Briggs, his contemporary and political agent and collector of Khandesh. Briggs was a Persian scholar, then engaged in translating Ferishta's *Tarikh*, a monumental history of Muslim monarchy in the medieval Deccan. Grant Duff calls him a 'Pathan Turk'. Duff's contention was that he could not find the 'smallest proof, 'a vestige of' Deshmukh, Deshpandya or Deshlekuk before the Bund of the Umraos which ended in the establishment of the Bahamani dynasty'.[4] He argued that many powerful *naiks* or chiefs in this country, who had established their authority during the earlier period, joined the insurgent Muslim nobles and secured in return for their services confirmation of their authority over those portions of their native country. He maintained that the naiks who supported the Muslims were the original *deshmukhs*.[5] Briggs challenged this theory and asked him:

How do you account for the same officers being known and held office under the Mysore government, before a Mohammedan ever set his foot in those territories? And from whence have sprung the Dessays of Ceylon, which was never conquered by the Indian Mohammedans.[6]

However, he expressed his inability to deliver a 'Deshmookh of the old Raj precisely circumstanced as the Deshmookh with whom we have lately come into contact.'[7] This did not satisfy Grant Duff, and he still maintained that 'the institution of Deshmukh, if not prior to the rise of the Bahamani dynasty, is at least coeval with it in Maharashtra.'[8]

It is true that we do not find the term *deshmukh* prior to the rise of the Marathas, in either literature or inscriptions. It is a Sanskrit word. But modern researches in the early history of the Deccan have enabled us to establish the link between institutions of the pre-Muslim and Muslim periods in the Deccan. In the age of Rashtrakutas (eighth–tenth centuries) the *gramakuta* and the *deshgramakuta* were performing the duties of *patil* and *deshmukh* respectively.[9] The office of the *deshgramakuta* was in vogue under the Yadavas, and it must have been replaced by the term *deshmukh* in course of time. It was simply a verbal change, and the functions of the office remained the same. The Muslims did introduce Persian terms for some offices of the village community, for example, *muqaddam* for *patil*, *riyaya* or *muzarian* for *praja*, but they did not have any Persian equivalent for *deshmukh*, a purely Sanskrit term.[10]

The Deshmukhs of Indapur

It seems from the records of the eighteenth century that the *deshmukhi* and *patilki* rights of Indapur belonged to Shahu Chhatrapati and his successors. An *ajnapatra* of 5 December 1704 issued by Shivaji II, the son of Rajaram, instructs the *shete, mahajan, kulkarni* and *rayani* that the *patilki watan* of *qasba* Indapur belonging to the *swami* (king) is being transferred to the Aisaheb that is, Tarabai, the widow of Rajaram, along with the rights and perquisites attached to the *watan*. It emphasizes that the *watan* especially belongs to *the swami*.[11] It is well known that Indapur formed a part of the original *jagir* of Shahji, which he bequeathed to Shivaji in the early decades of the seventeenth century. It is, therefore, likely that the *deshmukhi* rights of Indapur continued with the Bhonsles in spite of the changes in political power in that region.

Shahu appointed a *mutalik* to act on his behalf as the *deshmukh* of Indapur pargana. Under the Maratha, *mutalik* is the deputy of any person holding a hereditary office. A royal decree of 18 December 1724 issued to the *deshpande* of Indapur mentions that the king had appointed Madhavrao Shankar as his *mutalik* in the vacancy caused by the death of Shankaraji Vedaji. As we do not have the genealogy of Shankaraji Vedaji as well as of Madhavrao Shankar, it is very difficult to establish any relationship between the two. It is very likely that

Madhavrao was the son of Shankaraji, and succeeded his father in 1724. If this is true, the office of *mutalik* also becomes a hereditary one. The royal decree which gives *mutalki* to Madhavrao also asks the *deshpande* to work in unison with the new incumbent, while transacting the business of his pargana. It further says that all privileges and perquisites due to the *deshmukh* should be transferred to the new *deshmukh*.[12]

The *deshmukh* of Indapur pargana was also holding the *patilki watan* of both Peth and Qasba. Moreover, the king had granted him the full revenues of two and a half villages in the pargana, which have been referred to as *isafat gava* to the *deshmukh*. Three documents from the Poona Jamav section dealing with the 'Accounts of the Deshmukh' of the years 1774–75, 1780–81 and 1791 have been consulted in the present paper.[13] However, as the document of the year 1795 is more exhaustive and complete, it has been fully used in this study. The account papers give a more accurate picture of the income of the *deshmukh* than the *sanads* or firmans conferring such rights and perquisites on him. The *sanads* or firmans give broad categories of the sources of income of the officers to whom the document was issued, and hence they are sometimes vague; the account papers, on the other hand, give the actual receipt of the person concerned, and are hence more realistic.

The document of 1791 shows three broad sources of the income of the *deshmukh*, namely, the revenue from two and a half *isafat gava*, the income from the *deshmukhi haks* (privileges and perquisites) from the pargana, and lastly the *patilki watan*. In 1791 the total income of the *deshmukh* from these sources amounted to Rs 7,379-8-0. This, in the final analysis, was a burden on the village communities. The total revenue collection of Indapur in the year 1791 was Rs. 1,09,114-1-0 and the income of the *deshmukh* amounted to its 6.7 per cent.

Let us consider the nature of these three sources of income of the *deshmukh* with the help of these account papers.

Isafat or *izafat* literally means more or additional, and an *isafat gava* is a village held permanently by a person, usually an *inamdar* or *wantandar*. As it is added to his original *watan*, it is called an additional grant. The *deshmukh* of Indapur was favoured with a grant of the revenues of two and a half villages (Nhavi, Bori and half Rui) from the pargana by the state. The payment he received from these villages called *tanakha* was an assignment on the revenues of the villages. Under the Maratha system, while assessing the revenue of a village, its maximum was fixed, and it was *kamal akar*. While fixing the *kamal akar* of a village, its entire arable land including fallow land was taken into consideration. *Kamal akar* thus shows the maximum revenue which the state expected from a particular village. The *kamal akar* of these two and a half villages was Rs. 5,640- 11-0, from which various deductions were made and the balance was paid as *tanakha* to the *deshmukh* as the holder of the *isafat gava*.

Mention of the sharers or *hakdars* of this *kamal akar* has been made in the document itself. The first and foremost *hakdar* was the *deshmukh* himself and his share has been estimated at Rs. 254-4-0. The second *hakdar* was the *mutalik*, who enjoyed a typical *hak* called *nadgaudi*. The *mutalik*, acquired this right from Shahu in 1744.[14] *Nadgauda* is a Kannada word and is equivalent to *deshmukh*. His share was Rs. 83-3-0. The clerical staff employed by the *deshmukh* such as the *mujumdar* (accountant) and the *phadnis* (clerk) together received Rs. 52-8-0 for their services. The state sometimes assigned a portion of its revenue to the *kamavisdar* for his services in revenue administration. Ganpatrav Jiwaji the *kamavisdar* of Indapur, was allowed to receive Rs. 914-8-0 from these villages. This amount has been shown under the title *baje patiya*, that is, other taxes. Thus the income of the sharers was:

Haks of *deshmukh*	Rs. 254-4-0
Mutalik	Rs. 83-3-0
Mujumdar and phadnis	Rs. 52-8-0
Kamavisdar Ganpatrav Jiwaji	Rs. 914-8-0
TOTAL	Rs. 1,304-7-0

The *kamavisdar* granted a remission in the revenue of these *isafat* villages in 1795, as that year proved to be one of drought. This remission amounted to Rs. 2,310-5-0. Thus after deducting the dues of the sharers and the remissions granted by the *kamavisdar*, the *tanakha* of the *deshmukh* from these villages was Rs. 2,025-15-0 only.

Kamal akar	Rs. 5,640-11-0
Hakdars	Rs. 1,304-7-0
Balance	Rs. 4,336-4-0
Remissions	Rs. 2,310-15-0
TOTAL	Rs. 2,025-15-0 *Tanakha* of the *deshmukh*

The *deshmukh*, as mentioned earlier, was entitled to get Rs.254-4-0 as the share from his villages. But due to famine conditions, he could not recover his entire share, and got only Rs. 224-8-0. The *deshmukh* had appointed a peon called *naikwadi* in this area to collect his dues. This *naikwadi* usually belonged to the Mahar or Ramoshi community. The villagers were made to pay for his services which has been referred to as *masala*. The income of the *deshmukh* from this source has been shown as *siwaye jama* or additional income. Thus the total income of the *deshmukh* from these *isafat gava* was as below:

Tanakha	Rs. 2,025-15-0
Deshmukhi	+Rs. 224-8-0
Siwaye jama	+Rs. 80-8-0
TOTAL	Rs. 2,330-7-0

The pargana of Indapur comprised eighty-five villages[15] and the *deshmukh* enjoyed privileges from all these villages as its *watandar*. His income during normal times from this pargana was Rs. 5,081-6-0, but due to famine in 1795 he could realize Rs. 3,678-12-0 only.

The privileges of the *deshmukh* from each village have been referred to as *gavagana hak* which included a variety of items collected both in cash and kind from the cultivators, artisans, shopkeepers, etc. He used to charge certain fees for some specific duties.

Besides this *gavagana hak*, the other sources of income of the *deshmukh* were *kabulat pati, bhet,* Dasara and Samkrant, *masala,* etc. The *kabulat pati* was a tax on agreement transacted by the residents of the pargana. It may be a sale-purchase deed, or any other type of agreement. The *deshmukh* was entitled to get a present *(bhet)* at the rate of one rupee per village from the eighty-five villages, except the village of Narsipur which was assigned to a deity. Dasara and Samkrant are the major Hindu festivals, in which the elders are respected. The *deshmukh* being the seniormost person by virtue of his position in the *pargana* was entitled to receive presents from all the villages during these two festivals. He was also entitled to *masala* charges, that is, fees which he had to pay to the *naikwadi* (peon), who collected his dues from the villages. From all these heads he was expecting an amount of Rs.5,081-0-6, but due to conditions of scarcity in 1795 the *kamavisdar* gave remissions to the ryots which amounted to Rs. 1,780-10-0. Thus in 1795 he got only Rs.3,300-12-0 by way of his *haks* from this pargana. This has been referred to as *ain jama* in this document The break-up of this *ain jama* is given below:

Hak	Rs. 3,233-14-0
Kabulat pati	Rs. 1,269-4-0
Bhet	Rs. 84-0-0
Miscellaneous	Rs. 494-4-0
Remissions	Rs. 5,081-6-0
	Rs. 1,780-10-0
Ain jama	Rs. 3,300-12-0

Siwaye jama, that is, extra or additional income of the *deshmukh,* included such items as *jakat,* that is, transit duties, a levy on petty shopkeepers, bazars and festivals, a levy for feeding the servants on the Dasara day, and certain indirect fees. In the year 1795 the transit duties amounted to Rs. 296. The *deshmukh* did not collect all these dues for himself, but had sold the right of collection to a third person who paid him a fixed amount. This is called *makla.* Some fifty-two families of petty shopkeepers called *vani* had pitched their tents in the open space of *qasba* Indapur, and the *deshmukh* charged four annas per family, collecting Rs. 13 from them. The *deshmukh* had a right to share the charitable contributions made by the devotees to a temple. In one of the villages

in the pargana, Nirgava (a fair) was annually held in the month of Caitra, and
the villagers generally offered small coins in the box placed in the temple. The
deshmukh was entitled to get a handful of coins from this box, but had sold this
right, perhaps to a local man, for eight annas only. He used to get betel-nuts
and vegetables from the *vanis* who gathered at the weekly bazars of some
villages of the *pargana*. This right was also sold for Rs. 3-4-0 only. The messages
of *deshmukh* were carried to the villages by some peons employed by him. These
peons severally received one goat per village for the *deshmukh*. But instead of
receiving this payment in kind, the *deshmukh* preferred cash, and got Rs. 29
from all the villages under his charge. The villagers refered some of the local
disputes to him for decision as he was the chief of the pargana. He settled such
disputes, but claimed certain fees for his services. For instance, in a dispute over
the partition of the property of a *patil*, the *deshmukh* received Rs. 23 from the
parties concerned as his fees, which has been referred to in the document as
shela pagote. In the settlement of a dispute of a Kunbi (cultivator), he got Rs.
12. The wife of a Dhangar committed suicide for which her husband was held
responsible and fined. This fine was known *asgunhegari*. The *deshmukh* got Rs.
12 as his share out of the fine inflicted on the Dhangar. The wife of a washerman
was divorced, for which the *deshmukh* received Rs. 1-8-0 as his fees. All these
extra collections of the *deshmukh* have been shown under the head *siwaye
jama*.

The *deshmukh* collected Rs. 604 as *potagi* or maintenance allowance from
all tne villages of the pargana. His total income from various sources, therefore,
could be summarized as below:

Deshmukhi hak gavagana (including *kabulat pati*, *bhet* and other charges)	Rs. 3,300-12-0
Siwaye jama (including *jakat*, levy on shopkeepers, fairs, bazars, *masala*, judicial fees, etc.)	Rs. 378-0-0
Potagi (maintenance allowance)	Rs. 604-0-0
TOTAL	Rs. 4,282-12-0

The *deshmukh* of Indapur pargana was also the *patil* of Indapur *qasba* and
Peth in which he held one-fifth *bigha* as *bagait* (garden) land and four *bighas* as
jirayet. The *patilki* of Indapur, which was assigned to Tarabai in 1704, seems to
have been resumed by the king after her death in 1761. These holdings were
leased out to the tenants for Rs. 397-8-0. As *patil* of the village, he enjoyed a
peculiar privilege called *ghugari*, a grain share from each holding in the village.
This levy was usually collected in kind, but in this particular case he preferred
cash to kind. The rate was two maunds by measure per *chavar*,[16] which brought
him Rs. 248-2-0 both from the *bagait* and *jirayet* lands. It was customary not
to collect *ghugari* from the lands of other *watandars* of the village like *deshpande*,
kulkarni, *caugula*, a few cultivators who had brought waste land under cultivation

and religious endowments. The document under scrutiny mentions a convention that *patils* and *kulkarnis* should not collect *ghugari* from each other.

The *deshmukh* as *patil* collected Rs. 120-11-0 from a number of other sources, an enumeration of which would give an idea of the various sources tapped by these *watandars*:

1.	Weavers (This right was called *pasodi*, that is, one garment from each weaver. He got twelve garments, the value of which seems to have been Rs. 1-4-0 per piece.)	Rs. 15-0-0
2.	Oil-presser (*teli*)	Rs. 6-8-0
3.	*Vanis* or petty shopkeepers (There were twenty-three *vanis* at these two places, who supplied betelnuts to the *deshmukh* on weekly bazars and jaggery on two festivals, Nagapanchami and Holi.)	Rs. 1-13-0
4.	Dhangars (blanket weavers) (He received eight blankets at the rate of eight annas per piece.)	Rs. 4-0-0
5.	*Lohkar* or salt-merchant	Rs. 1-8-0
6.	Kernel of coconuts from the lower castes collected at the time of marriage	Rs. 0-6-0
7.	Discount on exchange of copper coins	Rs. 3-8-0
8.	Divorce fee	Rs. 3-0-0
9.	*Patilki haks*	Rs. 35-0-0
10.	Fodder	Rs. 50-0-0
	TOTAL	Rs. 120-11-0

This statement is also useful for knowing the prices of certain articles that were current in the market. The income of the *deshmukh* as *patil* of two places was as below:

1.	*Patilki watan* lands (rent)	Rs. 397-8-0
2.	Ghugari	Rs. 248-2-0
3.	Miscellaneous	Rs. 120-11-0
	TOTAL	Rs. 766-5-0

Thus, when we add up all these three different sources of income of the *deshmukh* of Indapur, we get the following figures:

1.	Isafat gava (Nhavi, Bori and half Rui)	Rs. 2,330-7-0
2.	*Deshmukhi haks* (from the pargana)	Rs. 4,282-12-0
3.	Patilki haks (from Indapur and Peth)	Rs. 766-5-0
	TOTAL	Rs. 7,379-8-0

A question may be asked here: how much income of the *deshmukh* was ploughed back in the pargana in either agriculture or manufacture? The ratio of his income going back to the villages under his charge cannot be proved statistically, but one can argue that he must be spending a part of his income on administration, and for the maintenance of peace and order in his pargana. He was expected to try to protect the ryot during the period of inroads of armies, and he must have incurred some expenditure on this account. As the *deshmukh* held some land in his name in the pargana, he may be using a part of his income from the sources mentioned above for its improvement. However, we do not come across any *deshmukh* engaged in either manufacture or moneylending business.

The analysis of the *deshmukhi watan* of Indapur clearly indicates the feudal basis of the Maratha society in the eighteenth century. The change in the government had little influence on the social structure of the village. The *watandars* were the real leaders, both socially and politically, of the Maratha country in the seventeenth and eighteenth centuries. The government had to solicit their support for its civil and military functions. The institutional set-up of the social organization, therefore, remained unchanged and the *watandars* exploited the situation to their advantage and continued to enjoy their privileges uninterrupted for a pretty long time.

Notes

1. S.N. Joshi and G.H. Khare, ed., *Shiva Charitra Sahilya*, III (Poona), 1930, Letter no. 611.
2. S.N. Banhalti, *ta.*, *Ajnapatra*, p. 92.
3. *Aitihasika Samkirna Nibandha (Quarterly)*, (Bharat Itihas Samshodhak Mandal, Poona, 1943), 1, 62.
4. MSS, EUR B 109, Grant to Briggs, dt. 15 August 1820, India Office Library, London.
5. Ibid.
6. MSS, EUR B 109, Briggs to Grant, dt. 24 August 1820.
7. Ibid.
8. Grant Duff, *History of the Marathas*, I, pp. 35, 38.
9. A.S. Altekar, *The Rashtrakulas and Their Times*, pp.178, 180; cf., M.G. Panse, *Yaavakalin Maharashtra*, pp. 50, 52–3.
10. For a detailed discussion of this topic, see my article on 'The Origin of *Deshmukh* and *Deshpande*' in the *Proceedings of the Indian History Congress*, Varanasi session, 1970.
11. Poona Jamav Section (unpublished), Rumal no.1784, Alienation Office, Poona.
12. *Shiva Charitra Sahitya*, III, Letter no. 615, 616.
13. Poona Jamav Section (unpublished), Rumal no.64, Alienation Offce, Poona. There are a number of similar documents of other years as well, but the nature of all these documents is almost the same. These documents are useful for micro-analysis. For a macro-approach to the subjects, refer to the author's *Maharashtra in the Age of Shivaji*, pp. 39–43.

14. Poona Jamav Section (unpublished), Rumal no.710, Alienation Office, Poona.
15. Surprisingly the present taluka of Indapur also comprises eighty-five villages.
16. A *chavar is* 120 *bighas,* and a *bigha* is approximately half an acre.

12

Taxation and Hindu Temples in the Telugu Districts Under the Vijayanagara Empire

R. Soma Reddy

THE FAMOUS empire of Vijayanagara is acclaimed in history as the custodian of Hindu religion and culture in South India for nearly three centuries. During this period, the development of Hindu temples in South India and especially in Andhra Desa, received an impetus, unknown either to the preceding or the succeeding period. The Hindu State of Vijayanagara was the main prop of the Hindu temples and the State patronage was the mainstay of their finances. Of course State activity with regard to the temples was not confined to mere patronage, but touched many other aspects of temple life.

This paper is an attempt to probe the nature of certain taxes collected by the government from the Hindu temples in the Telugu districts of the Vijayanagara empire. It takes into account some of the major and minor temples, belonging to both the Saiva and Vaisnava persuasion and their sub-sects, and is based mainly on inscriptions and local records.

At the outset, it is to be noted that all the districts of modern Andhra Pradesh were not under the political sway of the Vijayanagara empire throughout its period. While the ceded districts were more or less constantly under Vijayanagara rule, almost from the beginning to the end, the other two regions of Andhra Pradesh formed a part of the empire only in its palmy days.

While the kings and their feudatories granted lands, proceeds of revenue, cash etc., to the temples, they did not exempt these institutions from the financial regulations of the State. It is known from temple epigraphs and local records that the properties of the temples and temple functionaries, though recognized in principle as *Sarvamanya* or tax-free endowment, were liable to pay various taxes and contributed considerably to the State exchequer. And

*39th Session at Hyderabad, 1978.

even the devotees, visiting these shrines, had to pay certain taxes. Epigraphic evidence[1] relating to the conversion of temple endowments, granted to them in the previous period, into *Sarvamanya* by the rulers, also makes it clear that they did not always necessarily enjoy tax exemption.

Land revenue, being one of the basic sources of income to the government, was collected from all cultivable land whether owned by private individuals or institutions. Of course, the lands in Devagramas and Agraharas, i.e., lands owned by religious establishments, got a preferential treatment in this regard compared to the lands owned by the peasants in *Bandaravada* villages, i.e. villages owned by the government. It is difficult to give the exact rates of taxation in these two cases; yet it can be stated that religious establishments paid land tax at a lower rate than the ordinary peasant. During the Vijayanagara period, the government collected the land tax, known as 'Srotriyas' or a low quit-rent, on all the cultivable lands owned by the Hindu temples in the Telugu districts. An inscription of AD 1563 from Siruvalla village[2] says that these Srotriyas were collected by the government of Sadasivaraya from the *manya* villages belonging to gods and brahmins and the service inams. The tax paid by temples in the Tamil districts of the Vijayanagara empire is known as 'Jodi'.[3]

An important tax paid by temples is 'Durgavartana' or 'Durgadannayivartana', a tax paid to the commandant of the neighbouring fort in return for the protection offered by him to the temple villages. For example, there is a reference to sixty *varahas* being fixed, in AD 1541 as the annual 'Durgavartana' to be paid by some eight villages belonging to the temples of Puspagiri to the Gandikota fort.[4] An inscription of AD 1530 from Mopuru[5] (Cuddapah district) refers to Durgadannayivartana amounting to 235 *varahas* per annum, payable from villages belonging to the temple of Bairesvara of Mompuru to the same fort. But a record of AD 1545, again from Mopuru,[6] refers to 'Durgavartana' and 'Dannayivartana' as two different taxes, payable to the fort by the Devata gramas (temple villages) and Agraharas in the Gandikota sima. The difference between these is not known. In any case, the collection of this military cess from the temples, implies the responsibility the government of the day felt for the protection of the immense wealth of the Hindu temples, both movable and immovable, from thieves, robbers and even foreign invaders.

The government collected a tax known as 'Kavali kanike' on the inam lands held by various functionaries of the temples. As its name indicates, this tax was probably paid to the State for performing police functions; that is, for the protection provided to the service lands of the temple servants. A damaged inscription[7] from Palugurallapalli village (Cuddapah district) refers to this tax on the lands granted to the donees for rendering musical services to the temples of Somesvara and Chennakesvara, and its remission for the temple services. The difference between 'Kavali kanike' paid by the temple servants on these inam lands and 'Durgavartane' paid by the temples on their villages to the government is shown by a simultaneous reference to both of them in an inscription of AD 1545 from Mopuru.[8]

Even the *Jeevadhanam,* or property in livestock, of the temples was not exempted from government taxation. The Hindu temple maintained a large number of cattle which included cows, bullocks, buffaloes, sheep, etc., for their use. And, they had to pay a tax called 'Pullari' or 'Sulavari' to the government for grazing their cattle on government lands. There is a reference to 'Sulavari' in an epigraph of AD 1427 from Tiruttani village (Chittoor district),[9] levied by the Vijayanagara government from the temples of that place. An inscription of AD 1336[10] from Tangeda (Guntur district), forming a part of the Reddi kingdom of Kondavidu, also records the remission of 'Pullari', for the sheep, due from the herdsmen of the temple of Ghantala Ramanathadeva.

The government collected 'Perayam' of 'Kanike' from the devotees who came, in thousands, to the Hindu shrines on festival days. At Tirupati, Perayam was levied during the days of 'Puruttasi-Tirumal' or Brahmotsavam. The proceeds of this tax are said to have been granted for the services of Venkateswara temple of the same place by Krishnadevaraya.[11] An epigraph of AD 1405 from the village of Tamballapalli (Chittoor district)[12] refers to 'Kanike' (of 25 honnu) being charged from the devotees during the Sivaratri festival and to the grant of these proceeds for temple services. An inscription of AD 1553[13] also refers to this tax on the pilgrims of eighteen castes visiting Tirupati and Srisailam; the collection being made at the fort of Ketavaram on the river Krishna.

It is not clear whether this tax amounted to the 'Pilgrim tax' collected during the Mohammedan period. It is known that in the 12th century AD pilgrim tax was collected at Bahuloda (Gujarat) by the municipality on behalf of the Hindu government.[14]

There are references, in some of the inscriptions of the period of Devaraya II, to a tax called 'Vibhuti-kanike' as a royal due from the devotees visiting the Hindu temples. This tax appears to be a voluntary fee paid by the devotees while receiving the sacred ashes and collected by the temples on behalf of the government. These inscriptions, coming from both Telugu and Tamil districts,[15] give us to understand that this fee, collected from all the Saiva and Vaisnava temples of Chandragiri rajya till AD 1427, was remitted by the royal order in that year.

The government derived some income from prostitutes during temple festivals. There is a reference to 'lanja sunkam', i.e., a levy on prostitutes, collected by the government during the temple festivals at Markapuram (Kurnool district), in an inscription of AD 1555 from the same place.[16] It records the grant of the proceeds of that tax for temple services by Maharaja Narapadeva, a Vijayanagara official. This would show that prostitution was under government regulation and, like any other professions in the empire, it, too, was taxed.

The government also collected various professional and other taxes from the Devadana villages as from ordinary villages. An inscription of AD 1555 from Markapuram village (Kurnool district)[17] refers to taxes like Illari (House-tax), Pullari (Grazing-tax), Ganugari (Tax on oil mills). Maggari (Tax on looms), Mudrayam (A duty levied to stamp the heaps of grain brought for sale in the market), and Andi Santi sunkam (meaning not known), paid by 18 villages belonging to the temple of Chennakesava of Markapuram. There is also a reference to Mangala-pannu (Tax on barbers) and Dommara pannu (A tax on acrobats), collected by the government from the villages of Tiruvengalanatha temple of Mutukuru (Cuddapah district) in an epigraph of AD 1546[18] from the same village. And a few more taxes like Nagari birada, Asavachehalu and Birudulu, payable to government from the lands owned by the temple of Chaudesvari of Krotta cheruvu, are referred to in an inscription of AD 1581–82 from Anantapur.[19] Their nature is not known.

Besides the income derived from the taxes on temple properties, pilgrims etc., the government got considerable income from temples indirectly. It used to levy tolls on various articles of merchandise sold at the temples on normal days as well as on festival days and even on the roads leading to these shrines. An inscription of AD 1443 from Singarikonda[20] (Prakasam district) refers to the tolls levied by the government, on various articles of merchandise, including livestock like slaves, horses, bullocks, cows, buffaloes, etc., carried for sale on the road leading to the temple of Narasimha of the same village, and their remission by an official of Devaraya II during the 7 days of the festival of the God. Another epigraph of AD 1515 from Srisailam[21] also refers to the tolls levied on the loads of pack-horses, bullocks, asses and head-loads, collected from the merchants coming to Srisailam jatra, and their remission by Krishnadevaraya when he visited that place along with his queens.

Sometimes even the merchandise meant for temple services and even when carried by the temples' own transport system (bulls), was not exempted from government tolls. An epigraph of AD 1547 from Porumamella[22] (Cuddapah district) refers to the tolls collected by government on articles of merchandise, meant for the services of God Ahobaleswara of the same place.

It is to be remembered that the government sometimes granted, exemptions and remissions of these taxes and tolls, especially during festival. Almost all the epigraphs mentioning these taxes also refer to their remission either by the rulers or their representatives on various occasions and for various reasons. These exemptions and remissions were made at times on a large scale, affecting a number of temples, and sometimes they benefited one or two individual temples only.

Though the amounts of some of these taxes are mentioned in inscriptions, it is very difficult to give the rates at which they were levied. Nor is it possible to know the exact nature of their collection. We know from inscriptions that, sometimes, the tax-gatherers became oppressive and exacted, without the knowledge of the government, certain taxes that had been exempted in temple villages. Such oppressiveness resulted sometimes in desertion of people from the temple villages. This adversely affected worship in the temples and necessitated government intervention. An inscription of AD 1547 from Kommuru[23] (Guntur district) records such intervention and remission of certain taxes from the villages of the Agastesvara temple which had been deserted due to unjust collections.

Notes

1. An inscription from Chejarla (Guntur district) records the remission of taxes, by Krishnadevaraya, on the properties of temples and Brahmins who did service in them—no. AR 335/1915.
2. Mackenzie, MSS. 260, pp. 64–65.
3. The Punjai Inscription of Krishnadevaraya of AD1517–*EI*, XXV, p.297.
4. Mack, MSS. 140, p. l01.
5. *SII*, XVI, no. 91.
6. *SII*, XVI, no. 139.
7. *BAR*, 1942, no. 46.
8. *SII*, XVI, no. 139.
9. *BAR*, 1943, no. 131.
10. *BAR*, 1926, no. 388.
11. Tirumala Tirupati Devastanam Epigraphical Series, no. 46.
12. *SII*, XVI, no. 17.
13. *Further Sources of Vijayanagara History*, III, p. 253.
14. Altekar, *State and Government in Ancient India*, p. 223.
15. (a) A record from Sattravada (Puttur tq.) Chittoor dt., *AR 1912*, p. 78.
    (b) A record from Jambukesvaram (Tiruchinapalli), *AR 1937–56*, p. 82
16. *SII*, XVI, no. 201.
17. Ibid.
18. *SII*, XVI, no. 149.
19. V. Rangacharya, I, Anantapur no.143, p. 23 (Inscription of Madras Presidency).
20. Butterworth and Setti, inscription of Nellore district vol. III, p. 112.
21. *SII*, XVI, no. 52.
22. *BAR*, 1942, no. 34.
23. *SII*, XVI, no. 160.

13

The Jagirdari System of Maharaja Ranjit Singh in the Light of His Orders

Indu Banga

THIS PAPER is based on Persian documents belonging to what may be aptly called the Sita Ram Kohli Collection.[1] This Collection consists of 462 office copies of royal orders issued by Maharaja Ranjit Singh and some other documents. Over 400 of these are addressed to Sardar Tej Singh as the officer commanding the *campu-i-mu alla*,[2] and cover a period of thirteen months and six days, from November 14, 1833 to December 18, 1834. All of them bear the date and place of issue.[3]

We know from contemporary evidence that most of these orders were issued when Ranjit Singh was anticipating an attack on Peshawar from Dost Muhammad Khan of Kabul.

As it may be expected a *priori* these orders contain fascinating information on the way Ranjit Singh organised his campaigns.[4] Furthermore this information gives a clear idea of the organization of his army: recruitment and promotion, distribution of pay, leave rules, drill and military manoeuvres, maintenance of the army horses, bullocks and camels, their feed and its procurement and prices, the purchase and manufacture of military stores, uniform of the ranks and the officers, discipline in the army, for instance. There is information also on the royal workshops, procurement of raw materials, wages of skilled workers, prices of various articles, cost of cartage and the like. These documents afford a glimpse into the complicated system of credit and debit, and the adjustment of accounts, controlled and coordinated by the central *diwan*.

For the present, we propose to analyse about a hundred of these royal orders with a bearing on the *jagirdari* system: the types of assignees, nature of the services of *jagirs,* their transfer and their resumption. They provide some insight also into the *dharmarth* or charitable grants and land revenue administration.[5]

*40th Session at Waltair, 1979.

Among the assignees we find the military *jagirdars* like Sardar Jai Singh Atariwala and Chatar Singh Kalianwala maintaining horsemen (*idar-naukari-i-sawaran*),[6] and the civil functionaries like Misar Beli Ram, the *toshakhania*.[7] Some persons were in receipt of lands for the maintenance of mares (in all probability as a stud farm)[8], or for supplying gram for the horses and bullocks of the artillery.[9] There are references to some other categories of assignees also: the irregular horsemen known as the *ghurcharas*,[10] ordinary troopers,[11] time-keepers (*gharyalis*), elephant-drivers (*filvans*), and persons in-charge of the tents and floorings (*shamianawala* or *farrash*).[12] The personal servants of the Maharaja, like the ewer-bearer or the gadwai,[13] and the wine-sellers (*bada-farosh*) attached to the army also got paid in *jagir*.[14]

In certain situations, assignments were allowed to continue after the recipients ceased to perform formal service, primarily to provide the means of subsistence.[15] There are instances of *jagirs* given almost as *in'am* or pension.[16] An interesting case is that of a *jagir* given for taking the Sikh baptism of the sword (*pahul*).[17] On the whole, we find three categories of *jagirs* in these documents: service, subsistence and *in'am*.

The units of assignments ranged from an entire *ta'alluqa* to a single-wheel well (*cha-i-yak-rehta*). There are references to grants of one, two or three irrigation wells to individual troopers, lancers or cavalrymen or to the personal attendants of the Maharaja.[18] In one case, a whole village is given to two troopers who happen to be the father and son.[19] The *khidmatgars* and *gadwais* too are mentioned occasionally among the recipients of entire villages.[20] Many a *jigir* consists of more than one village.[21] The important *sardars* like the Sandhanwalias or the Atariwalas, and Prince Sher Singh held *ta' alluqas* in *jagir*.[22] Sometimes the *jagir* included income from other sources like justice.[23]

The *jagirdar* had generally to pay *nazrana* to the Maharaja before he was allowed to take over the *jagir*.[24] The state functionaries are ordered in some cases to first realise the *nazrana*. The amount depended probably on the value of the *jagir*.[25] It was not always easy for the assignee to get hold of the land granted and the Maharaja had to instruct his officials to establish the assignee's possession over the *jagir*.[26]

The documents frequently refer to the transfer of *jagirs*. The *jagirs* of princes also were not exempt from this practice.[27] The *jagirs* were usually transferred with effect from the *rabi* or the *kharif* harvests.[28] Occasionally, the *jagir* was transferred or resumed in the middle of the collection for a harvest. Then only the balance of the revenues due from the cultivators was realised by the new *jagirdar* or the state.[29] Sometimes the resumed lands were held by the state to ascertain their income all afresh.[30] The distinction between the *jagir* and *khalisa* lands was clearly maintained.[31]

The transfer or resumption of *jagirs* was not always peacefully effeted. To oblige the *jagirdar* to relinquish control, wells sometimes were not allowed to work.[32] Wherever armed resistance by the *jagirdars* was expected the officials concerned were ordered to go prepared at the head of adequate number of soldiers.[33] A *ta'alluqa* held by seven *jagirdars* in one case was to be recovered with the help of a battalion of infantry consisting of eight companies.[34] For resuming the *jagirs* of Prince Sher Singh, the Maharaja's orders were to take two cavalry regiments and some pieces of artillery, besides an infantry battalion.[35] However, in all such cases the officials are advised to handle the situation tactfully and to avoid the use of force.[36] The collectors of the *jagirdar* were to be allowed to leave honourably.[37] If the *jagir* had been held by a family for a long time, it was sometimes considered expedient to allow the garrison of the *jagirdar* to continue, while the officials deputed by the state took over the revenue administration.[38] Occasionally, the *jagir* of the deceased *jagirdar* was allowed to continue for sometime with his widow or mother, apparently as a subsistence *jagir*, before it was partly or wholly resumed.[39]

The royal orders also refer to the case of resumption of *jagirs* without the express orders of the Maharaja. In fact, Sardar Tej Singh was reprimanded several times by the Maharaja for taking over the lands held in *jagir* without his permission,[40] or for stationing his men in the villages of another *jagirdar*.[41] Cash or kind unduly collected in such cases had to be returned to the *jagirdar* concerned and a receipt had to be taken from him to be sent to the central office.[42]

Disputes between the *jagirdars* about appropriation of revenues or wells also figure in these documents.[43] The officials were expected to take cognizance of disputes and obviate them.[44] After due investigation, the *jagir* was to be restored to its authorised holder.[45] Even in cases where the matter had been settled through mediation, the Maharaja ordered further investigation to identify the 'aggressor'.[46]

Once in possession, the *jagirdars* appear to have managed their lands, either personally or through their agents.[47] The big *jagirdars*, including the princes had their own garrisons (*thanas*) and civil functionaries or *kardars*.[48] However, they do not appear to have enjoyed altogether a free hand in the administration of their *jagirs*. An eye was kept even on the influential *sardars* like the Sandhanwalias who happened to be the Maharaja's collaterals.[49] In case or any mismanagement, action was taken against their *kardas*.[50] Presumably during Prince Sher Singh's absence from his *jagirs*, Sardar Tej Singh was specially ordered to ensure that the prince's *jagirs* were 'really well-managed and looked after'.[51]

The *jagirdars* were expected to make good the demand-order (*tankhwah*) for cash frequently made on them, to take receipts and to get the accounts adjusted afterwards. They were expected similarly to provide fodder and grain for the animals of the army,[52] They were not expected to interfere with the cattle preserves (*rakh*) or the ancestral property of another *jagirdar* or the *dharmarth* grants located in their *jagirs* [53]

With reference to *dharmarth* grants (*waguzar* or *kharij az jama'*) in particular, 'all revenue officers' are ordered that 'they must not interfere with this class of grantees as they are worthy of respect and reverence.'[54] The grantees were expected to 'offer prayers for the health and prosperity of the *hazur-i-wala*.[55] The officials were ordered to restore lands wrongly resumed and the revenues unduly collected in cash or kind and to send receipts from the grantees to prove that their share had been returned to them.[56] There are references also to the harassment of the grantees by the local *chaudhari* or the *jagirdar*.[57] Among the various categories of grantees figuring in these orders are the *grant his*, the *bhais*, the *udasis*, some *Sodhi* and *Bhalla* descendants of the Sikh Gurus, Brahmans, *faqirs* and *dhadhis*.[58]

These royal orders do not contain much direct information on the assessment and collection of land revenue. There are references to *kankut* and *batai* and to the collection of land revenue in both cash and kind.[59] There are references also to the restraints imposed by the Maharaja over the *kardars* at the *ta'alluqa* level.[60] The officials were sometimes asked to submit a report on the conduct of a *kardar*, or to take him into custody or to send him to the Maharaja.[61] The Maharaja was very strict about the realization of arrears of revenue due from the *kardars*.[62] However, the *zamindars* undertaking to pay the revenues directly appear to have been given much greater latitude in the clearance of the arrears which, as the records maintained at the *daftar-i-mu'alia* showed,[63] were allowed to accumulate various kinds of cesses (rasum) were also levied in addition to the land revenue: *moharana, zabitana, abkari, adalatana* for instance.[64] one document there is a reference to *sa'irat*, as distinct from both grain and revenue in cash but the exact nature of the *sa'irat* is not clear.[65]

On the administration of *ijara*, however, the documents throw an interesting light. The *ijaradar* undertook to pay a certain stipulated sum before he was authorised to collect revenues due to the government from a given source of income like *abkar*,[66] or a given area.[67] His charge generally commenced from the *rabi* or *kharif* harvest, and the amount stipulated was generally less for the first harvest and reached the normal expected figure in the subsequent ones.[68] The amount of *ijara* was fixed after verifying the estimated income of the given area and was thus close to the revenues due to the government.[69] The *ijaradar* was not allowed to interfere with the *dharmarth* grantees or any other concessions given by the government.[70] The *ijaradars* who find mention in these documents, including Sardar Tej Singh himself, appear to be connected with government and administration,[71] although the practice of giving *ijara* to the *zamindars* too appears to have been prevalent.[72]

Finally, the administration of *jagirs, dharmarth* and *ijara* understandably could not be carried out without the existence of detailed records at the local level as well as the centre. These royal orders assume that the returns of the revenues of almost every village in the kingdom were available in the *daftar-i-mu alia* at Lahore.

Notes

1. Just a few weeks before his death Sita Ram Kohli had passed this Collection on his former student, Dr. S.N. Rao. The editor is grateful to Dr. Rao for making this valuable Collection available to her.

2. Of the remaining documents, five are addressed to some other functionaries, with copies sent to Sardar Tej Singh for information; thirteen documents are copies of office memoranda, and the rest are addressed jointly to more than one functionary.

3. Although in Persian these documents contain many Punjabi words and expressions, some English and French words too have found their way into the vocabulary.

4. This, in fact, is the only information of its kind available so far. The Maharaja kept almost an hourly tag of the movements of his men and officers all along the long line of communications between Lahore and Peshawar. His instructions cover even the selection of sites for encampment; the order to be observed by the troops while crossing over a ferry; the time for calling halt or resuming march, or the length or marches. All movement orders told the officers concerned in very clear terms that it was their personal responsibility to ensure that crops and wooden frames of wells were not damaged, and stragglers were not left behind to harass the people.

5. The following references to the documents are illustrative and not exhaustive. The royal orders are dated in the Bikrami Sammat.

6. Document 271, dated 30 Har 1891; Document 182, dated 20 Baisakh 1891.

7. Document 187, dated 24 Baisakh 1891; Document 193, dated 28 Baisakh 1891.

8. Document 190, dated 27 Baisakh 1891.

9. Document 9, dated 1 Maghar 1890; Document 192, dated 28 Baisakh 1891.

10. Document 218, dated 20 Baisakh 1891.

11. Document 90, dated 27 Phagun 1890.

12. Document 135, dated 28 Chet 1891; Document 205, dated 31 Baisakh 1891; Document 324, dated 19 Bhadon 1891.

13. Document 164, dated 12 Baisakh 1891.

14. Document 218, deted 20 Baiskh 1891.

15. Document 227; dated 11 Jeth 1891. The lands given to Gul Begam may also be termed as a subsistence jagir: Document 102, dated 6 Chet 1891.

16. The revenue-free grant of Chanda the hajjam, the attendant on Jugni the dancing girl (kanchani), may perhaps be considered as an instance of an in'am jagir: Document 287, dated 15 Sawan 1891.

17. Document 157, dated 9 Baisakh 1891.

18. Document 122, dated 20 Chet, 1891; Document 330, dated 27 Bhadon 1891.

19. Document 219, dated 28 Baisakh 1834.

20. Document 197, dated 30 Baisakh 1891.

21. Document 107, dated 9 Chet 1891.

22. Document 132, dated 14 Jeth 1891; Document 144, dated 6 Baisakh 1891. It appears that the princes' jagirs were generally larger than those of the other sardars: Document 132, dated 14 Jeth 1891; Document 138, dated 2 Baisakh 1891.

23. Document 168, dated 13 Baisakh 1891; Document 197, dated 30 Baisakh 1891.

24. Document 131, dated 26 Chet 1891; Document 189, dated 26 Baisakh 1891.

25. Document 186, dated 23 Baisakh 1891; Document 206, dated 2 Jeth 1891.
26. Document 107, dated 9 Chet 1891; Document 134, dated 27 Chet 1891.
27. Document 107, dated 9 Chet 1891.
28. Document 186, dated 23 Baisakh 1891; Document 205, dated 31 Baisakh 1891.
29. Document 182, dated 20 Baisakh 1891.
30. Document 113, dated Chet 1891; Document 141, dated 3 Baisakh 1891.
31. Document 164, 12 Baisakh 189; Document 169, dated 14 Baisakh 1891.
32. When resistance was reported from the agents of Gul Begam the Maharaja had to order that the wells of their jagir shall not be worked till further orders; Document 105, dated 8 Chet 1891.
33. For example, for taking over the jagir of Chaman Singh, one company of infantry were despatched, and for that of Diwan Kirpa Ram, the Maharaja's express orders were to take four companies: Document 127, dated 23 Chet 1891; Document 141, dated 3 Baisakh 1891, respectively.
34. Document 135, dated 28 Chet 1891.
35. Document 132, dated 26 Chet 1891.
36. Document 135, dated 28 Chet 1891.
37. Document 138, dated 2 Baisakh 1891.
38. Document 182, dated 2 Baisakh 1891.
39. Document 227, dated 11 Jeth 1891; Document 299, dated 23 Sawan 1891.
40. Document 192, dated 28 Baisakh 1891; Document 205, dated 31 Baisakh 1891.
41. Document 16, dated 12 Maghar 1890.
42. Document 219, dated 28 Baisakh 1891; Document 231, dated 1 Jeth 1891.
43. Document 136, dated 29 Chet 1891; Document 187, dated 23 Baisakh 1891.
44. Document 144, dated 6 Baisakh 1891; Document 58, dated 11 Magh 1890.
45. Document 163, dated 13 Baisakh 1891.
46. Document 255, dated 21 Har 1891. In fact, the suggestion is that such disputes were often settled by the disputants without reference to the Maharaja, and that the wanted to curb this tendency.
47. Document 16, dated 12 Maghar 1890; Document 145, dated 6 Baisakh 1891.
48. Document 138, dated 2 Baisakh 1891; Document 182, dated 20 Baisakh 1891.
49. Document 363, dated 17 Asuj 1891.
50. Document 146, date 5 Baisakh 1891; Document 148, dated 7 Baisakh 1891.
51. Document 165, dated 13 Baisakh 1891.
52. Document 253, dated 4 Jeth 1891.
53. Document 155, dated 9 Baisakh 1891; Document 273, dated 2 Sawan 1891; Document 141, dated 3 Baisakh 1891, respectively.
54. Document 262, dated 1 Har 1891; Document 14, dated 3 Baisakh 1891; Document 168, dated 13 Baisakh 1891.
55. Document 323, dated 11 Bdhadon 1891.
56. Document 123, dated 20 Chet 1891; Document 21 Chet 1891; Document 162, dated 12 Baisakh 1891; Document 199, dated 30 Baisakh 1891.
57. Document 327, dated 21 Bhadon 1891. Document 162; dated 12 Baisakh 1891, respectively.
58. Document 123, dated 20 Chet 1891; Document 186, dated 23 Baisakh 1891; Document 199, dated 30 Baisakh 19; Document 202, dated 31 Baisakh 1891;

Document 238, dated 11 Phagun 3891; Document 244,dated 4 Jeth 1891; Document 299, dated 4 Jeth 1891; Document 262, dated 11 Har 1891; Document 299 dated 23 Swan 1891; Document 323, dated 11 Bhadon 1891; Document 327, dated 21 Bhadon 1891; Document 372, dated 21 Asuj, 1891.

59. Document 164, dated 12 Baisakh 1891; Document 234, dated 15 Jeth 1891.

60. Document 442, dated 18 Maghar 1891.

61. Document 146, dated 5 Baisakh 1891; Document 148, dated 7 Baisakh 1891; Document 363, dated 17 Asuj 1892.

62. Document 171, dated 15 Baisakh 1871.

63. Document 311, dated 1 Bhadon 1891.

64. Document 168, dated 13 Baisakh 1891; Document 197, dated 30 Baisakh 1891; Document 201, dated 29 Baisakh 1891; Document 295, dated 21 Sawan 1891; Document 448, dated 23 Maghar 1891.

65. Document 155, dated 9 Baisakh 1891.

66. Document 447, dated 23 , Maghar 1891.

67. Document 206, dated 13 Baisakh 1891; Document 211, dated 20 Baisakh 1891.

68. Document 322, dated 5 Bhadon 1891.

69. Document 234, dated 13 Jeth 1891.

70. Document 168, dated Baisakh 1891; Document 186, dated 23 Baisakh 186, 1891.

71. Document 211, dated 20 Baisakh, 1891; Document 234, dated 15 Jeth 1891; Document 322, dated 5 Bhadon 1891.

72. Document 234, dated 15 Jeth 1891.

14

The Economy of Gujarat, c.1600:
The *Ain's* Statistics

Shireen Moosvi

THE ECONOMY of Gujarat, owing to its prominent position in India's overseas trade, deserves special attention. The extension of Mughal rule, in 1572, into Gujarat made it a part of the larger Mughal economic system; Gujarat received Mughal coinage and perhaps many elements of the Mughal revenue system. As for other province of the Mughal empire, a large amount of statistical material is provided also for Gujarat by the *A'in-i Akbari* in its section entitled 'Account of the Twelve *Subas*.'[1] The information here furnished by Abu'l Fazl has not so far been interpreted to assess the 'status' of the economy of Gujarat,[2] though it is so common to hear generalizations made about it.

It would be logical to begin with the agrarian sector, for which the *A'in* offers us detailed statistics of measured land and estimated revenue. The *Zabt* system of revenue assessment which implies measurement[3] was not extended to Gujarat; as Abu'l Fazl tells us.[4] Yet the entire Suba barring the *Sarkar* of Saurath is assigned area (*arazi*) figures in the *A'in*.[5] All *mahals* under each have the *arazi* recorded against them, except for the *bandar* (port) Gandhar, and *balda* (town) Broach in *sarkar* Broach, and *balda* Ahmadabad, *bandar* Gogha and three other *mahals* in *sarkar* Ahmadabad, out of a total of 29 parganas in the *sarkar*. It is possible that in practically all these exceptional cases the *mahals* were purely urban and there was no agricultural land to be brought under measurement.

These extensive *arazi* figures suggest some modification of the obvious sense of Abu'l Fazl's statement that Gujarat was mostly *nasaqi* and measurement was rarely undertaken.[6] Perhaps what he means is only that annual re-measurement was rare; in other words, figures of area once measured in a locality continued to be accepted in subsequent years (a practice that was a recognised form of *nasaq*).[7]

The *arazi* (lit. area), in Mughal revenue terminology signified 'measured area' and such measurement may be presumed to have covered gross cropped

*44th Session at Burdwan, 1983.

area, current fallows, cultivable waste and some portion of uncultivable waste.[8] The measurement was not necessarily complete in all those regions for which the *A'in* offers *arazi* figures.[9] But in Gujarat the measured area is so large that one must suppose that a very high proportion of the total area had been surveyed. This can in fact be verified by comparing the *arazi* (A) with the map-area (M) of the individual *sarkars*.[10] Table 1 offers such a comparison; in its column 2, it gives the estimated revenue (*jama*) or J per unit of measured area, through J/A.

TABLE 14.1

Sarkar	A as% of M	J/A
1. Ahmadabad	57.55	25.90
2. Patan	48.04	15.17
3. Nadaut	27.85	16.28
4. Baroda	73.83	44.63
5. Broach	41.02	22.95
6. Champaner	19.62	13.13
7. Surat	57.69	14.53
8. Godhra	29.24	6.83

The extent of measurement relative to map-area in various *sarkars* is uneven, but the unevenness is in surprising conformity with the actual geography of Gujarat.

Within *sarkar* Baroda, the *arazi* covered almost three-fourths of the map-area, while in the hilly and forested Champaner, partly falling in 'Mahindra Range'[11] it did not reach even one-fifth of the map-area. Similarly, in *sarkars* Nadaut and Godhra, with a hilly and forested terrain,[12] the *arazi* was a little over a quarter of the map-area. Since the extent of cultivation in these *sarkars* could not have been high, it is natural that the *arazi* covered a small portion of the whole map-area. Clearly, Akbar's officials were interested only in measuring the cultivated land, and left large tracts of waste alone. The comparatively low *jama arazi* ratios for these *sarkars* lend further strength to the assumption that the low *arazi* relative to map-area here is a result of low cultivation and not of an incomplete measurement of the actual cropped area. Had the *arazi* been small owing to incomplete measurement we should have obtained a high J/A, but this is not the case in any of the three *sarkars*.

In the *sarkars* of Ahmadabad, Patan and Surat, the *arazi* covered around one half of the map-area, and in Broach nearly that. This too is not unexpected, since large portions of *sarkar* Ahmadabad and Patan fell either in the sandy tracts bordering the Runn or were covered by grass lands inhabited by wild cheetahs.[13] The cropped area therefore, could not be as high as in Baroda.

One may thus say that the measurement of cultivated land in Gujarat was practically complete (in respect of the cultivated or cultivable area) in all *sarkars* (except, again, Saurath). If so, the *arazi* statistics of the *A'in* should be reliable index of the relative extent of cultivation.

Table 14.1, suggests the influence of yet another important geographical feature of Gujarat. On the basis of rainfall Gujarat can be divided into three distinct regions. The eastern tract (Sorath and portions of the *sarkars* of Patan and Ahmadabad) forming a zone of low rainfall; the central and southern parts of *sarkar* Ahmadabad, and the *sarkars* of Baroda and Broach, of moderate rainfall (between 30" and 40"); and the southern and western portions, including the whole *sarkar* of Surat of high rainfall (above 40"). It is the region of moderate rainfall that contains the cotton producing area and is the most fertile area of Gujarat. It is interesting to note that the incidence of *jama* per *bigha* in the *A'in* is the highest here. In Baroda it reaches the maximum, viz., 44.63 *dams* per *bigha* of *arazi*, while in Ahmadabad and Broach it respectively comes to 25.90 and 22.95. The revenue incidence in *sarkar* Baroda thus stands out. However, if we consider only the parganas falling in the central and southern parts of the *sarkar* of Ahmadabad and exclude the parganas in the low rainfall zone the J/A for these parganas works out at 39.01 *dams* per *bigha*, i.e., quite close to that of Baroda.[14] One can thus safely assume that it was the high fertility of the region that was responsible for higher incidence of the revenue here. However, in *sarkar* Godhra, a portion of which was a part of this fertile tract, J/A is very low, viz., 6.83 *dams* per *bigha*. Partly this must be due to the presence of hilly and forested tracts within the *sarkar*; but there seems to have been an additional factor. In this *sarkar*, the zamindars' share in the peasant surplus works out to a considerably high figure (namely, 44 per cent of the *jama'*).[15] It appears, therefore, that here the total claimed revenue was low also because the Mughal administration had to concede a larger share to the local *zamindars*

TABLE 14.2

Suba	JIM dams/bigha
Bengal	2.69
Orissa	7.84
Bihar	4.34
Allahabad	5.76
Awadh	7.14
Agra	5.56
Malwa	1.96
Malwa (excluding *sarkar* Garh)	4.31
Gujarat	7.91
Gujarat (excluding Saurath)	10.48
Ajmer	2.24
Delhi	8.43
Lahore	9.76
Multan	2.23
Thatta	2.24
Kashmir	5.19
Kabul	2.01

The revenue in the low and high rainfall zones varies within the range of 13 to 16 *dams* per *bigha* of *arazi*.

A somewhat intriguing feature of Gujarat's *jama* statistics is the comparatively high incidence of revenue. The *jama* incidence per unit of *arazi* in the various *sarkars* ranges from 6.83 to 44.63 *dams* per *bigha*, while for the *Suba*, (excluding Saurath) it comes to 22.21 *dams*.[16]

Incidence in Gujarat approximates to that of the two 'central' *Subas*, viz., Agra and Delhi, where too the area under measurement was very large in relation to the map-area, the J/A being respectively 20.69 and 19.44 *dams/bigha*.[17]

Even if we set the *jama* against the entire map-area, the higher incidence in Gujarat among North Indian provinces continues to be evident.

This high revenue-incidence might perhaps be attributed to certain peculiar features of the economy of Gujarat. The incidence of revenue, owing to the prevalence of cash nexus, was naturally affected by prices. Since Gujarat was the main entry-point for bullion and most of the imported silver was coined there,[18] this would naturally have increased the money-supply in the region. Since it channelled a large part of the Mughal Empire's sea-borne trade, commercial activity too must have been extensive in Gujarat, contributing to the greater velocity of money here. Moreover, Gujarat was a large importer of food-stuff,[19] and food-grain prices at least ought to have been higher in this *Suba* than in the surrounding area.

Furthermore, as we have noted above, a portion of the *Suba* falling in the moderate rainfall zone—the cotton tract—was very fertile and the larger yeilds too could have been responsible for the high revenue-incidence. The widespread cultivation of high quality cotton in itself could have been a source of larger revenues, since the revenue rates for cotton in the *zabt* provinces, were 25, to 40% higher than those for wheat.[20] In spite of the fact that Abu'l Fazl mentions jowar and bajra as the staple crops of Gujarat, the region was also known for production of high quality rice and indigo.[21] Sarkhej indigo, though inferior to the Bayana variety was still an important export variety.

Another possible reason for the high incidence af *jama* in Gujarat could be a larger state claim over produce. In the seventeenth century Geleynssen (166–73) says that in Gujarat the demand was closer to three-fourths of the agricultural produce instead of one-half or one-third.[22]

Besides all these factors that might have contributed in raising the land-revenue demand in Gujarat, there could be yet another possible factor not related to land-revenue-incidence. The share of the proportion of taxes other than land-revenue in the *jama'* of Gujarat might possibly have been higher than in other provinces of the Empire. In the absence of any straightforward data on urban taxes., we may seek help from the *jama'* and *arazi* statistics in the *A'in*, to work out the magnitude of urban taxes in total revenue. The means by which the sizle of urban taxation may be determined is based on the simple assumption that since the *jama'* recorded in the *A'in* included urban taxes as well, the *jama' arazi* ratio for the *mahal* comprising a large town should be higher than J/A for the adjoining rural parganas. If we further assume that generally the parganas containing large towns contributed their share of land-revenue according to the recorded *arazi,* the component of land-revenue in the *jama'* of these parganas can be worked out by multiplying their *arazi* by J/A calculated for the remaining parganas in the *sarkar.* On subtracting the result (representing the estimated land-revenue) from the *jama'* of the urban pargana we should get the total amount of realization expected from taxes collected in the towns situated within the pargana.

Proceeding on these lines we can calculate the urban taxes for various towns of Gujarat as follows:

TABLE 14.3

Town/Sarkar	Urban taxation from towns	Total urban tax in sarkar	% of jama
Sarkar Ahmadabad			
Ahmadabad	3,13,02,645		
Bandar			
Ghogha	6,00,000		
Khambayat	1,73,27,855		
		4,92,30,500	22.58
Sarkar Patan			
Patan ba haveIi	52,15,679		
		52,15,679	8.65
Sarkar Nadaut			
Nadaut			
ba haveli	24,48,001	24,48,001	27.83
Sarkar Baroda			
Baroda	1,01,76,136	1,01,76,136	24.73
Sarkar Broach			
Broach			
ba haveli	67,26,039		
Bandar			
Gandhar	2,40,000		
Hansot	13,36,875		
		83,02,914	38.08
Sarkar Surat			
Surat			
ba haveli	50,12,465		
Bulsar	5,19,235		
Rander	7,339		
Navasari	1,20,667		
		56,59,706	29.75
Sarkar Saurath			
Revenue of	26,02,060	26,02,060	4.10
the Ports of			
Saurath			
Total for Suha		26,02,060	18.65

The urban share in the total revenue in all the *sarkars* except Patan seems considerable. At the *Suba* level too it is only a little less than one-fifth of the total revenue. Moreover, the proportion of urban taxes in the total revenues of Gujarat turns out to be even larger than that in the *Suba* of Agra, in which the urban taxes accounted for 15.71 per cent of the total *jama* calculated on the same lines. In *sarkar* Agra itself urban taxes amounted to 28.53 per cent of the *jama* which compares favourably with its percentage in *sarkar* Ahmadabad. But in absolute figures the tax contribution of the city of Ahmadabad approaches that of Agra, which contributed 3,18,24,092 *dams* only, though it was the capital of the Empire. Moreover, *Suba* Agra had no towns comparable to the cities other than Ahmadabad in Gujarat, which show such high tax contributions. We can thus legitimately infer that the *Suba* of Gujarat was the most highly urbanized region in Akbar's Empire.

One may expect that the overseas trade of Gujarat played an important part in this high share of urban taxes in the *jama* of Gujarat through custom revenue. The *A'in* gives us *jama* for the ports of Saurath and the *mahals* containing other ports, viz., Ghogha, Gandhar Cambay, Surat, Broach, Hansot, Rander and Bulsar. The figures of urban taxation from these *mahals* add up to 3,26,39,949 *dams*, a figure which, even if the whole of it was from custom, accounts for 39.03 per cent of the total urban income of the *suba*.

It is to Pearson's credit that he has tried to make use of revenue statistics to gauge the significance of overseas commerce in the economy of Gujarat. But his quantification is based on extremely weak data. He puts the port-revenues from the *A'in* at Rs. 80,000—a figure certainly not supported by the actual entries in the *A'in* which really give us Rs. 8,15,999 (the equivalent of *dams* given above). He then, not surprisingly, rejects his own figure from the *A'in* as an unconvincing underestimate and relies on figures which the *Mirat-i-Ahmadi* assigns to the Gujarat Sultanate.[23] But these statistics are at best very dubious, at least in respect of the rupee equivalents of amounts given in *tankchas* (a hundred of which the author takes as equal to the rupee).[24] Apart from the small further discrepancies, such as that Pearson overlooks the figures assigned by the *Mirat* to the customs of Cambay,[25] he omits to notice that the *Mirat*'s figures for the Sultanate in rupees are hopelessly inflated, so that the total for the revenue of Gujarat comes to 5,47,00,000 for the province proper[26] as compared to the equivalent of Rs. 1,12,08,492 given in the *A'in*. In fact if we roughly scale down the total revenues to get the total given by the *A'in*, and deflate the customs revenues given in the *Mirat* by the same ratio, we would get a figure in close proximity to that of the *A'in*. In other words the port-revenues of Gujarat *c.* 1595 was much less than one million rupees and nowhere near the four millions accepted by Pearson. Even at the lower figure the customs revenue form a fairly respectable component of the total urban taxation of Gujarat (nearly 40 per cent as we have seen).[27]

Our study of the *A'in*'s statistics thus brings out a few major facts about the Gujarat economy towards the close of the sixteenth century. It was very extensively cultivated; that is in many areas gross cultivation reached the limits of the possible extent. The revenue incidence in money terms was high, suggestive of high productivity in cash crops like cotton, and relatively high prices. This ties in with what we can judge from our evidence about its commerce, and the numismatic fact of large coin mintage in Gujarat. Part of the reason for its high revenue lay in its large urban taxation, amounting to over 18% of the whole. Of the urban taxation, in turn, nearly two-fifths came from custom or ports. This suggests that Gujarat not only had a large urban sector, but within this sector sea trade accounted for a high degree of urbanization. These data largely confirm the common generalisations about Mughal Gujarat. But it is good to know that for once the expectations from impressions are fulfilled by quantification.

Notes

1. Abu'l Fazl, *A'in-i Akbari*, I, ed. Blochmann, pp. 485–500.
2. The *arazi* figures have however, been used to assess the extent of cultivation in Gujarat, in Irfan Habib, *Agrarian System of Mughal India*, pp.18–20.
3. *Zabt* signified revenue assessment based on cash revenue-rates, fixed for each cropper unit of area. It, therefore, implied prior measurement of land sown with the crops on which the rates were fixed.
4. *A'in*, p. 485.
5. Ibid., pp. 493–500. I have collated the figures in this edition with those of B.M.MSS Add. 6538 and 7658.
6. *A'in*, l, p. 485.
7. *Agrarian System*, p. 225.
8. *Agrarian System*, p. 3. see also Shireen Moosvi, 'Magnitude of Land-Revenue Demand and Income of the Mughal Ruling Class Under Akbar'. *Medieval India—A Miscellany*, IV, p. 106. Moreland, however, assumes *arazi* to be identical with the gross cropped area, *Jonrnal of UP. Historical Society*, 11, pt. 1.
9. cf. S. Moosvi, *Medieval India—A Miscellany*, IV, p. 102.
10. Since most of the parganas of Suba Gujarat have pretty firmly been identified in Irfan Habib, An *Atlas of the Mughal Empire*, Sheet 7A, it is now possible to work out the map-area of different *sarkars* with a degree of certainty.
11. *Atlas of the Mughal Empire*, Sheet 7B and notes. Wild elephants were found in the region, *Tuzuk-i Jahangiri*, ed, S. Ahmad, pp. 224–5.
12. *Atlas*, Sheet 7B; Abdul Hamid Lahori, *Badshahnama*, I, p. 331.
13. *Atlas*, Sheet and Notes 7B.
14. The parganas of *sarkar* Ahmadabad falling within the fertile zone are *Haveli and balda* Ahmadabad, Urhar, Matar, Bahiel, Piplod, Paranti, Pellatil, Thamna, Chhola Barcha, Dholk, Sarnal, Kavi, Khambayat, Kaparanj. Mahmudabad, Masudabad

and Nariod. See for their location *Atlas of the Mughal Empire*, Sheet 7 A. The total *jama* of these parganas is 17, 87, 23,062 *dams* and *arazi*, 45, 81, 975 *bigha-i llahi*.

15. See S. Moosvi, *Indian Economic* and *Social History Review*, V.3, p. 373.

16. These calculations are based on the *A'in's* statistics for the two *subas, BI*, I, pp. 493– 500.

17. Ibid.

18. In the UP treasure-trove finds, out of a total of 2617 rupee coins, belonging to the period, 1575–95, the coins from Gujarat mints alone are 1014, or 39 per cent of the total.

19. Wheat was brought from Malwa and rice from the Deccan, *A'in*, I, pp. 485.

20. This may be seen from the tables of *dastur* rates set out in the *A'in*, I, pp. 349– 55.

21. *A'in*, I, p. 486; Finch in *Early Travels in India, 1583–1619*, p. 174.

22. *cf.* Agrarian System, p. 19.

23. M. Pearson, *Merchants and Rulers in Gujrat*, pp. 23–4.

24. Ali Muhammad Khan, *Mirat-i-Ahmadi*, I, ed, Nawab Ali, p. 17.

25. Pearson disregards the port-revenues for Cambay given in the *Mirat*, I, pp. 21–2, without assigning any reasons and against the figure of Rs. 4,00,000 in the *Mirat* accepts Rs. 6,00,000 for the Cambay port-revenue on the basis of Portuguese evidence.

26. *Mirat*, I, p. 18.

27. I am here not entering into a debate about Pearson's calculation of total turnover of trade and its comparison with the total agricultural produce, for which see *Medieval India—A Miscellany*, IV, pp. 217–19.

PART 2

TRADE, MARKET AND CURRENCY

15

Textile Industry and Trade of the Kingdom of Golkonda

P.M. Joshi

Introductory

It is not necessary for me to give any historical background for this paper as all of you know it so well, I will, therefore, straight plunge into my subject.

The most famous industry in the Kingdom of Golkonda was, of course, the Diamond Mining Industry. Also Golkonda steel in its day was world famous. But in my opinion the most important branch of the economic life of the kingdom was its textile industry. The chief centre of this industry was Masulipatam which was also the principal port of the kingdom from where Golkonda fabrics went all over the world and established a unique reputation for quality and finish.

It is reasonable to suppose that the kingdom was self-sufficient in the matter of raw cotton required for its thriving textile industry. Today cotton is grown almost all over the area[1] covered by the Kingdom of Golkonda during the sixteenth and seventeenth centuries, and we have evidence enough to show that the same conditions obtained three hundred years ago.[2] On occasions when the cotton crop suffered due to famine, Gujarat raw cotton was imported at Masulipatam from Surat.[3] On the carding and spinning side we have no information at all, but it is evident that these processes were carried out in the cotton growing districts and in the neighbourhood of the weaving centres.

Weaving Centres

Masulipatam was the most famous weaving centre of the kingdom and also its natural port. Immortalised by Ptolemy in his Tables and by the unknown writer of the Periplus, Masulipatam had been since the dawn of history famous for its manufacture and export of cotton piece-goods. Marco Polo noted it as a place which manufactured the finest cottons that are to be met with in any

*5th Session at Hyderabad, 1941.

part of India.[4] And this same observation is amply supported by European travellers and English and Dutch merchants during the sixteenth and seventeenth centuries.[5] The territory round about Masulipatam was also dotted with villages and towns engaged similarly[6] and these acted as feeders to the international market at Masulipatam.

A little to the south of Masulipatam along the coast is Nizampatam or Petapoli as it was known. This was second in importance to Masulipatam as a sea-port and was likewise a great centre of the textile industry. But its fame is mainly due to that branch of the industry devoted to the printing and painting of cotton goods.[7] It was one of the first places on the Coromandel at which both the English and the Dutch established factories which continued to exist with varying fortunes throughout the seventeenth century.

A little to the south of Petapoli are three coastal towns, Baptala, Vetapalli and Motupalli in that order. These and the villages surrounding them were also well-known manufacturing places and during the seventeenth century we find both English and Dutch factors engaged in exploiting their possibilities to the fullest extent.[8] Further south on the banks of the Munyeru is the port of Karedu with weaving centres about 20 miles up in the country. Karedu served the needs of this district[9] by transporting its goods to the markets at Masulipatam and Petapoli.

North of Masulipatam the whole of the Gingerlee coast was dotted with villages and towns engaged in the manufacture of various cotton piece-goods.[10] On the southern delta branch of the Godavari was Narsapur with its adjoining town of Madapollam. Narsapur, besides having a shipbuilding industry, produced coarse woven cotton cloths and also some painted cloths.[11] The English had a factory here for long cloth which they took to Masulipatam to print into chintz.[12] Madapollam produced a special veriety of cloth "chequered somewhat fine"[13] and gave its name to this class of cotton good still known as Madapollams.[14] Across was Tatipaka an island in the river mouth which produced "fine white dumgarees, called Pcta dungarees and betilles" or fine muslins.[15]

About six miles to the north is the town of Palakollu, called Policull by the English factors. This place produced a variety of cotton clothes, Calicoes, Lungees, Palampores, etc., and also manufactured painted cloth. All this material was sent on to Masulipatam where it had a ready market.[16] The Dutch had a factory here and they sponsored weaving of cloth[17] for their trade requirements. Further north were Vizagapatam, Waltair and Bimlipatam. These centres produced cotton cloth mostly for local needs and were not frequented by Europeans.[18] Late in the seventeenth century the Dutch had a small factory at Bimlipatam to buy up local cloth for the Batavia market.[19]

It will thus be seen that the whole coast-line of the kingdom was engaged in the textile industry. This was in fact the principal economic activity in this region. But the industry had also many centres inland. It seems that cotton goods were manufactured round about Golkonda itself,[20] and the Dutch had a factory here during the seventeenth century.[21] Twenty miles to the north of Masulipatam on the south bank of the Krishna was Kondavid, another twelve miles from here was Nagelwanch. There were Dutch factories at both these places engaged in the purchase of piece-goods.[22] At a distance of eight miles north of Nagelwanch was Virawasaram which according to the English merchants "is not only inhabited for the most parts with weavers itself but is environed with many other villages that are filled with people of the like occupation.[23] The English expected this district to supply them cloth both for Europe and the Far East.[24] They opened a factory at Virawasaram in 1635 and abandoned it in 1661[25] when the industry of the place started to decline.

Warangal was the most important weaving centre inland for white muslin cloth known by its Portuguese name beatilha, i.e. veiling. The commonest epithet applied to betilles is "Oringall" in English and "Orinael" in Dutch.[26] Besides betilles Warangal has a historical reputation for its carpets which were originally manufactured by Persian settlers who came into the Deccan with the early Muslims.[27] Another place which specialised in the manufacture of carpets was Ellore now a taluka town in the Godavari district. In 1679 Strynsham Master considered Ellore as 'one of the greatest towns in this country ...where the best carpets are made (after the manner of those in Persia) by the race of Persians, which they told us came over about 100 years ago.'[28]

Varieties of Cloth

All the centres enumerated above produced calicoes of various grades. The coarsest variety was known as Dungarees; it was a stout cloth used largely for sail making or packing and was manufactured in and around Petapoli.[29] One pagooda (i.e. about Sh. 7/6 in contemporary exchange) fetched three of these pieces which I am inclined to believe, measured about 30 yards in length and 40 inches in width. The next grade was ordinary long cloth produced in all centres. A piece usually measured about 30 yards by 40 inches and in 1660 the price of this cloth per 100 square yards to exporters was nearly 8 pagodas.[30] This cloth was obtainable bleached, unbleached or dyed in the piece and was used mainly for the wear of the people in the locality of production. The apparel of the men folk consisted entirely of pieces of this cloth 'on their shoulders a loose white callico cloth... sometimes a coat to their bodies unto the middle, from thence downwards to their ankles full of cloth.'[31] The nether garment is the well known Lungi from which the English word long cloth comes.[32] The sarees of women were made of cloth of better grade described by Linschoten as 'some being mingled with threads of gold and silver, and such like stuff of a thousand sorts, very beautiful to behold, wherewith they cloth themselves in very comely manner.'[33] During the seventeenth century when the Dutch and English found that Far Eastern market could absorb more of long cloth they encouraged production of this variety.[34]

The next grade of calicoes was known as Salempores which was of two qualities. Ordinary Salempores were about the same price as long cloth. Fine Salempores, on the other hand were of a finer variety made with more threads to the inch. The average length of a piece of either kind was about 19 yards and its width between 36 and 40 inches. The price of the coarse cloth was the same as long cloth, whereas fine Salempores fetched as much as 16 pagodas per hundred square yards. The third variety was Moorees which had two qualities. Ordinary Moorees ranked with fine Salempores in price, but in size this cloth was 9 yards by 45 inches. Fine Moorees also had the same measurements but in price they were 25 pagodas the 100 square yards or about 2½ pagodas per piece. Perealles was the name of the highest grade of calico; a piece of this quality measured 8 yards by 1 and cost about 2 pagodas.[35]

The Muslins (*beatilha*) of Warangal which have been mentioned above were the finest kind of cotton goods produced in the kingdom. The usual length of a piece of this cloth varied between 14 to 20 yards and its width between 32 to 40 inches.[36] It was very well suited for turbans and was in great demand both in the Far Eastern countries and in Persia and Red Sea Ports. Another kind of cloth not so in great demand as the foregoing varieties but produced in many places was Ginghams,[37] a striped cotton cloth used for vizars or trousers. It should be remembered here that the Muslim section of the population of the kingdom was more elaborately dressed than the Hindus. The Muslims used trousers and wore coats and jackets. Most of the Gingham produce seems to have been used for local needs though a little quantity was at times exported. Other varieties of cloth were Allejas, a mixture of silk and cotton, Dymities, Dyapers, Boxshaes, Maraviues, Tape-shins, Sarassa Patola, Dragam Malaya[38] and few others including Baftas at Petapoli.[39]

Dyed and Printed Cotton Piece-goods

Calicoes of various grades were dyed brown, red or blue as the markets demanded. At Policull the Dutch factors 'dye much Blew Cloth, having about 300 jars set in the ground for that work.'[40] Brown long cloth was obtainable generally in all weaving centres.[41] Red Muslin or Salus was done at Golkonda to some extent,[42] but most of it came from the coast, more especially from Petapoli which produced a quality of red yarn and red cloth unsurpassed in colour.[43] The reason why the dying of piece-goods was localised on the coast round about Masulipatam and Petapoli was that the ingredient used in this process viz, the chay-root grew profusely and of the best quality in this region.[44]

The patterned goods were of two kinds, printed and painted. In printing a piece with the desired pattern blocks were employed which had a design on a cut or raised in relief, so that the raised parts when charged with colour transferred the design to the fabric when the block was stamped upon it. In painting a cloth the pattern was first drawn on paper and the outline pricked through with a fine point. This stencil was laid on the cloth and was treated with a small bag partially filled with charcoal powder. The outline of the pattern was thus faintly indicated by the charcoal powder on the cloth. The design thus obtained was then painted with a brush with the desired colour.[45]

The most famous printed or painted cotton goods were the well- known chintzes produced in and around Masulipatam and Petapoli. Bernier tells that the Imperial tent pitched outside the Diwan-i-Am at Agra had is 'inside lined with elegant Masulipatam chintzes, figured expressly for this very purpose with flowers so natural and colours so vivid, that the tent seemed to be encompassed with real parterres.'[46] Chintz or chites as it was called was used as bed-covers, table cloths, pillow cases, pocket handkerchiefs and especially waist coats for the use of both men and women, principally in Persia.[47] Chintz pillow cases and bed-covers were also in demand in England.[48] Palampores or chintz bed-covers may specially be mentioned as these were in great demand by the nobility both in the kingdom and elsewhere.

Printed goods were the customary wear in the Far East. The cloth used for these was mainly of the lower grade.[49] One hears occasionally of painted percalles, but as a rule long cloth, Salempores and betilles were used and early in the seventeenth century the English traders found the paintings of Masulipatam fit for Java, the Molucas, etc.[50] Later in the century these fabrics came into fashion in Western Europe for decorating rooms as a substitute for tapestry.[51]

Organisation of the Industry

Is it almost unnecessary for me to add that the weaving industry was in the hands of weavers who were a caste by themselves. Of weavers and painters of cloth Methwold remarks: 'all other mechanic traders are tribes by themselves, as painters, weavers . . . .'[52] The weavers and painters worked by themselves first to satisfy local needs and then to provide for the trade carried through the ports of the kingdom. But at no stage do they seem to have been in direct touch with the consumer. Between the weaver and the consumer and the European trader who bought for foreign markets was the local merchant who was usually a member of the Komati caste. Methwold describes the Komatis as "generally the merchants of this place, who, by themselves or their servants, travel into the country, gathering up calicoes from the weavers, and other commodities which they sell again in greater parcels in the port towns to merchant strangers, taking their commodities in barter or at a price."[53]

During the sixteenth century before the advent of the European traders, it was the Komatis who kept in touch with the export market and gave money in advance to the weavers to produce such goods as were in demand in the Far East and in Persia and the Red Sea Ports. Sometimes some rich Muslim merchants owning ships which plied between Masulipatam and Persia or Red Sea Ports would himself place orders with the weavers as he was aware of the tastes and fashions of the places where he wanted to sell the goods. I may mention here that there was always pilgrim traffic between Masulipatam and Mocha in Red Sea and the ships that carried pilgrims for Mecca also carried cotton piece-goods. Mocha acted as distributing centre for East Africa. This shipping was to a great extent controlled by Arabs, though the Kingdom of Golkonda did have some ships of its own. During the seventeenth century with the advent of the Dutch and the English the bulk of the export trade both to the East and West passed into their hands, though ships of various countries continued their contact with the Golkonda ports to some extent.

The English and Dutch merchants did their business through local agents who were mostly Komatis, but in some cases we also find Brahmins or Muslims engaged in this capacity. On their advent into the Orient the Europeans found that there was a great demand for Golkonda piece-goods in Persia, Arabia, East Africa and the Far Eastern countries and they also visualised the potentialities of these articles for the Western European market. The requirements of the various markets were already well defined, what the Europeans had to do was merely to enter the field as exporters of Golkonda goods. In order to meet the local agents on their own grounds they employed local people as buyers and Dubashes. The Dutch and English sometimes imported gold in specie or coins[54] to be paid as advances to the merchants. At times they used to borrow money from some influential businessman locally at a rate of 2 to 2½ per cent.[55] One of the best friends the English had at Masulipatam in their early days was a rich merchant and shipowner named Mir Kamaluddin who often advanced money to them.[56]

The local merchants or agents or middlemen as we may call them came to the export traders with samples of goods. After placing order according to the samples and giving advances to the merchants, it took four to five months for the goods to be delivered.[57] Sometimes it took even more, very nearly a year.[58] After the cloth was delivered it had to be bleached. The process of bleaching was done at the Dutch and English factories[59] and not by the weavers nor by the middlemen. Bleachers were employed for this purpose and the cloth was ready for export only after it was bleached. In case of printed and painted goods, however, the product delivered was properly finished and ready for the market Two interesting pieces of information in this connection may be mentioned. Some of the cloth purchased was tailored into articles of wear by the English merchants under their own supervision and for this purpose they engaged local tailors at Petapoli. They also engaged packers to pack cloth for export; these were paid at the rate of 2½ pagodas per month without any other allowance.[60]

Trade

The reason why the Dutch and English developed export trade in Golkonda textiles was (1) they were cheaper than at any other weaving centre both along the Western and Eastern coasts of India.[61] and (2) they were of unrivalled quality and finish for goods of their own class.[62] Also these goods had established themselves firmly in the Far Eastern Market. And, if the English and the Dutch wanted the spices from the latter source they had to take Golkonda piece-goods and get spices in exchange. Moreover, the whole trade, viz. taking cotton-goods to the Far East, exchanging them for spices and taking these to the European markets, was an extremely lucrative and profitable business which as a rule brought 100 per cent[63] profit to those engaged in it and at times this percentage was even double. The Golkonda authorities on their side were fully aware of the great advantage that accrued to their people and always made generous concessions to the Dutch and English traders so that they could exploit the resources of the industry to the fullest extent.

As already observed before the shipping during the sixteenth century was in the hands of Arabs, Golkonda shipowners and merchants from Sumatra, Java and other Far Eastern countries. During the seventeenth century when the Dutch and English entered the field they controlled major portion of the export and import trade, but the others also continued to ply their ships.

The most important centres in the Far East for Golkonda goods were Bantam and Batavia in Java. Moorees, Percalles, Salempore, white and red betilles, tapes or skirts were the chief varieties of cloth exported[64] from Golkonda ports to these two places which served as a distributing centre to the island of Java and beyond. Achin, Priaman, Teku and Jambi were the places in Sumatra which had a demand for long cloth, Salempores, white and blue Fine chintz, striped stuffs, cushion carpets or divan seats and Medapollam cloth.[65] The kingdom of Siam bought mainly callicoes and betilles though a demand for other goods also existed.[66] Adjacent to Siam was the kingdom of Patani and the Province of Kedah. The former absorbed as many as ten varieties of Masulipatam cloth and fine varieties of Petapoli.[67] The king of Patani we are told was very fond of betilles.[68] Kedah wanted mostly painted cloths of Petapoli.[69] Pegu, Tennasarim and Arracan in Burma wanted red cotton yarn, calicoes of various grades, white and dyed and printed and painted.[70]

The first country to the west to which Golkonda sent its cotton goods was the Maldive Islands.[71] The port in Persia to which all goods were sent was

Gombroon or the modern Bunder Abbas. This was of course the distributing centre of the whole of the country. All kinds of cloth, white, dyed and printed were in demand here,[72] and also finished chintz articles like pillow cases, pocket handkerchief, and waist coats for the use of men and women.[73] For Golkonda merchants who transported export goods in English ships the freight from Masulipatam to Persia was 1½ pagodas per maund.[74] The Red Sea Port to which piece-goods were exported was Mocha which was also the terminus of the pilgrim ships. Evidently many varieties of cloth were in demand at this place. Speaking of merchandise laden at Masulipatam for Mocha, Floris uses the generic term 'Indie cloth.'[75] Mocha in its turn served Arabia, Egypt and adjacent parts of North Africa which had a demand for Golkonda muslin and turban cloth.[76]

The Dutch and English also developed considerable export trade in high-grade cotton goods to Europe. Percalles, Moorees and Salempores had a very ready market in England, France, and Holland and printed and painted goods also were in great demand in these countries.[77] We find a special demand in England for 'Well painted counterpanes and pillowcases.'[78] Golkonda goods had established themselves so well in Europe that by the middle of the seventeenth century we find "callicoes of Coromandel making... are now preferred before any of the Surat clothing, because they fit best for French and other foreign sales"[79] and we also find that sale of these cloths in England 'yielded contentable profit.'[80] Early in the century about 1623 we find that the Danes too exported some cloth to Denmark.[81]

Besides cloth there was considerable export of cotton yarn from Masulipatam and Petapoli to England and Holland.[82]

The textiles imported into the kingdom were luxury goods from Europe and silk and other goods from the Far East broad cloth or scarlet cloth, Kerseys (a woollen cloth inferior to the former) and other woollen cloths of green, pale-blue and other colours were the chief imports from England.[83] The clothes were required for garments, to cover palanquins and for use on saddles; cloth of red colour was used for servant clothes.[84] The English factors also used broadcloth for giving presents to their agents, to nobles at the Royal Court and to Golkonda Officers at Masulipatam, Petapoli and other places.[85] Raw silk was imported at Masulipatam from China and Bantam in Java.(4) China also sent some silk thread and silk cloth, velvet, damasks and Chinese gold thread.[86] These were used for wearing apparel by the nobility and for their tents and tapestries. Bengal also sent some raw silk of a special kind called moonga silk. This was introduced in the apparel used by men and women and was also used in carpet.[87] apparently in imitation of gold thread.

Notes

1. Watts, *Commercial Products of India,* pp. 602, 603; *Dictionary of Economic Products of India,* IV, pp. 100, 132.

2. *EFI,1634–36*, pp. 40–41.

3. Ibid., p. 196.

4. Marco Polo, Marsden's edn., p. 658; Yule's edn., II, p. 298.

5. Linschoten, I, p. 91; Bowrey, p. 61; Thevenot, III, p. 165; *Relations*, pp. 61, 81.

6. *Letters Received*, II, p.84; Bowrey, p. 72.

7. *EFI, 1630–33*, pp. 229, 243, 280, *1634–36*, p. 45; Bowrey, p. 106, n.2.

8. *EFI, 1630–33*, pp. 77, 230, 234, 309; Bowrey, pp. 55–56; *DSM*, II, p. 135.

9. *DSM*, II, p. 178.

10. Bowrey, pp. 123–24; *Relations*, pp. 63, 80.

11. *Relations*, p. 63.

12. Alexander Hamilton, I, p. 374.

13. *Letters Received*, I, p. 74; *Hobson-Jobson*, p.532.

14. *Imperial Gazetteer of India*, XVI, pp. 227–28.

15. *Relations*, p. 80.

16. *Bowrey*, p. 106.

17. *DSM*, I, pp. 297–98.

18. Alexander Hamilton, I, pp. 375, 376, 381.

19. Alexander Hamilton I, p. 381.

20. *EFl, 1634–36*, pp. 48, 140; *1546–50*, p. 79; *DSM*. I, pp. 8, 257. .

21. *DSM*, II, p. 115.

22. *Relations*, p. 79; *DSM*, I, p. 298.

23. EFl, 1634–36, p. 45.

24. Ibid.

25. *DSM*, II, p. 107, n.2.

26. *IJE*, V, p. 235; cf., *Vestice of Old Madras*, II, p. 134.

27. Bilgrami and Willmolt, *Historical and Descriptive Sketch of His Highness the Nizam's Dominions*, II, p. 751. cf. Bowrey, II.

28. *DSM*, II, p. 171; cf. Bowrey *loc cit.*

29. *EFl, 1630–33*, p. 278.

30. *IJE*, V.

31. *Relations*, pp. 26–27 cf. also Linschoten, I, p. 91.

32. cf. *Hobson-Jobson* , p. 518.

33. Linschoten, I, p. 91.

34. *IJE*, V, p. 227.

35. Ibid., pp. 229, 230.

36. *DSM*, I, pp. 257, 272; *IJE*, V, p. 234.

37. *DSM, II*, pp. 113, 178.

38. *Letters Received*, II, p. 88.

39. *EFl, 1637–41*, p. 49.

40. DSM, II, p. 164.

41. Ibid., p. 114.

42. *DSM*, I, p. 257.

43. *EFI, 1634–36*, p. 145; Baldaeus, p. 655; *Letters Received*, II, p. 88.

44. *Relations*, pp. 35, 55, 77; Baldaeus, p. 655; Alexander Hamliton I, p. 374.

45. cf. Tavemier, II, p. 4.

46. Peter Mundy, I, p. 56; *EFI, 1634–36*, p. 161; Travemier, Crooke's ed., II, p. 4; Bowrey, pp. 71, 72 cf. also Linschoten, I, p. 91.

47. Bemier, p. 270.

48. Tavemier, loc. cit.

49. *EFl, 1630–33*, pp. 229, 280.

50. *IJE*, p. 238; *Letters Received*, II, p. 84.

51. *IJE*, loc. cit.

52. *Relations*, p. 19.

53. Ibid., p. 16, cf. *EFI, 1624–29*, pp. 8–9.

54. *EFI, 1634–36*, p. 48; *Dagh Register, 1640–41*, p. 113.

55. *EFl, 1634–36*, p. 140.

56. *EFl, 1630–33*, pp. 77, 167, 286.

57. *EFl, 1634–36*, p. 48.

58. *DSM*, II, 95; *EFI, 1630–33*, p. 235.

59. *EFI, 1634–38*, pp. 234, 235, 263; *1637–41*, p. 49; *DSM*, II, pp. 159–60; *Letters Received*, II, pp. 127–28.

60. *EFI, 1630–33*, pp. 231, 235.

61. *Letters Received*, II, p.99; *Relations*, p. 35; *EFI, 1651–54*, p. 263; *DSM* , I, p. 247.

62. cf. DeLaet, *Empire of the Great Mughal*, pp.76–77.

63. Bruce, I, pp. 342–43.

64. *Letters Received*, IV, p. 6; *EFI, 1618–21*, pp. 42–43; *1624–29*, p. 6; *1634–36*, p. 276; Floris, pp.17–18, 117; Alexander Hamilton, I, p. 38.

65. *Relations*, pp. 38, 60; Bowrey, pp. 288–89; *Letters Received*, I, pp.74–75; Bruce, I, pp. 188–90.

66. IJE, V, p. 242; Bowring, *The Kingdom and People of Siam*, I, p. 224.

67. *Letters Received*, II, p. 8.

68. Floris, p. 66.

69. Ibid., p. 71.

70. *EFI, 1651–54*, p. 265; *1668–69*, pp. 163, 280, *DSM*, II p. 130; *Relations*, pp. 39, 42.

71. *Pyrad*, I, p. 301; *DSM*, II, p. 113.

72. *EFI, 1630–33*, p. 289; *1634–36*, pp. 48, 139–40; *1637–41*, pp. 40, 42, 103–4.

73. Tavemier, Crooke's edn, II, p. 4.

74. *EFI, 1642–45*, p. 55.

75. Floris, p. 116, cf. also *Letters Received*, II, p. 116; *Relations*, p. 36.

76. IJE, V, p. 242, cf. *Letters Received*, IV, p. 35.

77. *Letters Received*, IV, p. 34; *EFI, 1622–23*, p. 336; *1634–36*, p. 45; *1651–54*, p. 99; *IJV*. p. 26; Bijdragen Tot de Taal-en Volkendunde vol. 94, p. 12.

78. *EFI, 1630–33*, pp. 229, 280.

79. *EFI, 1646–50*, p. 297.

80. *EFI, 1646–-50*, p. 164.

81. *EFI, 1622–23*, p. 337.

82. *Letters Received*, II, pp. 41, 59; *EFI, 1618–21*, pp. 41, 44, 49; *1624–29*, p. 181; Baldaeus, p. 655.

83. *Letters Received*, II, p. 154; *EFI, 1624–29*, p. 180.

84. *DSM*, I, p. 124, II, pp. 152, 168, 169, 384.

85. *Relations*, p. 62.
86. *EFI, 1624–29*, p. 25; *Relations*, p. 40.
87. *Letters Received*, II , p. 84; *EFI, 1624–29*, p. 80, *1634–36*, pp.49, 297; Floris, pp. 13, 19.

16

Surat in 1663 as Described by Fr. Manuel Godinho

G.M. Moraes

IN 1661 Portugal, threatened at home with the extinction of her independence by Spain and with the annexation of her dominions overseas by the Dutch, sought to save herself from a critical situation by concluding a defensive alliance with the English. The latter had long been casting covetous eyes on the Portuguese possessions in North Konkan. Already in 1626 they had all but succeeded in taking forcible possession of the island of Bombay. Twenty-six years later they had offered to purchase these territories. Consequently, when England demanded as the price of her help the island of Bombay, disagreeable though the prospect was, Portugal had no alternative but to agree.

In 1662 Charles II of England sent a squadron under Lord Marlborough to take charge of the island of Bombay. But the Portuguese governor, Antonio Melo-e-Castro refused to surrender it on the ground that the English admiral had failed to assist their fortress of Cochin, against the Dutch, who were besieging it. He defeated the efforts of Marlborough to siege Bhoyly force by marching all the Portuguese forces in Bassein to its defence. In the letters to the Portuguese Crown the governor and the administration of Goa defended their stand pleading that the cession of the island would deal a fatal blow to the Portuguese empire in India. As their arguments could not be driven home with sufficient force by correspondence, the governor despatched Fr. Manuel Godinho, an able and astute Jesuit, as his personal representative who would press before the Crown the point of view of the authorities in India. But few Portuguese ships were sailing to the East in those days and it was manifestly perilous to proceed by an English vessel on a secret and important mission which concerned English interests precisely. It was, therefore, judged safer to take the overland route through Persia. Accordingly, Fr. Manuel Godinho left Bassein in December 1662 for Surat to take ship to the Red Sea by which they generally went to Persia. To conceal his identity he entered Damaun dressed as a soldier. At Nargol he changed into Moorish clothes, as he ran the risk of being

*14th Session at Jaipur, 1951.

recognized as a Portuguese by inimical Arabs, and did not wish to attract undue notice from the Europeans. He was at Surat during the whole of January 1663 pending the departure of the ship. He reached Lisbon in October 1663. In his *Relacao do Caminho da India para Portugal* which describes his journey, he has left perhaps the very best account of Surat, pace his odium theological, by any writer of the 17th century.

Fr. Godinho was born in 1630 at Montalvao, a town in the district of Alentejo in Portugal. His parents were Manuel Numes de Abreu and Joana de Reis. He entered the society of Jesuits at the early age of 16. Assigned to the Indian Mission, Fr. Godinho worked in Goa. He left the society and became a secular priest, holding successively the post of prior of the Church of St. Nicholas at Santarem, and of beneficiary of the Church of the same saint at Lisbon. He was prior of the Church of St Mary at Loares, and was also Protonorary and Commissioner of the Holy Office. He died in 1712.

His chief work is the Narrative of the journey which Fr. Manuel Godinho made taking a new route by land and sea from India to Portugal in the year 1663. Published in 1665 it was reprinted in 1842 and again, in 1944. It is notable for the historical importance of the narrative, as well as for the beauty of its form, which reveals itself particularly in the vivid description of the journey. He also wrote a life of the Venerable Fr. Antonio da Chegas, the evangelical time-table showing the forty hours given in the Gospels with as many sacramental meditations for them, interesting descriptions of some events which took place at Constantinople after the March of the Turkish troops on Vienna which description he sent from Constantinople to a Maltese knight, and a panegyric on Saint Anthoney preached at the Church of St. Mary at Lisbon.

Description of the City and Port of Surat, the Major Emporium of India

In ancient times Surat was a poor town and the port was hardly known. But today, thanks to the patronage of the Hollanders and the English, it is the richest city and the most celebrated emporium in the whole of the Orient. It lies twelve leagues to the north of Damaun on the banks of the river Tapti, three leagues from its mouth and bar. It is not suitable for ships of heavy draft, which enter it only after first discharging their cargo. The river is not deep, but there are in it certain deep hollows excavated by human industry so as to allow heavy vessels to lie on the silt at low tide. The first Portuguese who sounded the bar was Antonio da Silveira, who proceeded thither by order of Nuno da Cunha with a fleet to destroy this city and that of Reiner which lies higher up the river on the opposite bank behind a promontory. The water of this river is sweet at low tide and brackish at high tide. In a hollow which the sea has made a league to the north of the river called Soali, the ships of the English and the Hollanders that come to Surat ride at anchor, and are under so close to the land that they can cover the landing place of their sloops with the artillery from their ships. There these two nations have their own custom-houses, through which they send their goods. In this hollow of Soali both the Hollanders and the English have been attacked by our fleet, but with little credit to our arms. The greatest of these reverses was suffered by D. Jernimo de Azevedo, the twentieth Viceroy of India who after attacking four Dutch vessels which were at Soali with a fleet of six galleons, three pinnaces and sixty rowing vessels had to withdraw with hardly three pinnaces which he left in flames.

The city is rather narrow, and surpasses our Evora in grandeur as in the number of its inhabitants which I reckon at more than 1,00,000 the white Mongals, the Hindustani Moors, Hindus of every class, Christians of various nations, in short, people from all over the world, who either live a settled life there or frequent that port on business. You can find at Surat Spaniards, Frenchmen, Germans, Englishmen, Hollanders, Flemings, men from Dankerk, Italians, Hungarians, Poles, Swedes, Turks, Arabs, Persians, Tartars, Georgeans, Scythians, Chinese, Malabarians, Bengalees, Ceylonese, Armenians, with other infinite variety of barbaric and strange nationalities. The buildings are generally simple with roofs of olas (which is the name given to interfaced palm leaves). This is the reason why, if by some accident a house is set on fire, it consumes many an entire street. But the city is not without some noble and stately houses belonging to the chief lords. The exterior is hardly imposing because these men as also other Moors take care to embellish the interior of their houses, purposely leaving the exterior uncouth, as they are building apartments for their women and not habitations for men. If you should look at one of these better houses from the street, they give an appearance of hell, but if you enter them they are like paradise because everything is of gold with rich paintings on their ceilings, exquisite decorations on their walls, the finest carpets on chairs, couches draped with the best of silk for reclining, cloisters, gardens, fountains and everything else that can help those to amuse who live there. On the other hand, the Bania gentoos of Surat build their houses curiously, paying greater attention to their exterior than to the comforts within. They build them of stone and lime up to the first floor. From there on nothing else is to be seen but works of carving in relief on teak embellished with enamel and lacquers of variegated hues.

There are in the city a large number of mosques for worship, and each nation among the Muslims has set apart for it a portion of the mosque where they gather on Fridays. The chief mosque is outside the city gates. It faces east, and is a majestic and lofty structure with imposing houses adjoining the minaret Here lives the Sheriff (as the Moors call the relatives of their Mafoma) universally respected and venerated by high and low alike, and it is deemed a merit to kiss his hand or even his tunic.

Not the least sumptuous of the buildings are the two caravanserais (that is to say public inns) built in the style of cloisters with living rooms on the side. The caravanserais have only one door which is closed at night and opened at daybreak so that the goods of the merchants who lodge in them may be the more secure. Another building worthy of mention is the public bath. It is a low spacious house which caters for a variety of baths, and is open to Muslims. It is staffed by a large number of servants who are paid for by the city to serve those who have their bath there, and to furnish them with hot water without return of any payment from individual visitors.

The city is not walled, but has a low enclosure pierced by four gateways. These are heavily guarded and whoever enters them with his goods is taken by the guards to the custom-house to see that the customs dues on goods they bring may not be lost. On coming out, he is further interrogated and required to produce the receipt of the assessor of customs, without which no one is allowed to proceed. There are two custom-houses in Surat. They are close to the river and face each other. Through the bigger are despatched the goods that are brought by sea, and through the smaller those that come to the city from inland. For export there are other custom-houses or rather other offices at the same place. The duties which they pay at the custom-houses are five per cent. To the Dutch, however, 1% is remitted by the present governor in consideration of a rich and exquisite present which Mansucar, the governor of Jacatara, made to him in the name of the Company in the year 1661.

The defence of the whole city rests with the citadel which stands on the banks of the river. The citadel has three bulwarks and a horseman in the centre with twenty pieces of artillery partly of bronze and partly of iron. But almost all these have been dismantled being either without gun-carriages or having burst. The ditch of this citadel is very deep, but narrow. The garrison consists of 200 native soldiers under a Mughal captain. The latter holds authority independent of the Nawab or Governor of the province. Nevertheless, save for the fact that he is a lord of that fortress, he cannot set foot outside its limits without the express permission of the king. The Captain is also treasurer of many millions; for in the fortress are deposited the revenues of the province, the custom dues and most of the coins that are struck in this city continuously. These coins are the finest in the whole of India because they are refined the *patakas* that come from Spain, and of the *larins* of Persia which are of the finest silver as their rupees are made, corresponding to our *crusados*. At sunrise, and at sunset they beat kettle drums in the fortress which are like tabalas and which the Moors use as tambors in battle. Around the fort there are no houses in order not to stand in the way of the artillery, but a beautiful square in which a fair is held every day in the evening, and everything that is asked for can be had there.

Surat is the greatest emporium in India and perhaps the richest in the whole world, because of the choice merchandise that is carried there by land

and sea. It is carried by the English and the Dutch from Europe, by the ships of the Red Sea from Africa and by the natives from Asia and Asia Minor. The best of the goods come into Surat from inland by caravans of bullocks and camels which every hour enter its gates. The merchants and those that have business dealings in this city are very rich, some of them computed to have more than 5 to 6 millions. They have 50 ships going to all countries and of the foreign ships that call at this port there is no count. There will be found at all times of the year in Surat ships from China, Malaca, Macassar, Malucas, Jacatara, Maldives, Bengal, Tenacerim, Ceylon, Cochin, Cananore, Calicut, Mecca, Aden, Suez, Magadaxo, Caxem, Mascut, Madagascar, Ormuz, Basra, Sind, England; in fact from whatever part of the world one is after.

The country of Surat abounds in wheat, pulses, and rice but grows hardly any food or coconut trees save the date-palm from which wine is produced by a class of people. These are fair-skined and are called *P arsis* because of their origin from Persia, whence they fled at the time when Persia was converted to Islam. These are gentiles who adore the sun, the moon and fire, which they tend as is related of the restal virgins of Rome. And if by any chance a house is set on fire, they would rather have everything burnt than put it out, because that would amount to killing God whom they adore in fire.

Outside the city to the west there are two wide pieces of ground with countless tombs of the Moors, separated from one another by stones at the head of each grave. Further still are two enclosures, in one of which the Dutch and in the other the English are buried. Some of the mausoleums of the Dutch commodores and the English presidents are worth a visit both for their structure and finish. The epitaphs in Latin, English and Flemish describe what persons they were who lie there, and what offices they held. There is a separate graveyard for Christians easily distinguished by the crosses which are planted on the glares.

I shall describe the dress, food and other customs of the people of Surat when I shall speak of the Mughals. The water which is used for drinking is from two wells outside the gates of the city. The gentoos use the water from the river, not because it is better but because once the carcass of a cow was found thrown into one of the wells and they have since taken such a disgust for it that no one drinks of it any more. The moorish and gentoo gentry of Suratride beautiful Arab steeds, but without the solar hats, as it is the royal headgear in the Mughal Empire. Some also go in carriages called arcolins which look like coaches and are drawn by stately and swift-footed bullocks of beautiful colours. The points of these cars shine with rings of gilded bronze for gallantry, their hoods are lined with silk and scarlet cloth, and for seats they have luxurious cushions on fine alcatifa. Nothing is known here of carts drawn by mules, because they have no mules, nor of coaches because there are many horses.

Ever since they first entered India the English and the Dutch (the former during the viceroyalty of Matias de Albuquetue and the latter during that of

Aires de Saldanha) have established themselves at the port of Surat. Here the English have their presidents and the Dutch their commodores. Their ships anchor at this port though the Dutch ships since that nation possesses better ports in their city in the south, do not visit Surat as frequently as did before. But the English having no ports of their own in India capable of harbouring their ships save the fortress of Madras–Patan on the inhospitable and high seas of Coromandel, have availed themselves of the ready welcome they have always received at Surat where their ships are in great demand. Here they discharge their goods and wait till they can return laden with the cargo of cloth, pepper, indigo, silk and other commodities which for this reason is purchased at this port beforehand or is sent from other ports by their ships which for this purpose go coasting all over from Surat. And so it is that the Dutch commodores and the English presidents fly their national flags from masts not only higher than the roofs of houses but also all the towns in the city.

The administration of the whole of this district is vested in one head called the Nawab. He is selected from among the *umars,* who used to be the titular lords of the Mughal Empire. He is treated with great deference and never stirs out of his palace unless accompanied by a brilliant company of cavalry and foot soldiers preceded by an armed corps of elephants and camels and followed by a large body of horse. At the time when I passed through Surat, the Nawab was a highly respected Persian but he was much given to hunting leopards, a weakness he paid for with his governorship. For when it was reported that in going out on the chase, he was neglecting his duty and was never present in the city as was expected of him, the Emperor relieved him of his charge and sent another governor.

Whenever a letter is expected from the Emperor the Nawab goes out from the city, awaits it arrival, receives it from the messengers and puts it on his head, and without opening it proceeds to his palace and reads it there. The great Mughal at Surat has a Moor whose duty is to spy on the Nawab and the ministers in political as well as in other matters, who keeps him informed of his doings, at times even to the minutest details such as among Christians as well as among the Moors themselves would be regarded as trifles.

In ancient days there was in Surat a house of the Fathers of the Society of Jesus, who had enough work in this mission and city. For besides the Portuguese and their slaves who had fled or been expelled from our territories, there are so many Christians here of the East and of the West, that even if there be a hundred religions, all of them would be fully occupied with them, administering sacraments to the Catholics, converting the heretics, and undeceiving the schismatics. The Society abandoned this mission, because every time the Mughals demanded satisfaction they would take the Fathers prisoner, compelling the viceroys to accede to their demand for fear of imperilling the life or liberty of the prisoners. Their place is now taken in Surat by two bearded French Capuchins sent by the Sacred Congregation of the Propaganda Fide who labour there much in the service of God, and have their chapel in their house, in which the Catholics hear mass on Sundays and holidays.

I saw at Surat among the gentoo Banyas a counterfeit of our religious orders, whom the devil makes them mimick so that he may take more source for himself to hell. I refer to the dervishes who live in a community in such poverty that not even the Order of St. Francis can equal it. They sleep on the ground with no other bed than the hard earth. They eat only rice with butter, and take no meat or fish all their lives. They wear a coarse saffron cloth, which covers only a part of their body. They go about barefooted and bare-headed with a staff in hand, always in two like the friars. They observe celibacy, live on alms, accompany the dead, and in this way live to a great age. Twice a day they go out to the river in community, each one with a pot full of water, which they call holy, and spend much time in praying in their manner and relating stories, to whomsoever wishes to hear them. They are governed by provincials and other local superiors.

But these religious men are not so strict as the *yogis*. The ancient call them gymnosophists. I would with greater propriety call them martyrs to the demon, or rather living demons. They go from place to place like the gypsies, some in torn and patched clothes, others without any clothes at all, others still with only a piece of cloth to cover their shame, leaving the rest of the body bare. And although it would appear that they cover a part of their body for shame, they have in fact very little of it, and in all human matters they obey nature wherever they are so disposed, and are not ashamed to be seen, saying with the cynics that nature can do nothing shameful. They go about with ashes smeared all over from head to foot including the eyes and mouth. These ashes are of cow-dung. The cow also gives them water with which they wash themselves. They have neither house nor bed. They sleep in the open on the bare earth. Not only do they despise luxury and all delicacies in eating and dress, but they lead penitential lives of such surprising rigour as to move one to pity. For some go about naked with heavy iron chains round their neck and body like hairshirts. Others bury themselves alive by the roadside, leaving only an air-hole, through which may be passed a piece of reed for directing into their mouth some *conjee* or rice-water. Others fall into a trance after mounting columns or wooden pillars, from which they do not descend save after death. Others still on days of great feasts in their temples hang themselves from poles by pointed hooks which are made to pass through their naked ribs, and remain suspended in the air singing in joy hymns to their gods. One of the *yogis* I saw at Surat had been holding his arms aloft and had not lowered them for ten years. The nerves and the joints had become so stiff that even if he had wished it would not have been possible for him to bring them down. His hands had their fingers clenched as in dealing a blow. His nails had grown so long that it turned round the hands they could serve as chords for tying them. The hair of the head covered part of the visage and all that was exposed. I saw another *yogi* with only one hand raised, another always in standing position whether by day or night, the only rest he took was when he caught a string, the ends of which had been tied to two windows, and balanced himself from side to side. Others went about charged with conches and rama beads about their neck. I was curious to go and see how these *yogis* with the upraised arms ate and slept, and I saw that certain boys of their company fed them; and when it was night the Banyas brought to them many sacks of cow-dung (cakes) with which they lit a fire and sitting round it they passed the night.

The credit of these *yogis* among the gentoos is very high. These gentoos think that they are the greatest saints on earth, who are doing penance for all the sins of mankind, and control the wrath of God with those hands lifted up to heaven. However, great may be the evils they see them commit, they take everything in good part, and if anyone harms them he is ex-communicated and loses both body and soul. The *yogi* carries a trumpet, which he sounds when he approaches a hamlet so that it may be known that the *yogi* is there, and that they may bring him food. If by any chance which is indeed very rare, *a yogi* is offended with people for failing to provide him with his needs he puts them under a curse, then forthwith all of them go in a procession taking with them whatever they have in the house in order to ask pardon of the *yogi* so that he may revoke his sentence which they think is already being executed on them. The *yogis* are more feared than respected, because to avenge a wrong done to any of their number, two or three thousand of them will collect together and stand in defence of the honour of their order. When they thus foregather, they elect a chief whom they obey just as the gypsies do in electing a count. The chief is generally of the highest lineage, since there is no dearth of such in their order. Indeed there are few gentoo countries in which there are no princely *yogis*, a fact which enables many to live free from danger from their brothers, and even to seize the reins of government from them with the help of their comrades. Not to speak of other instances, Bahadur Khan, the third son of Mudafar (Muzafar), king of Cambay was at first a *faquir* who usurped the kingdom from his brothers Muhammad and Latiff Khan. Again the present Grand Mughal, who today rules over more kingdoms than any other monarch in the world, became king from a *faquir* or *yogi* (the Moors call their *yogis* by the name of *faquir)*, and he secured his throne by putting to death a father and his three elder brothers.

All these *yogis* are very great sorcerers, and pretend to know medicine though in truth they are only herbalists. They make what is known as the cobra stone which is the best anti-venom for the bite of any poisonous animal. Many miracles are worked every day in India where the cobra is the most deadly and kills in a matter of hours. But whoever has the cobra stone saves himself by placing it on the wound; the stone at once adheres to the wound, and drops only after it has sucked all the poison off. The stone is cleared of this poison by immersion in milk. The *yogis* also bring some other green stones for which they claim the same properties as the cobra stone when put in the mouth. But I am not aware if this is proved by experience. These sciences which the ancient writers appreciated so much in the *yogis,* calling them on this account gymnosophists or naked philosophers, are to be found only in those of them, who having learned and practised them in the universities of Europe, entered the kingdoms of Madura and Mysore in the interior of India. Here they dress themselves as honest *yogis* to have easier access to, and be held in higher esteem by the natives, and they use their leaning in converting them to the faith of our Lord Jesus Christ, thus becoming gymnosophists of the soul.

The Society counts many such philosophers in these kingdoms.

17

Notes on Balasore and the English in the First Half of the Seventeenth Century

Jagadish Narayan Sarkar

BALASORE GREW to prominence as a manufacturing and commercial centre and as a seaport from the thirties of the seventeenth century. The destruction of the Portuguese Settlement of Hugli in 1632 attracted the Dutch and the English to open trade northwards. At the same time the growing scarcity of piece-goods at Masulipatam on account of the famous and widespread Gujarat famine of 1630–31 necessitated opening of new centres of trade and the advance of the English from the East Coast up the Bay of Bengal. Ralph Cartwright, the leader of the expedition sent by John Norris, English Agent at Masulipatam, was granted freedom of trade in May 1633 by the Mughal Governor of Orissa, Agha Muhammad Zaman of Tehran. Equipped with a 'parwana to trade free of all customs or duties, and to build houses or ships', the English merchants, Cartwright and Thomas Colley, returned from Cuttack to Hariharpur and started building a factory there (May, 1633). Leaving Colley in charge of it, Cartwright went to Balasore (June 16) and established a factory there also, at the invitation of Mir Qasim, the Governor of the district.[1] Like the English the Danes also wanted to establish factories at Balasore, in order to escape from the oppressions of the Portuguese.[2]

The importance of Balasore grew as a result of the expulsion of the Portuguese from Hijili by the Mughals in 1636 and the consequent decay of trade at Pipli and other neighbouring places. The silting up of the river Alanka and the Patua reduced the advantages of Harishpur harbour in comparison with the Road of Balasore. It also increased the difficulties of transporting down to the sea cotton manufactures of Hariharpur which could be brought to Balasore on land without much difficulty.[3]

In spite of these advantages of Balasore, the results of the efforts of the English there during the first decade were not very encouraging. Besides the opposition of the Portuguese there were other adverse forces working against the English and contributing to the decay of their settlements in Orissa, *viz.,*

* 14th Session at Jaipur, 1951.

the bad climate of the locality, the ravages of the Arrakanese pirates and worse still the opposition of the Dutch. The English also had their own internal weaknesses, namely, lack of funds and want of active servants, which naturally hampered their trade in these parts. There was even some talk of giving up Balasore. But this was opposed by Francis Day who, even during his short experience there (Aug. 13–Nov. 3, 1642) was convinced that Balasore (with adjacent places) should never be given up.[4]

Manufactures and Trade of
Balasore and Adjacent Places

Balasore was an emporium of cotton yarn, cotton and *tassar* manufactures of the interior hinterland and surrounding places. Most prominent among the centres, arranged in order of quality of goods manufactured, were Suro (Soro),[5] Harrapore (Hariharpur)[6] and Mohunpore (Mohunpur),[7] all specialising in the manufacture of *Sannoes*. Clavell writes in his account of Balasore that the weavers of Suro lived in the 'skirts of Balasore'. Sir Richard Carnac Temple, the editor of the *Diaries of Streynsham Master*, expresses doubt on this, saying that Suro can hardly be called outskirts of Balasore.[8] But does not Clavell's account imply that there was mobility of artisans and the weavers of Suro also arranged for disposal of their goods at Balasore by having a colony of theirs in the suburbs of that town?

Hariharpur was an important centre of manufacture of *Sannoes* and *Cassaes (Khasa)* which could be easily transported on land to Balasore.[9]

Again Balasore was near the country of the Raja of Tillbrichrumbung (Tribikrambhanj, *i.e.*, Mayurbhanj) where, as Walter Clavell wrote in 1676, 'the best quality and the largest quantity of Tester (*tassar*) or herba' was procurable. Further, '*Ginghams, Herba Tajfatyas, Herba Lungees (lungi* or loin-cloth) and other sorts of *Herba* goods,' manufactured in neighbouring places could be easily brought there. Another natural advantage of Balasore was that the waters of Casharry (Kasiari in Midnapur district) within two days' journey from Balasore, could be used to give 'the most lasting dye' to the textile manufactures of the neighbourhood.[10]

The following varieties of cheap, but well-made cotton manufactures were available at Balasore. In 1644 the Surat authorities wrote to the Company that they had asked the Balasore factors to invest money in 'Ginghams, *Sannoes, Cossaes,* and *Hummanees* proper for England, intended to be sent unto you as a testimony of what cheap and well-made cloth those parts afford.'[11]

1. *Sanas* or *Sanahs,* 'a kind of fine white cotton goods' (Sanu).[12]
   Luiller says 'Balasore is a place celebrated for trade in fine while calicoes called *Sanas*'[13] Sir Richard Carnac Temple thought that the *Sanah* of the seventeenth century 'exists as *Salu,* a cheap, fine cloth, generally red,

in common use in Bengal'.[14] But this seems improbable as the one is white and the other red. Can *Sana* be *Sahan* of Pelsacrt?

2. *Ginghams*, an Indian cotton cloth. The term, probably of Indo-European origin, denoted ' stuff made of cotton yarn dyed before being woven'.[15] The Orissan variety of *gingham* was superior to the Bengal variety available at Hugli, as Bridgman sending a bale of the latter to the Company in 1650 did not recommend it.[16]

3. *Orammalls*, or *Rumal*, handkerchief.[17]

4. *Cossaes* or *Khassa*[18]—a fine, thin cloth.

5. *Mulmull* or (*Malrnal*),[19] a kind of muslin.

6. *Humhum* (*hammam*),[20] a thick stout cloth used for wrappers.

7. Gurras.

8. *Neelaes* (or *Nillaes, Nillees*) or *Nila*: a kind of blue cloth.

Of the *Miscellaneous* goods produced in Orissa, may be mentioned: Sticklack (lac in a crude form),[21] *Turmerick*,[22] *Saltpetre*,[23] and *Rice*.[24]

Internal and Coastal Trade

Orissa had trade relations with Bengal and Golkonda:

(a) There was regular supply of Orissan cloth goods from Balasore to Patna in the seventeenth century. In the thirties of that century Peter Mundy noted that the following varieties of piece-goods of Orissa were available at Patna in Bihar.

　(i) *Cassaes* (*Khasa*), a fine and thin cloth, thicker than the Sonargaon variety: Size 16, 17, 18 coveds long and 1 broad.

　(ii) *Ambarees* (*Ambari, amari*, a turban, the canopy of an elephant howda) and *Chareconnaes*,(*Charkhana*, chequered muslin), linen striped with white silk; 16 coveds long and 1 broad.

　(iii) *Hamaones* (*hammam*), a thick stout cloth used for wrappers, linen, 11 coveds long, 1¼ broad.[25] Forty years later Thomas Bowrey observed that the various cotton manufactures of Balasore like *Sanas, Ginghams, Orammalls*, and cotton yarn and other goods were sent to Patna.[26]

Balasore also sent to Patna articles imported by the English, like broadcloth and lead, which could not be disposed of there.

(b) The close connection between Balasore and Hugli necessitated constant coastal trade between the two places.

About 1650 the following articles came from Hugli to Balasore, as we know from the letter of James Bridgman (abroad the *Lioness*) to the Company (Dec. 15, 1650): raw silk, saltpetre, sugar, dry ginger. Hugli could also supply bees-wax, long pepper, civet, rice, butter, oil and wheat, "all at about half the price of other places."[27]

(c) Balasore had trade relations with Dacca also.[28]

(d) In March, 1634 the *Thomas* (purchased from the Governor of Balasore) sailed towards Masulipatam filled with sugar, rice and other provisions.

In March 1638 (?) the Masulipatam factors Thomas Clark and Richard Hudson advised John Yard of Balasore that freight goods belonging to Mirza Taqi, *Dabir* of Golkonda, should be sent there.[29]

Foreign Trade of Balasore

(a) The foreign trade of Orissa, as conducted through Balasore, was not insignificant. She traded with Europe and Persia.

The commodities imported by the English into Orissa, Bengal and Patna, through Balasore, were (i) broad-cloth of various colours, (ii) scarlet, (iii) rials of eight, (iv) copper, (v) quicksilver, (vi) lead, (vii) vermilion, (viii) coral, (ix) glasses, (x) knives, (xi) brimstone. All these articles were not, however, in demand in Orissa. Some of them were transported to Bengal (including Patna), *e.g.*, broad-cloth and lead.[30]

The articles of (Bengal and) Orissa exported from Balasore were either (i) local products and cotton manufactures of Balasore and neighbouring centres in Orissa[31] or (ii) goods procured from Bengal (including Hugli and Patna).[32]

The general practice of shipment to England was that cotton goods and cotton yarn from Hugli and Balasore were embaled in factories; and according to the E.I.C.'s order, the various articles were loaded on the English ships coming yearly and anchoring in Balasore Road. From there these used to sail in November or finally laden and prepared there set out on the voyage to England about the end of January.[33]

(b) *Persian trade:* There was an active trade between Bengal (and Orissa) and Persia through Balasore. The English E.I. Company's factors used to utilise the ocean going ships coming from England during their enforced idleness on voyages to and from Persia, carrying articles of Indian merchants in return for freight and investing the proceeds in goods suitable for Persia.

In 1642–43 the English factors of Balasore sold or bartered their glasses, knives, lead, broad-cloth, etc., for sugar 'gurras' *Sannoes*, *Cassaes*, iron and *ginghams*, all except the last being intended for Persia.[34]

In 1644 the Surat factors sent to the Balasore factors one chest of rials with orders to provide for Persia 150 bales of sugar, 10 or 12 bales of gurras, and the same quantity of coarse *Sannoes*.[35]

The Dutch also had trade relations with Persia. In April, 1653, two Dutch ships from Balasore left Surat for Basra and Gombroon.[36]

Various factors influenced the nature of E.I.C.'s trade at Balasore:

(i) The first problem was that of *finance*. As elsewhere, the English merchants had to solve the problem of provision of purchasing power in the markets of Balasore and its adjacent places. They were not supplied regularly with funds by the authorities at Surat or Fort St. George, and even when money was sent it was not sufficient. Local borrowing in the Orissan markets was expensive, the rate of interest being high. The factors had to procure articles for the Europe as well as Persia investment, by sale or barter of the goods imported, as in 1642–43.

On account of lack of funds, timely purchase of necessary goods in advance of the shipping season could not be made at the cheapest markets, and the factors could not deal directly with the producers and weavers but had to contract with the town merchants. The Company suffered financial loss as a result of this arrangement.

Hence, the English factors concerned urged on the Company, the overmastering need of supply of funds, sufficient in amount and well in advance of the shipping season, for reasons of economy and early purchases. In November 1642 Francis Day suggested to the Company that nothing could be done to improve the prospects of trade at Balasore without doubling the supply of funds.[37] In 1650 James Bridgman (aboard the *Lioness*) explained to the Company (Dec. 15) that the prospects of trade at Balasore depended on sufficient stock of funds.

(ii) Second, Balasore suffered from want of efficient, hardworking and honest personnel. The English merchants 'preferred their own interests to those of the Company'. Many of them were engaged in private trade of their own. In 1663 Colley at Hariharpur deplored that 'the falsity and desaytfulness' of their 'new employed servants was such that they did not dare to trust them even for 10 rupees.' Francis Day suggested (Nov. 1642) the necessity of having two or three active servants.

(iii) Third, the system of contracting was another problem. Down to the seventies of the seventeenth century the English factors in Balasore, owing to difficulty in disposing of imported articles like broad-cloth, lead and to lack of funds, could not deal directly with the producers in securing articles for their investment, but contracted with the town merchants. From Clavell's account of 1676 we learn that on the arrival of the ships from England, the factors used to give the merchants half in money and half in goods and the latter contracted with them to supply the local products in October according to agreed musters or samples. The factors could 'make such abatements' as they considered reasonable. But generally the goods were supplied too late to allow the abatements to be made and the accounts to be adjusted before the departure of the ships. Hence the articles were invoiced home at the contracted price and 'the merchants were credited at the adjustment of accounts for the price concluded on and the difference carried to profit and loss.' The Company admitted that this system was causing loss, as all the white cloth procured at Balasore was 25% or 30% dearer than that at the coast. Clavell, therefore, suggested that:

(a) Direct dealing with the producers would be more advantageous than the system of contracting with merchants. The Company could send its own servants to Mucktapore,[38] Harrapore,[39] Mohunpore,[40] to make ready purchases of local manufactures and to Danton[41] and Jaleshwar[42] for the manufactures of *Oremara*[43] and *Kasiari,*[44]

(b) Balasore, being made a distinct factory, would have more leisure now to attend to such business. So an experiment should be made by advancing money to weavers of Suro for *Sannoes.*

(iv) *Attitude of the Governor:* The prospects of trade greatly depended on the attitude of the Governor. About 1642, owing to the non-arrival of Danish ships, the Governor of Balasore demolished their factory and seized their goods. In 1647 the Danes tried to settle their long-standing grievances against the authorities by force. A Danish fleet of 5 ships captured a Moorish ship laden with 8 elephants. At the request of Governor Malik Beg, the English twice attempted to persuade the Danes to release the junk but in vain. The English were told that they would have to compensate the damage inflicted by their co-religionists.

The war between the Danes and the Mughals in Bengal hampered the prospects of trade of the English and the Dutch at Balasore. In 1647, the English factors, Hudson and his party, buying cotton goods and rice at Balasore, were at first well received.

The necessity of offering presents to the authorities as a means of strengthening the foundations of trade and securing concessions was pointed out by James Bridgman (in his letter to the Company., Dcc. 15, 1650) and by Captain Brookhaven to James Bridgman (Dcc. 14, 1650). The latter instructed the Balasore factors that they should keep on good terms with the Governor of Balasore and Hugli and with other friends of the English ..... and that when the Nabbab of Cuttack came to Balasore, he should be presented with some fine cloth to the value of about 10 pounds and a swordblade or two.[45]

Bridgman wrote to Company: 'Presents must be given occasionally to the Prince (i.e., Shah Shuja) and Governors of the towns; and so a few rarities of low price should be furnished for the purpose, such as globes, glasses, multiplying glasses, and four or five good substantial house clocks.'[46]

(v) *An armed Convoy.* For reasons of security and of checking piracy, Bridgman suggested to the Company. (Dec. 15, 1650) that "'a small vessel of 30 or 40 tonnes, with 6 or 8 guns, would be very useful for carrying goods to Balasore and convoying other vessels.'[47]

(vi) *Undesirable practices in business:* The English E.I. Company's trade in broad-cloth and lead resulted, as we know from Clavell's account of 1676, in some undesirable practices and corruption on the part of the Company's factors, the merchants and the Government Officers, (a) though there was no demand for broad-cloth in Balasore, the company continued to send large quantities of it ordering the factors to sell as much as possible of the manufactures of England. This obliged the latter to continue the system of barter, i.e., exchange broad-cloth for local products. The merchants who took it from the English, used to sell it at 'underrates' either to Mughal officers at Cuttack, the capital of Orissa or to the armies that came to Cuttack at the time of change of a Governor in whose train there were merchants moving under protection with their goods, buying and selling without paying customs, (b) The transport of lead to 'the Rajaes countries' (?) Northern Circars and Orissa chiefships) was forbidden by the Governors, on the pretext that the rajas must not be supplied with articles of warfare, but really to make an illegal gain of 0/8/0 on every maund of lead so transported with connivance, (c) The merchants took recourse to another trick in disposing of lead and broad-cloth — 'to allow the king's officers so much per cent for taking of their goods on the king's account, and taking cowries in lieu thereof.' The English factors were also prepared to follow this trick, but the officers were afraid to have such dealings with them lest they might disclose them in case of any difference, whereas there was no such danger from the Hindu natives.[48]

Trade Privileges of the English
in Balasore Port

The commercial privileges of the English at Balasore were questioned about 1670 and the Mughal Customs Officers wanted to open and search the bales of goods of the English either out of motive of illegal gain or because they suspected some under hand dealings on the part of the English. So the latter secured 'an attestation given by the customers and brokers of Balasore concerning the English privileges in the import and export of their goods and disposing of them in that port.'

Private Trade at Balasore

The prosecution of private trade by the factors of European companies was a characteristic feature of commercial life in those days. Its volume was great, involving considerable loss to the companies concerned and immense profit to the private traders. Balasore was no exception to this practice.

In 1642 Francis Day agreed to carry freight goods and passengers to Masulipatam and Persia against the advice of Trumball at the following rates:

Balasore	Masulipatam : 16 passengers	Rs. 15/-per head
Balasore	Persia : 35 passengers	Rs. 40/- per head
76 bales of cloth at a freight of		Rs.15/-a md. (of 64 lb.)
335 bales of Sugar at a freight of		Rs. 7/-a md. (of 128 lb.)

They also embarked 118 bales of calicoes (at a freight of Rs. 15/- a maund.) possibly on joint account of Messrs. Day, Pcniston, Winter and Greenwill and only 700 bales of sugar and 34 of calicoes for the Company. Day arranged to load 'provisions' for the Persians in hampers, bales, chests and fardles, for which no freight was paid to the Company, but he himself received many gifts from them and 60 bales of the Company's cinnamon had to be left behind. Only Rs. 6,345/- was credited to the Company's account out of the freight money of Rs. 17,854/-.[49]

There were some Englishmen residing at Balasore who were engaged in private contraband trade. Two small ships belonging to Richard Hastings (Hastingh of Dutch records), a pilot of Bengal Junk and resident at Balasore, were seized near Nagapatam because they were carrying ammunition to Jafnapatam during the siege of Ceylon.[50]

Currency at Balasore

The nature of E.I. Company's trade at Balasore was largely determined by the prevailing currency. Orissa being a poor country, money was scarce, and as Abul Fazl informs us 'Money transactions are in *Kauris* which is a small white shell generally divided down the middle: it is found in the sea shore.'[51] John Marshall of the seventeenth century, giving further details, observes that these 'are little shell(s) which in England are called current shells (shell currency). They are taken at the Maldive Islands from the Rock and buried until all their fish is gone out of them and then sold. Some are sent for England to the Company, to be sent to Guiney, where they are of great value.'[52]

In the first half of the seventeenth century also cowries formed the usual means of exchange, the 'common pay' as Clavell wrote. Under the circumstances trade was at first carried on by the English factors by barter, i.e., exchange of goods; subsequently in the interloping period, i.e., from 1630 onwards, owing to keen competition among the factors of different interloping companies, trade was carried on partly by barter and partly by money.[53] By the middle of the seventeenth century the trade of Balasore came to be carried on in money. Capt. Brookhaven instructed the coast factors (Dec. 14, 1650) that 'the trade of Balasore being now carried on in rupees morees", they must continue their operations "in the same specie.'[54]

The establishment of a mint by the English at Balasore (Nov. 1658) resulted in raising the price of silver. The factors observed: 'This doth somewhat advance the price of silver in reference to sale: so that now a piece of eight will yield (if it be weighty rupees Chellena (*Chalani*, current) two and one anna.' When in 1660 the Governor of Balasore threatened to close the mint and prevent coining money by the English, the Company advised its factors (in their letter of 22 Feb. received in August 1660) that they might complain to the Prince (i.e., Shah Shuja) if complaint was of any avail, otherwise they must submit.[55]

John Marshall (*c.* 1670) found that the currency at Balasore consisted of (i) silver rupees, (ii) ana, 16 anas being equal to a rupee, but it was 'rare' (i.e., very scarce), (iii) cowries (*kauri*), forming 'small money'. Probably the perennial scarcity of coins accounted for the higher rate of exchange in Balasore as compared to other places. The rupee was 'valued here in the Company's books at 2s. 6d. per piece, but in no other place valued at more than 2s. 3d.' Eighty cowries always constituted a *pond* (*pan*) but the value of cowries in relation to rupees varied according to the availability or scarcity of the former (36 to 40 to a rupee).[56]

Balasore as Seaport

The economic importance of Balasore in the seventeenth century was due not only to its being (i) a source of supply of cotton manufactures which could be exported abroad, especially to Europe and Persia, (ii) a market for sale of goods imported from Europe, but also to its being invaluable as a seaport. The Dutch writer Schouten spoke well of it as a harbour.[57]

So long as the English had no settlement or factory in Bengal, their ships had to depend on Balasore as a port. It had, of course, several disadvantages. 'Sea Ports', observes Thomas Bowrey, 'this Kingdom affordeth only one, and that none to be admired, affording not water enough for a ship of 200 tunns in burden to goe into the river, and to ride out is very unnecessary and dangerous by reason, it is not better than a very very wild open bay that extendeth itselfe from Point Conjaguaree to Palmeris.'[58]

Thus big ocean-going ships could not sail up to Balasore town and had to halt at the Balasore Road, 2½ leagues from the shore. From there men and cargos intended for Orissa were transported in 'purgoes' and sloops. Further the bar of Balasore at 1 mile from the shore was 'a very dangerous place to sail over, being very narrow, and being very great seas.'[59]

Even after the subsequent establishment of English factory at Hugli and development of Hugli and Cassimbazar as sources of supply of merchandise of E.I.C.'s trade, Balasore retained its importance as a sea port. Thus in the seventies of the seventeenth century, Balasore constituted one of the three "most important English settlements in the Bay,"—Hugli and Cassimbazar for making sales and investments, and Balasore for loading and unloading the 'Europe' ships for Bengal (and Orissa).[60] Ocean-going ships could not, with safety, go up the Ganges to Hugli, on account of difficulties of navigation and had necessarily to halt at Balasore Road, and articles were transhipped to Hugli on small sloops and pinnaces. But this naturally proved to be very expensive. It was in 1660 that experimental trips up the river Hugli by ocean-going vessels were sanctioned by the English E.I. Company.

Balasore as Ship-building and Repairing Centre

In the seventeenth century Balasore was an important ship-building and repairing centre with suitable dockyards, which seemed to have developed further after the advent of the English. In the thirties the English factor Bruton described it as 'Bollasorye', a sea-town where shipping was built.[61] In 1634 the Governor of Balasore sold a small unfinished ship of his of about 100 tonnes to the E.I. Company's servants. The latter completed her construction as quickly as possible, and christened her the *Thomas*.[62] In 1638 the Masulipatam factors (Thomas Clerk and Richard Hudson) instructed Thomas Godfrey, Master of the *Coaster*, to proceed to Balasore for re-fitting the ship. In 1650–51 Captain Durson repaired his damaged *Loyalty* here. But she was totally wrecked by striking a second time in the Balasore bar. So he built a ship of 200 tons 'in partnership with a Moor of Balasore.'[63]

Notes

1. Wilson, *Early Annals on the English in Bengal*, vol. 1, chs. 1, 2, 3, p. 13n; *EFI, 1630–33*, XXXI, 307–8. Moreland, *Form Akbar to Aurangzeb*, p. 47.
2. *DSM*, II, p. 84.
3. Clavell's 'Account of the Trade of Balasore' in *Dairies of Sireynsham Master*, II, p. 84.
4. Wilson, op. cit., pp. 18–21; *EFI*.

5. Suro or Soro (Sohroh) in Balasore district (Lat. 16'21°, Long. 49'86°, is now a station on B.N. Rly., mid-way between Balasore and Bhadrak, 20 miles from Balasore. In the seventeenth century it was on the frontier of Bhadrak (Sarkar, *Studies in Mughal India*, pp. 228, 229; *Muraqaat-i-Hassan*, pp 41–59).

6. Harrapore (Hariharpur) near modem Jagatsimhapur, a town in the Mahanadi delta, about halfway between Cuttack and Harispur Gar, a port at which the English landed.

7. Probably Mohanpur in Midnapurdt. (Lat. 21'50°Long. 24'87°)

8. *DSM*, II, p.86.

9. Ibid., p. 84. The economic importance of Hariharpur depended not only on its being a centre of supply of cloth to the English but also on the fact that it was a market for sale of some articles brought by the English. The Hariharpur factory was probably withdrawn on Aug. 31, 1612, as its accounts closed on that date, *(EFI, 1612–45,* p. 126).

10. *DSM*, II, pp. 84–85. Casharry or Kasiari is in Midnapur dt. (Lat. 20'8°, Long. 87'16°).

11. *EFI, 1642–45*, p.207.

12. Wilson, I, Index, *EFI, 1655–60*, p. 188n.

13. Voyage au Golfe de Bengale, quoted in Prevost, *Histoire des Voyages*, XIII, p. 80, in Bowrey, p. 231n.

14. Bowrey, p. 231n.

15. *Hobson-Jobson*; Bowrey, op. cit.

16. *EFI, 1646–50*, pp. 337–8.

17. Ibid., Bowrey, op. cit., p. l33n.

18. Ibid., p. 279.

19. Ibid., pp. 237, 279.

20. Ibid.

21. *DSM*, II, p.70.

22. Ibid.

23. Ibid., p.279; *EFI, 1651-55*, pp.47,95,271.

24. Netlam in charge of Balasore was joined by Richard Hudson, sent to 'Bengalah' in July 1647 in the *Farewell* with 6000 rials of eight to buy cotton goods and rice. *EFI, 1646–50*, XXIX, p. 166.

25. Mundy, pp. 154–5.

26. Bowrey, pp. 231–2.

27. *EFI; DSM*, II, pp. 67–8.

28. *DSM*, II, pp. 67–8.

29. *EFI, 1634–6*, p. 43; *1637-42*, pp. 65, 66.

30. Bowrey, pp. 231–2; *EFI, 1634–36*, p. 42; *1642–45*, p. 65; *1646–50*, pp. 337–8.

31. Surat letter of 1644.

32. Letter of Capt. Brookhaven, Dec. 15, 1650.

33. Bowrey, pp. 231–2.

34. *EFI, 1642–45*, p. 65.

35. Ibid., p. 207.

36. *EFI, 1651–54*, p. 183.

37. *EFI, 1642–46*, pp. 65–66, cf. the following:

"Calicoes cannot be obtained at the Coast good and cheap unless funds are forthcoming to buy them before the ship arrives.... As for purchasing coloured *ginghams* in Bengal the only person available there is one William Netlam... but now unfit to make transactions. The Coast should be supplied yearly with £20,000 for investment for these parts. (Letter to Co., Jan 11, 1650; *EFI, 1646–50*)

38. Mucktapore is probably Matkadpur in Midnapur.

39. Hariharpur.

40. Probably Mohunpur in Midnapur dt. (Lat. 21'50°, Long, 29'37°).

41. Danton (Lat. 21'58° Long. 20'87°) in Midnapur dt. on the main road between Balasore and Midnapur. Here *'oftaes'* (*aftaba*, brasswares) and *'Chellamaches'* (Chilamchi basins) and other brasswares were manufactured. (*JM1*, pp. 63, 85n).

42. *Jellasore* (Jaleshwar), S.W. of Danton in Balasore dt. (Lat 21'44° Long. 15'87°).

43. *Oremara*, either Ulmara in Midnapur dt. or Urmullah in Balasore dt.

44. *Cashary* or *Kasiari*.

45. Bowrey, pp.182–190; *DSM*, I, pp. 318; *EFI, 1642–5*, p. 156; *1646–50*, pp. 174–75. The war between the Danes and Bengal continued for nearly 30 years. After the peace of 1674 the Danes established a settlement at Serampur on the Hugli.

46. Ibid., pp. 337–38.

47. *EFI, 1646–50*.

48. *DSM*, II, pp.85–86.

49. *EFI, 1642–45*, p.72 (details of the disposal of goods in Persia on p. 73).

50. *EFI, 1655–60*, P. 177n.

51. *Ain* (Jarrett and Sarkar), II, 138, see 'Revenue Regulations of Aurangzeb', in *Studies in Mughal India*.

52. *JMl*, p. 415–6, 419.

53. Vide Clavell's 'Account of Balasore': The E.I.C. found a formidable rival in the ships sent out by Sir William Courteen. *DSM*, II, p. 85.

54. *EFI, 1646–60*, pp. 333–4. 'Yule was puzzled by this term and could only suggest that a round rupee was meant, as distinguished from a square. This seems unlikely'. Foster in ibid., n.

55. *EFI, 1650–60*, pp. 192, 407–8.

56. *JMI*, op. cit. This does not wholly agree with the calculation given by Abul Fazl. "Four *Kauries* make a *ganda*, five *gandas a budi*, four *budis a pan*, sixteen or according to some twenty pans a *Khawan (Kahan)* and ten *Kahans* a rupee." *Ain*, II, 138-39. This makes 1 *Pan* equal to 80 *Kauries*, but 12,800 or 16,000 *Kauries* equal to a rupee.

57. Schouten, II, pp. l59f, quoted in Bowrey, 152n.

58. Bowrey, p. 152. See also Alexander Hamilton, I, p. 397.

59. *JMI*, p. 61; *DSM*, II, p. 67; I, p. 300.

60. Hedge, II, p. 236; Wilson, I, pp. 53, 56.

61. Wilson I, pp. 9, 12.

62. *EFI, 1634–6*, p. 43.

63. *EFI, 1651–54*, pp. 47, 92, 100.

18

Commercial Activities of the Mughal Emperors During the Seventeenth Century

Satish Chandra

THE COMMERCIAL activities of the Mughal emperors and their nobility has not yet received the attention it deserves from the students of medieval Indian history. It has sometimes been assumed that the interests of the Mughal emperors and the nobles in trade, particularly foreign trade, were largely confined to the procuring of rare and costly articles, and to the ensuring of a regular supply of Arab and Iraqi horses for their armed forces and for purposes of display. Already in the time of Akbar, the importance of trade, and the possibilities of making profit in commercial ventures and speculations, and thus supplementing the income from the *jagirs* had been realised by some of the more far-sighted observers. Thus, Abul Fazl remarks: 'When an appropriate means of maintenance is secured, it is a requisite condition of economy to husband a portion of one's means, provided that the household is not thereby straightened. The proper control of an estate is conditional on the expenditure being less than the income; it is permitted to indulge little in commercial speculation and engage in remunerative undertakings, reserving a part in goods and wares, and somewhat invested in the speculation of others, and yet a portion in lands and immovable estates, and a share may be entrusted to borrowers of credit.' Abul Fazl further says, 'Let such a one be frank in his commercial dealings and give no place in his heart to self-reproach.'[1]

The determination of the extent to which commercial profit formed a supplementary source of income for the ruling sections in the Mughal empire during the seventeenth century is important not only for a fuller understanding of the social and economic history of the period: the problem has to be studied as a background to the crisis of the Mughal Empire in the second half of the seventeenth century. This crisis, which had many aspects, in the economic sphere took the shape of an absolute shortage of lands available for assigning

*21st Session at Trivandrum, 1958.

as *jagirs* to the nobles, and of a wide divergence in the real and the paper income of the *jagirs*. The extent to which this crisis induced the nobles to turn towards commercial activities, and was a factor in the renewed expansion of the Mughal Empire towards the south and in the clash with various sections such as the Rajputs, Marathas, Jats, etc., has to be determined on the basis of a concrete study. The present writer has been engaged in studying some of these aspects. The purpose of this paper is to call attention to the direct participation of the Mughal Emperors and members of the royal family in trade, particularly sea-borne trade, during the seventeenth century as one aspect of the commercial activities of the upper classes during this period.

From scattered references in the English records, it would appear that at the beginning of the seventeenth century, Jahangir, Nur Jahan, Prince Khurram and even the Queen-Mother owned ships which plied between Surat and the Red Sea ports. While Khurram was viceroy of Gujarat, his ships carried on an extensive trade with Mocha, carrying mostly broad-cloth and textiles, but not averse to carrying even tobacco when no broad-cloth was available. His ships also went to Masulipatam which was one of the principal ports of south India at this period and carried textiles and gum-lac to the Persian ports.[2] Another commodity in which the Prince traded during this period was indigo.[3] An example of his trade in textiles with the English might be quoted:

In 1621, the English factor at Cambay contracted with Khizr Khan and the Prince's broker for the supply of goods to Mocha amounting to one lakh of *mahmudis*, a fourth part of which was to be delivered at Baroda, and the rest at the Cambay ports. The goods apparently consisted of 'baftas and buckar' which consequently fell in short supply and the original contract could not be fulfilled.[4]

During the same period, Jahangir's junks plied between Mocha and Goga. In 1622, the English, with a view to putting pressure on the Mughal Emperor to open the Red Sea trade to them, seized a number of Indian ships returning from Mocha, including one of which 'the shipper and goods only belonged to the King, the Normall (Nur Mahal), Assafcon (Asaf Khan), Suffichan (Safi Khan), and other greatte men.'[5] Jahangir also seems to have invested money in the Cambay trade.[6]

The Queens also invested in trade and even had junks of their own. We are told that Jahangir's mother was 'a great adventurer', and that the seizure of her ship 'Remewe' (*Rahimi*) by the Portuguese in 1614 was one of the causes of Jahangir's war on the Portuguese settlements.[7] However, at about the same period we find Nur Jahan, and a number of Mughal nobles trading from the Portuguese Settlements of Daman and Diu.[8]

When Shah Jahan ascended the throne, he continued to take interest in overseas trade. His ships, the 'Fettee' (Fath), and the 'Shahe' (Shahi) traded to the Red Sea ports, while at least another went to Achin (Sumatra) in 1636.[9]

Official pressure was sometimes used to procure cargo for these ships from the merchants. Thus, in 1643, the Governor of Swally Marine prohibited merchants, under great penalties, from landing any vessel "until both the great junks belonging to this King are full." On occasions, the English were forced to convoy the King's ships, or to carry his goods on their ships.[10]

Another method adopted by Shah Jahan for augmenting his income was to create monopolies. Thus, according to the English factory at Agra, in 1633 a contract was made between the Emperor and one 'Munnodas Dunda' by which the latter was granted the sole right of buying all indigo grown in the kingdom, and in return was to pay at the end of three years eleven lakhs of rupees, or rupees two lakhs a year out of his profits, and rupees five lakhs as repayment of the loan which had been made to him from the royal treasury. It was also stipulated that if the indigo remained unsold, he was to be excused all payment to the King except the repayment of the loan. The English and the Dutch were apprehensive that this would result in a rise in the price of indigo; and hence entered into an agreement not to buy any indigo except at their own price. The result was that the monopoly failed and had to be wound up by the Emperor after about one year. It would appear that the Emperor was not to have been the only beneficiary from this monopoly. According to the advice received by the English, 'Manoardas' 'bore the name of the prime monopolist, yet Meir Jombolo (Mir Jumla), High Steward to the King, was principally engaged in the project.'[11]

Tavernier mentions another kind of royal monopoly. He says:

'All the waggons which come to Surat from Agra or other places in the Empire and return to Agra and Jahanabad are compelled to carry lime which come from Broach, and which, as soon as it is used, becomes as hard as marble. It is a great source of profit to the Emperor who sends it where he pleases.[12]

Another commodity which was frequently sought to be 'engrossed' or monopolised was saltpetre. As an ingredient of gun-powder, saltpetre was apparently regarded a strategic goods. Its export from Gujarat was forbidden by Shah Jahan in 1630, and this ban was later reiterated by Prince Aurangzeb as viceroy of Gujarat. Mandelslo says that foreigners were not allowed to export gun-powder, lead and saltpetre except with the governor's permission.[13] However, the English were able to export fairly large quantities from Surat, and later Patna which soon became the main centre of the saltpetre trade. The trade was a very profitable one, and the King, the Princes, and provincial governors often traded extensively in it.[14]

An interesting development in Shah Jahan's reign was the granting to traders, both European and Indian, of loans from the mint and the local treasury for their business. Thus, Muizz-ul-Mulk, the Mughal Governor of Surat, Broach and Cambay advanced to the English in 1637, Rupees 20 or

30,000 from the mint and the Governor's treasury, and this sum was forwarded by the English by exchange to Agra. In 1646, the English factors complained of shortage of money at Surat, for as soon as money was coined, the merchants at Surat paid it to the King's *diwan* in satisfaction of advances made by him.[15]

It is not clear if this was done with the Emperor's sanction—it is scarcely possible to imagine that it could have been otherwise—and what interest was charged on such loans.[16]

Princess Jahanara also had ships of her own, and carried on extensive commerce with the help of the Dutch and the English.[17]

As the governor of Thatta Prince Dara carried on an extensive trade with the Red Sea ports. In 1647, his agent, the Shahbandar of Thatta contracted to buy two new ships from the Portuguese on his behalf for the Red Sea trade.[18] Of interest is another statement that one of the Prince's ships came to Thatta direct from Congo, not touching Muscat at all.[19]

Emperor Aurangzeb owned a fleet of ships which plied mainly to the Red Sea ports. Some idea of the numbers and tonnage of Aurangzeb's shipping interests may be formed by the request made by the English factors in 1663, asking for ten or fifteen anchors for 'the supply of the King's junks'. The request for ten anchors for the King's ships was repeated a few years later.[20] Even if each ship carried two anchors, it would not be unreasonable to assume that the King's fleet numbered at least five ships.

As for the size of the royal ships, Moreland concluded that a 'large' ship or junk for sea-borne trade averaged less than 200 tonnes.[21] However, we learn that the Queen Mother's junk in 1613 was 11 or 1200 tonnes, while of the two ships belonging to the King at the Surat port in 1668, 'the least of them was upward of 600 tonnes.'[22] However, further evidence would be needed before some definite idea can be formed of the average size of the royal junks.

It would appear that during the reign of Aurangzeb, the practice of provincial governors seeking to monopolise the trade in their provinces became fairly common. As the governor of Lahore, Wazir Khan got a commission on everything that was bought or sold at Lahore.[23] In Bengal, Mir Jumla, and following him Shaista Khan attempted to monopolise the trade in all the important commodities.[24] Even princes of blood could not escape the lure of making easy profit in this manner. As the viceroy of Bengal and Bihar, Prince Azim-ush-Shan declared the entire import trade to be his monopoly, styling this the *Sauda-i-Khas-o-Am*. Aurangzeb wrote him a stinging reproof, and reduced his rank by 500 *sawar*.[25]

From the brief review above, it should be apparent that the Mughal Emperors and members of the royal family continuously participated in commercial activities, particularly in the sea-borne trade to the Red Sea ports, and also, to some extent, with ports to the south of Surat up to Achin, and ports on the east coast of Africa. The royal ships not only carried goods purchased with the Emperor's money, but also the goods of nobles and individual merchants. The King and members of his family also freighted their goods on the ships of individual nobles or merchants as well as on English, Portuguese and Danish ships. While the trade on behalf of the Emperor and the princes was sometimes carried on by local officials, there is reference to the activities of their own agents and merchants. There is some evidence of the participation of the Emperors and members of the royal family in internal trade, particularly by way of creating monopolies.

Thus, there was an apparent growth of commercial interests and commercial morality among the upper sections of society including the Mughal Emperor and members of the royal family during the seventeenth century. This feature did not come to an end with the collapse of the Mughal empire, but seems to have been in evidence as late as the close of the eighteenth century.[26]

Notes

1. *Ain-i-Akbari*, vol. II, tr. H.S. Jarrett, pp. 57–58. Cf. the earlier outlook represented by Barani in his *Fatawa-i-Jahandari*'... whenever plenty of profit is seen in regrating and selling at high prices and not much profit remains in other professions, people discard their own professions by an instinct of nature. Soldiers take to agriculture; cultivators, seeing plenty of profit in it, take to trade; regrators, owing to the influence of their wealth, extend their hand to high posts; shop-keepers try to become officers; men of noble birth become merchants, and transport-merchants desire to become *amirs* and *sar-i-khail* (Advice, IX).

2. *Letters Received by the East India Co.*, ed. W. Foster, vol.III, p. 270; *The English Factories in India*, ed. W.Foster, 1914, *1618–21*, pp. 92, 106, 113, 177, 240, 328; *1622–23*, p. 273 et seq.

   Sir Thomas Roe, writing from Ajmere, thought that the Prince's, opposition to the English trade with the Red Sea ports was due to the fact that 'Coronne himself... had a ship to send to the Red Sea and was willing to wink, yea, to encourage his ministers to molest and hinder the despatch of our fleet until his ship were clear'. (*Letters Received*, vol. IV, pp. 13- 14).

   The English subsequently realised that the Mughal opposition to their trade with the Red Sea ports was due to the general opposition of the Indian merchants who had already suffered heavily by the encroachment of the English on the trade to Achin, Bantam, etc., and hence depended almost exclusively upon the Red Sea Trade. (*English Factories, 1618-21, p.* xiii).

3. Thus, when Prince Shahjahan rebelled against his father, all his goods were seized, including his junks and his indigo which was 'sould by armfulls.' (*English Factories*, *1622– 23*, pp. 218,233).

4. Ibid., pp. 148,149,152,168. The approximate value of the *mahmudi was* 5/9 rupee.

5. Ibid., pp. 204, 264, 271, 272.

6. Thus, in 1662, Jahangir sent to Cambay two lakhs of rupees to be invested in the goods for the Red Sea, the proceeds of which were to be given to the poor at Mecca. (*English Factories 1622–23,*vp. *144, 171*).

7. *Letters Received, vol. II, 1613–15, p. 213.*

8. *English Factories, 1622–23.* p. 81 (Customs paid to Portuguese by Nur Jahan's junk).
   The English were indignant at the trade of the Mughal nobles with the Portuguese, and Thomas Roe from Agra advised seizing their goods, and 'show ourselves a little rough and busy,' so that they 'feared to freight in the Portugal and rather offer themselves to us.' *The Embassy of Sir Thomas Roe*, Hakluyt Society, 1899, p. 506).

9. *Factory Records, Surat*, vol. I, pp. 134, 526; *English Factories 1634–36*, p. 255.

10. *English Factories, 1641–45*, pp. 10, 90, 91, 96, 101, 253.

11. *English Factories, 1630–33*, pp. 324–28,1634–36, pp. 72, 138. The *Dagh Register* gives the price of the monopoly as 400,000 rupees. The text of the *farman* dissolving the monopoly is given in *Hague Transcripts*, Series i, X, no. 324.

12. Tavernier, *Travels in India*, tr. V. Ball, ed. W. Crooke, vol. I, p. 35.

13. Mandelslo, *The Voyages and Travels of the East Indies*, tr. J. Davics, p. 28; *English Factories, 1630–33*, p. 21, *1646–50*, pp. 34 et seq. See also J.N. Sarkar's article, 'Saltpetre Industry in the Seventeenth Century in India, etc.', in *IHQ*, 1937, pp. 319–50.

14. Thus, the royal official stored up 10,000 double maunds of refined saltpetre at Ahmedabad in 1665, evidently with the object of forcing up the price. Two years later, Prince Murad Bakhsh attempted to monopolise its sale in Gujarat. Shaista Khan as Governor of Bihar did the same (*English Factories, 1655–60*, pp. 121, 299, 300; *1661–64*, pp. 395–96, 402 et seq).

15. Ibid., *1637–41*, p. 193; *1646–50*, p. 72.

16. For interest on loans (*musa'idat*) to nobles in the time of Akbar, *see Ain*, Blochman, pp. 275–76.

17. *Dagh Register*, 1644–45, p. 256; *English Factories, 1641–45*, p. 148 (Junk built for her).

18. *Factory Records, Surat*, vol. C, ii A, pp. 53, 142, *English Factories, 1646–50*, pp. 72, 90, 119.

19. *English Factories, 1646–50*, p. 30.

20. Ibid., *1661–64*, p. 211; *1668-69*, pp. 11–13. A letter from the English factor in 1660 alludes to 'the new King Orang Zeebe intending to land two great juncks this year from Surat *with his owen money*; besides other merchants lode one more of his jouneks.' (Ibid., *1655–60*, p. 302; *1661–64*, p. 80, my emphasis).

21. Moreland, *India at the Death of Akbar*, pp. 231–32. For the size of the ton for tonnes in the seventeenth century see, ibid., pp. 310–12.

22. *Letters Received*, vol. II, p. 213; *English Factories, 1668–69*, pp. 11–13.

23. *Maasir-ul-Umara, Bib. Ind.* vol. Ill, p. 936- (*Chun dar Lahore har kharid-o- farokhte ki mi-shud aksar az sarkar-iu-bud zarhai bisyar andokht*).

24. For the commercial activities of Mir Jumla in Bengal, sec J.N.'Sarkar, *The Life of Mir Jumla*, pp. 216–18; for Shaista Khan's activities, see *English Factories, 1661–64*, pp. 395–96 et seq.

25. *Ragaim-i-Karaim*, MS. Aligarh University Lib.,*Riyaz-us-Salatin*, Persian text ed. by Maulvi Abdul Haq, pp. 243–44.

26. Thus, see *Calendar of Persian Correspondence*, vol X, nos. 706; 1659, 1914–15, pp. 440, 1272, 1056, et seq. See also Introduction pp. xxi, xxii.

19

Mints of the Mughal Empire
(A Study in Comparative Currency Output)

Aziza Hasan

IT PERHAPS needs no stressing that the students of the economic history of Mughal India are faced with the paucity of data on a number of crucial aspects. Thus, for example we have had hitherto no data on which a continuous price index could be constructed. Similarly, there are very few materials on the basis of which the relative scale of economic activity in various regions, or the relative volume of trade carried on by sea and overland could be worked out. (There is considerable evidence for coastal areas and overseas trade in European sources, it is true; but, then, hardly any, or very little for overland trade and inland areas.)

It was in view of this that the present writer ventured to submit at the previous session of this Congress that an analysis of Mughal silver coins preserved in the major collections might yield data of value and suggest certain new lines of enquiry. The basic facts that give point to a quantitative analysis of the coins are that (a) the Mughal coins were of standard weight and uniform purity, (that is to say, they were never debased and so had a fixed ratio with bullion); (b) they bear the year and the mint of the issue; and (c) the Mughal coinage was free, so that any change in the quantity of rupees issued in various years or at various places would reflect variations, over time or localities, of the supply of silver bullion.[1]

In my paper last year I attempted to establish, tentatively, a curve of the silver-currency output of the Mughal empire, by arranging year-wise all the coins in the major catalogues, and then to suggest the significance of the curve for the study of imports of bullion and price changes during the seventeenth century.[2]

In the present paper, the aim is to arrange the coins of each year mint-wise, and then to analyse the varying proportions in which each mint contributed to the total number from decade to decade.[3] This, it is hoped, will show broadly, which regions or mints were receiving and coining larger or smaller quantities

*29th Session at Patiala, 1967.

of bullion (in relative terms), and it is proposed to discuss what possible significance this inferential information can have for a study of silver influx and the pattern of inland and foreign commerce.

Before explaining the principles on which our tabulation has been organised, we may broadly indicate what factors might be reasonably had to influence the relative size of the output of each mint. To begin with, the mints which stood on or near the coast, or which were situated on the termini of overland caravan routes would, in a large measure, be coining bullion brought by foreign merchants or importers. This was not only because it would have cost more to the merchants to transport the bullion further inland, but also because internal trade of the imported bullion was not free. It appears from the reports of the English factors that the bullion imported was first entered in the custom house records, where the duty was paid, then it was handed over to the imperial mint for minting in the currency of the country; after these preliminaries were fulfilled, it could be exported.[4] Internal trade of bullion was further discouraged by the occasional insecurity on trade routes.[5] Since the internal trade of silver was slow and on a smaller scale,[6] the re-minting of the coins, first minted in the nearer mints would probably have constituted a larger part of the issues of inland mints. The imports of bullion, thus, would have affected the issues of the distant mints on a much smaller scale and only much later.

The size of the coinage issued from a particular mint would naturally have been determined to a great extent by the volumes of its commercial activities, that is by its own importance as a commercial centre. From its being administrative headquarters, a mint too might derive its importance, since money might be needed there for remittance or revenues and taxes, and the expenses of the grandees and officials. Indeed, the presence of the imperial court for some length of time might greatly expand commercial activities at a particular town,[7] with resultant impact on the output of its mint. Again administrative measures such as a shift in the collection from kind to cash, would have also played some part in enlarging the output of a mint or mints within a Suba, or region. Political instability also can not be ignored in analysing the fluctuations of a mint's output.

If such factors might have determined the size of the output of each mint, the output of a mint, if established, would help us to determine whether, and to what extent, such factors existed. It is with this in view, that I have tabulated the surviving Mughal coins (silver coins only), catalogued in the five major collections.[8] The coins have been assigned the year in which they were minted, and these years (originally in the Ilahi or the Hijri calendar) have been converted into Christian years according to the principles that have been already set out in my paper last year.[9] I have taken only the catalogued coins of large collections, because of the risk that the collector's curiosity and hoards are much more likely to decide the character of the private collections. Issues of the Deccan and south Indian mints have been excluded, because they did not form a permanent part of the Mughal Empire, and the rise in total amount of coins in the last decade might be argued to be a result of inclusion of these mints.[10] Our confidence in the data is reinforced by the fact that the mints are represented in almost the same proportion in all the collections, thus reducing the role of accident and hoard in one collection for creating fluctuations. A striking   example of this is offered by issues of two small inland mints: all of them in all collections belong to the same two decades, again in case of the second, the substantial increase in the second of these decades is indicated by the numbers of issues preserved in practically all the five collections.[11]

Mint Town	Museum	AH 1096–1105 (AD1684–5–1693–4)	AH 1106–15 (AD1694–5–1703–4)
Itawa	British Museum	16	13
	Indian Museum, Calcutta	10	21
	State Museum, Lucknow	24	41
	Punjab collections	2	4
	Bombay collections[12]	9	10
Bareli	British Museum	5	10
	Indian Museum, Calcutta	2	8
	State Museum, Lucknow	7	18
	Punjab collections	—	2
	Bombay collections	11	4

The Ahmadabad and Surat mints are equally well represented (of course the figures vary according to the size of each collection) in all the collections in which their issues are highest.

Ahmadabad

Museum	1568–77	1578–87	1588–97	1598–1606	1607–16
State Mus., Lucknow	13	22	63	68	44
Indian Mus., Calcutta	2	11	20	20	9
British Museum	5	9	25	24	10
Punjab collections	7	8	20	6	5
Bombay collections	—	—	1	—	2

Surat

Museum	1656–66	1666–74	1675–84	1685–94	1695–1703
State Mus., Lucknow	23	20	33	29	35
Indian Mus., Calcutta	12	13	23	19	19
British Museum	17	20	15	14	8
Punjab collections	12	5	5	4	2
Bombay collection	17	22	27½	25	19

I have not included those coins in my data, which have lost the year of their minting or the mint name. However, their proportion is very insignificant. The percentage of the coins which have lost the year stamped on them is:

Akbar	4.9%;	Jahangir	3.4%;
Shahjahan	3.9%	Aurangzeb	0.7%

And the proportion of the coins whose mint name is missing or doubtful is:

Akbar	14.8%;	Jahangir	0.2%;
Shahjahan	2.3%;	Aurangzeb	0.08%

On the whole 4.6% of the coins have lost their mint name.

All the fractions and sawai and rupa-i-Jahangiri have been converted into the rupee weight, because we are mainly concerned here in a coin's silver content. *Nisars* have not been included because of their having no standard weight and standard of purity like the currency. Proceeding on these principles, I have prepared the first table marked 'A' (at the end of the paper). This table shows the absolute figures of rupee issued from each mint.

The arrangement of the table is Suba-wise.[13] Further the number of coins are shown for each of the fourteen decades, beginning with AD 1568.[14] This has been done mainly for convenience of comparison and presentation. Table 'A' is our basic table, from which the others have been prepared. Table 'B' shows the contribution of individual mints (arranged Suba-wise) in relation to the total mintage in northern India in each decade. Only the figures for mints with 100 or more issues in the collections, are stated separately and those represented by fewer issues have been combined under 'other mints'. Table 'C' is concerned only with the south Indian mints. It shows the absolute figures issued by each mint as well as its total's proportion to the grand total (including the issues of both the North and South Indian mints). The next table marked 'D' shows the contribution of the mints of different regions of northern India in relation to the total, in each decade as well as in the whole period.

The Subas have been grouped into four regions, largely on the basis of considerations of economic geography (particularly, the trade routes).

1. *North-Western Region:* The Indus and its tributaries form natural trade arteries making the entire region a closely knit economic area. This region is connected with the Middle East by Thatta, as a seaport, and by Qandahar and Kabul as two important points on the land routes.
2. *Inland Region:* The Subas which were distant from thecoast as well as the land frontiers have been included in this region. This, therefore, included the central parts of the empire, in particular the provinces of Agra and Delhi.
3. *Eastern Region:* This region includes the areas lying on or close to the Bay of Bengal and connected with the lower Gangetic river-system, this has been done only on the consideration that Patna was the largest commercial centre of eastern India and connected to the ports of Bengal through Ganges.

4. *Gujarat:* It is only one Suba but has been counted as a separate region because of its important role in India's overseas trade, especially, in respect of commerce with Europe during the seventeenth century.

Since our main objective in this attempt is to find out the effect of silver influx on the economy of different regions of India and the channels through which this influx occurred, we have naturally concentrated on the comparative increase and decrease in the issues of a mint or region (given in Tables 'B' and 'D') than the absolute figures issued from a mint (given in Table 'A').

A study of Tables B and D would immediately draw attention to one outstanding fact, namely, that of all the four regions, the north-western region turned out the largest number of coins. Total number of coins issued from the mints of north-western region constitutes 36.7% of the total coins issued from north Indian mints, i.e., nearly two-fifths. This strongly suggests that a very large amount of silver entered India from the Middle East. But the contribution of the region to silver-currency output was by no means uniform. Table 'D' shows that there were great fluctuations. There is a large increase in its share in the total coins issued during the first five decades (1568–1616). These amount to 62.4% of the total during the decade 1607–16. But the region contributes only 39.4% and 35.8% during the preceding twenty years. There is an increase again in its issues during 1636–45. Afterwards, the figures go on falling except for a small recovery in 1685–94. In the last decade (1695–1703) the region's contribution amounted to only 16.3% of the total.

A few comments are also called for in respect of the output of individual mints. The Lahore mint issued the largest number of coins not only among the mints of this region but among all the Mughal empire. Its contribution to the total was the greatest during the period, 1578–1626, in north-western region; and its own largest contribution was in 1607–16, there is a contraction in this mint's contribution to the totals of the preceding decades, except for a recovery in 1635-55. The second decline, starting from 1656, is steeper. During the last three decades (1675–1703) this mint shows an increasing tendency. The issues of the Qandahar mint belong naturally to a much smaller period only, the period during which the fort was included in the Mughal Empire. During the five decades, 1607–55, this mint issued quite a large number of coins. Its contributions form even 13.9% and 11.4% of the total of north Indian mints in the decades 1607–16 and 1636–45 respectively. This mint would have been certainly affected by the continuous rivalry between the Mughals and the Persians over its occupation. The absence of its issues after the decade 1646–55 is due to its final annexation by the Persians in the year 1648. One thing should be marked in this mint's behaviour, that, broadly, the rise and fall in its issues during the whole decades that it remained in Mughal occupation corresponds to the movements in the Lahore mint. There was a great increase in this mint's issues during 1607-16, which was accompanied by the peak in the share of the

Lahore mint. Its second increase was sharper than that of the Lahore mint, which too showed a simultaneous increase.

The Kashmir mint was represented by issues from the decade 1598–1606. Its highest contribution was in 1607–16; thereafter, it fell greatly and seldom contributed to even 1% of the total.

The issues of the Thatta mint begin in 1588–97 and its contribution was highest in the next decade, 1598–1606, when it contributed 21.3% of the total coins issued from the north Indian mints in that decade. There was a considerable decrease in its share in 1607–16, and afterwards the figures fluctuated between 12.3% and 6.4%. In the last three decades (1675–1703) there was a considerable fall in the contribution of this mint to the total.

The Multan mint was represented by small numbers in the decade 1588-97, and then after a gap, by a very large number of coins in 1627–35. It should be noted that mints of all other Subas of this region showed decrease in their share in total of this particular decade, and the total number of coins of north-western region, in proportion to the north Indian total, also fell during this decade. The Multan mint appeared to be issuing quite a large number of silver currency during the period 1627–74. In the last three decades (1675–1703) there appeared to be a fall in the issues of this mint, which is similar to that of the fall in the issues of all the mints of the north-western region except Lahore. The total of the coins of this region also fell during this period. The small rise in 1685–94 in the regional share seems to be caused by the increase in the issue of Thatta and Lahore.

The inland region was very large in area. It comprise the six Subas of Agra, Ajmer, Awadh, Delhi, Ilahabad and Malwa. The movement of the relative output of the mints of the inland region was very much different from that of the north-western region. Its issues represented 42.4% of the total in 1578–87, but falls to the comparatively very low level of 16.0% in the next decade, 1588–97. It continued to offer more or less the same share to the totals of the four succeeding decades; after which it rose slightly. During the three decades 1636–65, it contributed the least among all the four regions. In the next four decades, however, its share rises steadily; and the region becomes the largest contributor in 1685–1703. Except a small rise in the eastern region, the other two regions show great decline in their share during this period. This increase in the share of the inland region towards end of the period is accompanied by the emergence of several new mints in this region.

The individual mints of the inland region showed interesting changes and fluctuations in their shares of the total. Both Agra (Akbarabad; including Fatehpur Sikri) and Ilahabad mints showed a great decline in their share of the north Indian total. The Agra mint showed an increase subsequently but never contributes more than 12.8% of the total. Its share rose very slowly and steadily until 1635, whereafter it began to fall. Its issues increase only nominally in the last decade though the issues from the mints of the Suba of Agra increased greatly. The emergence of a number of new mints[15] seemed to have caused the rise in the total output of the Suba; the mints, other than Agra, in fact contributed about 16% of the north Indian total during these decades. The Suba of Ilahabad continued to issue coins continuously, but its proportion to the total was very insignificant after 1587.

The Delhi (Shahjahanabad) mint issues for most of the period the largest number of coins among the mints of the region, except Agra. Its share of the north Indian total fell only in 1598–1606 and 1636–55, otherwise it showed a constant increase, until the last two decades when a slight decline was noticeable. But there was an increase in the number as well as output of the Suba of Delhi during 1685–1703, as the other mints, Bareli, Saharanpur and Sarhind join in contributing to 5.2% and 9.1 % of the totals in 1685–94 and 1695–1703 respectively.

The Suba of Ajmer made only an insignificant contribution throughout the period. It is represented for the first time in 1607–16, and then, after a gap of four decades, in the decade beginning from AD 1656. It never contributes more than 1% of the total issues of the north Indian mints.

The Suba of Awadh appeared for the first time in the decade beginning since 1627. It remained insignificant until the decade ending in 1674, its issues never constituting more than 0.5% till 1656–65. There was a sharp rise in its output after the decade 1665–74. There emerged a new Mint at Muazzamabad in this Suba in 1685–94. The largest share of the Suba is in 1685–94; 6.8% of the total output of the north Indian mints in that decade.

The contribution of Malwa remained insignificant throughout except for small rises in 1578–97 and 1697–45.

Though a single province, Gujarat contributed a very large portion of the issues of the total. The issues of this region constitute a fairly high proportion of the total coinage of north Indian mints, viz., 24.7%. The proportion of the contribution of this region to the total issues of the north Indian mints in the respective decades until 1597 rose steadily. There is a large contraction in this region's contribution during 1598–1616. Its relative share increased from the decade beginning in 1617 and continued to increase until the decade ending in 1684, except for a small decline in 1627–35. The fall in the last two decades, 1685–1703, was very great, reducing its share in the total contribution of the north Indian mints to 18.3%.

Ahmadabad remained the largest mint of Gujarat until the decade ending in 1635. This mint showed an increase down to 1597, and then a decline. The proportion of its contribution to the total of the decade 1588–97 was 35.0, which was very large for an individual mint, even Lohore never contributed such a large percentage in a single decade. The share of the mint in the total started to decline from the decade beginning in 1598. The decline continued with a small increase in 1617–26 and 1656–65. Ahmadabad accounted for a very small portion of the total coins in the last decade.

Broadly speaking, the contraction in the output of the Ahmadabad mint is accompanied with arise in the Surat mint. It replaces Ahmadabad as the largest mint of the region since 1627.[16] But the issues of the Surat mint never formed as high a portion of the total as Ahmadabad did. Its highest contribution was 25.8% in 1666–74, after which there appeared a fall in the issues of this mint. In the period starting from 1636 other new mints started working in this region. Cambay (Khambyat) developed to be a very important mint in 1675–84. Other mints, too, go on contribute continuously till the close of our period. There was a great increase in the share of the Cambay mint from 1666–74, which was also seen in the contribution of the Surat mint. In the last two decades (1685–1703) all the mints of this region exhibit a considerable decline in relation to the total for north India.

The fluctuations in the relative output of the eastern region are very different from that of the other regions. Its contribution is very small until the decade ending 1597. Then the numbers increase and finally reach the proportion of 26.8 to the total in 1617–26. This is its highest contribution. Thereafter its share fluctuates very greatly, displaying distinctly a downward tendency. But even while declining the percentage never goes below that of the period previous to 1616. Although the region is very large in terms of area, its total issue constitutes the lowest portion of the total for north Indian mints, *viz.* 15%, for the whole period.

The Patna mint is represented from the very beginning of the period under study. This mint remains the largest mint of this region until 1655, though its share to the total starts to fall after reaching the peak in 1617–26. The Akbarnagar mint starts later in the decade 1598–1606. Jahangirnagar starts later (1607–16). The other mints of this region (Makhsudabad and Bangala) are too small to be considered; one of them, the Bangala mint, is represented only by issues belonging to 1588–1606, and the Makhsudabad mint by those belonging to 1695–1703. The combined contribution of the last two mints was negligible. The Akbarnagar mint's share of the total increases until 1665, with a fall in 1636–45. These fluctuations correspond to those of the Patna mint during the same period. Akbarnagar showed a slight tendency of decline during the rest of the century, which, too, is similar to the movement of the share of the Patna mint, except that Patna showed an increase in the last decade. The contribution of the Jahangirnagar mint to the total showed a great increase in 1617–26, which was similar to that of Patna. In the succeeding years the issues of this mint greatly fell. The consequent increase, decrease, and increase in the ratio of its issues and the north Indian total in 1675–84, 1685-94 and 1695–1703, respectively were similar to the movements of the issues of the Patna mint. The increase in the issues of the Jahangirnagar mint in the last decade was comparatively high.

The only mint of the Suba of Orissa, Katak, was poorly represented. And it was very difficult to compare it with other mints, except with the increasing tendency in its contribution in the last decade which was also present in the issues of the mints at Patna and Jahangirnagar.

The Deccan and south Indian mints behaved just in the manner that would be expected from them. As Table 'C' shows, the proportion of their issues to the total increases sharply during 1646–74, and afterwards showed some stability. The mint at Burhanpur was the only large mint of this region until the decade ending 1635. From 1646 new mints spring up and their number as well as increasing volume of coinage causes the great increase in its share in the total coinage of the Mughal Empire. Burhanpur is not very significant during this period, most probably, because it was replaced as the headquarters of the Mughal Deccan by Aurangabad in 1636.

After our calculations and descriptions of the tables, we may venture to suggest rather tentatively what inferences can be drawn from them.

The pre-eminent fact emerging from our analysis concerns the relative volumes of the streams of the silver influx into India. In accordance with our expectations, the share of the Gujarat mints in the total coinage of northern India was very large, and this was surely due to the silver entering this province through overseas channel was most of all from Europe directly. But what was surprising was the larger share still of the northwestern region, whose mints contributed, as we have seen, a little over 36 per cent of the total of northern India as a whole, during the entire period under study. The only reason for this can be that far larger quantities of silver bullion entered north-western India from the Middle East than has been supposed. Since there are few data about the overland trade, one is apt to underestimate the drain of silver from Europe through the Middle East into India. But some contemporary observers[17] did draw attention to this stream, for example, in 1694–95, Careri wrote that "nor Persia, Arabia and the Turks themselves to go without the Commodities of India, send vast quantity of money to Moka on the Red Sea, near Babel Mandel to Bassora at the bottom of the Persian Gulgh; and to Bander Abassi and Gomeron, which is afterwards sent over in ships to Indostan."[18]

This large amount of silver coming from the Middle East, would have entered the north-western region of India through Qandahar and Multan by land route and Thappa by sea route.[19] Some re-exports of silver even reached Bengal by sea; and might have contributed part of bullion that the eastern mints coined. Persia was exporting silver also to Bengal in return for sugar and other goods.[20]

As already noted, Gujarat's total contribution of 24.7% of the total silver coined during the whole period was not unexpected. The important role that Surat and other ports of Gujarat played in the European commerce, made it only natural. The considerable decline in its contribution to the total coinage of north-western India during the first half of the seventeenth century is less easy to explain. One possibility was that the opposition in Europe to the export of bullion, especially marked in England, hampered the direct export of bullion to India.[21] Quite possibly the rivalry among Holland, England and Portugal, often breaking into hostilities, obstructed their trade. The policy of the English Crown and Parliament towards the East India Company, however, underwent a great change during the second half of the century. Now much greater attention was paid to the commercial interest. Bullion export, in the view prevailing, was not making the country poor but, in the long run, increasing its wealth. The changes in the English policy greatly encouraged the East India Company's trade, hence increase in the amount of silver imports in India and later on (after 1680) the export of Indian manufactured goods to England.[22] Thus the great increase in the share of Gujarat in the total north Indian mints during 1656–84.

The decline in the last two decades (1685-1703) in the contribution of Gujarat, which was also reflected in the absolute numbers of coins preserved, might have been due to local factors. Commerce and trade of Gujarat was very badly affected by the Maratha raids.[23] This combined with the diversion in bullion imports to the newly established English factory at Bombay might have caused the decline in silver imports into Gujarat.

Another interesting point that emerged from our analysis was that the number of coins turned out of a mint was determined much more by the amount of the silver supply and to a smaller extent by the city's position in the commercial world or its administrative importance. This can be seen from a comparison of the number of issues from the mints directly in touch with the foreign commerce and the mints of the inland region.

The issues of the mints of the inland region, was true, constituted the highest proportion in the decade's totals until 1587. But during this period, the expansion of the empire was not complete, Gujarat, Sindh, and the whole of the north-western region and Bengal was brought under the full control of the Mughal emperor only during the next decade, 1588–97. When the full territorial extent of the empire was established, the contribution of the inland region to the total began to decline very sharply. For the whole period, its contribution to the total minting was by no means commensurate with its size. It contributed over the whole period 23.6 per cent of the total for North India, while the single Suba of Gujarat accounted for 24.7%.

Of the mints within this region, Agra was a very large commercial centre. It was in fact the headquarters for the European traders for buying the commodities and products of doab area. The large scale trade of Bayana indigo was carried on from here. It was also the capital of the Mughal Empire, the seat of the imperial court for almost a half of the seventeenth century. In spite of all this the Agra mint made comparatively only a modest contribution to the total currency output of the northern India. There was even a gap of a whole decade, 1588–97, of which no issue from any mint in this Suba has been preserved. Despite the substitution of the Ahmadabad mint by Surat after 1635, and a great decline in its issues, thereafter, the issues from Ahmadabad alone exceed those of the whole Suba of Agra.

Similarly Delhi was the capital under Shahjahan and Aurangzeb, and was therefore at times, the largest administrative centre of the Mughal Empire. Yet, the relative contribution of the Delhi mint individually and of the whole Suba were poor, being much less than Agra.

Mere distance from the sea, of course, did not by itself reduce the importance of a mint. The Patna mint issued far more coins than the mints of Bengal combined. This was probably because of its position as a great river-port, where the Bengal and Upper-Indian boats had their termini, so that silver was directly brought up to it from the Bay of Bengal.[24]

The tables also display very large fluctuations, for most of which no explanation can be offered. Some time a sharp increase might be due to the collection of revenue in cash, and some time to the replacement of earlier currency by the Mughals. The phenomenal rise in the output of the Kashmir mint during 1607–16, could have been the result of either or both of these factors. The tendency of the Mughal *jagirdars* in Kashmir was to shift from revenue collection in cash into collection in kind.[25] Similarly its old currency was being replaced by the Mughal rupee.[26]

Temporary seats of imperial court and administration certainly have led to an increased demand for use of money and expansion of trade.[27] This seems to be responsible for the increased coining in Burhanpur and Aurangabad. The issues of the Burhanpur mint decline from the decade beginning 1636, the exact year when it was replaced by Aurangabad as the headquarters of the Mughal forces. But the influence of this factor is not very apparent in the fluctuations of the issues in Kashmir, Agra, Delhi, and Lahore. For example Kashmir's contribution to the total increases only in the decade 1607–16. Although Akbar had visited it thrice in the single decade (1588–97) and Jahangir went there in 1618 and later, the number of issues increased only in 1607–16.

Of course the relative efficiency and too much burden on certain mints must also have played a part in shifts and fluctuations. Minting at the Surat mint was not speedy enough to satisfy the needs of the merchants of that city. Sometimes, especially during the reign of Aurangzeb, the mint remained closed for sometime. Minting at Ahmadabad, which would have been a good remedy, was not possible because of the restrictions on bullion trade. A better choice would have been Cambay, which was a good port, near Surat and, bullion could have been sent there without landing at Surat. This may explain the great rise in the Khambayat mint during the years 1666–84, apparently at the expense of Surat.

These do not by any means exhaust the reasons for which a change in the relative output of a mint might have taken place. What has been said above is by way of illustration only.

TABLE A: Silver Coins Issued from the North Indian Mints of the Mughal Empire, 1568-1703 AD

AH	976-85	986-95	996-1005	1006-15	1016-25	1026-35	1036-45	1046-55	1056-65	1066-75	1076-85	1086-95	1096-1105	1106-15	Total
AD	1568-77	1578-87	1588-97	1598-1606	1607-16	1617-26	1627-35	1636-45	1646-55	1656-65	1666-74	1675-84	1685-94	1695-1703	
	1	2	3	4	5	6	7	8	9	10	11	12	13	14	15
North Western Region															
1. KABUL															
Qandahar	—	—	—	—	88 ⅔	33	3	47	12	—	—	—	—	—	183
Kabul	—	—	—	18½	2¼	10	6	4½	—	7	3	2	5	3	62
Peshawar	—	1	—	—	—	—	—	—	—	—	—	—	—	—	1
Total	—	1	—	18½	90¹³⁄₂₀	43	9	51½	12	7	3	2	5	3	251
2. KASHMIR															
Kashmir	—	—	—	—	42⅕	8	2	5	2	1	1	—	2	1	65
Srinagar	—	—	—	12	—	—	—	—	—	—	—	—	—	—	12
Total	—	—	—	12	42⅕	8	2	5	2	1	1	1	2	1	77
3. LAHORE															
Lahore	18	24¾	109³³⁄₄₀	162¹³⁄₂₀	222½	5	70	49½	46	21	12	27	67	64	980
Rohtas	—	—	—	—	—	2	—	—	—	—	—	—	—	—	2
Total	18	24¾	109³³⁄₄₀	162¹³⁄₂₀	222½	87	70	49½	46	21	12	27	67	64	982
4. MULTAN															
Multan	—	—	7½	—	—	—	89	53	22	60	34	24	24	14	326
Sitpur	—	—	—	13	—	—	—	—	—	—	—	—	—	—	13
Bhakkar	3	—	—	—	—	—	24	11	6	11	4	2	1	—	62
Total	3	—	7½	13	—	—	113	63	28	71	38	26	25	14	402

(Contd.)

TABLE A (*Contd.*)

	AH	976-85	986-95	996-1005	1006-15	1016-25	1026-35	1036-45	1046-55	1056-65	1066-75	1076-85	1086-95	1096-1105	1106-15	Total
	AD	1568-77	1578-87	1588-97	1598-1606	1607-16	1617-26	1627-35	1636-45	1646-55	1656-65	1666-74	1675-84	1685-94	1695-1703	
		1	2	3	4	5	6	7	8	9	10	11	12	13	14	15
5. THATTA																
Thatta		—	—	49¼	118¾	43⅘	65	45	51	21	25	20	6	23	10	477
Lahri Bandar		—	—	—	1	—	—	—	—	—	—	—	—	—	—	1
Total		—	—	49¼	119¾	43⅘	65	45	51	21	25	20	6	23	10	477
Total		21	26	167	326	399	203	239	220	109	125	74	62	122	92	2187
Inland Region																
1. AGRA																
Agra		38	3	—	31	56⅗	39+6	24½	—	—	—	—	—	—	—	
Akbarabad		—	—	—	—	—	—	59	19¹/₁₆	25	9	10	16	15	28	413
Fatehpur Sikri		3	3	—	—	—	—	1	—	—	—	—	—	،	—	
Islamabad (Mathura)		—	—	—	—	—	—	—	—	—	—	—	—	1	3	4
Itawah		—	—	—	—	—	—	——	—	—	—	1	—	61	89	151
Namol		—	—	—	—	—	—	—	—	—	—	—	—	28	—	28
Sikandarah		—	—	—	—	—	—	—	—	—	—	—	—	1	—	1
Gwalior		—	—	—	—	—	—	—	—	—	—	—	—	6	—	6
Jalesar		—	—	—	—	—	1	—	—	—	—	—	—	،	—	1
Total		41	33	—	31⅕	56⅗	46	84½	19¹/₁₆	25	9	11	16	112	12	598
2. AJMER																
Ajmer		—	—	—	—	5	—	—	—	—	2	3	1	2	4	17
Sambhar		—	—	—	—	—	—	—	—	—	—	—	—	1	—	1

(*Contd.*)

TABLE A (*Contd.*)

	AH	976-85	986-95	996-1005	1006-15	1016-25	1026-35	1036-45	1046-55	1056-65	1066-75	1076-85	1086-95	1096-1105	1106-15	Total
	AD	1568-77	1578-87	1588-97	1598-1606	1607-16	1617-26	1627-35	1636-45	1646-55	1656-65	1666-74	1675-84	1685-94	1695-1703	
		1	2	3	4	5	6	7	8	9	10	11	12	13	14	15
Ranthanbor		—	—	—	—	—	—	—	—	—	—	—	—	1	—	1
Total		—	—	—	—	5	—	—	—	—	2	3	1	4	4	19
3. AWADH																
Lakhnau		—	—	—	—	—	—	1	2	1	—	4	20	41	30	101
Muzzamabad		—	—	—	—	—	—	—	—	—	—	—	—	3	—	6
Total		—	—	—	—	—	—	1	2	1	—	4	23	46	30	107
4. DELHI																
Delhi		13	7	48$^{9}/_{10}$	11	46	30	34	2	—	—	—	—	—	—	191$^{9}/_{10}$
Shahjahanabad		—	—	—	—	—	—	—	—	5¼	23½	30	48	65	52	223¾
Bareli		—	—	—	—	—	—	—	—	—	—	—	—	25	42	67
Saharanpur		—	—	—	—	—	—	—	—	—	—	—	—	2	—	2
Sirhind		—	—	—	—	—	—	—	—	—	—	—	—	8	10	18
Total		13	7	48$^{8}/_{10}$	11	46	30	34	2	5¼	23½	30	48	100	104	503
5. ILAHABAD																
Ilahabad		—	—	—	18	—	3	15	7	1	3	4	4	1	4	61
Jaunpur		30½	8	—	—	—	—	—	—	—	—	—	—	1	—	39½
Total		30½	8	1	18	—	3	15	7	1	3	4	4	2	4	101
6. MALWA																
Ujjain		—	8	9	5	—	1	13	2	1	3	3	1	2	1	49
Bhilsa		—	—	—	—	—	—	1	6	12	2	—	—	—	—	21
Total		—	8	9	5	—	1	14	8	13	5	3	1	2	1	70
Total		85	56	59	65	108	80	149	38	45	43	55	93	266	236	1404

(*Contd.*)

TABLE A (*Contd.*)

	AH	976-85	986-95	996-1005	1006-15	1016-25	1026-35	1036-45	1046-55	1056-65	1066-75	1076-85	1086-95	1096-1105	1106-15	Total
	AD	1568-77	1578-87	1588-97	1598-1606	1607-16	1617-26	1627-35	1636-45	1646-55	1656-65	1666-74	1675-84	1685-94	1695-1703	
		1	2	3	4	5	6	7	8	9	10	11	12	13	14	15
Eastern Region																
1. BENGAL																
Akbamagar		—	—	—	6⅗	30⅗	24	51½	17	22¼	30	22	28	44	26	302
Jahangimagar		—	—	—	—	1	30	21	9	—	3	1	7	12	34	118
Makhsu-dabad (Murshidabad)		—	—	—	—	—	—	—	—	—	—	—	—	—	2	2
Bangala		—	—	1	2	—	—	—	—	—	—	—	—	—	—	3
Total		—	—	1	8⅗	31⅗	54	72½	26	22¼	33	23	35	56	62	425
2. BIHAR																
Patna		1	6	3	25⅖	30⅖	97½	89	27½	32	28	20	27	23	30	444
Total		1	6	3	25⅖	30⅖	97½	89	27½	32	28	20	27	23	30	444
3. ORISSA																
Katak		—	1	—	—	—	—	1	4	—	7	—	5	8	12	38
Total		—	1	—	—	—	—	1	4	—	7	—	5	8	12	38
Total		1	7	4	34	62	152	171	58	55	68	43	67	86	104	907
4. GUJARAT																
Ahmadabad		27	41½	128¼	120 1/30	69 1/30	99	61	15	4	26	7	12½	6	1	617
Surat		—	—	1	—	1	30½	48½	69½	64½	80½	79½	100	91½	82	649
Khambayat		—	—	—	—	—	—	—	1	6	12	27	49	34	15	138
Junagarh		—	—	—	—	—	—	—	5	11	11	8	7	18	5	65
Pattan Deo		—	—	—	—	—	—	—	2	—	—	—	—	—	—	2
Total		27	41½	129¼	120 1/20	69 7/10	130½	109½	92	85½	129½	121	169	149½	103	1473
Total		27	42	129	120	70	131	110	92	86	130	122	169	150	103	1473
Grand Total	6101½	135	131	364	545	639	566	666	411½	303	372	294	371	324	562	6106½

TABLE B: Percentage of the contirubiton of an Individual Mint to the Ten Yearly Totals

	AH	976-85	986-95	996-1005	1006-15	1016-25	1026-35	1036-45	1046-55	1056-65	1066-75	1076-85	1086-95	1096-1105	1106-15
	AD	1568-77	1578-87	1588-97	1598-1606	1607-16	1617-26	1627-35	1636-45	1646-55	1656-65	1666-74	1675-84	1685-94	1695-1703
		1	2	3	4	5	6	7	8	9	10	11	12	13	14
North-Western Region															
1. LAHORE															
Lahore		13.4	18.8	30.1	29.9	34.9	15.1	10.6	12.2	15.3	5.6	3.8	6.5	10.0	11.4
Rohtas		—	—	—	—	—	3.5	—	—	—	—	—	—	—	—
2. MULTAN															
Multan		—	—	2.3	—	—	—	13.5	12.7	15.3	5.6	3.8	6.5	10.0	11.4
Other Mints		2.3	—	—	2.4	—	—	3.6	2.6	2.0	2.9	1.3	0.4	0.1	—
3. THATTA															
Thatta		—	—	13.5	21.8	6.9	11.5	6.7	12.3	6.9	6.8	6.4	1.4	3.4	1.7
Lahri Bandar		—	—	—	1.8	—	—	—	—	—	—	—	—	—	—
4. KABUL															
Qandahar		—	—	—	—	13.9	5.8	0.4	11.4	3.9	—	—	—	—	—
Other Mints		—	0.8	—	3.5	0.3	1.7	0.9	1.2	—	1.9	0.9	0.7	0.7	0.5
5. KASHMIR															
All mints		—	—	—	2.2	6.6	1.4	0.3	1.2	0.7	0.3	0.3	0.2	0.2	0.1
Inland Region															
1. AGRA															
Agra (including Sikri & Akbarabad)		30.0	25.0	—	5.7	8.9	8.0	12.8	4.6	8.2	2.4	3.2	3.9	2.2	4.9
Itawah		—	—	—	—	—	—	—	—	—	—	3.2	—	9.0	15.6
Other mints		—	—	—	—	—	0.1	—	—	—	—	—	—	5.3	0.5

(*Contd.*)

TABLE B (Contd.)

	AH	976-85	986-95	996-1005	1006-15	1016-25	1026-35	1036-45	1046-55	1056-65	1066-75	1076-85	1086-95	1096-1105	1106-15
	AD	1568-77	1578-87	1588-97	1598-1606	1607-16	1617-26	1627-35	1636-45	1646-55	1656-65	1666-74	1675-84	1685-94	1695-1703
		1	2	3	4	5	6	7	8	9	10	11	12	13	14
2. AJMER															
All mints		—	—	—	—	0.8	—	—	—	—	0.5	1.0	0.2	0.6	0.7
3. AWADH															
All mints		—	—	—	—	—	—	0.2	0.5	0.3	—	1.2	5.6	6.8	5.2
4. DELHI															
Delhi (including Shahjahanabad)		9.6	5.2	13.8	2.0	7.2	5.3	5.1	0.5	1.6	6.4	9.5	11.1	9.6	9.0
Other mints		—	—	—	—	—	—	—	—	—	—	—	—	5.2	9.1
5. ILAHABAD															
All mints		—	5.9	6.7	1.0	—	0.2	2.1	1.9	4.3	1.3	1.0	0.2	0.3	0.2
Eastern Region															
1. BENGAL															
Akbarnagar		—	—	—	1.3	4.8	4.2	7.8	4.1	7.3	8.0	7.0	6.8	6.5	4.5
Jahangimagar		—	—	—	—	0.2	5.3	3.1	2.2	—	0.8	0.3	1.7	1.8	5.9
Other mints		—	—	0.3	0.4	—	—	—	—	—	—	—	—	—	0.4
2. BIHAR															
Patna		0.7	4.5	0.8	4.6	4.6	17.5	13.4	6.8	10.6	7.5	6.4	6.5	4.0	5.2
3. ORISSA															
Katak		—	0.8	—	—	—	—	0.2	1.0	—	1.9	—	1.2	1.2	2.1
4. GUJARAT															
Ahmadabad		20.0	30.0	35.0	22.1	11.0	17.6	9.1	3.6	1.3	7.0	2.3	3.1	0.9	0.2
Surat		—	—	0.3	—	0.2	5.6	7.3	16.7	21.5	22.0	25.8	24.4	13.8	14.4
Khambayat		—	—	—	—	—	—	—	0.24	2.0	3.2	8.7	12.2	5.1	7.3
Others mints		—	—	—	—	—	—	—	1.7	3.6	2.9	2.5	1.7	2.8	0.9

TABLE C: Contribution of South Indian Mints

	AH 976-85	986-95	996-1005	1006-15	1016-25	1026-35	1036-44	1046-55	1056-65	1066-75	1076-85	1086-95	1096-1105	1106-15	Total
	AD 1568-77	1578-87	1588-97	1598-1606	1607-16	1617-26	1627-35	1636-45	1646-55	1656-65	1666-74	1675-84	1685-94	1695-1703	
	1	2	3	4	5	6	7	8	9	10	11	12	13	14	15
Ahmadnagar	—	—	—	1	1	1	5	—	4	—	1	1	8	4	27
Ahsanabad (Bijapur)	—	—	—	—	—	—	—	—	—	—	—	—	—	2	2
Aurangabad (Khujista Bunyad)	—	—	—	—	—	—	—	—	—	12	6	12	19	15	64
Alamgirpur	—	—	—	—	—	—	—	—	—	4	10	8	12	6	40
Bijapur	—	—	—	—	—	—	—	—	—	—	—	8	31	27	67
Barar	—	—	1	28	—	—	—	—	—	—	—	—	—	—	29
Barhanpur	—	—	1	29	19	14	48	5	2	3	3	11	16	23	17
Chinapattam (Mailapur)	—	—	—	—	—	—	—	—	—	—	—	—	3	16	19
Daulatabad	—	—	—	—	—	—	—	3	18	12	—	—	—	—	37
Elichpur	—	—	—	—	7	—	—	—	—	—	—	—	—	—	7
Gulkunda	—	—	—	—	—	—	1	—	—	17	40	32	17	—	107
Gulbarga	—	—	—	—	—	—	—	—	—	—	—	—	7	1	8
Haidarabad	—	—	—	—	—	—	—	—	—	—	—	—	12	6	18
Karnatak	—	—	—	—	—	—	—	—	—	—	—	—	—	2	2
Machlipattam	—	—	—	—	—	—	—	—	—	—	—	—	48	4	8
Makhsudabad	—	—	—	—	—	—	—	—	—	—	—	—	—	2	2

(Contd.)

TABLE C (*Contd.*)

	AH	976-85	986-95	996-1005	1006-15	1016-25	1026-35	1036-44	1046-55	1056-65	1066-75	1076-85	1086-95	1096-1105	1106-15	Total
	AD	1568-77	1578-87	1588-97	1598-1606	1607-16	1617-26	1627-35	1636-45	1646-55	1656-65	1666-74	1675-84	1685-94	1695-1703	
		1	2	3	4	5	6	7	8	9	10	11	12	13	14	15
Nusratabad (Dharwar)		—	—	—	—	—	—	—	—	—	1	—	—	—	3	4
Qamarnagar		—	—	—	—	—	—	—	—	—	1	—	—	—	—	1
Sholapur		—	—	—	—	—	—	—	—	—	—	6	5	23	5	25
Toragal		—	—	—	—	—	—	—	—	—	—	—	—	—	2	2
Zafarabad		—	—	—	—	—	—	1	—	—	9	4	3	3	6	26
Zafarnagar		—	—	5	—	—	—	—	—	—	—	5	—	—	—	—
Zafarpur		—	—	—	—	—	—	—	—	—	—	—	—	6	—	6
Total		—	—	2	58	28	15	64	8	25	59	71	81	161	124	682
Percentage contribution of South Indian Mints to the total of Ten yearly decades		—	—	0.5	9.6	4.2	2.6	8.7	1.9	7.6	13.7	18.5	16.5	19.3	17.8	

TABLE D: Percentage of the Contribution of the North-Western, Gujarat, Inland and Eastern Regions to the Ten Yearly Totals

	AH	976-85	986-95	996-1005	1006-15	1016-25	1026-35	1036-44	1046-55	1056-65	1066-75	1076-85	1086-95	1096-1105	1106-15
	AD	1568-77	1578-87	1588-97	1598-1606	1607-16	1617-26	1627-35	1636-45	1646-55	1656-65	1666-74	1675-84	1685-94	1695-1703
		1	2	3	4	5	6	7	8	9	10	11	12	13	14
North-Western Region 36.7%		15.5	19.8	45.8	59.8	62.4	39.4	35.8	53.4	35.9	33.6	25.1	15.8	19.2	16.3
Inland Region 23.6%		62.9	42.4	16.0	11.9	16.9	14.1	20.8	9.2	14.8	11.5	18.7	23.7	41.0	46.7
Eastern Region 15%		0.6	5.3	1.0	6.2	9.7	26.8	25.8	14.0	18.1	18.2	14.7	17.1	13.5	18.5
Gujarat 24.7%		20.0	32.0	35.4	32.0	10.9	23.1	16.5	22.3	28.3	34.9	41.4	43.2	25.1	18.3

Before closing this paper attention may be drawn to a peculiar phenomenon which may be of some help in interpreting the economic history of the Upper Gangetic area. There was a noticeable general increase in the issues (and their relative share in the total of northern India) from the mints of the Subas of the inland region during the last two decades, 1685–1703. This increase can be explained, at least partly, as the result of a phase of recoinage of bullion, minted at first at the points of their entry. But this cannot by itself be an adequate explanation for not only is there a rise in the number of coins minted, but also in the number of mints. Places like Itawa, Narnol, Sirhind, Sikandarh, Bareli, Saharanpur, Muazzamabad, Ranthanbhor, Sambhor, Gwalior, and Islamabad are now established as mints during 1685–1703. Jaunpur, after a gap of hundred years is represented in 1685–94. Docs this merely indicate dispersal of minting establishment as an administrative measure, or is it a possible index of rise of numerous medium size commercial centres all over the region during this period. This is a question to which the present writer has not been able to find an answer, but which may be offered to the students of economic history for their consideration.

Notes

1. 'Currency Output of the Mughal Empire and the Extension of Price Revolution to India', presented by the present author to the *Indian History Congress*, Mysore Session, Dec. 1966.
2. Since there was no internal production of silver in India, there was little scope for the currency being affected by the silver supplies available within the country.
3. Moreland introduced this method in *Akbar to Aurangzeb*, pp. 176–78 for the study of the relative output of the Ahmadabad and Surat mints. I am not aware of any other attempt at such comparative tabulation.
4. *English Factories in India, 1618–21*, p. 238; *1630–33*, pp. 102, 205. This restriction was sometimes relaxed by the special order of the Emperor, *E.F. 1618–21*, p. 331.
5. *Supplementary Calendar*, ed. Foster, p. 101; *Letters Received by the English Factories in India*, vol. VI, p. 131; *English Factories; 1637–41*, p. 262; *Travels of Tavernier*, tr. V. Ball, vol. I, pp. 33–34. Unsafe trade routes were one of the main reasons why the English factors used 'bills of exchange' rather than cash remittance, thus avoiding transport of treasure without hampering their trade.
6. Although there were many problems in the internal export of bullion, trade of coined money and bullion never ceased. There were some places where remittance, either due to urgent need or because the bills of exchange were not available, had to be made in cash, generally the coined currency. *English Factories, 1618–21*, pp. 98, 99, 119, 152, 160, 190; *1622–23*, p. 274; *1630–33*, pp. 96, 205, 302; *1634–36*, p. 35; *Supplementary Calendar*, ed. W. Foster, p. 139.
7. See the *Indian Travels of Thevenot and Careri*, ed. Sen, Bk. I, pp. 69–61, for a description of how much the life was changed and the commercial activities expanded by arrival of the Imperial Court.

8. (a) Catalogue of Coins in the Indian Museum Calcutta, vol. III, by N. Wright, and the Supplement to the Catalogue of Coins in the Indian Museum Calcutta, vol. Ill, by Shamsuddin Ahmad.
   (b) The Coins of the Mughal Emperors of Hindustan in the British Museum, by Lane Pool, ed. R.Stuart Pool.
   (c) (i) Coins of the Mughal Emperors of India, collected by C J. Rodgers, and published by the Government of Punjab.
   (ii) *Catalogue of Coins in the Government Museum Lahore, by C.J. Rodgers.*
   (d) (i) *Catalogue of Coins in the State Museum Lucknow, (two volumes on the Mughal coins).*
   (ii) *Supplementary Catalogue of Mughal Coins in the State Museum Lucknow, by C.R. Singhal.*
   (e) *Catalogue of Coins of the Mughal Emperors by M.K. Husain.*

9. Please see note 1, above.

10. Names of the South Indian mints which have been excluded are: Ahmadnagar, Ahsanabad (Gulbarga), Alamgirpur, Aurangabad (Khujista Bunyad), Bijapur, Burhanpur, Chinapatan (Mailapur), Daulatabad, Elichpur, Golconda, Haidarabad, Imidarabad, Imtiyazgarh (Adoni), Nusratgarh (Dharwar), Qamamagar (Kamol) Sholapur, Zatarabad (Bidar) and Zafarnagar.

11. Punjab collections, include Rodgers' personal collection and collection of Govt. Museum of Lahore. The two collections even when combined are very small, therefore their share in the coins of each mint preserved is also very small as compared to the other collections. See my paper, op. cit, for further details on the size and similarity of different collections. The information in *The Catalogue of Coins of the Mughal Emperors* by M.K. Husain, which has been published from Bombay, could not be used in that paper. It is, however, not a large collection. The coins are mainly of the reign of Aurangzeb (total number of silver coins of the period from AD 1556–1707 is 620 and of these 467 are of Aurangzeb). The mints of Gujarat and South India are, naturally, much better represented (out of the total silver coins catalogued 198 are of Gujarat mints and 100 of south Indian mints, both accounting for 51.9 of the total).

12. M.K. Husain, *The Catalogue of Coins of the Mughal Emperors*, is referred to as 'Bombay collection'.

13. The identifications of the mint-towns as given in the catalogues have been accepted in all cases. Their assignment to various Subas is based largely on the list of pargana in the *Ain-i-Akbari*. I have been greatly helped by maps prepared by Prof. S.N. Husain.

14. Our decades are essentially those of Hijri years, beginning from 976. Since the Christian year is longer than the Hijri Year by about 9 days, the years AD 1601, 1634, 1666 and 1699 consist of the larger parts of two Hijri years. Asa result, four of the decades (of Hijri years) correspond to only nine Christian years each. But this does not affect the data because the real periods remain the same.

15. New mints of the Suba are: Islamabad (Mathura), Itawah, Narnol, Sikandarah, and Gwalior.

16. Moreland points out the replacement of the Ahmadabad mint by Surat, in *Akbar to Aurangzeb, pp. 177–78.*

17. cf. Sir John Welstenholme, (member of the Commission appointed by the government to suggest remedies for drain of silver from England) memorandum to the Privy Council in 1621, in which he mentions the land routes of bullion export to the Indies. (K.N. Chaudhuri, *The English East India Company*, p. 120).

18. Sen, *Indian Travels of Thevenot and Careried*, p. 241.

19. The way in which the shares of Qandahar mint rises during 1608–1617, obviously at the expense of Thatta, probably indicates a shift in the direction of the major portion of silver coming from the Middle East, from Thatta to Qandahar. This might have been due to the increased Mughal Portuguese rivalry on the sea during the first quarter of the seventeenth century which increased the trade on Qandahar route four times (cf. Moreland, *Akbar to Aurangzeb*. pp. 57–8).

20. *The English Factories in India, 1668–69*, p. 179.

21. S.A. Khan, *The East India Trade in the seventeenth Century*, pp. 94, 188–89, 192.

22. Ibid., pp. 269–73.

23. *English Factories* (West Presidency), p. 200.

24. Irfan Habib, *The Agrarian System of Mughal India*, p. 63 n. 72.

25. Abul Fazl, *Akbarnama, Bib. Ind.*, III, p. 726, Akbar abolished the practice, but how far the prohibition was effective may be doubted.

26. Irfan Habib, 'Currency System of the Mughal Empire', published in the *Medieval India Quarterly*, nos. 1–2, p. 8. The indigenous local currency, Rup Sasnu, has been referred by Jahangir to be replaced by the Rupee.

27. *The English Factories in India, 1626–29*, p. 128; 1630–33, p. 12; 1634–36, pp. 68–69. Alexander Hamilton, *A New Account of the East Indies*, ed. W. Foster; vol. I, p. 118.

20

Cafilas and Cartazes

M.N. Pearson

THERE HAS been a considerable volume of tendentious writing dealing with the presence of the Portuguese in India. The aim of this paper is not to add another exercise in glorification or vilification, but simply to try and investigate objectively one aspect of Portuguese activities in the sixteenth century—that of trade on the West Indian coast. The situation in the fifteenth century will be sketched, so far as the limited sources allow. Then the methods by which the Portuguese tried to control West Indian trade will be described, and the differing reactions of the traders of two areas in India, Calicut and Gujarat, will be investigated.

In the absence of any detailed records it is difficult to be very definite about trading patterns in West India during the so-called Arab period, which ended in the early sixteenth century. It seems that after the Chinese stopped trading past Malacca the major route in South Asia was that from Malacca to the Red Sea via Malabar. The most important article carried over this route was spices from the Spice Islands, destined for markets all over Asia and, via the Red Sea and Egypt, for Europe. There were numerous feeders growing on to this Malacca to the Red Sea route. The following can be listed briefly from Malacca eastwards to China, Indonesia and the Philippines; from Coromandel, Bengal, Burma and Siam; from Ceylon; from West India North of Malabar, especially from Gujarat; from Ormuz; from East Africa. Of these six, the two most important were those from Malacca to the Spice Islands, which carried the crucial spices to Malacca and so onwards to the West, and from Gujarat, for from here came a large proportion of the cloths and piece goods which paid for the spices. There were also many other frequented routes outside this pattern, especially from Gujarat. From the great ports of this Kingdom ships sailed to the Red Sea, to South Arabia, to Malacca direct, to East Africa, to the Persian Gulf and to Indonesia.

It appears that Muslims dominated all these routes, except that to China and some minor coastal trade, but these Muslims were not all Arabs. Arab merchants did most of the trade from Malabar to the Red Sea, but Gujarat Muslims were most important on the second half of the major route to Malacca

*30th Session at Bhagalpur, 1968.

and the very large trade up the West Coast from Malabar to Konkan, Gujarat and Ormuz was handled by a great variety of Muslims, with some Jews and Hindus also participating. Thus at Ormuz, which was the great transhipment centre for horses en route from Persia and Arabia to the Bahmani Kingdom and Vijayanagar, Abd-er-Razzack in 1442 found merchants from Gujarat, Vijayanagar, Java, Bengal, and Malabar.[1] Varthema distinguished Muslims from twenty-one different areas at Calicut in 1505.[2] The same author had earlier found 400 Turks living at Diu, and indeed he calls the city 'Diuobandierrum', i.e. 'Diu, the port of the 'Turks'.[3]

The Portuguese in the sixteenth century did not try to take over much of this trade for themselves; rather they attempted to control and tax it. To do this, naval dominance was necessary, backed up by a string of forts situated at the great trade areas. In less than twenty years from the date of Vascoda Gama's arrival at Calicut in 1498, Portugal had achieved most of her aims. A combined Egyptian-Calicut fleet was held to a draw off Diu in 1509, and for the rest of the sixteenth century the Portuguese armadas were never challenged by a major fleet. Portuguese strongholds had been established at Malacca, Cochin, Colombo, Goa and Ormuz. By the time of the death of Albuquerque in 1515 the Portuguese had only two major desiderata left in West India—to establish a fort in Gujarat so that the flourshing trade here could be controlled as closely as was that of the rest of West India, and to end the resistance of Calicut to Portuguese dominance.

Before going on to consider these two centres of resistance to the Portuguese claim to control all the trade of the Arabian Sea, it is necessary to investigate more closely the mechanics of the Portuguese control. The first point to be made is that in general the Portuguese tried to control trade in West India, and indeed in South Asia in general, but they did not try to take it all over for themselves. Portuguese merchant ships did trade to Malacca, and further East, and also to Gujarat, and from Calicut to Goa, but the only route where the Portuguese alone sailed was that to Europe via the Cape of Good Hope. Further, a large part of the trade done by the Portuguese was handled by private traders, not by the State. The King attempted to restrict dealings in spices, silk, and horses to royal ships, but for the rest individual Portuguese are frequently heard of. Indeed, at least on one occasion a privately-owned ship sailed to Portugal, and on this route space on the royal ships was set aside for the goods of private merchants.[4]

The main instrument of control used by the Portuguese was the cartaz, or pass. Any ship found sailing in West India waters without one of these documents was liable at best to be confiscated, and at worst sunk with all hands. Such a policy was justified by the official Portuguese chronicler in these words: 'It is true that there does exist a common right to all to navigate the seas and in Europe we recognize the rights which others hold against us; but this right does not extend beyond Europe and therefore the Portuguese as Lords of the Sea are justified in confiscating the goods of all those who navigate the seas without their permission.'[5] These cartazes laid down when a ship could leave, where it could go, and what arms and cargo it could carry. One granted to the King of Bijapur in 1613 was for a voyage from Dadhol to Jiddah. It laid down in some detail what weapon could be carried, and forbade the ship to transport Turks, Abyssinians, cinnamon, pepper, ginger, iron, steel, copper, lead, tin, brass, timber, taboaco (?), coir, saltpetre, sulphur, or bamboo, or anything else forbidden. Nor could this ship transport any Portuguese, nor horses unless they were licensed, nor slaves, unless they were natives of Bijapur and not Christians. The ship was to be searched by the Royal Factor at Dabhol before it left.[6] In return, a ship carrying a cartaz was not to be molested by Portuguese ships, and would be protected by their armadas against pirates.

These cartazes had to be paid for, the tax on one pilgrim ship from Surat being Rs. 2,000, and in addition ships carrying cartazes were usually forced to call at ports controlled by the Portuguese, so that customs duties could be collected. Thus once the Portuguese held Diu, from 1535, all ships coming to Gujarat had to call at Diu first and pay customs.[7] This policy was very lucrative for the Portuguese. For example, at Goa the customs duty on horses was £80 each in 1567. Customs receipts at Diu in 1575 were reported to be £30,000.[8] Further, by forcing as many ships as possible to call at Portuguese ports, their enemies such as Calicut were denied trade and revenue.

To maintain this control the Portuguese employed numerous armadas, which sailed up and down the West Coast of India, and also to the Red Sea entrance, and around Malacca, Coromandel, and Ceylon. In 1523 a total of 46 warships of various sizes were engaged on this task.[9] These armadas checked all the ships they sighted for cartazes. Those that did not have them were captured, and later either sold at auction or ransomed back to their owners. Any ship suspected of being a pirate was sunk on sight.

Apart from issuing cartazes and enforcing them with their armadas, the Portuguese later in the sixteenth century began to organize cafilas, or convoys of merchant ships, which sailed on the West Indian coast and were guarded against pirates by Portuguese warships. This new form of control was necessitated by the opposition of Calicut to the Portuguese claim to control all trade in West India, and we must now consider the response from Calicut and Gujarat to the Portuguese pretensions.

The record of the dealings of Gujarati merchants with the Portuguese is one of considerable and successful flexibility. From the time of Albuquerque the Portuguese had coveted Diu, but it was only in 1535 that Sultan Bahadur under pressure from Humayun, allowed the Portuguese to build a fort there in return for their help against the Mughal King. The fort survived two epic seiges by Gujarat. Prior to 1535 the Portuguese had found the absence of a strong point off the Gujarat coast a great gap in their system, for as Portuguese domination spread in the early sixteenth century many merchants moved to this one remaining free area in West India. As a result Diu flourished greatly. Pepper was brought from Malabar to Diu, and from there was taken to the Red Sea by the fleet of Arabian ships which came each year. These ships paid for the pepper with goods very similar to those the Portuguese imported to India, such as copper, quicksilver, velvets, satins and weapons, and as a result Portuguese imports did not sell as well as they could have.[10] Diu also took over part of the valuable horse trade as the Portuguese consolidated their control of the seas around Dabhol and Bassein, which had been the chief points of entry. Other merchants from Gujarat traded to the Bay of Bengal, and Sumatra.

Once the Portuguese had established themselves at Diu, and in 1559 at Daman, it was clear that the merchants of Gujarat bent with the wind and accepted Portuguese cartazes for their ships when they could not do otherwise. By doing this their profits were perhaps reduced, but their trading operations continued. Nor could the Portuguese always force them to trade only to their settlements, for some Gujaratis traded, in Southeast Asia to Achen and Bantam, not Malacca. With their cloth they bought spices, and Chinese goods, and these they then took to Mocha and sold for cash. It is inconceivable that the Portuguese would have issued cartazes for such trade, for they claimed to monopolise the spice trade. Thus this trade in spices at least must have been done illegally, from the Portuguese point of view. But it seemed that most Gujarat merchants preferred to work within the Portuguese system; some even sailed on Portuguese ships to Malacca and Cochin.[11]

The most important trade of Gujarat in the Seconal half of the sixteenth century was evidently to the Red Sea. We have records for three years early in the seventeenth century of ships bound for Red Sea ports. Of a total of 67 ships observed. 31 were from Gujarat ports, including Diu, Daman, and Bassein (none of these were Portuguese ships), and 36 were from all other places, which included East Africa, the rest of West India, and Southeast Asia.[12] Generally it seems that the Portuguese presence hindered external trade based on Gujarat but this trade continued nontheless, in very large volume, in the sixteenth century.

The reaction of Calicut to the Portuguese claims was different, for the prosperity of this kingdom was based on the Muslim's use of it as an entrepot. For this reason the Zarnorin rejected a request by the Portuguese that he expel all Muslim merchants from his dominions. Further, Calicut's main exports were pepper and ginger, both of which the Portuguese King claimed as a royal monopoly. Thus the hostility between the two was fundamental. The whole existence of Calicut was threatened by the Portuguese, especially after they made an alliance with the Raja of Cochin, who had been loosely subordinate to the Zamorin, and directed all trade to Cochin while blockading Calicut. The peace treaties between the two in the sixteenth century never lasted long, and nor did a Portuguese factory at Calicut early in the century, or a fort which they were allowed to build by the terms of the peace of 1513. Throughout the century the Portuguese treated ships from Calicut, which they called 'Malavares', as pirates, and attacked them on sight. This was only to be expected when the two were at war, but even during the uneasy intervals of peace the Portuguese curtailed so strictly the articles in which the Calicut ships were allowed to trade that nearly any 'Malavare' inspected by the Portuguese was sure to be carrying something which the Portuguese considered contraband.[13]

It is necessary to try and clarify just who were these 'Malavares' or 'cossarios' whom the Portuguese attacked with such abandon. Some were actually light naval vessels under the command of the Kunjali admirals of Calicut, fighting a guerrilla war against the Portuguese and their allies the Cochinese. Others were mercenaries fighting for other Indian powers, as for Malik Ambar and the Mughals in the early seventeenth century.[14] Others again were undoubtedly pirates pure and simple. Malabar produced many pirates in the fifteenth century.[15] As Calicut weakened as a result of Portuguese attacks piracy increased, and the Zamorin refused to recognise such pirates as being in his service.[16] But there is no doubt that many of the 'Malavares' which the Portuguese sank were actually merchant ships engaged in legitimate trade, albeit in goods which the Portuguese claimed to monopolise. These traders had little choice but to resist. Gujarat produced articles over which the Portuguese did not claim a monopoly, which Gujarati merchants could trade with, but Calicut did not.[17] Thus, many of the pirates on the West Indian coast were actually created by the Portuguese, while others existed only in their minds.

Piracy increased as the despair of Calicut's merchants grew. By the late 1560s it was unsafe for a lone merchant ship to sail almost any where on the West Indian coast, even near Goa and in the Gulf of Cambay.[18] The Portuguese armadas could not be everywhere at once, and so in the 1560s the Goa government inaugurated a new method of controlling and protecting local trade. This was the Cafila or convoy system. There are indications that Muslim ships travelled together in the fifteenth century,[19] and earlier in the sixteenth Portuguese warships sometimes escorted merchant ships, but now the system was made regular. Large convoys of several hundred local merchant ships, guarded by a few Portuguese warships, came each year from the North and the South to Goa. By this means food and articles for export to Portugal arrived at Goa. A typical cafila of 1613 is described by the chronicler Bocarro. The Portuguese fleet collected some ships from round the area of Cape Comorin, and brought them to Quilon, where other ships from Quilon, and also Coromandel, joined. All these were taken on to Cochin. Then the protection fleet returned to Cape Comorin to collect stragglers, and then they all went on to Goa, collecting more ships from Mangalore, Barcelore, and Onor on the way.[20] The cafila from the North started only after the Mughal conquest of 1572–73. During the Sultanate period Portuguese merchants lived and traded at Cambay,[21] but their goods went via Diu. At least by the end of the century, however, a regular convoy came from Cambay to Goa, via Daman, Bassein and

Chaul.[22] It is to be noted that these cafilas apparently only operated on the West Indian coast. Elsewhere the Portuguese continued to sell cartazes to merchants who then travelled independently of any Portuguese supervision except casual inspection by armadas.

Finally, we must attempt to formulate some general observations on the effects of these methods of control on the local merchants, who are my main interest. First, how much trade continued outside the Portuguese system? It appears a considerable amount. By the 1560s the spice trade in the Mediterranean had regained its fifteenth century level, despite the Portuguese King's claims to a monopoly.[23] These are records of Gujarati and Turkish ships taking on pepper at Achen for the Red Sea, and some ships from Calicut succeeded including the Portuguese. Nevertheless, given the strategic locations of the Portuguese forts, and their armadas cruising in the Arabian Sea and elsewhere, it seems that many Asian merchants trading in West India did find it safer to buy Portuguese cartazes, although how closely their stringent conditions were observed, is another matter.

The Portuguese justified their issuing of cartazes, and their cafilas, partly on the strength of their self-proclaimed position as Lords of the Sea, and partly as they claimed that they provided protection from pirates in return. But to what extent did this protection compensate for the disadvantages attached to accepting the Portuguese control? Certainly there were considerable disadvantages associated with accepting a Portuguese cartaz or travelling in a Portuguese cafila. Indeed, the escort of the cafila had a dual function: to protect the cafila from pirates, and to stop members of the cafila from escaping.[24] Ships travelling in cafilas were quite at the mercy of the Portuguese, so that, for example, if the accompanying escort was needed elsewhere the cafila was forced to wait until the Portuguese ships returned from their mission. Cartazes were expensive, as were the customs duties at Portuguese forts. There were cases of ships carrying Portuguese cartazes being stopped and forced to pay an additional sum to another Portuguese ship.[25] It seems clear that most local merchants would never have travelled in cafilas, and certainly would never have taken cartazes, were it not that the Portuguese forced them to. Further, we may repeat here that many of the so-called pirates were actually legitimate traders driven to piracy by the Portuguese monopolistic policies, so that to a great extent the Portuguese provided protection from pirates whom they had themselves created.

In conclusion, we may ask what effect the Portuguese had on the composition of Asian traders in West India. We have seen that Muslims dominated this trade in the fifteenth century, but in the sixteenth century there is evidence that Hindus, especially from Gujarat, were increasingly trading overseas. This was not because the Portuguese discriminated against Muslim traders despite the complaints of the religious that Muslims were being allowed to travel on Portuguese ships from the Red Sea to Goa, and so to Southeast

Asia, where they proselytised for Islam, the Portuguese secular authorities seem to have been ready to allow Muslims to trade provided they had cartazes. Muslims, along with those of other faiths, settled in Portuguese towns such as Cochin, Goa, Malacca and Ormuz.[26] But it is clear that Hindus, once the Muslim dominance of the fifteenth century was broken by the Portuguese, began to trade and settle abroad increasingly. Banias are described in the late sixteenth and early seventeenth centuries as being important merchants at Goa, Diu, Achen, Mocha, and San'a an inland town in Yemen. However, it appears that Muslims of various races continued to be most important among Asian traders, outweighing all others, including Jews, Armenians and Hindus, in the extent of their seaborne trade.

Notes

1. R.H. Major, *India in the Fifteenth Century*, pp. 5–6.
2. L.Varthema, *The Itinerary of Ludovico di Varthema*, p. 61.
3. Ibid., pp. 37–8.
4. J. Linschoten, *The Voyage of John H. Van Linschoten*, II, pp. 225–6; Antonio da Fonseca to King, Goa, 18 October 1523, Corpo Chronologico, 1-30-36, MacGregor Papers, University of Singapore; J. Wicki, ed., *Documenta Indica*, II, 130.
5. Quoted in K.M. Panikkar, *India and the Indian Ocean*, p. 40.
6. J.FJ. Biker, *Colleccao de Tratados*, IV, 181.2.
7. Sa, Artur Basilio de, ed., *Documentacao para a Historia das Missoes de Padroado Portugues de Oriente*, V, pp. 218–19, 234; see also Diogo do Couto, *Vida de D. Paulo de Lima Pereira*, p. 76.
8. C. Frederick, *Travels*, in Richard Hakluyt, *Principal Navigations of the English Nation*, V, p. 381; J. Wicki, *Documenta Indica*, X, 135.
9. Fonseca to King, Goa, 18 October 1523, op. cit.
10. Ibid.
11. Samuel Purchas, *Hakluytus Posthumus, or Purchas his Pilgrimes*, 20. vols, III, 89; Linschoten, op. cit., I, 58; C.F. Beckingham, 'Dutch Travellers in the Seventeenth Century,' in *Journal of the Royal Asiatic Society*, 1951, pp. 71–2, 78; Fazlullah Lutfullah Faridi trans, *Mirat-i-Sikandari*, pp. 84–5, 295.
12. C.F. Beckingham, op. cit, pp. 79–81; S. Purchas, op. cit., III, pp. 152–5, 190–3.
13. M.J. Rowlandson, trans, *Tohfut-ul-Mujahideen*, pp. 111–12, 130–46, 150–4.
14. Antonio, Bocarro, *Decada 13 da Historia da India*, p.213; N. Downton, *The Voyage of Nicholas Downton*, p. 4.
15. R.H. Major, op. cit., p. 18; L. Varthema, op. cit, p. 63; Fazlullah, op. cit., p. 63.
16. Couto, Diogo do, op. cit., p. 47; J. Linschoten, op. cit., II, p. 169 MJ. Rowlandson, op. cit., p. 157.
17. See, for example, M.J. Rowlandson, op. cit., pp. 123, 126–7.
18. Ibid., pp. 157–8; J. Wicki, *Documenta Indica*, X, 3.
19. K.M. Panikkar op. cit., p. 42; O.K. Nambiar, *The Kunjalis—Admirals of Calicut*, p. 38.
20. Antonio Bocarro, op. cit., pp. 77–8.

21. C. Frederick, op. cit., V, 375.
22. For example, Bocarro, op. cit., p. 15; Thomas Best, *The Voyage of Thomas Best*, p. 34.
23. F.C. Lane, 'National Wealth and Production Costs' in *War as a Social Institution*, pp. 36–42.
24. P. Delia Valle, *The Travels of Pietra della Valle*, II, 393–4.
25. Fonseca to King, Goa, 18 Oct. 1523, op. cit.
26. J. Wicki, *Documents Indica*, I, 504–5; II, 548; III, 539, IV, 492; V.179.

21

The System of Bills of Exchange (*Hundis*) in the Mughal Empire

Irfan Habib

IN AN article entitled 'Banking in Mughal India', published in *Contributions to Indian Economic History*, ed. Tapan Raychaudhuri, Calcutta, 1960, I attempted a description of the Indian system of bills of exchange as it functioned during the Mughal Empire (pp. 8–14). Looking back today on that portion of my article the only defence I can offer for myself is that no one had written on the theme earlier. I committed certain elementary mistakes, such as thinking that two separate, exchange-rates existed, one for merchants, the other for *sarrafs*', that the *sarrafs*, when they drew *hundis*, always gained a premium, while merchants had always to pay discounts, and so on.

I owe it, therefore, particularly to the readers of that article, to make a fresh attempt, so as partly to eliminate the confusion that I may myself have caused. But the theme is, of course, of sufficient importance in itself to merit enquiry without much excuse.

While narrating the events of the 40th year of Akbar's reign, Abul Fazl digresses on the subject of the *hundi*, whose spelling he clearly sets forth by using the word-names of the consonants and noting the vowels. 'In this country', he says, 'when any one wishes to transmit money to a distant place, without undertaking the risks of journey and expenses of conveyance, he delivers the money to a financier (*khwastadar*). The latter gives him a written paper, which he draws on the place desired; and there he (the drawee) hands over the money upon sight of that hand-written paper. Wonderful it is that no seal or witness is required. That document they all know by the said name (*hundi*). In accordance with place and time, on some occasions the payment is made at par while on others gain accrues to one of the two parties'.[1] In other words, depending upon the stream of remittances and reverse-remittances between any two places, a *hundi*, drawn at one place upon the other, might carry either a premium or discount.

About a hundred years later (1695–96), the historian Sujan Raj Bhandari offered another description of this species of paper:

*33rd Session at Muzaffarpur, 1972.

If, because of dangers on the routes, a person cannot convey sums of money to a near or distant place, the *sarrafs* take it from him, and give him a piece of paper written in the Hindvi characters, without a seal or envelope addressed to their agents (*gumashta-ha*), who have their shops in the various towns and places throughout these lands; and this paper in the language of this country is known as *hundi*. The *gumashtas* of these honest dealers, pay out the money, in accordance with that document, without any argument or objection, though the distance may be two hundred leagues (*farsang*), and so they keep their dealings straight. It is still more wonderful that though that document is nothing more than a piece of paper, if its possessors wish to sell it at a place other than the one where payment is promised, it is sold for the sum that it specifies, and the purchaser, obtaining a small amount from the seller, receives the sum stated in it, at the promised place.[2]

Sujan Raj thus adds two further points of importance to Abul Fazl's description. One is that it was the *sarrafs* ('money-changers', the Indian bankers), who specialised in issuing *hundis* to enable remittances to be made. A similar statement is made in the famous dictionary, *Bahar-i-Ajam*, s.v. *hindui*.[3] The French traveller and merchant, also made a general statement to this effect.[4] These general statements are, in turn, corroborated in convincing detail, by the actual records of transactions, especially remittances through bills, made by the factors of the English East India Company, who had always to approach the 'shroffs' for the purpose.

The second point emerging from Sujan Rai's description is that the *hundi* was a negotiable document, usually transferred at a small discount. It was thus convertible from a means of remittance into an instrument of credit.

It is quite clear that the *sarrafs* specialised not only in issuing *hundis*, but also in discounting them. Indeed, in 1655, the English factors at Agra reported that the *sarrafs* were not lending out money at interest, for they were 'Finding more profit by exchange', i.e., by using their funds to discount *hundis*,[5] Whenever the English drew a 'bill', it was usually discounted by a sarraf.[6]

In circumstances when remittances and loans were few, or commerce was not extensively supported by credit, the rate of 'exchange', that is the amount of money paid at the place of issue of the *hundi* as against the drawn by *sarrafs* and on those discounted by them. But if extensive dealing in such bills had been established, the two rates were likely to converge. For, supposing the *sarrafs* were to demand a much larger amount against a *hundi* they had drawn, than what they themselves paid while discounting someone else's *hundi*, this would induce the two other parties, namely, the remitter and the borrower (one wishing to make payment at the place, the other desired to send money to) to dispense with the services of the *sarrafs* by seeking each other out—a process which would be so much the easier the larger the number of such remitters and borrowers.

It is an important fact, therefore, that in the English commercial records, only a single rate of 'exchange' is quoted for bills drawn at one place upon another, irrespective of whether it was on a *hundi* drawn by *sarrafs* to arrange remittance or on one drawn by a merchant seeking credit. It is, indeed, only by a rare good fortune that we come across a report in which the rates of exchange on these two kinds of *hundis* are distinguished. The English factors at Ahmadabad, writing in 1622, when there was apparently a premium on remittances made to Burhanpur, say that the rate of exchange for bills on Burhanpur "was, the takers-up shall receive 91½ and the deliverers to pay 92¾ rupp(ees) seccawes, to pay or receive 100 Brampore rupp(ees)."[7] In other words, a person who 'took up' money at Ahmadabad by drawing a bill on Burhanpur, would receive from the *sarrafs* Rs.91½ *sikka* as against the promised payment of Rs. 100, in rupees current at Burhanpur, whereas a person who 'delivered' money to the *sarrafs* was called upon to pay them Rs. 92¾ *sikka* to get a *hundi* on Burhanpur from them for 100 rupees current at Burhanpur. Similarly, for *hundis* drawn at Ahmadabad on Surat, the same report gives the following two rates: (a) for takers-up, Rs. 42¼ and 42 3/16, against *hundis* of 100 *mahmudis* payable at Surat; and (b) for deliverers, Rs. 42¾.[8] Thus in issuing a *hundi*, and discounting another, the *sarrafs* made a gain of about 1¼% in the case of those on Burhanpur, and a gain of 1¼% to 1 3/8%, on those on Surat. If the gain was equally shared between drawing and discounting, the *sarrafs'* charges, as brokers between the remitters and debtors, would come to about 5/8% on each *hundi*.

These charges do not appear to be high, and the small margin of difference between the rates for 'deliverers' and 'takers-up' suggests, for reasons explained above, that the business in bills was quite brisk. Just as the rates at which the *sarrafs* issued and discounted *hundis* were bound to come very close to each other, if commerce were brisk, so also it was natural that a close correlation should exist between the rates at which *hundis* were drawn at one place, say A, on another place, B, and those at which they were drawn at B on A. If the rates did not correspond, then a person who wished to send money from A to B, by *hundi* purchased at A, might find it more profitable to draw a *hundi* himself at B, redeemable at A[9]; or a person who wished to adopt the latter course, might choose the former. Thus if the transactions were numerous enough to make the choice of these alternative means possible, one would expect that when *a* represents the ratio between the payment received by *sarraf* at A and the amount at which his *hundi* was to be redeemed at B, and *b*, the ratio between the amount at which the sarraf sold his *hundi* at B and the payment to be made at A, then, in conditions of perfect competition, *b* should be 100/*a*.

A test for this is at hand in the English records of 1622. Here with A standing for Ahmadabad and B for Burhanpur, we find that *a* was as 92 3/4 Rs. *sikka* to Rs. 100 current, payable at B; and our simple equation given above should give the value of *b*, as Rs. 107.8 current to Rs. 100 *sikka* payable at A. We find that this time the English factor at Burhanpur had actually paid at the rate of Rs. 106 3/4 for Rs. 100 (*sikka*) at Ahmadabad.[10] The difference between the hypothetical and actual rates is small enough to show that competitive conditions were sufficiently strong to force the rates quoted at the two places to correspond (inversely) to each other.

Given such competition among the *sarrafs*, and a minimum development of commerce, the rates of exchange between any two places were likely to be determined by the total 'balance of payments' position of each place. A sudden spurt of payments made in any direction might create pressures upon the *sarrafs* for cash at one place, while leaving more in their hands at another—a situation that they could only rectify by discouraging remittances from the former to the latter and encouraging reverse remittances, through modifying the exchange rates. An instance of this is furnished by the English factors' reports from Patna. In the course of the month of March, the exchange rate on bills drawn at Patna on Agra altered from 98 1/8 Rs. *nuris* (*sikka*) to 98 3/4 Rs. *sikka* against Rs. 100 *hundi* payable at Agra. This fall in the discount was explained as due to the 'delivering' of Rs. 300,000 by Muqarrab Khan, the outgoing Governor of Bihar, for payment at Agra.[11]

The Gujarat famine of 1630–32 had a similar influence on the exchange rates, by accumulating balances due to Agra at Surat, on account of the grain supplied to that famished region.[12] As a result remittances to Agra had to be made at a heavy discount—2% in 1630,[13] and 'practically 7%' of the amount payable at Agra in 1631.[14] As late as 1634 when the English at Agra drew upon Surat, they had to pay a discount of 8 5/8%.[15] But as Gujarat slowly recovered, and no longer needed such heavy grain 'imports' its balance-of-payments position improved. Thus the loss to the remitter from Surat to Agra was only 1/2% in 1636[16]; and Tavernier, whose experience, belonged to the period, 1640 to 1667, says that such remittances were made at par.[17]

There were cyclical fluctuations too in the premiums/discounts on remittances, depending on the season's commodities came on the market atone place and were sold at another. A single quotation, from 1661, will serve to illustrate this:

To pay money in Cossumbazar (Qasimbazar) and receive it in Pattana (Patna), upon a bill of Exchange, a month after date, always yields profit. I have known it from 1 to 6 per cent. When the silk sells well at Agra; the produce (proceeds) is usually sent to Cossumbazar (the major silk-mart) in money overland, which is the reason that when great sums of money come frcm thence the exchange of money to Pattana in one day doth sometimes fall 2½ to 3%.[18]

One thing more is certain. Throughout the seventeenth century, India enjoyed an immensely favourable balance of trade with Europe and the Middle East, as a result of which silver and gold accumulated at the ports, and after being minted, had continuously to be transported inland. Remittances from the ports to places inland, therefore, always involved loss by exchange for the remitters (and a corresponding gain for the drawers). Since the English were almost invariably in the position of remitters, in this direction, it is not surprising that they suffered this loss constantly. They suffered this, of course, irrespective of whether they purchased a *hundi* at Surat drawn on any place in land, or drew one themselves at one of the inland places on Surat, to procure such remittance.

This situation can be seen by comparing the rates at which *hundis* were drawn at Surat on Agra and *vice versa*. We have already seen that the cost of remittance from Surat to Agra during the period of the famine was very high. But even when these extraordinary circumstances disappeared the remitter received his amount at par at Agra, while those milking the reverse remittance gained a premium of 4 1/4 and 5%. This is what Tavernier says.[19] The English records show, as we have seen, that in 1636 they lost 1/2% in remitting money from Surat to Agra;[20] but in drawing bills at Agra on Surat, they quoted discounts at 4 3/8% in 1645, 4 3/8% again in 1948 and 4 1/8% in 1632.[21] In 1655, possibly under exceptional circumstances, the Dutch were reported to be paying even 5 3/4 and 6 3/4% in discounts on *hundis* drawn by them at Agra, while others were allowing to 'sheroffs' discounts as high as 9 and 11%.[22] Interest, of course, has to be considered in analysing these rates; but it is clear that the conditions were far more favourable for remittance from Agra to Surat than for remittance in the opposite direction.

A pretty similar situation too prevailed in respect of remittances to and from Thatta, which again was a port of entry for large amounts of bullion brought in from the Middle East. On money remitted by exchange from Ahmadabad to Thatta, a gain of 2% was quoted in 1635.[23] In 1647, in order to remit money to Thatta, the English discounted a bill drawn at Ahmadabad on Thatta, at a net gain of 1½ to themselves[24]. On the other hand, a *hundi* drawn at Thatta, maturing after 61 days at Ahamadabad, carried a discount of only 1% at a time (1635) when the interest rate at Thatta was no less than 1 and 1¼% per month.[25]

The rate of discount/premium on a *hundi* was determined partly by the real rate of exchange depending upon the balance of payments between the places of issue and maturity. Partly, it was determined by the rate of interest for the period between its issue and redemption.

The *hundi* itself specified whether it was to be payable on sight, or payable at the end of a particular period *after* its presentation to the drawee.

This is established by two passages from the English factory records. In 1621 Hughes wrote from Patna to the factors at Agra that though they had written to say that the *hundis* were of 40 days 'bandye mudet' (*band-i muddat?*), the *hundis* themselves were made out at 45. He suggested that the period should be twice seven (=14) days 'berbust' (*barbast*, customary); this would save the Patna factors much in 'deheig', especially if a speedy 'cassad' (*qasid*, messenger) was employed, the last two *qasids* being praised for having arrived in 11 days.[26] I have not been able to trace the term 'deheig'; it seems to mean the interest or discount paid for cashing the *hundi*; before the date. Now, if the period before the date of maturity of the *hundi* was counted from the date of issue, the speed of *qasids* would have been immaterial, so long as they arrived before the due date. It could only have significance if the period after which drawee had to pay was counted from the date he had sight of the *hundi*. Thus in the case of the *hundis* mentioned by Hughes, the actual period before payment became due must at least have been 11+45 days.

A similar inference is to be drawn from an earlier letter, sent from Broach to Surat, in 1616. The Surat factors are reproached for not having insisted on payment on sight, but having allowed a period of 4 days. Had it been payable on sight, the drawees would have paid after 4 or 5 days (days of grace?). With 4 days allowed, they would now pay after double that time (8 days).[27] It is thus implicit, again, that the period specified in the *hundi* began after its presentation to the drawee.

The information on the customary periods for which *hundis* were issued suggests that the periods varied broadly with the distance. A bill drawn at Cambay upon Allahabad was payable 2 1/2 double days after sight.[28] A bill from Surat upon Burhanpur was described as 'payable at four double days as per custome'.[29] So also one from Ahmadabad upon Surat was 'payable four double days accustomed'.[30] It is to be assumed then, that *hundis* between these towns usually were payable 8 days after sight. It took a 'bazar cosset', *bazar qasid* (general messenger), less than 9 days to convey letters from Ahmadabad to Surat.[31] So that it may be further assumed that the discount/premium on the bill between these two places had to allow for interest for about 17 days.

Between Agra and Patna, as we have seen already, the period specified was 40 or 45 days, and allowing for 11 days for 'speedy' messengers to traverse the distance, this implied allowance of interest for a period of 51 or 56 days.

Between more distant towns the period seems to have been 60 days. '61 daies of payment' were specified for bills drawn at Thatta in Ahmadabad.[32] Tavernier gives two months as the customary period governing payment of bills from inland towns to Surat. But since he says that all bills from such places as Dacca, Patna and Benares, had first to be drawn upon Agra, and then only upon Surat, it seems that the period was generally customary for the bills drawn at Agra upon Surat (and, presumably, *vice versa*).[33] Since it took a messenger 34 days to cover the distance between the two places[34] the discount/ premium must have had to allow for interest for a period of more than three months.

It happens that we have considerable information about the interest rates prevailing at Surat during the period (1640–67) to which Tavernier's experiences in India belong. From 1635 to 1650 the rate at which the English could borrow was 1% per month, it then fell and fluctuated between 5/8 and 3/4% until

1665; though the rate at which the English couldlend to merchants was only
1/2%.[35] In Agrain 1645, the *sarrafs* paid 5/8% per month on deposits, but lent
out at 1% to 2 1/2%. Though the English had borrowed at 1% previously, now
they were able to reduce the interest on their debt to 3/4% and 5/8%.[36] One
would think, therefore, that the discount/premium on a *hundi* drawn at Agra
on Surat or *vice versa* must have had to allow between 2 and 3% for interest
(counting on the basis of the monthly rates of 5/8 and 1%, multiplied by 3).
We may further suppose that when the *sarrafs* drew *hundis* at either place on
the other, they allowed a rate of interest no higher than what they paid on
deposits placed with them, i.e., 5/8% per month and so about 2% on each such
hundi; while when they discounted *hundis*, they charged a rate closer to 1% per
month, i.e., 3% on each *hundi*.

Now, if with these data we look at the actual discount and premium rates,
interesting corroboration of our hypothesis is obtained. Tavernier tells us that
a merchant wishing to send money from Surat to inland places received it at
the latter at par.[37] We know that in 1636, remittance by *hundi* from Surat to
Agra involved a loss of only ½%.[38] Allowing for interest at 2%, conceded by the
sarraf drawing the *hundi*, it means roughly that the remitter paid Rs. 100 at
Surat to obtain Rs. 98 at Agra (the sum paid at Agra *less* interest). Conversely,
therefore, those engaging in reverse remittances should have obtained about Rs.
102 at Surat for every Rs. 100 paid at Agra. Since Tavernier (and the English
also) assume here the position of those who drew the *hundis* to be discounted
by the *sarrafs*, we can assume that the interest allowed for on the *hundi* was now
3%, not 2%. Thus the *hundi* drawn at Agra upon Surat by a merchant should
have carried a total discount of about 5%. We have seen above that in actual
fact the discounts on such *hundis* ranged from 4 3/8% to 4 1/8%., between
1645 and 1652; and Tavernier puts the usual discount at 4 1/4% and 5%.[39] The
hypothesis is thus broadly confirmed.

It appears that Tavernier considered the discounts to be rather high.[40] It is
not clear, however, why he should have thought so. In Europe too bills bore
quite large premiums or discounts. 'In 1680 the premium on an inland bill of
exchange from Newcastle-upon-Tyne to London, before the sailing of the coal
fleet was 5 per cent.[41] The distance between Newcastle and London is of course,
far less than the distance between Surat and Agra.

Possibly Tavernier had in mind the difference between the discount the
merchant obtained when he discounted a *hundi* drawn by a *sarraf*, to make a
remittance, and what he paid when drawing a *hundi* himself. This difference,
which was slight in short distance *hundis*, such as those drawn at Ahmadabad
on Burhanpur and Surat, being about 5/8% (see above) was likely to be higher
on long-distance ones, because of the larger allowance for interest, which was
calculated at two different rates. From Tavernier's words, it appears, furthermore,
that the difference not only arose out of the two separate rates of interest, but
also because the discount on a *hundi* drawn by a merchant, who had done so

to purchase and despatch goods for sale at the place where the payment was due, covered the cost of insurance of the goods as well. For, he says, 'those who lend the money (by discounting the merchant's *hundi*) must accept on their part the risk that if the goods are stolen, the money is lost to them.'[42] Such *hundis* are now known as *jokhami hundis*,[43] An actual instance of how the discount included costs of insurance is furnished by the report of the English factors at Ahmadabad, in 1647, that they had discounted two bills drawn on Thatta at 'two per cent profit, less half a rupee (per cent) for insurance.'[44]

Earlier in this paper we have quoted Sujan Rai Bhandari, who, writing in 1695, commented on the *hundi* being transferable. An established customary law appears to have governed the obligations of different parties involved. If the drawee refused to pay, then the *hundi* was returned to the drawer, and the latter had to pay 5% over and above the value of the *hundi*.[45] From another report, it seems that the drawee too was held liable, until the drawer paid up, and even after that the drawee might be called upon to pay 1% of the value of the *hundi*.[46] Where the *hundi* had passed through many hands, the person who presented the *hundi* to the drawee could on the latter's refusal to pay, demand its value from the person who had sold it to him; and so, up the chain, the principal could ultimately be claimed from the drawer. 'Now, the law of these nations (India) is in such a case that if a merchant cannot recover in what is due on such bills, that he shall return them to the persons of whom he bought them and receive his money without interest.' This custom of the country was recognised to be 'different... from all others', since elsewhere (and, in England, at any rate), a person who had once sold a bill was no longer under any obligation to pay anything if it was not honoured.[47]

The Indian custom had this significance, that a *hundi* which had been discounted by merchants of credit, could be confidently purchased in the knowledge that in the event of the drawee's failure, the amount of the principal could be claimed from those who had discounted it earlier. This explains the procedure adopted at Patna in 1621, when the English factor, Hughes, received a bill from the Agra factors, drawn by Kalyan, a *sarraf* at Agra, upon his 'gamoshtye' (*gumashta*, agent) at Patna. The *gumashta* had left the city. The other *sarrafs* cashed the bill, but only after Hughes had discounted (i.e., formally endorsed) it, which, in the light of our other information, means that he had made himself liable to compensate the *sarrafs* should they fail to receive satisfaction from the drawer.[48]

The negotiability of *hundis* led to a situation in which a large number of *hundis* were simply drawn and honoured against other *hundis* without the intermediation of actual cash payments. The simplest case is represented by the drawing of a *hundi* to meet another that is due.[49] One *hundi* may then be exchanged for another. But, of course, in actual practice much more complex conditions prevailed, with *hundis* constantly passing hands in adjusting payments, and thus becoming, in the process, a medium of payment. This situation is described in the *Mirat-i-Ahmadi* in the following terms:

Suppose a person having paid a fixed sum at the port of Surat to a *sarraf* of that place, brings a *hundi*, which in Persian is called *sufta*, drawn by him (the *sarraf*) on his partner or agent at Ahmadabad, he may, if he chooses, collect cash, paying the deduction on account of *anth* at the current rate or, in case another person has a claim against possessor of the hindui (*awarinda-i hundwi*), for that sum, he may give it to that person, and so free himself from that obligation. Similarly, he (the new holder of the *hindui*) may transfer it (the *hundi*) to another, until it reaches a person, against whom the drawee of the *hindui* (*sahib-i hindui*) has claims, and who, therefore, surrendering it to the latter, relieves himself of his debt. But cash is not used throughout.[50]

This was written about 1761. But the term *anth* occurs in an English document of 1652. In this it is pointed out that at Agra the coins used for the purchase of goods are called 'Cutche Ant' (*kachcha anth*), while 'the good exchange money rupees paid to merchants (are) called Pucka Annt (*pakka anth*) assignacian." The difference between the two amounted to 1%.[51] It thus appears that when a *hundi* was redeemed by other paper, its value was treated at par ('"good exchange money'), equal to the new-coined rupees (*sikka*),[52] but when it was paid for in cash, the cash would be in ordinary rupees (not *sikka*) imposing a loss of 1% on the seller of the *hundi*.

It is thus probable that during the seventeenth century, the system of book settlements of *hundis* already existed, so that the *hundis* served as alternative media of payment. The subsequent artificial inflation of *anth*-deduction, so as to discourage encashment of *hundis*, and then the issuing of bills not redeemable in cash at all, probably developed owing to the 'scarcity of cash' (*kami-i zar*), that originated from the fluctuations in the output of the mints of the eighteenth century.

In 1715 the sarrafs at Ahmadabad raised the rate of the *anth* deduction to 20% or, possibly 8% only, since the words for those numbers are liable to be con fused in Persian writing—for the pretended reason that there was 'scarcity of cash'. The merchants greatly resented this; and a small civil war between them and the *sarrafs* was on the point of breaking out, when a settlement was arrived at, and the increase in the rate of *anth* was cancelled.[53]

Writing in 1821, Malcolm noticed, as a rather disreputable practice, the creation of book-credit through the issue of *anth* ('oant'), or "accommodation bills." He thought that the creation of such 'unreal... .bill- currency' had become common in Ujjain and other towns of Central India only comparatively recently.[54]

If then, in the Mughal Empire during its classic period, the *hundis* or bills served as alternative currency, it was simply a voluntary process, arising out of commercial convenience. How far the *hundis* substituted for coins, or contributed to the money in circulation, is a question that is obviously very difficult to answer. Towards the end of the seventeenth century (1698), Davenent estimated that the assignable instruments in circulation in England totalled 15 millions and exceeded the coinage in the proportion of 5 to 4.[55] No such estimates are available for India. However, there is little reason to believe that at that time the *hundis* were any less used in Indian commerce than bills in England. If there were sometimes difficulties in remitting money to certain places by way of *hundis*,[56] in England too, at this time, the rents due to Oxford Colleges were sent to Oxford from London 'only with the greatest difficulty'.[57]

On the other hand, Tavernier had gone so far as to say, possibly with some degree of exaggeration, that 'in India a village must be very small indeed, if it has not a money-changer, called a Shroff (cheraf in the original) who acts as banker to make remittances of money and issue letters of exchange.'[58] Moreover, the transfers of very large sums by *hundis* attest to the vast volume of money carried by *hundis*, for obviously a single large transaction in one direction did not only imply a converse transaction in the other, but, generally speaking, a stream of such transactions.

Very impressive is the record relating to large transfers and remittances made through bills by the English East India Company. Out of the numerous instances, a few will serve. In 1636, the English at Surat report sending Rs. 50,000 to Agra, by bills, through a *sarraf* (Tapi Dass). What is interesting is that they had only two days earlier asked their colleagues in Ahmadabad to remit this amount to Agra. They wrote now, anticipating that it must have been remitted, and, therefore, directed the Ahmadabad factors to 'write to "Dangce" (their agent at Agra) to send the money back again by exchange. . .'[59] In other words such large transactions were not expected to involve any delay or difficulty. Similarly in 1641, the Surat factors informed the Persian factors that they had remitted to Masulipatam 10,000 pagodas (= Rs. 41,000) by bills, besides another 2,000 pagodas (= Rs. 8,400) by accepting bills drawn at Masulipatam — thus nearly Rs. 50,000 in all.[60] In 1647, again, under one date the Ahmadabad factors acknowledge the receipt of 'bills of exchange' for Rs. 50,000 from Surat.[61]

Not only merchants, but the administration and the nobles as well remitted vast sums through *hundis*. The valuable passage in the *Akbarnama* on the subject of *hundis* follows a reference to the despatch of Rs. 300,000 from the imperial treasury to the army in the Deccan, in 1599.[62] From another document it appears that the entire tribute of Rs. 10,00,000 paid by Golkunda to the Mughals was remitted through *hundis* drawn upon Aurangabad.[63] Similarly, the nobles used *hundis* to remit very large amounts. In 1621 Muqarrab Khan delivered Rs. 300,000 to *sarrafs* at Patna to be paid to him in Agra.[64] In the 40th regnal year of Aurangzeb, we find Sultan Ghakkar, an important chief in the Panjab, remitting Rs. 50,000, being part of his tribute (*peshkash*), through *hundis*, to the imperial court in the Deccan.[65]

Perhaps, the greatest tribute to the capacity of the *hundis* to transfer vast amounts is paid by Aurangzeb in his letter to Prince A'zam, where he orders that the accumulated treasure at Akbarnagar (Rajmahal, Bengal) and Bihar, amounting to 80 or 90 lakhs was to be transported to the Imperial Camp in the Deccan, because despatching it through *hundis* would involve much delay." In future, the surpluses in the treasury were to be sent partly by *hundis* and partly on carts.[66] Thus even a sum of nearly a crore could conceivably have been conveyed by *hundis*, though with some delay.

Notes

1. *Akbarnama, Bib Ind.*, III, p. 762.
2. Sujan Rai Bhandari, *Khulasaiu-t Tawarikh*, ed. Zafar Hasan, p. 25.
3. "*Hindui*. When money is deposited with the *sarraf*, in lieu of payment at another place, this written (paper) is issued. This is an Indian custom, and a Hindi word. In Persian it is called *sufia*" (*Bahar-i-Ajam*, II, p. 498). The. *Bahar-i-Ajam* was completed in AH 1152 (1739–40). *Hindui* is a variant of *hundi*.
4. Tavernier, *Travels in India*, tr. V. Ball., ed. W. Crooke, p. 24. cf. also Manucci, *Storia do Mogor*, tr. W. Irvine, vol. I, p. 241, speaking of "the 'saffafos'" as "the men who issue bills of exchange." Also S. Commissariat, *Mandelslo's Travels in Western India A.D. 1638–9*, pp. 27–28.
5. *English Factories, 1655–60*, pp. 18–19.
6. See, e.g. *English Factories, 1618-21*, p. 236; Mundy, *Travels of Peter Mundy in Europe and Asia*, II, ed. R.C. Temple, p. 290.
7. *English Factories, 1622–23*, p. 68.
8. Ibid., pp. 68–69.
9. An instance of this is furnished by the English at Cambay in 1621, drawing a short- dated bill (payable 'at 2 1/2 double days after sight') on Ahmadabad rather than wait for remittance from the latter place, because, the discount they had to allow on the bill, *viz.*, 6/10%, was less than 'the exchange from Amadavads to Cambaya', which was 7/10%. (*English Factories, 1618–21*, p. 329. It is to be remembered, while checking this passage, that in the English accounts 80 pice made a rupee).
10. *English Factories, 1622–23*, pp. 40, 54, 68. It may be noted that the exchange rates here also covered the difference between the values of the *sikka* Rs. and the current Rs. In 1616 it was reported that 100 *sikka* Rs. were worth 105 Rs. of the kind; current at Burhanpur (Foster, *Supplementary Calendar*, pp. 65, 66).
11. *English Factories, 1618–21*, pp. 236, 248.
12. *English Factories, 1634–36*, p. 225.
13. *English Factories, 1630–33*, p. 96.
14. Ibid., p. 154.
15. *English Factories, 1634–36*, p. 70.
16. Ibid., p. 168–69.
17. Tavernier, tr. Ball, ed, Crooke, I, p. 30.
18. 'Kenn's, etc., advices about Bengal, etc.' in Wilson, *Early Annals of Bengal*, I, p. 376. The punctuation has been slightly altered.

19. Tavernier, I, p. 30. His experience in India belonged to the period, 1640–67.

20. *English Factories, 1634–36*, p. 169.

21. *English Factories, 1642–45*, pp. 302-3; *1646–50*, p. 224; *1651–54*, p. 122.

22. *English Factories, 1655–60*, pp. 18–19.

23. *English Factories, 1634–36*, p. 131.

24. *English Factories, 1646–50*, p. 103.

25. *English Factories, 1634–36*, p. 131.

26. *English Factories, 1618–21*, pp. 247–48.

27. Foster, *Suppl. Calendar*, p. 78.

28. *English Factories, 1618–21*, p. 329.

29. Ibid., p. 104.

30. *English Factories, 1622–23*, p. 172.

31. *English Factories, 1655–60*, p. 197. The *qasid* delivered on Feb. 1, 1659, a letter given to him by the Ahmadabad factors, dated Jan. 22.

32. *English Factories, 1634–36*, p. 131.

33. Tavernier, tr. Ball, ed., Crook, I, pp. 30–31.

34. *English Factories, 1622–23*, p. 79.

35. See my article, 'Usury in Medieval India', *Comparative Studies in Society and History*, The Hague, IV, 4, July 1964, p. 402.

36. Ibid., p. 403.

37. Tavernier, I, 30.

38. *English Factories, 1634–36*, pp. 168–69.

39. Tavernier, I, p. 30.

40. Ibid., p. 31.

41. A.H. John in *Essays in Economic History*, ed. E.M. Carus-Wilson, II, London, 1966, p, 372.

42. Tavernier, I, p. 31.

43. A *jokhami hundi* "contains certain conditions, in accordance with which if the goods are lost or destroyed in transit, the drawer or the holder of the *hundi*" who buys it with full knowledge of the risk, "has to suffer the loss" (L.C. Jain, *Indigenous Banking in India*, p. 78).

44. *English Factories, 1646–50*, p. 103.

45. *English Factories, 1655–60*, p. 363.

46. *English Factories, 1622–23*, pp. 110, 115–16.

47. *English Factories, 1668–69*, p. 177. *cf.* L.C. Jain, *Indigenous Banking India*, pp. 81–82.

48. "The shroffs (at Patna) intend to 'natcare' the bill if necessary, and 'use our cusmonna for the recovery of the debt there from the said Calyane'. (*Engligh Factories, 1618–21*, pp. 247–48). I am not able to trace the term 'natcare'. 'Cusmonna' is obviously *khasmana*, a (written) complaint.

49. "In order to pay two bills, amounting to 12,000 rupees on account of the Agra merchants, they (English factors at Ahmadabad) have drawn on Surat for that sum. . ." (*English Factories, 1646–50*, p. 103).

50. Muhammad Ali Khan, *Mirat-i Ahmadi*, I, ed. Nawab Ali, p. 411.

51. *English Factories, 1651–54*, p. 105.

52. Cf. ibid., p. 81.

53. *Mirat-i Ahmadi*, I, pp. 410–11.

54. "The person who accepts these from the drawers, enters the amount against him in his books at interest, which it continues to bear and be transferable, but without giving any holder to enforce payment. It is a kind of floating credit introduced by individuals to supply the place of capital; but when that abounds it falls to the grounds, being unreal. The dealings in this bill-currency are limited to soucars and money-brokers". (John Malcolm, *A Memoir of Central India*, II, p. 90).

55. K.G. Davies in E.M. Carus-Wilson ed., *Essays in Economic History*, II, p. 277.

56. The English, for example, report from Agra, in 1622, of the difficulty of remitting Rs. 10,000 to Samana by *hundis-*, they could only remit Rs. 4,000 by that means (*English Factories, 1622–23*, p. 9).

57. A.J. John, op. cit., p. 372.

58. Tavernier, I, p. 24.

59. *English Factories, 1634–36*, pp. 168–69.

60. *English Factories, 1637–41*, p. 300.

61. *English Factories, 1646–50*, p. 102.

62. *Akbarnama*, III, p. 762. The amount was distributed among the nobles who were than to dispatch it through hundis.

63. Y.H. Khan ed., *Selected Waqai of the Deccan 1660–1671*, Central Records Office, Hyderabad, 1953, p. 17. The document records the remittance of an instalment of Rs. 1,25,987 1/2 by this means.

64. *English Factories, 1618–21*, p. 236.

65. *Akhbarat*, 4 Safar, 40 R.Y.

66. *Ahkam-i Alamgiri*, letters and orders of Aurangzeb collected by Inayatullah.

22

Aspects of Business in Northern India in the Seventeenth Century

Ramesh Chandra Sharma

THE PRESENT paper attempts a study of Indian business in the seventeenth century on the basis of the information supplied by the *Ardha-Kathanak* of Banarasidas[1] written in 1641. Banarasidas was a medium-class businessman, hailing from Jaunpur, who came to Agra for business and settled there. His memoirs, supply first-hand information on indigenous middle-class business in north India during the seventeenth century.

The Business Community

Internal trade in those days was generally in the hands of the Hindus. Among them the Vaisyas and Jains were particularly engaged in it. Banarasidas's family were originally Rajputs,[2] who after conversion to Jainism took to business. It was his grand-father Muldas, who adopted *banik vrtti*[3] profession of a Vaisya, i.e., business) for the first time in his family. Although, the ideas of business and trade were instilled in the minds of the children of this section of the medieval Indian society, from the beginning, their training and education was not neglected. They studied both Hindi and Persian.[4] Generally speaking, along with general competence in reading, writing, and arithmetic, practical knowledge concerning their profession, namely, testing the coins, keeping accounts, maintaining records of loans given and taken, and learning *sarafi*,[5] was considered enough for them and this practical training was provided in the business establishments along with literary education at school.[6]

Jeweller's Trade

Banarasidas, his family, and relatives, all were primarily jewellers, and dealt in gems, precious stones and ornaments hira (diamond), lal (ruby), moti (pearls),

*33rd Session at Muzaffarpur, 1972.

manik, chuni, mani (kinds of precious stones).[7] Some of them were sarafs (money changers) and sold gold.[8] Banarasi had contacts with others of this trade.[9] The reason for the popularity of the jewel trade appears to have been the high profits that accrued from it, as is clear from Banarasidas's own conclusion on the basis of his personal experience in business, after selling a pearl necklace, purchased for rupees forty, for rupees seventy, thus earning rupees thirty in this bargain.[10]

Medium-Size Business

Yet Banarasidas belonged to the middle-class, and he, his father, and relatives were medium-size businessmen. As it were, businessmen of this class could not afford to undertake specialised business. Therefore, besides their primary dealings in jewels and ornaments, they also took other commodities for sale. Thus they were sundry or general merchants. While giving him a start in his career, Banarasidas's father gave him jewels, ornaments, ghee, oil, and cloth to sell at Agra.[11] Again, while making preparations at Khairabad for restarting business, Banarasidas purchased jewels and cloth,[12] and the similar thing he did while undertaking business for the third time.[13] Goods for sale were collectively, called *saunja*.[14] The trade in sundry goods appears to have been adopted to minimise the risk in dealing in one or two commodities.

Capital Formation and the Credit System

Due to cheapness of prices average class business required small investments. Banarasidas started his business twice with the initial capital investment of rupees two hundred or so,[15] and twice that of rupees five hundred.[16] Own savings and loans were the principal means of capital formation.[17] Capital advances were also available.[18] Interest on loans was charged.[19] At times people paid many times more than the principal, by themselves out of obligation for allowing them credit in dire necessity, as Banarasidas did in the case of the *kachauriwala*.[20] Much of the business used to be on credit.[21] Credit instruments were in use. *Hundi*,[22] a very important instrument of credit in the Indian banking system, like the bill of exchange is especially mentioned.

Markets

Market was the usual area of exchange. There were general markets, *bazaar*,[23] and specialised markets, such as:

> (i) *mandi*,[24] which was a wholesale market, usually for provisions or grain, named after the chief commodities sold or after its founder.[25]

(*ii*) *nakhasa*,[26] which was a daily market, where at Agra among other things cotton goods were also sold;[27]

(*iii*) *katra*,[28] defined as an enclosed market, named after the article sold there or its founder,[29] also appears to have been a ward in the city in Banarasidas's references.[30] In big cities their number used to be quite large. Jaunpur is said to have had fifty-two *bazars* and the same number of *mandis*.[31] Numerous shops—*hai*,[32] *fari*,[33] were kept in the markets for daily business, and were also imparted practical training in the businessman's arts to the children, as stated above. But sometimes the small traders had to go round selling their wares. In the beginning this required hard labour; but once established it could be easily managed through agents, as Banarasidas did with Dharamdas at Agra and with Narottamdas at Varanasi.[34] Even otherwise services of agents and brokers were engaged.[35]

Centres of Trade

Trade was centred in cities. Agra, being a capital city, appears to be the destination of all traders, big or small. The business at Agra was very well organised and it was not easy for a new trader to understand its complex working.[36] Allahabad, Varanasi, Patna, and Jaunpur[37] were other centres falling within the range of the business activities of Banarasidas and his men. At these places there used to be big business establishments—*Kothi*, where ware-housing facilities were provided for small businessmen.[38] Those owning these *kothis* were known as *kothiwal*.[39]

Ups and Downs in Business

Profits and losses are usual in business. There were rejoicings on profits which could be at times cent per cent.[40] Losses were also very heavy rendering the trader almost a pauper. Banarasidas usually incurred losses and had to sell all his belongings for making his both ends meet.[41] He lost especially in cloth trade.[42] Only once he could make some profit in it.[43] Losses in business were greatly lamented.[44] Usually goods could be sold at profitable rates in the Agra market, but on knowing that the seller was in urgency it became difficult even to get adequate return.[45] Thus many of the losses suffered by Banarasidas were owing to his hasty sales. Jewel trade was comparatively more profitable, as already noted.

Partnership

Partnership appears to be the most prevalent mode of business. As his father and he himself did business in partnership, *sir*,[46] we get many details about its working from the *Ardha-Kathanak*. Four partnerships, two entered into by Banarasi's father,[47] and two by Banarasidas[48] himself, are described in the book. These partnerships functioned according to definite rules. Partners had equal share in profit and loss.[49] Proper accounts were kept,[50] in common, and separate statements were prepared when partners decided to part.[51] For terminating a partnership the presence of all partners was required. Before dissolution of it, the partners were required to clear all accounts and appropriate measures were taken to prevent future disputes. This may well be explained by considering the way in which the two partnerships into which Banarasidas had entered, were dissolved. In the first case, when after two years Banarasidas wanted to dissolve the partnership with Dharamdas and to repay the capital advance given to him by his creditors, he was advised to make a clearance sale, to collect all money, and then, accounts were finally settled.[52] Thus the partnership was dissolved with the consent of the parties and accounts were settled after clearance sale. In the second case, in spite of Banarasidas and his partner having settled accounts at Jaunpur,[53] the partnership was not terminated till a final account was made in the presence of the creditor sponsoring the partnership. It was for this purpose that Sabal Singh called Banarasidas to Agra. The accounts were settled by Angan- das, brother-in-law of Sabal Singh, on the request of Banarasidas to redress his own misery and the plight of his deceased partner's father. Angandas 'called for all the papers and gave clearance to both the partners. In order to avoid the possibility of future disputes, he got the concurrence of the two partners recorded and gave these papers to each of them.[54] Thus besides the presence and consent of the partners, the satisfaction of the person sponsoring it was required for terminating a partnership and services of a mediator could be engaged at times.

Journeys for Business

Long journeys had to be undertaken in connection with business. Journeys were made in groups—caravans,[55] through regular stages,[56] on horses,[57] on *dolis*,[58] rathas,[59] carts[60]— mainly used for carrying loads. These were available on hire as well. Sometimes travelling was done on foot also.[61] Arrangements for crossing streams existed.[62] Porters could be hired for carrying loads.[63] *Serais* existed for the benefit of travellers.[64] Journeys were commenced on auspicious days,[65] and *tika* was put on the forehead before that.[66] Journeys began in the morning.[67] Roads were infested with robbers and thieves—at places even their whole villages existed,[68] with thugs and cheats.[69] Hence, it was a real problem for people— especially the well-to-do, to journey. Due to this at times they travelled in disguise and took the round about way.[70] Valuables had to be carried either hidden in the underwear or in hollow belts of tough cloth tied round the waist.[71] Other problems faced by travellers, especially businessmen, were inclement weather[72] cold, rains, etc., over—crowded inns,[73] corruption of government officials,[74] etc. Thus travelling in those days used to be quite troublesome.[75] But traders without caring for these undertook long journeys for business. Banarasidas and his men travelled often in northern India between Agra, Jaunpur, Khairabad, Varanasi and Patna.[76]

Rich Merchants

Some of the merchants had grown very rich. Sabal Singh was one such merchant, who was 'intoxicated with prosperity. The singers sang, the *pakhavaj* was sounded constantly in his court, which resembled that of a prince.' Banarasidas found it impossible to draw his attention towards accounts of his partnership, for setting which he had been summoned from Jaunpur, as 'for one engrossed in carnal pleasures the sun neither rises nor sets.'[77] In fact, lavish luxury among the upper classes was the order of the day, and in this respect kings and the nobility set the pace, which others strived to catch with. Another wealthy merchant mentioned was Hiranand Mukim, the jeweller of Prince Salim.[78]

Businessmen and Officials

It may not be out of place here to put in a word about the relationship between businessmen and the government officials. Some princes,[79] and provincial officials[80] patronised businessmen and encouraged business, while there were others who perpetrated oppressions on people in general and businessmen in particular.[81] Under such circumstances the only alternative left for people was to fly away from the place.[82] Reference to corrupt officials has already been made above but there were quite a few considerate officials as well.[83] In times of uncertainty people either flew away or assumed pauper's disguise, hiding their valuables under the ground.[84]

Notes

1. Banarasidas, *Ardha-Kathanak*, ed. by N.R. Premi *(hereafter A-kth)* For an English translation of it with notes see *Indica*, vol, 7, nos. 1 and 2, hereafter Bombay, March and September 1970, pp. 49–73 and 105–20.
2. *A-kth.* 9–10, p. 2.

3. Ibid., 14, p. 3.

4. Ibid., 13, p. 3.

5. The type of language in which the Indian businessmen keep accounts. It is Hindi without head lines and *matras*. Also money-changer's trade.

6. *A-kth.* 46–47, p. 7; 98–99, p. 12.

7. Ibid., 39, p. 6; 76, p. 10, 100, p. 12; 145, p. 17; 283–84, p. 32; 319–23, p. 36; 327, p. 37; 355, p. 40; 369–70, p. 41; 385, p. 43; 392, p. 44; 400, p. 45; 445, p. 50; 519, p. 58.

8. Ibid., 67, p. 9.

9. Ibid., 224, p. 25; 353, p. 39.

10. Ibid., 392–93, p. 44.

11. Ibid., 281–84, p. 32.

12. Ibid., 385 and 388, p. 43.

13. Ibid., 494 and 497, p. 55.

14. Ibid., 285, p. 33; 309, p. 35.

15. Ibid., 284, p. 32; 375, 379 and 384, pp. 42 and 43.

16. Ibid., 354, p. 40; 494, p. 55.

17. Ibid., 285, p. 33; 494, p. 55.

18. Ibid., 407, p. 47.

19. Ibid., 403, p. 45.

20. Ibid., 356–57, p. 40.

21. Ibid., 16, p. 3; 145, p. 17.

22. Ibid., 316, p. 36; 494, p. 55.

23. Ibid., 198, p. 23; 335, p. 38; 349, p. 39; 485, p. 54.

24. Ibid., 31, p. 5.

25. H.K. Naqvi, p. 76.

26. *A-klh.* 314, p. 35; 390, p. 43; 571, p. 63.

27. H.K. Naqvi, pp. 75–76.

28. *A-klh.* 310, p. 35; 389–390, p. 43.

29. H.K. Naqvi, p. 77.

30. Cf. fn. 34 *infra*.

31. *A-kth.* 31, p. 5.

32. Ibid., 70, p. 9; 81, p. 10; 200, p. 23; 252, p. 29; 293, p. 33; 335, 338–339, p. 38; 390, p. 43.

33. Ibid., 391, p. 44.

34. Ibid., 355, p. 40, 446–48, p. 50; 458, p. 51.

35. Ibid., 497, p. 55; 579, p. 64.

36. Ibid., 318, p. 36.

37. Ibid., 31, p. 5; 133, p. 16; 197, p. 23; 407, p. 45; 434, p. 48; 439, p. 49; 458–59, p. 51.

38. Ibid., 309, p. 34; 313, p. 35; 393, p. 43; 519, p. 58.

39. Ibid., 468, p. 52; 499, p. 56; 518, p. 58.

40. Ibid., 208, p. 24.

41. Ibid., 318–24, p. 36; 333–34, pp. 37–38; 338–42, p. 38; 364–66, p. 41; 373, p. 42; 458, p. 51.

42. Ibid., 314, p. 35; 391 and 394 , p. 44; 402, p. 45.

43. Ibid., 573–571, p. 63.

44. Ibid., 331, p. 37.

45. Ibid., 362, p. 40 364–66, p. 41.

46. Ibid., 68, p. 9; 354, p. 40.

47. Ibid., 68, p. 9; 75, p. 10.

48. Ibid., 352, p. 39; 407, p. 45.

49. Ibid., 361, p. 40; 489–90, pp. 54–55.

50. Ibid., 356, p. 40.

51. Ibid., 489–90, pp. 54–55.

52. Ibid., 358–63, pp. 40–41.

53. Ibid., 489–90, pp. 54–55.

54. Ibid., 475, p. 53; 495, p. 55; 567–69, p. 63.

55. Ibid., 289, p. 33; 498, p. 55; 499–500, p. 56.

56. Ibid., 289, p. 33; 410, p. 46; 498, p. 55; 502, p. 56.

57. Ibid., 33, p. 7; 73, p. 10; 198, p. 23; 227, p. 26; 498–99, p. 55; 552, p. 61.

58. Ibid., 140, p 16; 183, p. 21; 193, p. 22; 198, p. 23; 432, p. 48.

59. Ibid., 73, p. 10; 410–11, p. 46.

60. Ibid., 289–90, p. 33; 396, p. 44; 408, p. 45.

61. Ibid., pp. 46–48; 464, p. 52.

62. Ibid., 471, p. 52.

63. Ibid., 140, p. 16; 411,413–14, p. 46; 428, p. 48.

64. Ibid., 117, p. 11; 411, p. 46; 429, p. 48; 503, p. 56.

65. Ibid., 408, p. 45.

66. Ibid., 407, p. 45.

67. Ibid., 548, p. 61.

68. Ibid., 78, p. 10; 417, p. 46.

69. Ibid., 505–44, pp. 56–60.

70. Ibid., 64, p. 9.

71. Ibid., 288, p. 33; 319–21, p. 36.

72. Ibid., 291 and 294, p. 33; 295, p. 34.

73. Ibid., 292, p. 33.

74. Ibid., 300, p. 34; 540–44, p. 60.

75. Ibid., 239 and 241, p. 27.

76. Ibid., 66, p. 9, 115, p. 14; 134, p. 16; 197, p. 23; 434, p. 48; 558, p. 51.

77. Ibid., 557–62, p. 62.

78. Ibid., 224, p. 25.

79. Ibid., 145, p. 17; 224, p. 25.

80. Ibid., 443–50, 454–55, pp. 50 and 51.

81. Ibid., 110-13, p. 13; 467–73, p. 52.

82. Ibid., 114, p. 14; 462–68, p. 51; 470–471, p. 52.

83. Ibid., 503–46, pp. 56–61 gives important details about the working of the governmental machinery at the district level and the behaviour of the officials.

84. Ibid., 503–46, p. 56–61 give important details about the working of the government machinery at the district level and the behaviour of the officials.

23

Saltpetre Trade and Industry in Bengal Subah, 1650–1720

Sushil Chaudhuri

IN THE second half of the seventeenth century, saltpetre was an important item in the export list of the European Companies trading in Bengal. As an essential ingredient of gunpowder it was in great demand in the West. Besides, as it could be used as saleable ballast, its export was of additional advantage to the Companies which otherwise had to take the uneconomic method of using iron as ballast to make the deep-sea ships sailworthy. It was only in the early twenties of the seventeenth century that the shortage of saltpetre in England and the increasing difficulty in obtaining supplies of gunpowder had turned the attention of the English Company to the possibility of importing this chemical from India. The first supply however reached England only in 1626.[1] And once established the saltpetre trade displayed a consistent growth, though the real expansion did not take place till after the Civil War.0

The chief sources of saltpetre supply till the beginning of the forties were mainly Coromandel and Gujarat. Thevenot, the French merchant, recorded in 1666 the process of its manufacture in Ajmer from whence it was carried to the sea ports for Western India and purchased by the Europeans 'to ballast their ships and to sell elsewhere'.[2] But Coromandel seems to have supplied the main bulk of this commodity to the Europeans before 1640s. In 1624 and 1625, 270,000 lbs. (Dutch) and 286,434 lbs. (Dutch) respectively of saltpetre were exported to Batavia from Coromandel. In the late thirties however Bengal saltpetre supplemented those from the Coast.[3] From the fifties Bengal definitely replaced Coromandel as the chief source of supply.

Saltpetre was produced in Bihar mainly in the neighbourhood of Patna where it was available in abundance. The discovery of this source revolutionized the Company's saltpetre trade and led to its tremendous expansion in the second half of the seventeenth and first half of the eighteenth centuries. A Dutch report of 1688 gives interesting details regarding the annual output, the

*34th Session at Chandigarh, 1973.

names of the parganas producing saltpetre, and the officials who owned or administered these tracts. According to this, the total output a year amounted to 226,200 mds. (raw) and when refined (*dobara-cabessa*) the figure stood at 127,238 mds. Of this amount, as the report runs, 1,200 mds. were sent to Hugli, 3000 mds. to Dacca, and 7,000 mds. were retained for Patna gunpowder factory. The rest amounting to 105,238 mds. were left for export.[4]

The saltpetre procured at Patna was considered the best in quality for the manufacture of gunpowder. Moreover the price of Bengal saltpetre was cheaper than that of other places.[5] It was reported in 1650 that saltpetre cost only Re. 1 per maund at Patna, though the customs and freight for bringing it to Hugli would raise the price to Re. 1.12 annas per maund.[6] Again from the point of transportation, Bengal saltpetre enjoyed another advantage. The cheaper and more convenient transport down the Ganges enabled the Company to despatch cargoes of saltpetre from Patna to Hugli for lading Europe-bound ships and also for supplying Madras with ballast for its vessels. All these considerations coupled with the enhanced demand from England and Europe encouraged the Company to drive an extensive trade in Bengal saltpetre.

There were generally three varieties of saltpetre—the refined one called *dobara cabessa or culmy*, the twice boiled or *dobara* and the crude variety termed *cutckha* or raw.[7] The European companies generally exported refined saltpetre as otherwise it could not be used for making gunpowder. Moreover the export of raw or crude variety was uneconomic as it increased freight charges while custom duties remained the same on both refined and crude varieties.[8] The companies often undertook the refining in their own factories. The Dutch Company procured large quantities of saltpetre from Patna and shipped it direct to Batavia after refining it at Hugli or Pipli. As a matter of fact, as early as 1640–41, the Dutch set up a refinery at Pipli with copper kettles imported from Holland.[9] Tavernier stated in the sixties of the seventeenth century that the Dutch refined saltpetre at a 'large village called Chapra, situated on the right bank of the Ganges', about twenty miles above Patna.[10]

The English Company too, it seems, refined its saltpetre at Singhee or Patna.[11] The refining, in order to remove impurities, was usually done by the Indian methods of evaporation in which earthen vessels were used. In 1652 the English factors reported that the great difficulty in refining was for want of convenient copper pans. Refining in great earthen pots was tedious and troublesome because those pots very often broke in the middle of processing. As suitable copper pans were not locally available, the Company decided to divert to this purpose appliances which had been sent out for making sugar at Assada in Madagascar.[12] The cost of refining, however, was very small being only ¼ of an anna per maund.[13] The English Company once attempted to refine saltpetre at Calcutta but abandoned the experiment as it was found to be too expensive.[14]

An examination of the orders for saltpetre sent from England reveals that the quantities ordered depended on two main factors. First, in times of war the quantities required to be sent from Bengal naturally went up while in peace time they were greatly reduced. Second, the quantities ordered depended on the requirement of the ships for their ballast or 'kinteledge'. Saltpetre was used as ballast not only for Bengal ships but also for ships sailing from Madras, Masulipatam, Bantam or Bencoolen. The order for Bengal saltpetre increased steadily from the foundation of the English factory in Hugli in 1651 till 1681 when for the first time there was sudden decline in the quantities ordered. There were two obvious reasons for this reduction in the order. There was then little demand for saltpetre in Europe which by then was temporarily relieved of war. Second, it was from 1681 that there was a sudden boom in the demand for Bengal silk and piece-goods which shifted the emphasis in the Company's export trade in favour of the latter commodities.

In the early years of the Company's trade in Bengal, saltpetre definitely ranked as the primary object of commerce, and not merely a make-weight. In 1651, the factors in Bengal were instructed to invest half of their capital in saltpetre alone and in case the factors ran up debts the Court gave special instruction that 'let it be for this commodity.'[15] In the early years of its trade, the order was generally for 200 to 600 tonnes, while in the eighties it went up to 800 to 1000 tonnes a year, the highest order being for 1500 tonnes in 1682. The Dutch East India Company's order for saltpetre from Bengal for Holland itself far surpassed that of the English Company throughout the period, and the former also supplied its other Asiatic factories, specially Bantam and Ceylon from Bengal. In the first two decades of the eighteenth century the demand for Bengal saltpetre for Holland only stood consistently between 3,000,000 to 3,500,000 Dutch pounds.[16]

The supply condition in saltpetre trade was more or less smooth enough for securing an extensive trade in that commodity. The only inhibiting factor was the occasional attempts by local officials to monopolize the trade. Mir Jumla made such an attempt but with little success.[17] The next *Subadar* Shaista Khan tried to monopolize the trade and sent his agents to Patna who 'obstructed and hindered' the procurement of saltpetre by the Europeans. When the English appealed to him, he demanded 20,000 maunds. of saltpetre from them on the pretext of his Arakan war.[18] Prince Azim-us-Shan made a similar attempt in 1699. He sent an agent to Patna to buy between 40,000 and 50,000 maunds. of saltpetre on the plea of making gunpowder for his intended attack on Arakan. But ultimately his initial plan of making cent per cent profit on an investment of rupees one lakh failed miserably.[19]

The saltpetre was generally produced through *assomies* or petremen to whom money was advanced in the right season.[20] Often merchant middlemen were also employed for procuring saltpetre. In May 1683, the Company contracted for 4120 maunds. of saltpetre (at Re. 11/4 per. maunds.) with three able 'petremen': 'Bucktmall,' 'Muluckchand' and 'Siabray' who had provided all the Company's saltpetre in the previous year, and now gave good security against fulfilment of the contract.[21] But official capacity occasionally made the petremen hide out in which case the Company had to deal with the merchant-middlemen who demanded a greater price than the ordinary petrcmen or *assomies*. Thus in 1684, the Patna factors reported that they dealt with one merchant, namely Probhat ('Perevott') who would not deal at the same price as the *assomies* on the ground of the trouble given by the *nawab* and his officers.[22] In general, the competition in the saltpetre market was confined mostly among the European companies, specially the English and the Dutch. Both these companies were apprehensive—not without a reason—that the others try to engross the trade. As a consequence the English Company asked their factors to carry on with the investment in saltpetre even in the time of war when they could hardly send the commodity for want of shipping.[23]

This competition amongst the Europeans had often its impact on the prices. The English factors once claimed that the price of saltpetre was much reduced when the Dutch had left Patna.[24] The interlopers too were competitors in the market specially in the eighties of the seventeenth century. In 1684 the Patna factors reported that Purusuttom Das and Jadu Das—who were formerly Dutch *gomasta*, and provided the interlopers with saltpetre in the various years—again procured for the interlopers great quantities of refined saltpetre which made the coarse variety scarce and raised their price. But when the interlopers failed to come, the two merchants, hard pressed by the creditors for money, tried to sell the commodity for whatever price they could get. But the English and the Dutch companies 'plagued them sufficiently' and agreed not to buy an ounce of them so that 'they might be sufficient losers and be made examples to prevent others' from following their steps in future.[25]

An analysis of the price of saltpetre shows a general upward trend throughout the period, though with exception during certain years.[26] Of course, it is difficult to find out precisely the cost price of saltpetre as it depended on certain factors, e.g., the place and time of purchase as also on the variety bought. As noted earlier, the price of saltpetre at Patna in Dec. 1650 was Re, 1 per maunds. while with charges for freight, it amounted to Re. 1¼ at Hugli. But the English bought the same variety for the ships despatched that year at Re. 1 5/8 per maunds.[27] In other words, the English had to pay 5% more for the commodity during the shipping season. The price at Patna was about 40 to 50% cheaper than that in Hugli.[28] In 1659–60 the English factors procured saltpetre at Re. 1 1/8 per maunds. at Patna which indicates a 12½% rise in price than that in 1650–51.[29] At the end of our period, i.e., in 1719–20 the average price of saltpetre was about Rs. 5 per maunds. This was generally the price in Hugli and definitely it shows a rise of about 300% from that in the beginning of our period. This tremendous rise in the price over the period can only be explained by the competition among the European companies and their heavy demand on the supply. When the English first began trade in saltpetre in 1650–51, there was only the Dutch Company who used to export the commodity from Patna. So the former found saltpetre very cheap. But with the growth of the English trade and the heavy demand by the Europeans on the market, the price soared accordingly. The other contributory factors for fluctuations in prices appear to be the occasional attempts at monopoly by local rulers as also the uncertain weather condition. It was reported that more slatpetre was procurable in dry seasons than during the rains.[30]

During 1663–64 and 1664–65 the price of saltpetre was Rs. 3 per maunds. while the treble refined variety cost Rs. 3¾. It ranged between Rs. 2 to Rs. 3.2 from 1668–79 to 1675–76 with a sudden rise to over Rs. 4 during the years 1676–77 and 1678–79. In the eighties however the average price was about Rs. 2 with the lowest figure of Rs. 1.6 in 1682–83. But in the nineties the average price was over Rs. 3 per maunds. During the first decade of the eighteenth century it went up high and stood at Rs. 4 per maunds. which was the trend in the second decade too, only with the exception of 1712–13 when the price went up to Rs. 6 per maunds. However, it must be pointed out that fluctuations in cost price of saltpetre did not have any determining influence on the amount procured by the European companies. The main considerations were the ballast requirements for the returning ships and the market conditions in Europe.

The quantities of saltpetre actually exported by the English Company from Bengal over the period under review show fluctuations though the general trend was one of expansion, reaching the peak in the eighties and then sloping downwards in the nineties, only to rise gradually again in the subsequent years. These fluctuations depended on various factors which can be generalised as the demand from England, the available supply and the requirements for the Company's shipping from Bengal. In 1663–64 the Company exported 943,650 lbs. of saltpetre which rose to 990,450 lbs. in 1664–65. There was a phenomenal rise in 1668–69 when 1,977,300 lbs. were exported from Bengal though the figure fell to as low a level as 712,950 lbs. The boom in the export of saltpetre began in 1681–82 and continued up to 1685–86. The following table will indicate the fluctuations in the export of saltpetre from the eighties till the end of the period under review.[31]

Saltpetre Export: Quinquennial Total

Years	Quantities	Average
1681–82, 1685–86	6,298,208 lbs	1,259,641 lbs.
1690–91, 1695–96 (excluding 1691–92)	2,652,964 lbs	530,592 lbs.
1696–97, 1700–01	2,226,132 lbs.	445,226 lbs.
1701–2, 1706–07 (excluding 1703-04)	3,785,486 lbs.	757,097 lbs.
1710–11, 1714–15	4,202,514 lbs.	840,502 lbs.
1715–16, 1719–20	5,352,689 lbs.	1,070,537 lbs.

The Dutch East India Company exported a far greater quantity of saltpetre from Bengal than its English counterpart. In 1669–70 the Dutch export to Holland and the Asiatic factories amounted to 3,343,440 Dutch lbs.[32] Even in the first two decades of the eighteenth century the Dutch export to Holland far surpassed that of the English. During the three years — 1701–2, 1702–3, 1704–5 the Dutch exported to Holland 8,494,754 lbs. (Dutch) at an average of 2,3 81,918 lbs. yearly. The average annual export to Holland during the quinquennial periods 1705–6,1710–11 and 1711–12 to 1715–16 was 2,999,789 lbs. (Dutch) and 3,884,405 lbs. (Dutch), respectively, which indicates that the Dutch trade in Bengal saltpetre was far greater than that of the English.[33]

Though the quantities of saltpetre exported annually by the English Company seem to be impressive, the total value of this annual saltpetre trade in proportion to the value of total exports of the Company was not so. In the sixties the total value of saltpetre exported annually from Bengal constituted about 20 to 25%. of the total value of export, rising to 50% in 1668–69. But its share during the slump which began in 1681–82 was only 4% of the total value of the Company's exports from Bengal, though that year witnessed a boom in the absolute quantities of saltpetre exported by the Company. This decline in value continued till 1685–86 when it formed only 1.5% of the total value of the exports. There was a sudden rise in 1704–5 when it stood at 22.7% but gradually went down again. Then onward it varied between 3 to 4 p.c. of the total value of the Company's exports.

Manuscript Sources and Abbreviations

A.G.D.	Accountant General's Dept., India Office Library, London
Beng. Public Consult.	Bengal Public Consultations, India Office, London
DB	*Despatch Book*, India Office Library, London
KA	*olonical Archief* Rijksarchief, The Hague
EFI	nglish Factories in India, ed. W. Foster
Fact. Records	*Factory Records*, Hugli, Calcutta, Patna, Misc., I.O.L., London

Notes

1. Court Book, IX, p. 320,5 Jan. 1627.
2. S.N. Sen, *ed, Indian Travels of Thevenot and Careri*, p. 74.
3. T. Raychaudhuri, *Jan Company in Coromandel*, pp. 168–69.
4. KA., 1343, ff. 748–49; for pargana-wise breakdown, see Table 1.

5. Price of Patna Salpetre was just half of that of Ahmedabad saltpetre, cf., Moreland, *From Akbar to Aurangzeb*, p. 121; Price of saltpetre at Hugli was £6 per ton while at the Coast it was £8 to £9 in *1659–60, DB;* vol. 84, ff. 411–12; vol. 85, ff. 334.

6. OC, 15 Dec. 1651, no. 2188, vol. 22.

7. *Fact. Records, Hugli,* vol. 10, f. 235.

8. *DB,* 5 vol. 95, f. 232.

9. T. Raychaudhuri, op.cit., pp. 169–70.

10. Tavemier, *Travels in India,* trans. V. Bali, vol. 1, p. 122.

11. *Fact Records, Misc.,* vol. 3, f. 63; vol. XIV, ff. 331–32.

12. OC, Jan 13, 1652, no. 2246, vol. 22. *EFI, 1651–54,* p. 95.

13. *Bengal Public Consultations,* Range 1, vol. 6, f. 488a.

14. *DB,* 3 Feb. 1720, vol. 100, f. 224.

15. OC, l0 Feb. 1651, no. 2208, vol. 22; ibid., 25 Feb. 1651, no. 2210, vol. 22. *EFI,* 1651-54, pp. 45, 47.

16. For the list of Dutch Company's orders for Bengal goods, see *KA,* vols. 1556, 1581, 1584, 1622, 1636, 1653, 1669, 1688, 1720, 1734, 1746, 1776, 1804.

17. *EFI, 1661–1764,* pp. 69–71.

18. *Fact. Records, Hugli,* Consult. 11 July 1674; *EFI, 1661–64,* pp. 395–96.

19. *Fact. Records, Calcutta,* vol. 3, pt. II, f. 87.

20. *Fact. Records, Hugli,* vol. 10, f. 194.

21. *Fact. Records, Patna,* vol. 1, pt. IV, f. 18.

22. *Fact. Records, Hugli,* vol. 10, f. 194.

23. *DB,* vol. 86, ff. 504–5; vol. 86, ff. 522–23, vol. 87, f. 39.

24. *Fact. Records, Calcutta,* vol. 11, pt. II, ff. 2–3.

25. *Fact. Records, Hugli,* vol. 10, f. 235.

26. See Table 11.

27. OC, 15 Dec. 1650, no. 2188, vol. 22; *EFI, 1651–54,* pp. 337–38.

28. *DB,* 28 Jan. 1659, vol. 84, f. 414.

29. OC, 15 Dec. 1659, no. 2833, vol. 26; *EFI, 1655–60,* p. 29.

30. OC, 1 Sept. 1665, no. 3069, vol. 29.

31. See, relevant volumes of A.G.D.

32. *KA,* 1164, f. 380–82, The Dutch lb. is equivalent to 1.09 English lb. approx. cf. T. Raychaudhuri, op. cit., p. 223.

33. For the list of Dutch export from Bengal, see *KA,* vols. 1556, 1581, 1584, 1622, 1653, 1669, 1688, 1720, 1734, 1746, 1776, 1804.

24

India in Asian Trade in the 1730s—
An Eighteenth Century French Memoir

Indrani Ray

GROWING EUROPEAN participation in India's overseas trade during the seventeenth and eighteenth centuries was a significant phenomenon in the pre-colonial commercial structure of India. The role of the various European East India Companies and of European private merchants as carriers of Indian commodities to European markets for local consumption or re-exportation has so far attracted more attention than Asian trade proper—trade between the various regions of Asia, as well as the coastal trade of India. This, despite the fact that down to the middle of the eighteenth century Asian trade largely retained its autonomous existence and was of greater importance than the Europe-bound trade to Asian and European merchants carrying on trade in the Indian ocean.

The European Companies themselves participated, according to their ability and with varying success in this trade. Their main aim was to supplement their import of bullion, always inadequate, by money made out of Asian trade. Moreover, administrative needs of the growing establishments like Madras or Chandernagor or Chinsura, involving a great deal of expenditure forced them to look in this trade for a steady source of 'auto-financing' of these factory towns. Their prosperity depended on the presence of merchants interested in Asian trade. That servants of most of these companies, employed in India with ridiculously low salaries, found their sole *raison d'etre* in participation in this trade as private merchants is a fact too well known to be repeated in greater details. This was the surest 'remedy against poverty, the epidemic illness of Pondicherry', prescribed by Dupleix from Chandernagor, in his letter of eighteenth January 1733 to La Bourdonnais urging him to follow 'the recipes of captain and supercargoes' and suggesting 'a little of the syrup of Surat, with

*34th Session at Chandigarh, 1973. I am grateful to the Centre d'Etudes Indiennes, Paris, for having made available tome a microfilmed copy of the present document (Ref. No. C (2) 197, ff 1–18).

a few drops of drinking gold from China' which, he hoped, 'would have a marvellous effect' on him.

Since Moreland drew our notice to the 'puzzling phenomenon that merchants who came to buy Eastern goods should devote so much of their energies to the conduct of purely Asiatic trade' (N), we have had quite a few illuminating studies of participation in Asian trade in the seventeenth and eighteenth centuries by some of the companies. But these are concerned mainly with the policies and fortunes of the Companies. Asian trade, however, was mainly an affair of the private trader. Second, till about the second half of the eighteenth century, it was truly international in character. Third, in the European factory towns the Company's officials played a much more important role than free merchants. Finally, it was not yet affected by the mid-eighteenth century 'commercial revolution' intimately connected with the beginning of British dominion of Bengal, which turned the main stream of Asian trade from western to an eastern direction (N). So far we do not have any comprehensive study of India's trade with Asia immediately preceding the colonial period, although its importance in understanding the economic history of the time is underlined by both Furber and Dermigny. All the same, so far we do not know how far there has been any important change in the trade-pattern, so far as the composition of participants, the cargoes and the main trade links are concerned. What were the roles of Indian and European participants in the various branches of activity? What was the specific contribution of Asian trade to the prosperity of each of the colonial towns? Professor Furber's study of mid-eighteenth century Bombay and Surat throws a good deal of light on some of these questions; but there is no comparable study about the situation in Bengal. If we have learnt to modify our former concept of Europe oriented trade being the one all-absorbing issue in the trading community of eighteenth century India, we still have to understand what constituted the special attraction of Asian trade at this period, to what extent was it really the panacea for all and everybody drawn to the Indian mediterranean.

As mentioned already all the companies participated in this trade; all in fact began by trying to keep out the private trade from here also; but all, excepting the Dutch East India Company came to relax their control over it sooner or later. It was easier for the European trading Companies to leave it largely to their employees and free merchants, and to profit from the duties and other charges they would have to pay at the colonial port towns, or wherever they might have a factory, such as, in Surat.

Needless to say, this involved all sorts of complications, depending on the attitude and ability of a certain company, as well as on their officials in India who really controlled the trade within their jurisdiction. The case of the French East India Company reveals some of these complications. Excessive dependence on the state and shyness of the French merchant capital-offspring of French mercantilism and the French social system led to chronic financial problems and a more than average share of indecision on the part of the Directors of the Company. They were accused of "starting a thousand projects and not continuing a single one", of "changing all plans and all orders." Employees in Pondicherry and Chandernagor had to face indecision or rather inconsistency at every conceivable level. Pondicherry could not help turning sarcastic at times at the insistence on novelty not only in goods but in all affairs. But perhaps nowhere was it more evident that in its policy concerning Asian Trade. Competent and observant employees at Chandernagor or Pondicherry as well as free merchants and captains visiting India have all harped on the "one sure path to prosperity" of the French colonial towns in India, namely participation in Asian trade by the Company—or rather, creating a favourable situation for private traders in these colonies. Francois Martin, the founder of Pondicherry, Deslandes, the first Director of Chandernagor had both attracted the Company's attention to this, at turn of the century. Since then, the utility of Asian trade featured prominently in letters, memoirs and deliberations of the Councils of Pondicherry and Chandernagor. In all this nobody claimed originality. Rather, arguments were often supported by descriptions of Calcutta or Madras, thriving on private trade. The Company, having at First prohibited this trade to its employees, threw it open to them in 1722, with the exception of trade with China and Mocha. In 1734 China trade was also permitted to its employees. But throughout 1730s the Company kept on changing its mind about its own participation in this trade, shifting from total withdrawal, to participation for 1/4 of the total capital invested by the French colonies—then again to withdrawal—within a span of five years.

The 1730s were however years of optimum and brisk activity for French private traders, because, Dupleix, the new Director of Chandernagor had decided to "rouse the colony from its torpor" immediately after his arrival in June 1731. We are not concerned here with his achievements as a private trader nor with the impact of his activities on the development of Chandernagor. But his successes seem to have affected the Company sufficiently to make it a little more curious about the whole business of Asian trade. Probably this would explain the writing of several memoirs in the 1730s by French merchants resident in India or by officials on a special mission. They are much more detailed, concerned more with practical aspects of Asian trade, and less with the usual theoretical enumerations and generalisations, a common feature of much of the previous writing.

The document which is studied in this paper is one such memoir, written in 1733, informing the Company of the trade it could do in India for Europe as well as with outer parts of the Indies. Fortunately for us it speaks less about the prospects of the Europe-bound trade of the Company and dwells mainly on the advantages or disadvantages of the various branches of India's coastal trade as well as Asian trade that could be carried on from India, from the standpoint of the Company. It was written by Jacques Vincens, a Frenchman in service of the Company, residing in India since 1717. A close friend and trusted associate of Dupleix since their stay in Pondicherry, Vincens was persuaded by the former to come away from Pondicherry. He settled in Chandernagor in 1733 and took part in many of Dupleix's ventures till his death in September 1739.

He begins his memoir with the conviction that the only way to establish solidly the French colonies in India, and to enable them to bear their expenses would be to attract rich private merchants, European and Indian, to these towns by creating favourable condition of trade for them. Absence of such merchants was in fact the main reason behind Pondicherry's failure to develop into a prosperous commercial centre. Ships often turned away with unsold goods from Pondicherry as there was no buyer. Madras had become rich only through her private traders, realising as much as 90 thousand pagodas a year simply from the export and import duties paid by them (N). Trade with Europe offered in fact little attraction to the richest Indian merchant there. Vincens does not mention Calcutta in this context, most probably because he was still not quite familiar with the situation in Bengal. While giving his idea about bringing Pondicherry out of her present depressed condition, Vincens suggests that the Company should invite European merchants to set up business houses there, or invest more capital in this trade on its own account. He does not suggest any definite plan for attracting the Indian merchants— probably he sees no possibility of the company being able to entice them away from Madras. Moreover it was evidently his aim here primarily to encourage the Company in playing a more positive role in Asian trade, and to provide with a guideline and as such he could not really make a plea for private traders. Vincens, moreover, belonged to that period when the Director and the officials of a Company were the principal private merchants in the European colonies and he would not think in terms of permitting equal facilities to free European merchants or Indian traders who would try to trade on their own.

The basic attraction of the memoir is a description of the main structure of India's coastal and Asian trade, which would hold good more or less for the first half of the eighteenth century. It picks up, one after another, the important Asian trading centres and then gives details. He also deals with the trade connection between different regions of India, i.e., between Bengal and Surat or Bengal and the Malabar coast. Tentative schemes are suggested in great details concerning those connections which are considered important by him for example, trade with Manila, or trade between Mahe and Mocha.

One single document like this can by no means claim to offer a comprehensive picture of the Asian trade, with answers to questions which seem pertinent to us. It is lacking in personal experience which he must have gathered later as a supercargo. On the other hand, as a member of the Pondicherry Council, he had stakes in this trade—and had also come across detailed information on this trade from local participants, from employees in other French colonies, as well as from private ships moving along the coast. It is moreover more concerned with the European participants and the general structure than with factual details of the internal organisation of Asian trade. It only occasionally indicates the number or ownership of ships that took part in this trade; there is no mention of names of important Indian or European merchants. Neither do we get any description of the ports and their hinterlands. As explained already, Vincens was aiming at informing and convincing his masters in Paris of the nature and importance of this trade for the Company and ultimately it was a matter of his personal observations and judgement. This accounts for certain omissions and preferences. In spite of this, the memoir is of undoubted value first as it presents a framework to be used for more minute studies involving the career of important private merchants. Second it reflects the attitude of an employee turned merchant in service of the French East India Company, at the beginning of the famous and controversial 'Dupleix decade', with great optimism and enthusiasm about the drive and resourcefulness of the energetic new Director of Chandemagor. Evidently, more studies, based on such records as well as on commercial activities of European and Indian traders would be necessary before one could assess the contribution of Asian trade to the fortune of a private trader or to the prosperity of any given colonial town such as Chandernagor.

Of the principal trading regions in India, directly involved in coastal and Asian trade—Surat, the Malabar coast, the Coromandel coast and Bengal—Surat gets the greatest attention in the Memoir (ten out of a total of thirty-four folios are devoted to various aspects of trade in Surat) for several reasons. It was still the 'richest and most trading city in India' being the only port which was also the entrepot "of the whole of Hindusthan" absorbing everything that was brought there. In India it had ships from Bengal, the Coromandel coast and the Malabar coast, of which the Bengal-Surat link was the most important. About 30 ships: English, French and Indian ('Maure') came annually from Bengal to Surat. European ships generatelly carried freight belonging to "people of the country, Maures and Armenians" who had greater faith in these ships which were superior in both arms and officers to the Moslem ships. Sugar was brought as ballast which always fetched a good price in Surat, the commodity being transported throughout the Mughal empire and reexported to Persia and the Red Sea. The ship-owners had recourse to sending raw silk and textile products on their own account only when freight was lacking. Vincens, rather unusually for him, waxes eloquent for a brief moment over the 'merchandise of Bengal...produced in the villages and along the Ganges', which it will take 'volumes to describe'. Most of these goods were absorbed by the region between Ahmedabad and Delhi; the rest was inserted into the cargos described to Persia, Bassorah, Mocha and Jedda. Trips from Bengal to Surat were considered "very advantageous" only if one could load his ship completely with freight, since it invloved very little capital. We come across repeated emphasis on the necessity of freight specially in trade with regions in the Persian Gulf and the Red Sea. Superior shipping, not greater command over capital seems the main point in favour of the Europeans. The ships from Bengal went back mainly loaded with cotton, which was however not always easily available, a lot depending on the "vigilance" of the supercargo or the correspondent of the merchants. Pepper was the next choice, part of which was sold at the coast of Coromandel. 'Maure' ships going to Bengal from Surat were generally owned by the 'big merchants orbanias' of Surat exported the same goods as taken away by English and French ships—the main difference between these and the Europeans being that they loaded their ships on their own account and carried very little freight.

The English private ships figure largely on the Bengal-Surat route. In the very year, 1733, ten to twelve ships left Calcutta for Surat, of which six belonged to the Governor and private traders of Bombay, the rest to those of Calcutta. One proof of the domineering position of high officials in European private trade is to be found in the fact that none of the Calcutta ships was carrying any freight, the whole being reserved for the Governor of Calcutta who was sending a ship of 700–800 tonnes to Surat. Members of the Chandernagor Council have been sending one ship annually to Surat between 1727–31, with little profit Since Dupleix's arrival therein 1731 things were improving, Dupleix managing again by dint of his "vigilance" to draw away a part of the freight destined to Surat, and adding a second ship on his own, in 1732 as well as 1733. Vincens is sure that French ships will be preferred to the English ones in future through better management and more attention to the freight-owning passengers.

Besides the ships going directly from Bengal to Surat, the English also tried to develop another line of trade from Bengal via the Malaccan detour. They fitted out ships of 150–250 tonnes mainly with cargos of opium and would bring powdered Javanese sugar and Calin in return—to be sold at Surat. This trade was not of assured profit, the opium quite often fetching hardly the cost price. This penchant of the English private trader to hit at every possible source, without being necessarily guarded by very lucrative prospects is something merely noticed by Vincens; he does not seem to be aware of the implications. It was the English again, who owned the rare ships coming from Pegu to Surat mainly with rice, Calin, elephant tusk and wax. One object of these ships was to sell rice between Cochin and Malabar on their way to Surat, where they loaded cotton for Bengal. We shall see later how they traded from Bengal to China via Surat.

Direct trade from the Coromandel coast to Surat was quite infrequent. Since his arrival in India (in 1717) Vincens had never seen more than one ship being fitted out to Surat directly from the coast. This took place only when there was excess of such goods as Calin, wax (arlatte?) and elephant's tusk on ships arriving at the coast from Pegu, Junk Ceylon or Malacca. This excess cargo furnished the trip to S urat where it always sold well. The return cargo was in pepper when it was available. This description leaves out the role of Madras in re-exporting Chinese goods such as sugar or china-wax to Surat, as described by Captain Hamilton earlier in the 18th century. Trade from the Malabar coast, conducted by local people was also hardly worth mentioning according to Vincens.

While European private traders, above all the English occupied a prominent position in Surat's trade with Bengal and with trading areas in the east in general, Surat's trade in the west with Mocha, Jedda, Bassora and Persia was largely controlled by the 'Maures and Bagnans' of Surat. (Vincens does not mention the trade of Europeans from Surat to those regions). Formerly, he said, they were the masters of this trade sending at least thirty ships to those directions, excluding those sent to Bengal. They also traded with China and Manila (there is no reference to the once important trade of Surat with Achin or the Maldives), which has been abandoned since the last ten years or so and trade with the western regions had also 'greatly diminished'. No reason is however suggested for this decline. To Mocha they sent three to four ships annually, weighing 400–600 tonnes, sometimes even more, with very considerable cargos. These were mainly composed of piece-goods (most probably there were more of coarse than fine piece goods); a considerable quantity was manufactured for Mocha at Surat. This is one clear example of a rigid consumption pattern dictating the sellers market, who responded by throwing up a specialised group of weavers who could not be found anywhere else in India. The French were sufficiently aware of the possibilities of trade in these piece-goods to the extent of getting samples from Mocha, together with weavers (he does not mention from where) to Pondicherry; goods produced on this basis sold well at Mocha; the Surat merchants tried to persuade the Imam to forbid their importation from the coast, and the French agent at Mocha only succeeded in importing these goods by agreeing to pay a higher duty—3¾, while 2¼% was the rate for all other merchandise imported by them. Surat's trade with Mocha in fact did "a lot of harm" to trade of other Indian regions sending ships to Mocha, but above all to the trade from the Coromandel coast.

Surat's trade with Persia was according to Vincens, practically nonexistent at this time, due to wars; the caravans were no more coming to Bandar Abbas, the port as well as entrepot of Persia. Did he mean by 'the wars' the conflict that had brought about the downfall of the Safavi dynasty? Dupleix however had already sent ships there for two consecutive years, and as far as known at least the first trip was quite good. Anyway, so far as trade from Surat was concerned, it seems to have been diverted to Bassora, according to Vincens, to do trade with the caravans coming from Turkey. Indian merchants of Surat generally sent two big ships to Bassorah annually. The cargoes were similar to those sent to Mocha. Piece-goods from Bengal and sugar were also added to these cargoes, when the latter was abundant and cheap in Surat. The return cargo generally included Persian horses, date, almonds, raisin, rosewater and Persian wine—the last three items having become extremely rare since the wars. All articles were sold with very high profit at Surat, specially the horses. The recent dislocations in Persian trade had thus provoked different reaction among the various trading groups of India. While trade with Surat is said to be totally abandoned, traders from Cutch, Laharibunder, etc., had found new outlets in Calicut, Cochin and other centres in Malabar—leading the 'northern boom' as described by A. Dasgupta in his study of Malabar. No idea can be formed from the memoir as to factors helping the continuation of this trade from Bengal. Vincens was not well-informed about Surat's trade with Jedda, as so far the French had not attempted this; as far as he knew. Surat merchants sent one to two big ships there annually with goods similar to those sent to Mocha and Bassora.

Vincens dwells at length on certain features of European trade in Surat, mainly with a view to persuading the French Company to reestablish its factory there. It was at Surat, that the Company had established its first Indian factory in 1668, but huge debts contracted by the Company had always hampered business there. By the late 1720s there were only a few employees, deprived of any of the privileges accorded to other European Companies. The Pondicherry Council was still against any idea of reviving trade there, always putting up the arguments of huge debts, uncooperative local merchants and a possible pressure to be brought about by the Mughal Governor in favour of the ancient creditors. Vincens strongly argue against these, as a misconception, and assures the Company that local merchants and banias had really no authority in the city, and that the Mughal representative had no intention to support the claim of previous creditors since Muslim law was against usury. One ship named 'al' Europeene' in fact was more than a match for fifteen ships armed by the Muslims. So far no French private ship had been harassed in any way on the pretext of the ancient debt. And, above all, it was Indian merchants and banias themselves who had approached a personal friend of Vincens in April 1733 to request the Director of Chandernagor to send ships there regularly, assuring him of unhindered business and even better prospects than those enjoyed by the English private traders. The latter, not their Company, represented the English private trade in Surat although they enjoyed 'privileges of the company'. But they were absolutely at the mercy of the English Governor of the Surat factory. They had to do trade through the Company's broker, Indian merchants being prevented to approach them, were forced to sell all their goods to him and to the Governor who was "the master of all goods after the departure of the ships", sometimes buying up to 800,000 rupees. worth goods. Intervention of the Governor and the Company's broker pushed up the duties payable by the English to about 12% while it could not be more than 8% for the French.

All this explains Vincens' optimism as well as the Indian merchants' eagerness to do business with the latter. Vincens' observations and comments support the picture drawn by Holden Furber, of English country-trade being dominated by the Governors of Surat and Bombay. The situation in Pondicherry was not too different. All in all, private European trade was still too much restricted by the Company's officials in authority throughout the ports and colonial towns of India; the position of Indian merchants *vis-a-vis* them is not clear from this memoir but could it be much different in the factory towns? The entire project of developing them as prosperous centres of Asian trade perhaps should be re-examined from this point of view. While Surat's unquestioned prominence is based on the east-west orientation of the bulk of India's Asian trade, and on her role as the emporium of the Mughal empire, Bengal on the other side of India is declared to be "the centre and source of trade", because of the striking abundance and variety of goods. She moreover supplied provisions to the Malabar and Coromandel coasts. Up to 100 ships ranging from 100–500 tonnes left the Ganges laden with goods for Europe or other parts of Asia. One could, in fact, have as much goods as desired provided necessary cash was available; and ships navigating in India and coming back to Bengal could always depend on selling off all their important cargo.

This description would sound rather generalised or idealised. Vincens moreover does not deal with the trading world of Bengal in any detail, most probably because he was not yet familiar with it. He also admits having no knowledge of the inland trade of Bengal as it was controlled by the local people. But a more concrete image of Bengal's important position in the structure of Asian trade is provided by Vincen's description of the trading links in India and other Asian ports. Bengal figures prominently on every one of them, a distinction not shared by any other region of India. This was obviously due to the volume and range of her manufactured goods, already referred. Another factor could be the development of carrying trade by Europeans who faced less competition in Bengal than on the west coast. But it was probably Indians who supplied bulk of the capital as well as goods.

The essential part of Bengal's coastal and Asian trade was, with Surat on the west coast, and with the Red sea, the Persian Gulf coming next. This was done with the European ships, largely with freight provided by the Indians; there is no indication of Bengali merchants sending goods or their own ships to those areas. It was only the English who traded directly from Bengal to Mocha, carrying sugar, rice or priment or artalle, ginger and coarse piece-goods; formerly three or four English ships went to Mocha, but part of the trade having been attracted to Jeddah, they were now sending one to two ships of 250 to 300 tonnes. Profit was not certain; Surat competed in coarse piece-goods while rice also came to Mocha from the Malabar coast; so profit in any given season depended on the number of ships from these two areas and there

were years when the English barely realised the cost price. From time to time
the French to loaded some goods from Bengal on ships fitted out at Pondicherry
but they had always incurred loss on them.

The English trade from Bengal to Bassora was also of long standing. They
did not seem to be bothered by the Dutch who sent there two ships annually,
since the latter's cargo was composed mainly of spices, and rarely of any goods
from Bengal or the Coromandel coast. But the annual appearance of one
French ship of 400–500 tonnes for the last four or five years had, according to
Vincens, affected them considerably, even to the extent of reducing their
number of ships to two while eight or ten years ago they sent five to six ships
of 300 to 600 tonnes. This would mean a severely limited buyers market, unless
we admit that Vincens was perhaps giving a little too much importance to
French rivalry. Dupleix of course showed considerable skill in securing 28,000
rupees. worth freight the year before. Vincens makes it very clear that freight
was the basis of Bengal's trade with Bassora. It was paid in advance and did not
involve the shipowner in any extra cost for wintering, if all the goods were not
sold off within the same season, which was quite often the case. Sugar and
coarse cloth were the main items brought from Bengal. The return cargo of
dried fruits, nuts, etc., was of very little significance, so far as the coast and
Bengal were concerned; dates and sugar were the only items with good profit
but enormuous amounts were needed to make it worth while, because of their
low prices. Silver seemed to be the only article in constant demand, but it was
very rare at times; a lucky supercargo would sometimes be paid in copper,
always selling well in Bengal; but its supply was uncertain, as it was only
secured by soldiers plundering in wartime.

English private traders also figured prominently in Bengal's trade with the
Malabar coast. They sent at least five to six ships including frigate of 100 to
150 tonnes to that coast, mainly with goods destined to Mozambique and
Brazil which they sold to Portuguese ships at Goa. The rest was made up with
rice, wheat and some piece-goods to be sold at various points between the Cape
Comorin and Goa, for cash or pepper and arak fit for consumption on the
Coromandel coast and in Bengal. They also took cowries from Tellichery. Some
years profit from this trade went up to 15–25%. But 'it is enough if there seems
to be something doing any where' to prompt the English 'to send such a number
of ships there as ruin all of them'. This in fact is a recurring note in description
of trade conditions in many of the places described by Vincens. This account
leaves out Mahe where Tremisot was already helping Dupleix in his private
trade.

Bengal's trade relations with ports and regions in the east—Pegu, Manila,
Achin, and China were less regular and on the whole less profitable than those
with the west. Vincens is however quite optimistic about prospects of trade
with Manila and Pegu. Trade with Manila consisted of supplying the Mexican
galleons, and was generally good, ships going there from Bengal having often

made 25–40% profit. So far the French had not attempted this from Chandernagor and the English in Calcutta seem to be controlling it. No details of export cargoes are mentioned but there are indications of Bengal piece-goods being in good demand. Manila trade was important also because it supplied gold to traders from the Coromandel coast, or silver to be sometime converted in gold in China; to Bengal it furnished cowries, so much in demand there, that on some years when goods were sold at cost price in Manila, the cowries brought back by these ships had saved the trip and had even yielded some benefit. There is no indication as to what proportion of the cowries was absorbed locally or how much of it was going to be reexported for the 'Guinea trade'. Vincens shows his interest in the trade for the Company by his usual way of sketching a detailed project of how it could be attempted from the Coast and Bengal.

Trade with Pegu was mostly done from Bengal and Coromandel. The exact extent of Bengal's share in this trade cannot be ascertained, only the English merchants being mentioned in this context; their main object was construction of ships to be employed in country trade; the problem of securing an adequate return-cargo in Burma faced by the Dutch in Coromandel in the previous century thus no more plagued the European trader; there is also no mention of trade in rubies 'the best in the world', according to Captain Hamilton who was there earlier in the thirteenth century. Vincens rates Pegu very highly for the purpose of the Company's trade. Achin on the other hand, had lost her previous attraction as an important supplier of spices; fine gold powder was now her main item of export. Trade with Achin, 'one of the best trade in India' was now very much on the decline according to Vincens, which he attributed to both troubles within the state and a greater number of ships, mainly English. English competition in fact seems the more pertinent of the two; would it suggest once more a limited market, or the necessity to have a high margin of profit, impossible to maintain without an undisturbed monopoly? Bengal anyway fared better than the Coromandel coast or Surat, not only she sent there some piece-goods not manufactured on the Coast, which sold well; moreover, her cargoes to Achin included opium, prohibited in the entire Malaccan region, but in high demand all the same. The success of Dutch trade in Patna was also attributed to their business in opium shipped to these regions. Were these the first steps towards the east illegal opium trade, to reach China within a few more decades? Already, trade with some places in the east, to be successful, was depending on contraband goods.

Vincens' observations of India's trade with China gives only a slight indication of its future predominance in India's Asian trade. There is for example the allusion to China trade being no more as profitable to the English traders as it had been previously, as the Companies were sending a large number of ships there directly from Europe. The English East India Company had recently prohibited it to its employees, having sent three ships to Madras in 1733 for China trade, only one of them assigned to private trade, which interested nobody. There was also news of French ship carrying a great amount of silver to China that year. All this would push up the price of gold in China exorbitantly, rendering the trips unprofitable, gold being the main article sought by ships going to China from India. These developments dissuaded Vincens from taking part in a projected trip to China that year, although according to him, only trade from Bengal could make something out of it in such a situation. For, Bengal's trade with China was as yet dependent on Surat. The English would carry their freight of sugar there, to ensure a good fund in rupee or piastre; they would add a little Surat cotton, and pepper and sandal from the Malabar coast. Silver was the essential commodity, to be exchanged for gold; but Bengal ships could always avoid being affected by a steep rise in the price of gold, by investing a good deal of their bullion in buying sugar, porcelain and tutenag to be sold with profit at Surat. They would return to Bengal with a cargo of Surat cotton, or pepper from Malabar. Thus Bengal-China trade was advantageous but only as an important link in a wider network, without any autonomy. Trade with the Maldives is the only one in the context of Bengal, that is considered by Vincens to be totally unsuitable, not only to the Company but to Europeans as a whole. The growing demand for cowries notwithstanding, Europeans from Chandemagor found the climate of the Maldives too unhealthy to risk the trips. Only 'the Metis born at the Ganges' could stand the climate and at the time there was only one man in Chandernagor 'born in Bengal' who was sent to the Maldives as supercargo. He had already made 14 trips there when Vincens wrote the memoir. The high percentage of profit did not take away from this problem; moreover, huge quantities were needed to make up for the low price of cowries. Hence, this trade was best left to Indian traders. There is no discussion of Calcutta's role in the cowrie trade. But the English were the only Europeans to attempt from time to time the trade in dry fish from Maldives to Achin, repeating a trend already familiar to us in connection with their trade in Achin and in the straits of Malacca.

Then Bengal's position in Asian trade is thus determined, first by the abundance and variety of her goods and second by the growing importance of European, specially English carrying trade. They dominated not only the more advantageous trade with the west, but were trying to capture trade in areas which involved greater risk such as with Achin, or with region in the straits of Malacca; they also showed ingenuity in building up the Bengal-China trade around Surat. The impact of Dupleix's commercial activities had only just started to make itself felt. The most important lacuna is the absence of any reference to Indian or Armenian merchants who must have been supplying the bulk of freight as well as captital.

One would expect to find a good deal about trade in Coromandel from the memoir. It was there, in Pondicherry that Vincens spent 15 out of his 22 years in India. The emerging picture, however, is not very clear, partly because

Vincens is more preoccupied with the details of Pondicherry's participation in this trade than with the general condition. Even so, thanks to the concrete nature of some of his brief statements, some distinctive features emerge, of trade in the coast. The first impression one gets is of a distinct fall off from days in the last century, when the European Companies joined the rank of Asian merchants carrying "coast cloth" to the spice islands. The growth of Dutch control over the spice growing areas, reduced demand for pepper in Europe, as well as dislocation of economy on the coast due to repeated droughts as well as continuous warfare, all had weighed upon production and trade in cotton cloth.

Second, her main trade links were oriented to the east—China, Pegu and the Philippines still holding out better prospects for her than trade with Mocha or Bassora. The Dutch seems to have lost out completely. Apart from the English, Armenian, Moslem and Danish merchants seem to be rivals of some importance in the eastward trade at least so far as Pondicherry was concerned. Nothing however can be asserted with any degree of certainty without more information about Madras, although his brief references to Madras, evoke a picture of solid opulence and brisk commercial activity based on Asian trade.

The composition of cargoes exported and imported also suggests important differences with Surat and Bengal. Coromandel had nothing unique to offer to foreign markets, excepting certain variety of piece-goods to the east; to some extent perhaps the export trade of the entire coast deserved the analogy drawn between Madras and the Dutch 'supplying foreign markets with foreign goods'; needless to say, in the case of Coromandel this was a necessity and not a deliberate policy supported by vastly superior carrying power of a European merchant navy. Her imports were determined more by her own deficiencies in bullion, and in food, than by a well-organised policy of re-exportation, excepting, to some extent, to Surat.

The list of places linked in trade with Pondicherry, which would certainly hold good for the entire coast is an impressive one. China, Manila, Achin, Mergui, Pegu, Surat, Bassora and Mocha all figure on it. However, Vincens points out in a marginal note, that only trade with China, Manila, Pegu and Mocha was of some advantage; cargoes destined to all other regions had to depend on "goods drawn from Ganges" which greatly increased the cost of fitting out. Bengal is not mentioned in the list, but we know, that she supplied provisions regularly to the coast, so often a victim of drought and famine. This was one regular source of profit to European traders in Bengal. Arakan and Ceylon where trade was pushed from the coast by the Dutch Company in the seventeenth century find no mention.

Trade with Manila consisted of carrying the piece-goods manufactured at the coast and bringing back piastres. The principal gain to the Company was from export and import duties paid by Indian and European merchants, at Pondicherry. The English at Madras also once considered Manila trade to be the best as they were assured of at least 1000 bales of cloth to be freighted by Armenians and other inhabitants of Madras to Manila. According to Vincens Armenians had really become masters of this trade at the period when the memoir was written. Pondicherry so far had made poor show in Asian trade, even with the east. Her inhabitants, European and Indian although large in number, were too poor to attempt by themselves an expedition with 30,000 pagodas, without the Company's participation. Vincens suggests a tentative project for rendering this trade profitable, which involved equal participation by the Company and the Councils of Pondicherry's and Chandernagor, and a trip to China from Manila. Pondicherry's success in this trade, in short, depended largely on Bengal and China.

A note of regret over better days in the past runs through Vincens' description of trade with China, Achin and Pegu. This seems general, so far as China is concerned. Formerly this trade yielded so much profit to the English that they considered trade with Manila as of no importance. (Vincens contradicts himself here.) As explained before, increased competition had raised the price of gold exorbitantly in China. This affected Coromandel particularly, whose ships mainly sought gold in China, to be secured against goods like pepper, Calin redwood and sandalwood, which generally brought a profit of 10.15%. But these goods constituted only a part, at least ¾ of the export cargo was to be formed of silver at a maximum rate of pagodas 18 fanam a serre. Chinese gold would bring the expected profit of 26.27% at Pondicherry only if it did not cost more than 106–7 taels of silver for 10 taels of gold in China. Tutenague, procelain, tea and sugar which made up the rest of the return cargo, also sold well, but profit ultimately centred around securing a favourable price for gold. Limited markets for other goods, as well as limited capacity of the French to develop other lines of trade around China led to this dependence—a clear contrast with Bengal. There is no allusion of the important role of Madras as a centre of transhipment of part of Chinese goods to Surat, observed by Hamilton. But even private traders in Madras were feeling the impact of the growing interest of the English and the French companies in China, according to Vincens. Even so, Vincens considers China trade worth giving more attention for the Company, as it would bring 25–30% profit, expenses would always be covered, and it would relieve the French colonies from going to others to buy goods from China.

Coromandel's trade with Pegu, for once does not evoke unfavourable comparison with Bengal. Some low price piece-goods such as betille, manufactured at the coast were preferred apparently to similar goods from Bengal. But while Bengal was primarily interested in wood for shipbuilding, the return cargo to the coast was more varied; apart from wood, it included calin, wax, elephants' tusk and copper partly to be re-shipped to Surat; there was also plenty of rice always in demand along the coast. One disadvantage of trade with Pegu was the inability of local people to furnish in the same year the goods in payment for what they bought from merchants from Bengal and Coromandel. This involved an extra cost of wintering. Even so this trade had enriched a number of inhabitants of Madras; not even ten years ago 15–20 vassels, ships as well as frigates left Madras (for Pegu). The recent 'decline' in trade is attributed to the control of Armenians settled there, who became favourites of the King (Hamilton had also referred to Armenians monopoly of trade in 'rubies' but that concerns a much earlier period. Pondicherry fared badly in trade with Pegu as well; lack of capital or understanding or a combination of both had prevented merchants there to employ a double fund in this trade to defray the cost of wintering. The 'governments' of Calcutta and Madras maintained two agents in Pegu who looked after their business, so the English did not have to incur this expense. Most English private traders had to arrange their affairs with them.

A tone of general regret of the past, mingled with frustration due to the poor level of performances put up by Pondicherry marks also the observation on Coromandel's trade with Achin. Unbleached and blue guinee cloth manufactured at the coast had a good market in Achin. But trade there had gone from bad to worse; on top of the Moslem and Danish ships who generally did these trade from the coast, the English were sending a number of ships there annually, which had reduced the profits greatly. The complaint is familiar. Another factor adding to the difficulties was the scarcity of gold in Achin, causing delay in payment by the local merchants, and involving costs of wintering, which always ate away profits. Pondicherry as usual had failed to gain so far from the reduction of duties (by 1/3) granted to the French at Achin. Vincens advises the Company to attempt no more than sending one ship with freight to Achin, to winter there instead of at Merguy; this would involve no risk on the part of the Company. Such trade as this was best left to the local people, who could do it with more experience and more economy—a familiar argument reflecting the altitude of the Companies, interested only in trades yielding maximum profit. The English once more proved an exception, sending ships to Achin and even to the straits of Malabar at the risk of being massacred by local pirates, 'I do not know how they do it' Vincens confesses frankly 'since it is true that if one such expedition succeeds there are at least ten that are ruined' and grudgingly admits, at the same time that 'one has to be as enterprising as the English to attempt a second time' ventures even more risky than this.

Mergui seems to be mentioned only to enumerate the difficulties involved in this trade, with the expected advice to leave to the "Maures and local people" who did the trade with greater economy and greater risk. They traded mainly in rice and elephants, neither suited to Europeans. Trade in elephant was practically a monopoly of the King of Siam, who sent two ships to Madras and St. Thome annually. Vincens' lack of enthusiasm for the rice trade is to be explained, obviously, in terms of difficulties involved, as he had cited trade in this very commodity as one of the attractions of Pegu. On the whole one gets an impression of relatively reduced prospects so far as this area was concerned, due most probably to growing English rivalry, although non-European competition is not negligible. The coast had also lost out to some extent to Bengal. But the role of Madras is not at all clear, and a good deal of the pessimism reflects condition in Pondicherry, which up to that time had failed to develop into a centre of Asian trade.

Coromandel's trade with western India and with Mocha and Bassora is clearly less favourable than with the east, even if it is often about Pondicherry that Vincens speaks more than the coast. Demand for coast goods is more limited and competition greater in this region. Only the blue cloth of the coast had a little demand on the Malabar coast, but in such little quantity that it was not worth fitting out a ship only for that. She was a mere link in the chain of Bengal's trade with the Malabar coast. We have already seen that its trade with Surat was irregular, fed by occasional glut of merchandise brought by ships from the east. There was no trade from Coromandel in her own goods to Mocha before 1713, according to Hamilton. At the beginning of the 1730s only the English and the French traded from there with Mocha. Surat's cloth trade with Mocha 'harmed' this trade from all regions, as already mentioned; but trade in coarse blue and unbleached cloth, the main export of Coromandel suffered most in the competition. So, success in this trade seems very often to have depended on an occasional failure of Surat ships to turn up at Mocha in the trading season. This happened in 1730 which encouraged the English and the French to send two ships each, between October 1730 and January 1731. The resulting glut, thanks to the arrival of Surat ships left ¾th of the goods unsold till 1733; even then it was due to another year of troubles and war, now more and more frequent in Surat that prevented merchants of that city to send their ships to Mocha. The English had stopped sending any ships since 1732. The French had sent a ship with cargo valuing 26–28,000 pagodas, only with the Company's participation amounting to half of that sum. Markets in the east as well as in the west were thus limited—unless this reflects refusal of the Europeans to sell their products below a certain rate. Vincens saw no reason for the Company to maintain a factory at Mocha, unless it intended to use it as a centre for Asian trade, not merely a place to supply it with coffee for its Europe-bound ships.

Trade from the coast to Bassora was also of little importance at least for the French. Its demand for coarse cloth was met largely by Surat, to some extent by Bengal. Only unbleached and blue guinee cloth had some market in Bassora; this did not involve more than 20,000 pagodas. So far the French had not attempted it directly from Pondicherry, loading their ships on their way to Mocha from Chandernagor with this cargo, either at Pondicherry or at Mahe on the Malabar coast. Problems concerning the return cargo from Bassora have already been explained. Bassora was not considered suitable for the Company's trade either. According to Vincens, the Directors were misinformed about the possibilities of selling French cloth, transhipped from Chandernagor and Pondicherry at Bassora. Such cloth, imported also by caravans into Bassora was of the same quality and sold at a lower price. Vincens, however, suggests one way of making Bassora useful to the Company, by developing it into a centre of trade in Mascarin coffee.

The least attention is paid to trade in the Malabar coast. Neither the commercial boom hitting the port of Calicut in the 1730s nor the Dutch participation in Asian trade from this coast features in the memoir. We do not meet the bombaras from Porbandar, Sind, etc., seeking new outlets for their trade, the one in the Persian gulf having been seriously disturbed in the previous decade. We have already met with conditions of trade in Goa, which attract a good deal of attention from Vincens. He also takes note of the menace to ships between Mahe and Surat from the Angrias. This was obviously one of the reasons behind the small volume of trade conducted by local merchants from the Malabar coast to Surat.

Vincens briefly mentions the trade from Malabar to Persia, Bassora and Mocha, done by local traders—'Moslems and natives'. They carried Mangalore rice, pepper, cardamom and sandalwood to Bassora which sold well; this, added to the little cost involved in their trade made up the expenses incurred. Similar cargoes were shipped to Mocha, one added attraction being arak, always fetching a good price at Mocha. In spite of obviously bright prospects, only the English had so far attempted this trade, one more proof of their leaving no source untapped. The year before Vincens had planned along with the French agent Tremisot this trade from Mahe, to Bassora and Mocha in the same monsoon but gave it up on being informed of a great fall in the price of pepper, cardamom and arak in Mocha. Such a project, according to him suited only private traders — most probably he did not have faith in the French Company sticking to such a project, involving repeated short and fast trips between Malabar and Mocha and Bassora over a couple of years, whereas, continuation over a certain period was essential for success in this undertaking. Nevertheless, he suggests the measures to be followed by the Company in case it wanted to try this branch of trade.

This memoir does no more than illuminating one point in the history of India's Asian trade in the late pre-colonial period—more specifically the half century or so preceding definite establishment of British commercial monopoly in Bengal. A study of several such vantage points is necessary to know how far the emerging picture represents the entire period. It is an absorbing study, in spite of its obvious incompleteness. If Asian trade retains here on the whole the character of 'thin golden thread' linking ports and countries around the Indian ocean, without the backdrop of the hinterland, it evokes all the richness and confusion of a seventeenth century painted wall decoration produced by Coromandel artisans. Porcelain, ivory and gold move from one sea to another along with coarse cloth, rice and sugar, to destroy once more the image of the 'splendid and trifling' oriental trade. Presence of a greater number of rivals rather than any grave dislocation of commerce due to internal disorder or decay accounts more for all the references to 'better days before'. There is an atmosphere of brisk activity all round, to a considerable extent due to the presence of Europeans.

Vincens does not seem conscious of two new developments characterising the period, the rise of Bombay and the beginning of Surat's decline; the first is mentioned only in connection with its profitable trade with China; ominous signs of the decline of Surat can be read in the frequent references to 'troubles and war' disrupting her trade. The Europeans in fact figure more than the Indians in this picture, although so far they seem to be following an existing pattern, rather than introducing any striking change so far as routes or cargoes were concerned. They were moreover as much dependent on Indian freight and capital, as the Indian on their ships. Finally, the 'freedom' of the free European merchant is still severely limited *vis-a-vis* the control of private trade by higher officials of the various companies, specially the English, wherever they had factories, not to speak of the factory-towns. Vincens has suggested the granting of greater privilege to private merchants by the Company, but, understandably though, does not refer to the domineering and coercive attitude of Directors and Governors of the various European Colonies. Indian merchants in Surat show their eagerness to deal with the French, as this would improve their bargaining position; these must be traders with less command over capital and shipping than the ones organising trade to the west or with Bengal. Armenians in Madras were quite prominent in her overseas trade with Manila, and the richest Indian merchants there could afford to stay aloof from providing goods for the Europe oriented trade. They would not mind some extra business as long as trade was regular and offered sufficient scope for all. This, according to La Bourdonnais, another contemporary observer, also prevented the Bengali merchants of Calcutta from coming to settle in Chandemagor. But no image of the Bengali merchant emerges, even as the subordinate partner to take his place beside the Moslem and Hindu traders of Surat, or the Armenians of Madras.

Prominence of the English among European private traders, already known, also comes out of Vincens' description. One main factor of this prominence, as seen in this memoir, was their readiness to try all the possible trade links, even those considered unsuitable, for the Europeans by Vincens.

Nothing reflects better than such a document the difficulty of somebody in Vincens' position, obliged to convince his incompetent and indifferent masters at home about possibilities of Asian trade, since he was one of the witnesses of the poor level of the Company's performances in that sphere for the last twelve years. Bound by his loyalty to do the best of a bad job, he nonetheless gives himself away in his remarks about the activities of Dupleix in Chandemagor. The note of hope and optimism is in striking contrast to his references to Pondicherry, a failure as a commercial centre. Even his detailed projects, for the Company's trade which China or Manila in the east, or with Surat and Malabar remain only interesting models, and seem quite unreal, in spite of all the specific details when we remember how the Company responded to this and similar suggestions by pursuing a policy of indecision through the most notable decade of French trade in the first half of the eighteenth century. The tragedy of Vincens lies in his realization of the Company's limitations and a failure at the same time to suggest an alternative.

25

Position of the Local Merchants of Orissa, 1550–1757

Pinaki Ranjan Mahapatra

THE LOCAL merchants of Orissa played a significant role in Orissa's trade. They took active part in its trade with different parts of India as well as with Asiatic countries. They also acted as middlemen between the producers and the European merchants.

The local merchants of Orissa belonged to both the Hindu and Muslim communities. The English factory records mention the names of Khemchand, Chintaman Shah, Suraj Shah, Hira Shah, Kalyan Rai, Rajaram, Ram Narayan, Gangaram and Gopal as the principal merchants of Balasore. All of them were Hindus. We have also reference to some Muslim merchants of Balasore with whom the English contracted for purchasing goods in 1684.[1] But there is no mention of the names of these Muslim merchants. Some merchants were wealthy while others were insolvent. Even after promising to pay Rs. 30,000 to *nawab* Saf Shikan Khan in 1672,[2] Khemchand had resources to indemnify the English and others and this consideration led the English to deliver to Khemchand Rs. 7,500 which was his share in the investment.[3] Again in 1674 Khemchand paid Rs. 50,000 to Rashid Khan, the *nawab* of Orissa.[4] These details go to show the wealth of Khemchand. In 1679 the English considering the insolvency of Gopal abated a portion of money that he owned to the Company.[5]

The local merchants of Orissa carried on trade with different parts of India e.g. Calcutta, Dacca, Pulicat and Cochin. We have reference to the merchants of Balasore carrying on trade with Calcutta in the sixties of the eighteenth century. They used to send iron, stone plates, rice and some other commodities the names of which have not been mentioned. Their imports from Calcutta to Balasore consisted of tobacco and certain other articles regarding the name of which we have no information.[6] Sometime before 1684 a *gomastah* of Khemchand purchased huge quantities of *cassas* at Dacca.[7] There is mention of the ship of the merchants of the Gingelly coast being burnt by the Portuguese

*35th Session at Jadapur, 1974.

in the Road of Pulicat in the early twenties of the seventeenth century.[8] This ship certainly went there on a commercial mission. In the thirties of the seventeenth century Manrique found at Pipli a ship belonging to the local shiqdar being sent to Cochin laden with merchandise.[9]

The merchants of Orissa also carried on Asiatic trade, viz. with Ceylon, Tenasserim and the Maldives. Bowrey in the seventies of the seventeenth century referred to the merchants of Balasore and Pipli sending their ships every year to Ceylon, Tenasserim and the Maldive Islands for the purpose of trade.[10] In 1680 Khemchand brought elephants from Tenasserim to Balasore.[11]

The European companies trading in Orissa had to depend on the local merchants regarding the supply of goods for export. Some of them acted as brokers of the European companies and helped them in financing their purchase. At the initial stage of commercial operations of the English in Orissa when lack of ready money and difficulty in selling European goods were the main hindrances to their trade[12] the merchants took part-payment for goods supplied by them in the articles imported from Europe.[13] In 1673 Khemchand alone had in his stock broad cloth worth Rs. 30,000.[14] The merchants sometimes acted as brokers between the English and the Government officials. In 1673 the Hooghly factors directed Hall, the English factor at Balasore, that Malik Kasim the 'Governor' of Balasore, must either pay cash for the guns that he would purchase from the Company or Khemchand should buy them for him. The English factors wanted to make this arrangement in order to avoid difficulties in realising the price of the guns.[15]

Besides paying much customs duties[16] the merchants were subjected to many other exactions. During the Subahdarship of Shaista Khan the merchants of Orissa had to make contributions towards strengthening the naval defence.[17] The merchants belonging to the Hindu Community had sometimes to make extra payments. The Hindu merchants of the Gingelly coast besides paying the usual taxes and duties had to pay many extra taxes that the Muslim Governor of the place used to charge from them. Although some of the richest Indian merchants lived there, they could not display their wealth for fear of extortion by the Muhammedan officials as well as for the fact that after their death their properties would belong to the emperor and their descendants could inherit these only by the mercy of the emperor.[18] The Subahdars considered the merchants as 'fill'd sponges' and extorted money from them.

Both Saf Shikan Khan and Rashid Khan exacted large amount of money from Khemchand.[19] The latter also demanded from other merchants at Balasore money varying from Rs. 10,000 to Rs. 50,000 according to their capacity to pay.[20] Besides being forced to pay large amount of money to the Subahdars, the merchants were harassed by the local officials in some other ways. When Malik Kasim became 'Governor' of Balasore in 1673 Walter Cavell, the Chief of the Bay factories and his Council feared that he would give trouble to the local merchants, at Balasore and force them to wind up their business. Their fears came to be true and in August 1673 Malik Kasim created such conditions as would make the merchants prefer to leave the place.[21] In the sixties of the eighteenth century the merchants of Balasore who traded with Calcutta were so much oppressed by a *gomastah* that many of them left the place, and transacted their business at Kunka (Kanika).[22] Some who remained at Balasore were greatly distressed.[23]

The merchants exercised considerable influence on the local government. In 1654 at the insistence of the local merchants Malik Beg, the local 'Governor' opened the godown of the Dutch at Pipli which was previously sealed by him as the Dutch refused to grant passes to the Indian ships to go to the countries in the Malay Peninsula and Achin which were then under the control of the Dutch.[24] The English sometimes solicited the intervention or mediation of the merchants in the hour of need and trouble. The former attempted to procure a *parwana* from the *nawab* Saf Shikan Khan in 1672. Though the *parwana* was procured through the intervention of Boremul (Puran Malla) the Governor of Balasore, during the transaction the merchants, Haricharan, Khemchand and Suraj Shah accompanied Boremul (Puran Malla) taking with them some presents for the *nawab's diwan* and other officers and this "smoothed the way"[25] (i.e. the way of obtaining the *parwana*). In 1679 there was a dispute between the English and the Dutch over a house and a piece of land at Balasore. The English decided to procure Kanungo's stamp through the mediation of Khemchand if it be necessary to validate their claim. They also sought, the good offices of Khemchand and Chintaman Shah in 1685 to settle an affair with the local officials.[26]

Notes

1. *EFI, 1678–84*, New Series, IV, p. 346.
2. *EFI, 1670–77*, New Series, II, p. 339.
3. J.N. Sarkar, "A Seventeenth Century Hindu Merchant and Broker of Balasore" in *JBRS*, 1954, pp. 123–24.
4. Bowrey, pp. 152–56, *EFI, 1670–77*, New Series, I, 339m.
5. Master, II, p. 254.
6. Long, op. cit., I, p. 250.
7. J.N. Sarkar, op. cit., in *JBRS*, 1954, p. 126.
8. *EFl, 1622–23*, p. 260.
9. Manrique, I, pp. 440, 441.
10. Bowrey, pp. 179–80.
11. J.N. Sarkar, op. cit., in *JBRS*, 1954, p. 126.
12. Bowrey, pp. 232–33; *EFl, 1670–77*, W., II, p. 345, Master, I, p. 54; II, pp. 86–87.
13. Master, I, p. 306; *EFI, 1668–69*, pp. 309–11.
14. *EFI, 1670–77*, New Series, II, p. 358.

15. Ibid., p. 365.
16. *EFI, 1668–69*, pp. 309–10. They paid customs both for what they bought from and sold to the English.
17. Bowrey, pp. 161–63.
18. Ibid., pp. 126–27.
19. Bowrey, pp. 152–56; *EFl, 1670–77*, New Series, II, pp. 339, 339n.
20. Bowrey, p. 155.
21. *EFI, 1670–77*, p. 361. There is no clear reference to the nature of oppression to which the merchants were subjected by Malik Kasim.
22. Kanika; Qila Kanika, situated along the sea-coast on both sides of the Dharma estuary and extended about 20 miles inland. Its area was 440 square miles. (*Chullak Dist. Gazt.* p. 218).
23. Long, op. cit., I, p. 250.
24. *EFI, 1651–54*, pp. 269–70; *Valentyn*, vol. V, part I, p. 162a; T. Raychoudhury, op. cit., p. 78 based on Kononisal Archief Algeman Rijksar chief, the Hague.
25. *EFI, 1670–77*, New Series, II, p. 339.
26. J.N. Sarkar, op. cit., in *JBRS*, 1954, p. 125.

26

The Nagarsheth of Ahmedabad: The History of an Urban Institution in a Gujarat City

Dwijendra Tripathi and *M.J. Mehta*

I

In whatever manner the traditional division of Indian history into ancient, medieval, and modern periods might have helped the study of political history, it has positively hampered a proper understanding of the evolution of social institutions. This is because political developments—succession of kings and change of dynasties—had little effect on the day-to-day life of the common people. As such certain social institutions displayed a remarkable degree of resilience and continuity, untrammelled by political changes, which cannot be adequately appreciated without transcending the narrow limits of conventional periodization.

A case in point is the mercantile associations. As has been shown by R.C. Majumdar, A.S. Altekar and others, traders' organizations, roughly comparable to trade guilds in medieval Europe, existed in India at least from the sixth century BC up to the end of the thirteenth century AD.[1] Known variously as *shreriis, sanghas, pugas, naigamas* and *mahajans* in different parts of the country or at different points of time, these organizations played a very important part in the economic and social life of the country during the period. A typical city could have several guilds, each presided over by a headman known in most of the cases as *shreshthin*. The *shreshthin* was neither appointed by a superior authority nor was he elected. He owed his position to popular acknowledgement as a result of his economic and social standing on one hand, and his demonstrated concern for his community or occupational group on the other.

What happened to the institution of trade guilds after the conventional terminal point of ancient period of Indian history, we do not know thanks to

*39th Session at Hyderabad, 1978.

the lack of scholarly scrutiny into the phenomenon by the specialists of the subsequent periods. But if the experience of the Gujarat cities is any guide, the guilds continued and flourished well up to the end of the nineteenth century. Gujarat being, in the words of Jadunath Sarkar, 'the gateway of India to the western world,'[2] its cities had become prominent centres of trade and commerce, and the wealth and prosperity of its merchants had made them into powerful pressure groups.[3] Their associations, known as *mahajans* each headed by a *shreshtha* or *sheth*, continued to remain an integral and important part of civic life in Gujarat.[4]

Founded in 1411 by Sultan Ahmad Shah, Ahmedabad became the beneficiary of this tradition. Though it started as an administrative and military headquarters of the province, by the end of the sixteenth century it had become a great manufacturing and commercial centre. Its cotton, silken and woollen goods of various varieties as well as its gold and silver brocades were in great demand in India as well as abroad, and its gold and silver jewelleries were considered as the best specimens of craftsmanship and manual dexterity. Other flourishing industries included dyeing and bleaching, embroidery and needle work, and inlaying of precious stones. One of the principal commodities of Ahmedabad market was indigo which was produced in plenty in its vicinity, and the neighbouring town of Sarkhej (now a suburb of Ahmedabad) had emerged as a principal mart.

Another factor which invested Ahmedabad with great commercial importance was the fact that it was situated at major trade routes connecting it with other commercial centres like Multan in the north and Agra in the east, and principal port towns like Cambay in the West and Surat in the South. In fact trade routes connected the city, directly or indirectly, with every part of the country. As a consequence, the capital city of Gujarat gradually emerged as an emporium of goods from various parts of India and the world, and 'there is not in a manner in any nation nor any merchandise in all Asia which may not be had in Ahmedabad....'[5]

By the end of the sixteenth century, the city had become one of the largest and most populous in the country with a heterogeneous population and a rich and variegated mercantile class. It had become a veritable 'confluence of most nations in the world'.[6] The merchants immigrating into the city from other cities in Gujarat and other parts of the country brought with them the tradition of *mahajans* and this institution took firm roots in Ahmedabad at a very early stage. The mention of a 'shresta' in a *khatpatra*, or sale deed, of 1627 clearly indicates that this institution had already come into being.[7] A Moghul *farman* of 1644 also refers to some *mahajans* implying that they had been in existence for quite some time.[8]

II

In developing the institution of *mahajans*, Ahmedabad was simply replicating the experience of other urban centres in Gujarat. Ahmedabad wentonestep further. It evolved gradually the position of the *nagarsheth*, or the chief merchant of the city. There is some ground to believe that certain urban centres in ancient India did have positions comparable to the *nagarsheth*,[9] but even if it was so, the position had fallen into disuse much before Ahmedabad came into being.

Maganlal Vakhatchand's classical history of Ahmedabad, first published in 1851, attributed the origin of the position to an imperial order. According to him, Emperor Jehangir had conferred this title on one Shantidas Jhaveri and his descendants in perpetuity.[10] Shantidas, the son of an immigrant merchant from Marwar,[11] undoubtedly was a great jeweller and a man of enormous wealth. He had extensive business dealings with the imperial court and occasionally helped the Moghul emperors with money in their hours of need. It is said that he won the title because of his services to the empire. This theory of the beginning of the *nagarshethship* in Ahmedabad has remained in vogue for more than hundred years. But a closer examination would indicate that it is of questionable validity.

Maganlal or his followers give no clue to the basis of their thesis. Shantidas has been mentioned as a *nagarsheth* in no contemporary document. It is significant that though a large number of imperial Moghul *farmans*, still in the possession of Shantidas's descendants, prove the grant of several favours of much lesser significance to Shantidas, there is none to back up the *nagarsheth* claim on his behalf.[12] Also, the title is never prefixed with Shantidas's name in *Mirat-i-Ahmadi*, a history of Gujarat in Persian completed in 1761, which almost never refers to Khushalchand, Shantidas's grandson, without the title.[13] It is also noteworthy that none of the *khatpatras* pertaining to the years before 1660 makes reference to any *nagarsheth*, though several of the subsequent years do so.[14] That the title was not hereditary to begin with, as the royal charter theory would have us believe, is clear from the fact that several individuals, not belonging to Shantidas's family, became *nagarsheth* after Shantidas's death. Supplementing these arguments of silence is the existence of a Gujarati document of 1633 which refers to one Udhavaji as the *nagaradhyaksha*, or the city chief,[15] challenging the assertion that Shantidas was occupying a similar place in the city on the orders of Jehangir who was dead in 1627.

The fact is that the position of *nagarsheth* was not a part of the Moghul bureaucracy, nor did it connote a purely honorific title the like of which the Moghul emperors used to confer on their favourites. As such it is extremely doubtful that such a position would have been created by an official fiat or would have been the creature of the pleasure of an emperor.[16] What seems more plausible is that the position evolved over a period of time in response to the peculiar conditions prevailing in Ahmedabad.

Two groups—Jain and Vaishnava banias — emerged the most prominent in the business field with Muslims as an important minority group. The various *mahajans* that sprang up in the city remained independent of each other and regulated trade matters in their respective spheres. There was no formal link between one another and there was no formal authority or agency to speak for the entire business community as a whole at least up to the middle of the seventeenth century. Of course, Udhavaji is referred to as *nagaradhyaksha* or the city President in 1633. But the fact that there is no reference to this position in any earlier or later document indicates that even if an attempt was made to institute a system of formal leadership, it seems to have made very little headway in the first half of the seventeenth century.

There is no doubt that during this period, the mercantile community of Ahmedabad accepted or at least acquiesced in the leadership of Shantidas Jhaveri. The English factory records speak of his great influence on the imperial court.[17] Shantidas, an Oswal Jain, had used his influence to win a series of privileges and concessions for his religion from Jehangir and Shah Jahan, and even Aurangzeb, whose bigotry had led him in 1645 to defile a Jain temple built by the Jain magnate in Ahmedabad, thought it necessary to reconfirm these concessions and grant new ones when he came to power.[18] Formally, Shantidas was the head of the jeweller's *mahajan* alone, but because of his unassailable position in the business world he acted as a link between the city as a whole, particularly the merchant groups, and the state. It is because of this that Aurangzeb after assuming power, but still seeking legitimacy for his imperial position, chose Shantidas, 'the best among compeers', to convey his message of 'conciliation and consolation' to all merchant *mahajans*, common inhabitants, and general residents" of Ahmedabad.[19] It may be appropriate to mention that in other Gujarat cities, too, at this time, the wealthiest and the most influential businessman acted as the leader of the entire city though without any formal authority. Virji Vora, for instance, was the undisputed leader of the business community of Surat without having ever been formally acknowledged as such.[20]

The death of Shantidas in 1660 removed from the scene a very powerful figure. The city was left without a personality who, throughout his life, had been accepted as the spokesman of all the diverse groups in the city. It is around this time that phrase *nagarsheth* came in vogue to signify the leadership of the entire city. In a *khatpatra* of 1660 Sundardas, Shantidas's brother, has been referred to as the *nagarsheth*.[21] This is the first mention of this position in any contemporary document. It is possible that Shantidas's powerful personality had prevented Sundardas from making any mark on the life of the city during the former's life time. The latter, therefore, needed this impressive prop to reach the position left vacant by Shantidas. It is also possible that the family feud, which had started during the life time of the Jain magnate,[22] led Sundardas to assume this title to denote the supremacy of his line against the direct descendants of his deceased brother. Significantly, none of Shantidas's five sons has ever been referred to as *nagarsheth* in any contemporary record.

Sundardas's attempt to emerge as the leader of the entire community did not go unchallenged. The Vaishnava banias who had accepted, grudgingly or otherwise, the supremacy of Shantidas were no more prepared to continue playing a second fiddle in the affairs of the city. They, by this time, had become a prominent mercantile group themselves, and it was natural for them to aspire for the city leadership. The title of *nagarsheth* was still without much substance, but the fear that the lustre of the designation gave unfair advantage to the Jains in their bid to retain their pre-eminence led the rival group to claim this position for its own members. This marked the beginning of a period of bitter competition between the two groups for the coveted position.[23]

The outcome of this conflict is by no means clear on the basis of available records. But it seems that either the position alternated between the two rival communities or each recognised a separate *nagarsheth* of its own. We have already seen that in a *khatpatra* of 1660 Sundardas is mentioned as *nagarsheth*, but the *khatpatras* of 1677, 1678, 1685 and 1712 indicate that one Vanmalidas Tapidas bore this title at least from 1677 to 1685, and his son, Kika, was *nagarsheth* in 1712.[24] The names of these persons suggest that they were Vaishnava banias. We do not know whether the Jains ever accepted Vanmalidas as their leader or recognized Sundardas or some other member of their community as the city chief, but there is little doubt that they increasingly challenged Kika's position as *nagarsheth*. For, according to *Mirat-i-Ahmadi*, one Ka-purchand Bhansali, an Oswal Jain, was the *nagarsheth* in 1713 and continued to be so till he was murdered in 1719.[25]

In the meantime, Shantidas's son, Lakshmichand, who had succeeded to the family affairs after his illustrious father, was dead and his son Khushalchand had assumed charge. Able and ambitious, the new head of jewellers' *mahajan* decided to regain the position which his grandfather enjoyed in the city affairs. His opportunity came when the Marathas, taking advantage of the constantly weakening Moghul power after Aurangzeb's death, attacked the city in 1724 in alliance with the former deputy governor Hamid Khan who had turned rebel following his ouster. The Marathas needed money, and they were about to destroy the city when Khushalchand paid a huge amount as ransom to the invaders from his personal pocket and turned the greedy invaders back.[26] Khushal's gracious act won for him the gratitude of the city population, specially of the business class which was the hardest hit by the Maratha presence. To express their appreciation, therefore, the heads of 'all the *mahajans* of the city of Ahmedabad' representing all communities and trades resolved that hence forward Khushalchand and his descendants would receive in perpetuity a levy of a quarter per cent on all goods stamped in the municipal weighing yard.[27] This was a great compensation. More importantly, this was a virtual acknowledgement of Khushal's supremacy in the civic affairs by all the trading guilds.

Khushal's enemies, however, were not to accept defeat so easily. During all these years since the beginning of the struggle for the *nagarshethship*, the imperial governors had stood scrupulously aloof. But the death of Aurangzeb heralded an era of political instability and intrigues and counter intrigues in high places. Taking advantage of this kind of environment, Khushal's rivals poisoned the ears of the provincial governor, Mubarizulmulk Sarbuland Khan, against him. The infuriated governor ordered the imprisonment of the Sheth in 1726 and appointed the head of the silk merchant *mahajan* as the *nagarsheth*.[28] Perhaps, the troubled political climate offered a unique opportunity to the provincial governor, to throw all conventions overboard to bring the holder of the prestigious title under his absolute control.

Gangadas whom Sarbuland Khani designated as the new *nagarsheth* was Khushal's cousin.[29] Most probably he belonged to the Sundardas branch of the family. This as well as the fact that prior to Khushalchand, another Jain, Kapurchand, held the position indicates that not only various communities—Jain and Vaishnava banias being the principal rivals—but also different individuals belonging to the same community were competing for supremacy. Be it as it may, by recognizing Gangadas as the city chief, the Governor ensured the assistance of a principal citizen in extracting illegally a large sum of money from the merchants and tradesmen.[30] Gangadas's cooperation in Sarbuland's oppressive acts must have cost whatever little goodwill he might have enjoyed in the city.

Khushalchand, in the meantime had bought his release and fled to Delhi. It was clear to him that the effect of Sarbuland's action in designating Gangadas as *nagarsheth* could be contracted only by an imperial *farman*. He waited for his chance till Sarbuland fell from the imperial favours and was dismissed from his post because of his tyranny and oppressiveness. The new governor, Abhay Singh Rathor, easily suppressed the revolt of the incensed Sarbuland. One of his first acts was to imprison Gangadas for his complicity in the misdeeds of the previous governor. Abhay Singh, however, emulated the example of his predecessor at least in one respect; he too appointed a *nagarsheth* of his choice in 1731. The new *nagarsheth* was a Muslim the head of the Bohra community—whose name was Ahmad.[31]

A little later in 1732 Khushalchand, who had stayed in Delhi all along after his fall from grace, returned to Ahmedabad with an order issued in the name of the emperor by his *Amirulumarah*. Addressed to the Maharaja it said that emperor Muhammad Shah had appointed Khushalchand as *nagarsheth* and instructed him to return to Ahmedabad. The royal charter charged the new *nagarsheth* with the responsibility to "attend to welfare of the people, prosperity of the city, well being of the common-folk, and manage affairs with such diligence that persons may devote themselves with satisfaction to their respective work and profession."[32] It was not possible for Abhay to ignore the imperial order completely. At the same time he did not want to eat a humble pie by disgracing his own appointee to the position. As a compromise, as it were, he recognised Kushalchand as the 'nagarsheth of the Hindus'; Ahmad, too, continued to hold the title simultaneously. For sometime, Ahmedabad seems to have had two *nagarsheths*.

For all practical purposes, the compromise tilted heavily in favour of Ahmad. During Khushal's absence, the Muslim *nagarsheth* had endeared himself to Abhay's deputy and treasurer (*bhandari*), Raten Singh.

The new rulers of the state were in no way less corrupt than Sarbuland Khan, and their ways to extract money from the local population were in no way dissimilar. The Bohra chief was willing to be an instrument of illegal exaction in the hands of Ratan Singh, as Gangadas was in the hands of Sarbuland's. Khushal, on the other hand, could not countenance such acts. Naturally, therefore, the ruling authorities threw their weight on Ahmad's side. Khushal's protests against illegal collections were ignored. So inconvenient did the Jain leader become to the deputy governor that he was inclined to put him in jail. But instead of doing so, Ratan Singh asked the Hindu *nagarsheth* to leave the city. An angry Khushal prepared for a fight, but was eventually persuaded to comply with the orders. Four years after this incident, Ahmad died[33] and the period of dual *nagarshethship* came to an end.

Khushal returned to the city. His return almost coincided with the fall from power of the Rajput governor and his deputy. The imperial authorities, unwilling to let his tyrannies continue any longer, dismissed Abhay and appointed one Momin Khan in his place to take charge of the province. Khushal had little problems with the new rulers for sometime, but after Momin's death in 1743, the Mughal-Maratha authorities, too, put him in jail and he was released only after he had paid them a considerable amount of money.[34]

The Jain leader, no doubt, had an eventful and stormy career. Successive Moghul governors, irrespective of their caste and religious backgrounds, illtreated him and extracted large sums of money, and he had to spend several years in exile. He, however, achieved what none of his predecessors had done. Thanks to his sacrifice and influence in the imperial court, he had established an undisputed claim to the *nagarsheth* position not only for himself but also for his descendants. By the time he died in 1748, the honour had definitely come to rest in his family. This is clear from the fact that none in the long line of subsequent *nagarsheths* belonged to any other family. According to the available information, after Khushal, his eldest son Nathusha or Nathumalsha (1720–93) became *nagarsheth*; he was followed by his younger brother Wakhatchand (1740–1814), and after Wakhat came his son and grandson, Hemabhai (1785–1858) and Premabhai (1815–87) respectively.[35] It is significant that though there was a division in the family after Wakhatchand, Motibhai, the founder of the splinter branch or his descendants, never questioned the right of the main branch to the *nagarshethship*. There is no doubt that after Khushal, the position had become hereditary. However, the eldest son did not necessarily have a claim over it. From the time of Shantidas, the family had established a tradition of entrusting its supreme management to the ablest member[36] and whosoever was accepted in this role also inherited the title. None of the three *nagarsheths* following Khushalchand, for instance, was the eldest son of his parents.

The development of the *nagarshethship* in Ahmedabad was thus nothing short of an innovation in urban institution. The evolution passed through three different stages. The first phase was symbolized by Shantidas Jhaveri, who was accepted as the informal spokesman for his class—in fact of the entire city—without having ever been formally appointed to the position. The word *nagarsheth,* to signify this kind of leadership, came to be used after the death of Shantidas in 1660 which marked the beginning of the second phase which continued up to 1725. This phase was marked by the conflict between various groups and individuals for popular acceptance as the city chief. The political confusion and instability that came to characterize the Gujarat politics in the wake of disintegrating Moghul authority made the political power join this conflict on one side or the other. And this marked the beginning of the third and the final phase. The issue was finally clinched in favour of Shantidas's descendants when Khushalchand, aided by an imperial charter, won the title for himself and his descendants. What started as a purely informal institution was finally formalized and legitimized with the aid of the state power.

III

It is tempting to believe, as M.N. Pearson has done, that the *nagarsheth* was the head of a city-wide *mahajan* 'on which sat representatives of all the occupational *mahajans.*'[37] The fact, however, is that at no stage did a city-wide corporate organization in Ahmedabad on the lines of individual *mahajans,* come into being. In fact the mention of the word *sarva mahajan* in the *khatpatras* definitely indicates that the individual *mahajans* never submerged their separate existence into any other corporate body. Referring to the situation as it existed in the last quarter of the nineteenth century the *Gazetteer of the Bombay Presidency* observed that the 'phrase Ahmedabad Mahajan is a misnomer, there being no permanent aggregation of the guilds which can claim to represent the whole of that city. The influence of the *nagarsheth* can generally command the adherence of all, but in such a case the various merchant guilds merely unite for a temporary purpose. They do not amalgamate into one guild.'[38]

The *nagarsheth*, being a principal merchant and the head of his own guild coupled with his acceptance as the spokesman of the city, became an informal link between the city and the state at a time when representative of urban institutions were yet to develop.[39] He was frequently consulted by the ruling authorities about the affairs of the state and represented to them the grievances of the people. Kapurchand Bhansali, for instance, led a delegation to Delhi after a communal riot in 1713 to apprise the imperial authorities of the details.[40] Likewise when Raghunathrao Peshwa (Raghoba) occupied the city in 1753, another *nagarsheth*, Nathusha, accompanied by some other merchants discussed the problem of future administration of the city with the conqueror. But later in 1780 when General Goddard took possession of the city, the same Nathusha led a delegation to prevail upon the British soldier not to harm the city in anyway. Without beating about the bush, the *seth* candidly maintained that he and the merchants supported the earlier government because they could not "in common honour act adverse to the ruling authorities" and, by the same logic, they had come 'forward to pay their obeisance to the conqueror, not so much for themselves as for their fellow citizens....'[41]

Besides being a link between the city and the state, the *nagarsheth* performed several other roles. He used his influence to settle disputes between various guilds or individuals, helped the state authorities to raise funds in the city, and played some role in the collection of the town cess as indicated by the assignment of a part of the town duties to the *nagarsheth* family by all the *mahajans*. A Gujarati poem of 1725 indicates that probably he had access to the key of the city gates.[42] On occasions a *nagarsheth*'s action was guided by his own sense of responsibility towards the city as Khushalchand's action in saving the city from the Maratha invaders in 1725 doubtlessly was. Sometimes he performed purely ritualistic acts. For instance, one *nagarsheth* led a batch of citizens pouring milk on the earth to propriate the rain god when the monsoon failed.[43] On the other hand, if a *nagarsheth* misused his position, as Gangadas and Ahmad indeed did, there was nothing anybody could do. But normally a sagacious *nagarsheth* performed such acts which legitimized rather than compromised his position.

The *nagarsheth*, in short, was a sort of father-figure to the city. After the Moghuls, the Marathas continued the tradition of treating the *nagarsheth* with deference during their sixty years rule over the city after 1758. When the city came under the British occupation in 1818, the new rulers, seeking to consolidate their position, readily recognized all the privileges which the *nagarsheth* family had traditionally enjoyed. Perhaps the only ostensible change that the British effected was that they computed the *nagarsheth*'s share of the octroi into an annual pension of a little more than Rs. 2000.[44] Both Hemabhai and Premabhai fully supported the British and the new rulers in turn extended their patronage to them.[45]

The beginning of the British rule, however, marks the decline of the *nagarshethship*. Slowly and gradually, the position became incongruous with the new forces which the British rule generated. Two developments need particular mention in this connection. One, the new rulers who believed in more formal institutions established municipal administration on modern lines the roots of which can be traced back to 1834, though in a more real sense the municipal government did not develop until the last quarter of the nineteenth century.[46] As the formal structure of the civic administration strengthened itself, the informal link between the city and suite, symbolised by the *nagarsheth*, became superfluous. Simultaneously the emergence of an industrial leadership in the later half of the nineteenth century began to offer an effective though subtle challenge to the supremacy of the trading and commercial groups which the *nagarsheth* represented. It is no accident that the first president of the Ahmedabad Municipality was Ranchhodlal Chhotalal, who had founded the first textile mill in the city and had risen to be the most prominent industrialist. Throughout his life, Ranchhodlal's position in the business and governmental circles remained unrivalled.[47] This was a clear signal that the institution which had survived several centuries of vicissitudes was incapable of meeting the challenge of new political-industrial forces. The result was that the position lost all substance, though the title still continued as an irrelevant relic of the past and the reminder of an old order. The title, too, disappeared recently when the last holder died in 1977 and nobody could inherit it under the new dispensation of the government.

We do not know how many more cities emulated Ahmedabad's example in developing institutions like that of *nagarsheth*. There is no doubt that some did[48] but our knowledge about the forces that influenced the evolution and decline of such institutions elsewhere is scanty indeed. Further research may also reveal that, like the *nagarshethship*, several other social institutions survived political changes and upheavals. But a proper understanding of their rise and fall would require problem oriented rather than period-based enquiries into India's past.

Notes

1. R.C. Majumdar, *Corporate Life in Ancient India*, pp. 135; A.S. Altekar, *A History of Important Towns and Cities in Gujarat and Kathiawad*, pp. 52–53; Radha Kumud Mookerjee, 'Economic Conditions' in R.C. Majumdar ed., *History and Culture of the Indian People*, II, pp. 601–2; U.N. Ghoshal, 'Economic Conditions' in ibid., III, pp. 603– 5; IV, pp. 605–7; V, pp. 524–26.
2. Quoted in M.R. Majumdar, *Cultural History of Gujarat*, p. 63 fn.
3. An example of the power of the merchants in Gujarat is provided by an incident of 1669. The nephew of a famous merchant of Surat, Tulsidas Parckh, was converted to Islam and another bania committed suicide to escape conversion. To protest

against the policy of religious coercion, about 8,000 banias left the city, and the *mahajans* ordered all their members to close down their shops. This action eventually led the government to revise its policy. For details see M J. Mehta, 'Some Aspects of Sural as a Trading Centre in the seventeenth Century', *Indian Historical Review*, I, no.2, 1974, p. 258; for a general discussion on the place of the merchant in Gujarat see Majumdar, *Cultural History of Gujarat*, pp. 188–89.

4. Altekar, *History of Important Towns*, p. 53.

5. Observation of German traveller J. Albert de Mandelslo who visited Ahmedabad in 1638. See M.S. Commissariat, *Mandeslo's Travels in Western India*, p. 26.

6. Observation of Nicholas Downtun who visited Ahmedabad in 1615. See W. Foster ed., *The Voyage of Nicholas Downton*, p. 151. B.G. Gokhale, 'Ahmedabad in the XVII Century', *Journal of the Economic and Social History of the Orient*, XII, pt. 2, April, 1969, pp. 187–97 is a concise but excellent account on the subject. Ratnamanirao Bhimrao, *Gujaratnun Patnagar Ahmedabad* in Gujarati is more comprehensive. For historical account see pp. 23–185.

7. *Khatpatra*, no. 91. The original manuscripts of more than 100 of such documents are preserved in the B.J. Institute of Oriental Research, Ashram Road, Ahmedabad. Most of these are written in old Gujarati; only a few are in Persian. They record the sale and purchase of various kinds of properties. They have, mentioned among other things, the names of various officials and people holding important positions, including *sheth* and *nagarsheth* at the time of the transaction. This source is cited here as *khatpatra* along with the appropriate number and the year of the document in question. The years given in the original documents are in the Vikrama era. The authors have converted these into the Christian era. For the historical value of these *khatpatras*, see Hariprasad Shastri, 'Vidyasabha Sangrahalaya na Marathakal in Khatpatra' in Gujarati, *Buddhiprakash*, March, 1978, pp. 121–24.

8. M.S. Commissariat, *Imperial Mughal's Farmans in Gujarat, reprinted from Journal of University of Bombay*, IX, pt. I, pp. 36–47.

9. Radha Kumud Mookerjee in his chapter "Economic Conditions' in Majumdar ed., *History and Culture of the Indian People*, II, pp. 601–2 refers to the existence of the *Mahasetthi*, the president of a commercial federation with numerous *Anusetthis* under him. According to U.N. Ghoshal, the north Konkan cities under the Rashtrakutas had *purapatis* or *nagarpatis*, but these positions were probably a part of official bureaucracy. See Ghoshal's chapter 'Political Theory' in Majumdar, *History and Culture of the Indian People*, IV, 246. Prof. J.N. Asopa of the University of Rajasthan mentioned to the authors, on the basis of epigraphic evidences, that some cities in ancient India had 'pratham-shreshthas'.

10. Maganlal Vakhatchand, *Amdavadno Itihas*, in Gujarati, pp. 125–27.

11. Mohanlal Dalichand Desai, Jain Aitihasik Rasamala, in Gujarati; for career of Shantidas see. M.S. Commissariat, History of Gujarat with a Survey of Its Monuments and Inscriptions, II, 140–49: Also see Ratnamanirao Bhimrao, Gujaratnun Patanagar, pp.733–37.

12. The authors have seen most of these *farmans* in original still in possession of Miss Priayamvadaben Nagarsheth, Ahmedabad. English renderings of some of these are contained in Commissariat, *Imperial Mughal Farmans*.

13. M.F. Lokhandwala, *Mirat-i-Ahmadi: A History of Gujarat*, translated from the original Persian of Ali Muhammad Khan, pp. 210, 212, 213, 446, 447, 487, 708.

14. See for example, the *Khatpatras*, nos. 84, 42, 23.

15. P.C. Devanji, 'Three Gujarati Legal Documents of the Moghul Period', *Journal of the Gujarat Research Society*, IV, no. I, p. 26.

16. We owe the clarification of some of these issues to our discussions with Professor S.C. Misra of the M.S. University, Baroda.

17. William Foster, ed., *The English Factories in India, 1634–1636*, pp. 28–59, 196–97.

18. Commissariat, *Imperial Mughal Farmans*, pp. 50–55. The earliest of Aurangzeb's *farmans* was issued in 1658 and the last in 1660.

19. *Mirat-i-Ahmadi*, p. 213.

20. M.N. Pearson, 'Political Participation in Mughal India', *Indian Economic and Social History Review*, IX, no. 2, pp. 122–23; D. Tripathi and M.J. Mehta, 'The Profile of an Indian Businessman in the 17th Century: Virji Vora', Case no. I-Eco. 107(R), Indian Institute of Management, Ahmedabad.

21. *Khatapatra*, no. 84.

22. That Sundardas was Shantidas's brother is mentioned in a representation made by Nagarsheth Premabhai to the British government in 1862. The same document also refers to the division in the family in the lifetime of Shantidas. A copy of this document is still available with Miss Priyamvadaben Nagarsheth, Ahmedabad.

23. There is a reference to the traditional "deep enmity" between the "followers of Vishnu" and the Jains in House of Commons, *Parliamentary Paper*, no.615 of 1853, pt. II, p. 1008.

24. *Khatpatra*, nos. 15, 23, 24, 31.

25. *Mirat-i-Ahmadi*, pp. 358–59; 398–99.

26. Commissariat, *History of Gujarat*, p. 420.

27. Ibid., pp. 420–21. The original resolution of the *mahajans* is still available with Miss Priyamvadaben Nagarsheth, Ahmedabad.

28. *Mirat-i-Ahmadi*, p. 446.

29. Ibid., p. 487.

30. Ibid., p. 488.

31. Ibid., p. 489.

32. Ibid., p. 505. The *farman* makes no mention that the title had been conferred on any of Khushalchand's forefathers. In view of the fact that imperial *farmans* reconfirming certain privileges to the family normally refer to earlier grants, the 1732 order becomes yet another proof against the view that the *nagarsheth* title had been earlier conferred on Shantidas arid his descendants in perpetuity.

33. Ibid., p. 517.

34. Ibid., p. 621.

35. The *Khatpatras*, nos. 39, 57, and 17 of the years 1801, 1806 and 1813 respectively, mention Nathusha's grandson, Malukchand as *nagarsheth*. However, he has not been mentioned as such in any other contemporary document. It is possible that after the title became hereditary, it came to be loosely applied to prominent members of the family.

36. It is noteworthy that Lakshmichand, who came to the helm after Shantidas, was the third son of his parents. Khushal was the only son of his parents. The next *nagarsheth*. Nathusha, was the eldest son of Khushalchand and was followed by his younger brother, Wakhatchand.

37. Pearson, *Political Participation in Mughal India*, p. 120.

38. Bombay Government, *Gazetteer of the Bombay Presidency IV, Ahmedabad*, 112 fn. This is cited henceforward as *Ahmedabad Gazetteer;*, also see *Khatpatra*, no. 87.

39. For a comprehensive discussion on this role of the *nagarsheth* see Pearson, *Political Participation in Mughal India*, pp. 113–31; also see Balkrishna Govind Gokhale, 'The Merchant Community in XVIIth Century India', *Journal of Indian History*, LIV, pt. I p. 138.

40. *Mirat-i-Ahmadi*, 358–359.

41. H.G. Briggs, *The Cities of Gujarasthra*, 211–13.

42. "Abhramkulina Shlokovishe" *Buddhiprakash* (September, 1849), 194–200. It is mentioned in the poem that it was written in Samvat 1781 (1725 AD) and it was composed by one Shamalji Bhatt. The poem says that when the Marathas invaded the city they found that the city gates were closed on the orders of the provincial authorities. But it was Khushalchand who opened these gates.

43. *Ahmedabad Gazetteer*, pp. 113–14.

44. Ratnamanirao Bhimrao, *Gujarat nun Patnagar*. p. 739.

45. For careers of Hemabhai and Premabhai, see Bombay Government, *Representatives Men of the Bombay Presidency* (Bombay, 1900), 197; Vlaganlal Narottam Patel, *Mahajan Mandal*, in Gujarati (Ahmedabad, 1896) 1016–1018; Briggs, *Cities of Gujarashtra*, pp. 234–35; Ratnamanirao Bhimrao, *Gujarat nun Patnagar*, pp. 739–41; Mohanlal Desai (ed) *Jain Aitihasik Rasamala*, pp. 17–23.

46. For the history of Ahmedabad Municipality see, B.K. Boman Behram (ed), *The Rise of Municipal Government in the City of Ahmedabad*.

47. B.P. Badshah, *The Life of Rao Bahadur Ranchhodlal Chhotalal C.I.E.* (Bombay, 1920); on the rising challenge to *nagarshethship* from industrial leadership see, E. Washburn Hopkins, *India, Old and New*, pp. 169–79.

48. Poona, for instance, came to have a *nagarsheth* around the last quarter of the eighteenth century. Significantly enough, the position came into being after the Gujarat banias, who had migrated to the city, assumed great importance. For details sec, D.R. Gadgil. *Origins of the Modern Indian Business Class' An Indian Report*, pp. 28–29.

27

Portuguese Trade with India and the Theory of Royal Monopoly in the Sixteenth Century

K.S. Mathew

WITH THE definite aim of establishing trade on the Malabar coast and dominating the Indian Ocean, Pedro Alvares Cabral obtained the permission from the Zamorin of Calicutto found a Portuguese factory at Calicut, the biggest emporium of spices in the East.[1] As usual, the Zamorin gave a Gujarati merchant to give instructions to the 'Portuguese Factor regarding the customs and manners of the country and other details of trade.[2] As far as the Zamorin was concerned, this did not mean anything extraordinary since merchants from all over the world used to come and establish themselves at Calicut and he, on his part, gave all the possible assistance by appointing his officers to give protection to the merchant communities and also to serve as brokers.[3] Intent on establishing a perfect dominion on the Indian Ocean especially on the Malabar coast Vasco da Gama arrived at Calicut with a fleet of twenty-five vessels and demanded the Zamorin to evacuate all the foreign merchants from Calicut and to permit no one to land at any of the ports in his kingdom.[4] The Zamorin, however, made it clear that the port of Calicut would always remain open to all and it, would be simply impossible to prohibit any one from trading with Calicut whether he be a Muslim or not.[5] These incidents at the dawn of the sixteenth century marked the struggle for supremacy over the Indian ocean backed by some theoretical framework and the reaction of the Indian rulers who were used to free movements of merchants. The present paper is aimed at highlighting the theory of royal monopoly developed by the Portuguese concerning their trade with India in the sixteenth century. Contemporary documents in Portuguese, Italian and Latin are consulted in the preparation of this study. Calicut was the chief emporium of the Oriental commodities and held the premier position on the Western coast of India at the time of the arrival of the Portuguese.[6] The Chinese merchants had their own factory called *cina kotta*[7] at Calicut in the

*40th Session at Waltair, 1979.

fifteenth century.[8] Between twenty and twenty-five Chinese vessels used to visit the port of Calicut with fine linen-cloth and brasswares and took spices in return every year.[9] Calicut was the heaven of various merchants from Mecca, Bangella, Tornasseri, Pegu, Coromandel, Ceylon, Sumatra, Dabul, Bhatkal, Gujarat, Ormuz, Persia, Syria, Ethiopia, Turkey and so on.[10] When the Portuguese vessels under Vasco da Gama arrived at Calicut in 1498, they were greeted by Muslim merchants from Seville in Spain.[11] The merchants in large numbers from Cairo were found in Calicut and other ports on the west coast of India engaged in spice-trade at the time of the arrival of the Portuguese.[12] The Gujarati merchants who were compared to the Italians in the matter of trade in spices[13] extended their commercial operations in the region between Malacca and Aden. They went even up to the coast of Africa with the Indian products and it was one of their pilots who guided Vasco da Gama and his companions in 1498 to Calicut from Melinde telling them that pepper, ginger and other spices and drugs came from Calicut and not from Gujarat as they were told.[14] There were four Indian vessels in Melinde while the Portuguese were on their way four Indian vessels in Melinde while the Portuguese were on their way to Calicut. Thus, trade in the Indian Ocean was not at all closed to any merchant, but on the contrary all the interested parties had their freedom to navigate and land at any port of their choice for conducting trade.

Subsequent to the discovery of the sea-route to India and the attempts at establishing trade on the Indian coast, King Manuel I of Portugal assumed the title "Lord of Navigation, Conquest, and Trade with Ethiopia, Arabia, Persia and India" (Senhor da Navegacao, conquista, e comercio da Ethiopia, Arabia, Persia e India) in 1501.[15] From 1502 a definite number of Portuguese vessels were employed in the Indian Ocean to patrol the coast, to chase all other vessels from the coast and prevent others from having trade on the Malabar coast.[16] In addition to this, fortified fortresses were established in the main trade centres on the west coast of India to have strict watch on the movements in the Indian Ocean. Dom Lourenco, the son of Francisco de Almeidia, the Viceroy, was found in Chaul in 1507 with eight vessels to guard the Indian coast against other merchants.[17]

With a view to prevent the merchants from using routes away from the Malabar coast, the Portuguese made Ceylon tributary to the King of Portugal in 1507.[18] The ruler of Ormuz was also compelled to pay tributes to the Portuguese King in 1508.[19] The foothold in Ormuz helped them to stop the flow of spices from the Indian coast through the Persian Gulf. Goa, being the most important point for controlling the movements in the Indian Ocean, was conquered in 1510. Another important centre in the South, which was a great emporium of spices where Arab merchants flocked together, was Malacca. Since it was necessary to have hold over Malacca to bring the entire Indian Ocean under the Portuguese control, Afonso de Albuquerque attacked Malacca in 1511 and forced the ruler to enter on a commercial treaty with him. A

Portuguese fortress along with a factory was constructed there in due course.[20] Though Afonso de Albuquerque made an assault on Adel in 1513 and tried to conquer it with a view to block the Arab trade passing from India to Cairo and Alexandria via the Red Sea, he could not meet with success. The capital of the Portuguese in India was shifted from Cochin to Goa in 1530 to have greater hold on the Indian Ocean and especially the trade centres in the North By 1535 they established their fortress at Diu which gave them a better position to control the trade with Gujarat and the Persian Gulf. Various other posts like Chaul, Dabhol, Bhatkal and so on were brought under the Portuguese so that they might have a better hold on the Indian Ocean and the trade with India.

By 1510 the King of Portugal declared royal monopoly on spices, drugs, sealing wax, dyes, indigo and benzoin.[21] On account of frequent violations, every now and then the Portuguese King reiterated the prohibition to trade in spices especially in pepper and ginger under severe punishments.[22] This royal monopoly was so disgusting to the Indians that a native of Malabar in the sixteenth century gave vent to his feelings by complaining that if anybody needed a corn of pepper for some medicine, he should approach the 'Feringis' who gave it powdered and packed in a piece of cloth.[23]

Even the local rulers and merchants who used to send ships loaded with commodities to various places were at the mercy of the Portuguese from whom they were obliged to take permits or *cartazes*[24] failing which their ships were captured by the Portuguese. The name of the vessel and that of the Captain, the nature of cargo, its origin, destination and the name of the authority issuing the *cartazes* were the particulars to be entered in this sort of passes which were purchased from the Portuguese officials in the respective places against payment to the Portuguese government and the issuing clerks.[25] The Zamorin of Calicut[26] and several other rulers of India including the great Akbar used to collect *cartazes* from the Portuguese for the security of their ships in the Indian Ocean. Even those ships furnished with Portuguese *cartazes* were confiscated at the whims and fancies of the Portuguese officials.[27]

Side by side with the activities in the East, the Portuguese developed their own theories regarding the right to supremacy over the Indian Ocean and the royal monopoly on trade. The prevailing ideas that were current in Portugal during the early sixteenth century found expression in the writings of the official chronicler Joao de Barros who tried to justify the assumption of the title by King Manuel I in 1501 and the issuance of *cartazes*. He argued as follows:[28] The Popes through their bulls (such as 'Romanus Pontifex', 'Inter caetera' and 'Aeterni Regis') had granted the Portuguese Kings the right to appropriate the territories they had discovered or would discover. With the voyage of Vasco da Gama and especially with that of Pedro Alvares Cabral, the King had taken possession of what had been discovered and thus the newly discovered territories became the property of the Portuguese. The juridical titles, besides the papal grants, for the right to the oriental territories were discovery, usucaption or occupation, conquest and prescription.[29] The lands inhabited by Muslims as well as Hindus (Gentios) were to be taken out of their hands as they were unlawful possessors, being infidels who did not acknowledge the glory of God, the creator and redeemer of the Universe. This has been done by Dom Manuel I and he, moreover, discovered the trade in spices that was in the hands of the Muslims. Since he was the lord of the route to India and the conqueror thereof, it was fitting that he should be the lord of trade too. Once he took possession of the lands discovered and conquered by him, they by the right of occupation belonged to him. Moreover, there was no one from among the Christian powers to claim any right over these lands and so the King of Portugal enjoyed peaceful and unperturbed possession for several years and hence the title of prescription.[30]

Though the high seas were common to all since there was no other public route, this law was not acceptable in the case of India. Because, it was valid only in Europe with regard to the Christians who, by faith and baptism, became members of the Roman Catholic church. The Hindus and the Muslims being outside the law of Jesus Christ and being condemned to eternal damnation had no right to the high seas. Thus Barros held the view that there was no *Mare Liberum* in India, in other words, the Indian Ocean became *Mare Clausum* by the arrival of the Portuguese, a Christian power.[31] It was in the light of these considerations that he explained the necessity of *cartazes* for the alien ships in the Indian Ocean.[32]

The theories propounded by the Portuguese writers regarding their right over the Indian Ocean had been called into question by another Christian power by the end of the sixteenth century and especially at the beginning of the seventeenth. It was the Dutch who challenged the Portuguese in the Eastern waters and from the same quarters came the first theoretical exposition of *Mare Liberum*. Hugo Grotius, the proponent of the freedom of Seas, refuted the arguments of the Portuguese theoreticians. He denied that the Portuguese could have sovereignty over the East Indies on account of the title of discovery. Because, as India was famous for centuries before the arrival of the Portuguese and merchants used to come to India by sea to find means to escape poverty, the Portuguese could not say that they discovered India. Even granted that they discovered it, it did not bring about the possibility of appropriating it as long as it was not 'res nullius' unoccupied by any one.[33] Because the famous theologians like Thomas Aquians[34] and the Spanish writer Victoria held that on the basis of religious beliefs no infidel could be deprived of his possessions and so the proprietary right of the infidels could not be taken away by the Portuguese.[35]

Hugo Grotius very clearly denied the right to the Portuguese to the Oriental territories based one the papal grants. Because the Pope should not have any temporal authority and even granted that he could have, he had nothing to do with the infidels and to expropriate them in so far as they did not belong to the Church and consequently to his jurisdiction.[36] He refuted the argument that the Portuguese had right to the Oriental regions on the basis of war and conquest, except in case of Goa. The Indians being unbelievers could not be subjugated by force just because they were infidels.[37] Nor could the Portuguese be justified in saying that they fought the Indians for the sake of spreading the Christians faith, because the Portuguese were amassing wealth even to the neglect of their religious duties.

Grotius refuted also the theories regarding the right claimed by the Portuguese for dominion over the Indian Ocean since the titles such as papal donation,[38] occupation,[39] and prescription or custom[40] did not hold good in this regard. In the same way, claim to the monopoly of trade based on the titles of occupation,[41] papal donation,[42] and prescription[43] had been denied. Thus it was argued by Grotius that the trade with India as well as the right to navigate in the Indian Ocean should not be considered a monopoly of the Portuguese but on the contrary open to all.

Once the work of Grotius was published and began to be discussed, the Portuguese took up the challenge and Frei Serafim de Freitas upheld the right of the Portuguese to the East Indies especially India on the basis of the right to freedom to propagate the Christian faith in non-Christian areas and thus evaded the objections raised by Grotius. He admitted that the Pope did not have direct jurisdiction over the infidels in India, but he affirmed the indirect jurisdiction. The Pope, being the universal pastor, had the right and duty to send missionaries to the areas of unbelievers and force the infidels to hear the word of God preached by the missionaries.[44] He could also insist on the infidel ruler not to prevent the preaching of the missionaries and the conversion of the people even by waging war against the ruler.[45] Thus the Pope had indirect jurisdiction on the infidels. Freitas added that the Pope who had indirect jurisdiction over the infidels and the right to send the missionaries, could delegate the power to any particular nation of his choice as he did in the case of the Portuguese and he was empowered to restrict the right of navigation to these areas only to a certain nation as the missionaries were to be taken by ships. Moreover, the Pope also had the power to assign the monopoly of trade to these people and exclude others since the missionary activities needed money for their survival.[46] This was the most fundamental argument Freitas had to offer in support of the validity of papal grants to the Portuguese in regard to their jurisdiction over the infidels of India, the navigation thereof and the commerce with India,[47] against the objections raised by Grotius. He added that the Papal grants regarding these points would not have any relevance if they were prescinded from the missionary activities and that the King of Portugal consequently could not claim the monopoly if he did not send the missionaries to India.[48]

Similarly, regarding the occupation of the Indian Ocean which by its nature was not a thing to be occupied[49] by any particular power, he seems to have admitted the possibility of quasi-possession or quasi-occupation by reason of the privileges granted by a sovereign authority such as Pope for the sake of the activities of the propagation of faith, since he had jurisdiction all over the world.[50] Therefore, one could acquire the right to prevent anyone from causing trouble to the peaceful navigation of the occupant of the Ocean.[51] The explanation given to the system of *cartazes* in the Indian Ocean also was based on the papal grant, which implied that nobody else should navigate in the Indian Ocean without the permission of the Portuguese.[52]

Freitas held that the right of the Portuguese to navigate in the Indian Ocean was founded on the title of occupation before any one else, prescription and custom,[53] because they discovered India and occupied it through it was known for centuries. The activities of Bartholomeo Dias in 1493 to discover the route to India via Cape of Good Hope and the final attempt of Vasco da Gama in 1497/8 are adduced to corroborate the fact of discovery.[54]

Thus, one could conclude that the strongest argument for Freitas to prove the Portuguese claim to supremacy over the Indian Ocean lay in the duty and right to propagate the Christian faith delegated exclusively to the Portuguese by the Pope. This could be considered the weakest point in his argumentation.[55] It is to be noted that he deviated considerably from the opinion current among the Portuguese in the sixteenth century as expressed by Joao de Barros.

It can be affirmed that the sixteenth century witnessed the greatest interest shown by the Europeans to dominate the Indian Ocean and to reap profits from the flourishing trade in spices carried out in the Indian Ocean. Towards the end of the sixteenth century the other European powers came forward challenging the Portuguese claims and finally the Indian Ocean became the scene of continuous international conflicts. One power after the other tried to establish its supremacy over the Indian Ocean and the adjacent territories. This constant struggle for the mastery lasting throughout the colonial period speaks for the importance of the Indian Ocean in the international trade and balance of power. A scientific study of the seaborne trade of the Portuguese will definitely throw considerable light on the economic history of India during the pre-industrial period.

Notes

1. Fracanso Montalbodo, *Paesi Nouvamente Retrovali and Novo Modo da Alberto Vesputio Florentino Inlitulato*, p. 86.
2. Ibid., p. 90.
3. Duarte Barbosa, *The Book of Duarte Rarbosa*, vol. II, p. 77.
4. Thome Lopes, 'Navegacao as Indias Orienlaes' in *Colleccao de Noticias para a Historia a Geografia das Nacoes Ultramarinas que vivem nos Dominios Portugueses ou lhes sao vizinhas Tom II.* nos. 1 and 2, p. 187; *Cronica do Descobrimento e Conquista da India pelos Portugueses*, p. 33.

5. Thome Lopos, ref. no. 5, p. 188.

6. Raymundo Antonio de Buihao Pato ed., *Cartas de Affonso de Albuquerque*, tome I, pp. 137, 320; Gasper Correa, *Londas da India*, torn I pp. 75–6; 744.

7. Garcia da Orta, *Coloquios dos Simples e Drogas da India* ed. by Conde Ficalho, vol. I, p. 205.

8. Montalbodo, ref. no. 1, p. 162.

9. Ibid, p. 71.

10. Ludovico di Varthema, *The Travels of Ludovico di Varthema*, p. 151.

11. *Gaspar* Correa, ref. no. 7, p. 79.

12. Ibid., p. 75.

13. Tome Pires, *Suma Oriental of Tome Pires*, vol. l, p. 45.

14. Gaspar Correa, op. cit., p. 57.

15. Joao de Barros, *Da Asia*, Decada I, p. II, pp. 11 ff.

16. Ibid., p. 21.

17. Ibid., p. 181.

18. Valentim Femandes, *Uma Carta inedita de Valentim Fernandes*, p. 19.

19. Barros, op. cit., Decada II, pt. I, pp. 109 ff.

20. Ibid., Decada II, pt. II, pp. 40 ff.

21. *Archivo Nacional da Torre do Tombo, Lisbon MSS. Corpo Chronalogico*, pt. I, Maco 8, Document 68.

22. *Historical Archives of Goa*, MSS. Regimentes, Provinses of Alvaras, no. 3027ff, 4ff.

23. Muhammed Ibn Abdul Aziz, *Fathul-Mubiyn* trs. by M.A. Muid Khan in P.M. Joshi ed. *Studies in Foreign Relations of India from the Earliest Times to 1947*, Hyderabad, p. 177.

24. The word 'cartaz' takes its origin from the Arabic word Quirtas' meaning paper or document ref. Sebastiao Rudolfo Dalgado, *Glossario Luso-Asiatico*, vol. I, p. 220.

25. J.H. Cunha Rivara, *Archivo Portuguese Oriental Fasciculo*, V, pt. 1, p. 31.

26. Ref. no. 7, p. 321.

27. Ibid., torn II, pp. 401–2, torn III, pp. 14, 17.

28. Barros, op.cit., Decada I, pt. II, pp. 14–17.

29. Ibid.

30. Ibid., p. 17.

31. Ibid., pp. 16–17.

32. Ibid., p. 15.

33. Hugo Grotius, *Mare Liberum sive, de jure quod Batavis competit ad Indicana commercia Dissertatio* trs. by *Ralph Van Deman Magoffin and James Brown Scott* as *The Freedom of the Seas or the Right Which belongs to the Dutch to take part in the East Indian Trade*, p. 13.

34. *Summa Theologica*, II-a, II-ae, Questio 10, Article 12.

35. Hugo Grotius, op. cit., p. 13.

36. Ibid. p. 16.

37. Ibid. p. 20.

38. Ibid., pp. 45–46.

39. Ibid., pp. 22–44.

40. Ibid., p. 65.

41. Ibid.

42. Ibid., p. 66.
43. Ibid., pp. 67–68.
44. Frei Serafim de Freitas, *De Justo Imperio Lusitanoru*, vol. II, pp. 90–91, 113–14.
45. Ibid., p. 114.
46. Ibid., p. 93.
47. Ibid., p. 94.
48. Ibid.
49. Ibid., p. 121.
50. Ibid., p. 150.
51. Ibid., p. 126.
52. Ibid., p. 106.
53. Ibid., p. 172.
54. Ibid., pp. 172–73.
55. C.H. Alexandrowicz, *An Introduction to the History of the Law of Nations in the East Indies, 16th, 17th and 18th centuries*, p. 70.

28

Vyaparis and *Mahajans* in Western Rajasthan During the Eighteenth Century

G.D. Sharma

VYAPARIS AND *mahajans* constituted the most influential and dynamic class in the economic structure of Rajasthan during the Mughal period.[1] In an agrarian society, such as Marwar, the commercial undertakings by this class provided an extra source of revenue to the State particularly in a period when the State parted with the bulk of its revenue to the *jagirdars* and *ijaradars*. So far, no serious attempt has been made to understand the commercial activities of the *vyaparis* and *mahajans* and their role in promoting trade and commerce in Marwar and the involvement of the State in such activities. In the following pages an attempt has been made to examine these aspects of the economy of Marwar in the light of the policy adopted by the State towards the *vyaparis* and *mahajans* and the hurdles faced by the latter in the smooth operation of their business.

The present study is based on the information available in the *Khas Rukka-Parwana bahis, Sanad bahis* and the *Jarna-bandis* of *Sair* available in the Jodhpur Records of the Rajasthan State Archives, Bikaner, and its Jodhpur Branch. Most of these records have been tapped only recently and furnish information on the various aspects of economic and administrative history of Western Rajasthan during the eighteenth century.

I

In a period of political disorder which prevailed in Marwar, the State resorted to the promotion of trade and commerce to enhance State revenue. The *dasturs* related to Sair speak about the nature of taxes imposed on the sale and purchase of goods[2] and the duties levied on the transition of goods from one region to another.[3] They also inform us about the commercial practices prevalent during the seventeenth century and their continuation or alteration during the eighteenth century.[4]

*41st Session at Bombay, 1980.

The Rathor rulers took an initiative in this direction by entertaining the complaints lodged by the traders and merchants against the local authorities who used to impose forbidden taxes on them.[5] There are a number of *parwanas* throwing light on the nature of complaints, the attitude of the State towards these complaints and the concessions given by the State to the traders and merchants.

The *vyaparis* and *mahajans* were favoured by the State by granting free trade facilities and reduction in the taxes levied under the name of *sair-dan, mapa* and *rahdari*. The prominent traders were granted permission to conduct trade without paying transit duties and sales tax.[6] In this category were included big *ijaradars-cum-traders* and *vohras* from whom the Rathor rulers used to borrow money on credit at the time of emergency. Some outside traders were also granted these free trade facilities in Marwar, particularly those who belonged to Bikaner.[7] However, these facilities of free merchants. Another category of traders and merchants was of those who were enjoying fifty per cent reduction on *mapa-dan* and *rahdari*. Both, the local and outside traders were given this concession. The state also permitted the traders and merchants to conduct commercial activities with twenty-five per cent concession on *map-dan* and *rahdari*. Sometimes the concession could be limited only to *dan-mapa* or *rahdari*.[8]

There was another course of extending favour to the merchants and traders by providing them better conditions at big *qasbas* or villages. Bikaneria Kanha, Radha, etc., were asked to open a shop at Nagor with necessary requirements.[9] Rathor Amar Singh and other *mahajans* were assured of concession if they started business in Marwar.[10] Similarly Bhatt Ramchandra Roop Chand were asked to open a shop at Pali and assured concessions from the Darbar.[11] Bania Vinay Chand Santokchand was granted permission for opening a shop of *pashmina* cloth at Jalor.[12]

Besides granting permission to the merchants to conduct business in Marwar liberally, the State provided them facilities for constructing *havelis* (houses) and starting cultivation on *mukata*.[13] The *mahajans* and Chaudharis of village Ahuwa, a patta village, were allowed to purchase fields, shops and *arhats* and to sell them to others if they desired to do so.[14] *Parwanas* were also issued to the effect to providing haveli to the leading *mahajans* and *vyaparis* of the the town.[15] The concessions thus given to the *mahajans* and *vyaparis* are of immense importance in the light of the political situation faced by the State of Marwar.

The State also took an initiative to encourage *mahajans* and *vyaparis* belonging to the neighbouring State to participate on a large scale in the fairs of Marwar.[16] References are made to the holding of a fair annually at Mundawa (near Nagor) where merchants and traders of Jaisalmer, Fatehpur, Nawalgarh, Churu, Bikaner, Kisangarh, Bhilwara and Ghaneroa were invited to participate along with Zinas (*jinsi*) and articles. They were assured of the reduction of one-fourth of the duties levied in the fair normally.[17] This attempt was quite successful during the time of Maharaja Vijay Singh and shows that the merchants and traders were participating in big numbers from the five neighbouring States of Marwar.[18] It is worth mentioning that the *parwanas* issued by the Maharaja were always addressed to the *mahajans* and *vyaparis* of towns and not to the State. This implies an inter-state trade contract in which the merchants and traders were free from State interference. Further references are available regarding the allotment of the *havelis* in big commercial towns to the prominent traders — *mahajans* known as *seth*.[19] These references tend to suggest that in each of these cities and towns there were associations of traders and merchants.

II

The state patronage enjoyed by the traders and merchants could not make them free of the hurdles they faced due to the changes introduced in the politico-administrative structure of the State of Marwar.

In fact these changes were contrary to the flourishing of trade and commerce in any of Rajput States. Like the neighbouring State of Jaipur (Amber) the *ijara* practices became quite common in Marwar, particularly during the latter half of the eighteenth century.[20] This practice was not limited to land revenue only but had its hearing in *sair-jihat*, *rahdari* as well as minting. Vyas Santokhi Ram, Manroop etc. were granted the right of *chaweri* and *chungi* of Nagor[21] Vyas Malook Chand and Foohad Masheshdas Motiram were given the *taksal(mini)* of Jodhpur for Rs.4501/- for three months on *ijara*; the amount was to be paid in instalments.[22] Similarly the *taksal* (mint) of Nagor was given to the same person for Rs. 2801 ¼ for three months.[23] *Dan-mapa* and *rahdari* of pargana Merta were granted to Joshi Pannalal and Muhta Udai Chand on *ijara*; for Rs. 41001 for 13 months from Phalgun Sudi 1, 1813 to Phalgun Vadi 15, 1813. The amount was to be paid in 14 instalments. He was entitled to collect these taxes in the pargana and those who were granted *mapa, dan* or *ijara* of the villages falling in the pargana were asked to pay instalments to the said *ijaradar*.[24] There are many *sanads* which record the grant of *dan, mapa (sair)* and *rahdari* on *ijara*, separately or on the whole, of a few villages or pargana. In the case of the parganas of Ajmer and Didwana which were incorporated in Marwar, the practice of *ijara* was adopted more widely. This has similarities with the *ijara* practices adopted by Maharaja Jai Singh of Amber in the newly incorporated territories in Amber.[25]

Another change instituted was the practice of fixing a lump sum on the *pattadars* and, as a result of this, the *jagirdars (pattadars)* assumed more *power,*[26] and the right of levying *rahdari* or *dan-mapa* in their respective territories. These *jagirdars* had a tendency of levying taxes frowned upon by the State. The diwan office received a number of complaints made by the *mahajans* and *vyaparis* against the *jagirdars* and State officials.[27]

On the whole, reviewing the practices of *ijara* or commercial taxes, the increasing power of the *jagirdars* and the tendency of local officials to levy illegal taxes, there arise doubts about the implementation of the orders issued by State sanctioning the various concessions to the *mahajans* and *vyaparis*.

It may be noted that the leading merchants were getting concessions on taxes levied as *mapa-dan, rahdari,* etc., on the one hand and the *ijara* of these taxes in a pargana as a whole or some villages, on the other. Malook Chand was given the mint of Jodhpur on *ijara* while he enjoyed twenty-five per cent concession on the *sair, dan, rahdari* in the territory of Marwar.[28] Vyas Santokhi Ram was granted the *chungi* on salt at Didwana on *ijara* amounting to Rs. 1000 annually. He and his sons were also permitted free trade facilities or exempted from *dan, rahdari* etc. in Marwar.[29] The concessions provided to the *ijaradars* who were also operating trade and commerce in Marwar could have been implemented if there was political stability in the State. In a state of political disorder, there emerged a variety of rights which were overlapping. The *jagirdars* were assuming more power and the State was losing its effect on their areas. The assignment of commercial taxes on *ijara* ultimately posed problems of dual rights. Both, the privileged and underprivileged traders and merchants had to bear the burden of taxes levied on them by *ijaradars* and *jagirdars*.

III

The foregoing discussion makes it clear that the traders and merchants were enjoying protection as well as encouragement from the Rathor rulers of Marwar. In a state of changing politico-administrative scene, the trade and commerce showed its decadence and in the beginning of the nineteenth century this trend had become quite obvious. The explanation for this setback could be traced to the changes infused in the political and administrative institutions which had inherent contradictions in themselves. The trader and merchants, as *ijardars,* who had employed their capital in *ijara* failed to organise agriculture to enhance its produce and to systematise practices of commercial taxation for the smooth operation of trade and commerce. On the contrary, they practised illegal extortions which furthered the problems both for the peasantry and the commercial class. The State failed to provide coordination between the claims of *ijaradars* and *jagirdars* or *thikanadars*. The traders and merchants, as *ijaradars,* could not sustain their rights due to the counter-claims made by the hereditary landholders.

Thus, while they failed to turn this newly opened avenue of investment into money spinning ventures, their traditional occupation showed hardly any progress in spite of concessions offered by the State and the advantageous position they had acquired during this period of transition.

The capacity of traders and merchants to advance money on credit to the rulers and invest it in acquiring *ijara* indicates that they (at least big merchants and traders) had enough capital in hand to employ it for producing further gain. In Rajasthan, where the economy was primarily based on agriculture, they found no other sector of investment than *ijara*. This experiment proved futile and as a result they turned to their old profession, but in safer places other than Rajasthan, where they found better opportunities.

The impression of the existence of merchant-traders' associations and the institution of *nagar seth* is quite revealing. The survival of such institutions had been experienced by Col. Todd during his visit to Western Rajasthan in 1819. According to him:

Commerce in these regions is the basis of liberty: even despotism is compelled to leave it unrestrained.[30] Pali, like Bhilwara, Jhalra, Pattan, Rinnie and other marts, enjoyed the rights of electing its own magistrates, both for its municipal regulations and the arbitration of all matters connected with commercial pursuit.[31]

Such professional institutions had their existence in Gujarat during the Mughal period[32] and therefore it is quite tempting to see the relevance of Col. Todd's description regarding Marwar as well as Rajasthan as a whole. However, our existing knowledge, and sources we have at our disposal, give only indirect support to the prevalence of such institutions in Marwar during the eighteenth century. Further study of these problems may throw more light on this subject.

Notes

1. James Todd, *Annals and Antiquities of Rajasthan*, vol. I, pp. 543–44 and vol.11, pp. 127–29; Brijkishore Bhargava, *Indigenous Banking in Ancient and Medieval India*; Dilbagh Singh, 'The Role of Mahajan in the Rural Economy of Eastern Rajasthan during the 17th Century,' *Social Scientists*, May 1974; G.D. Sharma, 'Indigenous Banking and the State in Eastern Rajasthan during the 17th Century,' *Indian History Congress*, 40th Session, Waltair, 1979, pp. 432–41; Iqtidar Alam Khan, 'The Middle Classes in the Mughal Empire,' *Proceedings of Indian History Congress*, 36th Session, Aligarh, 1975, pp. 113–41.

2. *Parwana* dated Phalgun Sudi 10, 1763 issued by Maharaja Ajit Singh to the *mahajans* of Sanchor. The *parwana* dated Paus Vadi 5, 1822 issued by Maharaja Vijay Singh to the *mahajans* of Sanchor confirmed the dasturs levied during Ajit Singh's reign. *Parwana* dated Baishakh Sudi 12, 1823 issued by Vijay Singh to the *mahajans* of Jaitaran confirming the practices of dasturs of the time of Maharaja Abhai Singh. *Khas Rukka Parwana Bahi*, no. 1, Rajasthan State Archives, Bikaner (*RSAB*).

3. Levies on internal trade comprised: (a) duties on the sale of local produce known as *dan* which was imposed on the local traders; (b) *mapa* which denoted the weighing or quantity or *mal* (articles) subject to import and export from a pargana. Different

rates under this name were prevalent, which were charged according to the weight or quantity of articles; (c) *rahdari* which was a road police tax or inland transit duty, formerly a right of the State, levied by the local officers, *zamindars* (*thikaandars*), *jagirdars* and *ijaradars*. The term *sair*, although used separately in the *parwanas* and *sanads*, includes taxes covered by *dan* and *mapa* or "imports, including all those on grain whether on foreign importation or the homegrown, in transit from one district to another" (cf. *Pargana Sanchor ki Jama Bandi*, year 1826 w 266/1733 and *Pargana Jalor ki Sair Jamu Bandi*, year vs 1826, Rajasthan State Archives, Jodhpur Branch (*RSAJ*)

4. Supra, fn. 2.

5. *Parwana* dated Vaishakh Sudi 9,1838 issued to the *mahajans* and *vyaparis* of Merta; also *parwana* dated Baishakh Sudi 12, 1823, op. cit.

6. *Parwana* dated Asoj Vadi 12, 1813 records that Vyas Santokhiram Manroop Bhav were exempted from *Dan, Rahdari*, etc., in Marwar; *Sanad Bahi*, no. 285, *RSAJ*.

7. The *parwanas* and *sanads* relating to the trade facilities provided to the *mahajans* and *vyaparis* indicate this trend of migration, cf. *Khas Rukka Parwana Bahi*, no. w, *RSAB* and *Sanad Bahi*, no. 285, *RSAJ*.

8. *Parwana* dated Phalgun Sudi 14, 1812 records that Muhata Gulalchand Moolakchand would get 1/4 reduction on the *dan mapa, sair* and *rahdari*; for the trade conducted by him. Similarly, Lohio Samo and Ram of Nagor 1/4 got exemption on *sair dan, rahdari* etc. (*Parwana*, dated Asoj Vadi 7, 1814). Rathor Devi Chand. Vijay Chand of Bikaner were given 1/2 reduction on the transit duty for the trade conducted by them in Marwar (*Parwana* Asoj Sudi 1, 1814), *Sanad Bahi*, no. 285, *RSAJ*.

9. *Parwana*, dated Maha Vadi 3, 1827.

10. Ibid., dated Baishakh Vadi 6, 1827.

11. Ibid., dated Baishakh Vadi 5, 1829.

12. Ibid., 1838.

13. *Mukata*—the *mahajans* and *vyaparis* were permitted to conduct cultivation on the land belonging to them through a contract basis, which was known as *Mukat* in Marwar. Those who cultivated the land on behalf of the *mahajans* were given 1/3 or 1/2 portion of the produce.

14. *Parwana*, dated Maha Vadi 9, 1822 issued to *jagirdar* of Ahuwa *Khas-Rukka Parwana Bahi*, no. 1, *RSAB*. There are other *parwanas* of similar nature showing such facilities to the Chaudharies and *mahajans*.

15. *Parwana*, dated Phalgun Vadi 14, 1125 issued to Bhandari Manekchand and Singhvi Sawaimal of Didwana informing them that Sami Sawaj would be given possession of *haveli* at Didwana and paid the same respect as enjoyed by him earlier.

16. Tood has recorded the importance of the fairs of Mundwa and Bhalotra—"the first was chiefly for cattle. The merchandise of . . . was exposed and purchased by merchants of the adjoining states. It commenced with the month of Magh, and lasted during six weeks. The other was also for cattle and the merchandise enumerated amongst the imports and exports of Palli. Persons from all parts of India frequented them; but all these signs of prosperity are vanishing" (*Annals*, vol. II, p. 129).

17. Such *parwanas* were issued every year from vs 1822 to vs 1840. The fair was held in the month of Asoj. *Khas-Rukka Parwana Bahi,* no. I, RSAB.

18. *Khas-Rukka Parwana Bahi, no. I, RSAB, Sanad Bahi, no. 205, RSAJ.*

19. *Supra,* n. 15.

20. *i.e.* in case of pargana Nagor, out of a total revenue of *mapa* Rs. 1982 annas 15 pai 3, the revenue of Rs. 1537 annas 13 pai 1 was given on *ijara* which constituted about 77 per cent of the total revenue of *mapa. Sarkar Nagor des ma Kachedi Talaqe Jama Kharach* p. 1, *Bahi,* vs 1813, no. 1280, *RSAJ;* similarly, the *sair* (including *rahdari*) of pargana Sanchor—Bhinwar was given on *ijara* in Rs. 29251 for thirteen months, *sanad,* dated Shravan Sudi 1, 1846. *Pargana Jaloz Ki Kachedi Talaqe llala navis Ri Bahi,* no. 2, *RSAJ.*

21. *Sanad,* dated Jaishta Vadi 3, 1813, *Sanad Bahi,* no. 285, *RSAJ.* The figures of the rates of taxes levied on various articles have been mentioned in this *sanad.*

22. *Sanad,* dated Asad Sudi 13, 1812.

23. *Sanad,* dated Shravan Vadi 1, 1813.

24. *Sanad,* dated Phalgun Vadi 8, 1813, *Sanad Bahi,* no. 258 ff. 259.

25. C.U. Wills, *A Report on the Land Tenures and Special Power of Certain Thikanadars of Jaipur Stale;* G.D.Sharma, 'Political Change and the Rajput Nobility during the 18th Century' Paper presented at the Seminar held at the Deptt. of History, Guru Nanak Dev University, Amritsar, in March 1980.

26. *Rajput Polity.*

27. *Pargana Jalor Ri Kachedi Talaqe Italanavisi Ri Bahi,* no. 2. *RSAJ.* of vs 1146 contains the copies of the *Sanad* furnishing information regarding the illegal activities of the *zamindars* and *ijaradars* against the traders and merchants. *KhasRukka Parwana Bahi,* no. 1, Jodhjiur Records, *RSAB.*

28. *Parwana,* dated Chaitra Vadi 5, 1813, also *Sanad,* dated Asad Sudi 13, 1813. *Sanad Bahi,* no. 285.

29. *Parwana,* dated Asoj Vadi 13, 1813, *Sanad Bahi,* no. 285.

30. In connection with the freedom of traders and merchants and their influence Col. Tood has cited an example of the habitants of Pali and Bhilwara who opposed the construction of a city wall in those commercial towns. (*Annals,* vol. 1, p. 555).

31. *Annals and Antiquities,* vol. 1, p. 553.

32. S.C. Misra, 'Urban Structure and Change: A Study of the Impact of Tradition of Indian Towns with Special Reference to Ahmedabad and Sural' , Paper presented at the *Urban History Seminar,* held at the Department of History, Guru Nanak Dev University, Amritsar, in 1976.

29

Mint-Technology and Mint-Output in an Age of Growing Commercialization
(An Interim Balance Sheet for seventeenth and eighteenth Century India and Some Comparisons with the European Case)

Frank Perlin

FOR AN understanding of society and economy in the last centuries before colonial occupation, the mint is one of a number of little understood, little researched, but central problems. It is situated at a key point in the supply of money to hinterland economies, during a period of substantial change. It is at this time that imports of coinage media-silver, copper, *cauris* and *badam*—become substantial, and fairly constant over a long period, and that domestic and urban manufactures, oriented towards distant markets, spread through a number of regions of the sub-continent. A large number of measures, undertaken by different regimes, lead to the progressive monetization of land taxation; peasant settlement extends considerably, and state administrations develop the means for exercising greater control over their subjects.

The classic image of currency supply in the Mughal period is of a well ordered and centralized system, while in the eighteenth century we read of growing anarchy, marked by decline in purity, quality of fabrication, the appearance of a bewildering and random variety of coin types, and by failure to control the number of mints in operation. This image correlates directly with the orthodox perception of the eighteenth century as the period of dismantlement of the Mughal Empire—of growing political decentralization and of consequent economic disorder. This view should be discarded together with the assumptions upon which it is based (the links between political authority and economic order; confusion of things Mughal with the whole sub-continent). Instead I wish to argue that the career of the mint in this period expresses a differentiation of the pre-colonial economy: the increasingly patrimonial character of the various nobilities of the sub-continent (and of the property forms on

*42nd Session at Bodhyaga, 1981.

which they depended), the extension of money-use among the humbler sections of the population, and the growing commercialization of the pre-colonial economy. The argument is based on an analysis of available data on currency supply and minting during the period, but it remains highly provisional. Such data is at present too inadequate for the task of solving many of difficult issues facing a study of monetization, including minting. At the least, we can assemble hypothesis, using for this purpose the surprising results of comparison with certain features of minting in pre-industrial Europe.

A Typology of Currency Forms

The first problem concerns the coins, themselves. Why, in the eighteenth century, do we see such a variety of different qualities and types of coinage, and why, at the turn of the eighteenth/nineteenth centuries, coinages of especially low, or shoddy manufacture?

The problem of increasing heterogeneity of coin issues is partly explained by the increasing variety of uses to which money was put, and especially its extension to broader sections of the population. It is thus an expression of the differentiation of the economy itself, and although especially characteristic of the eighteenth century is not confined to it. For example, in the precocious commercial and manufacturing economy of seventeenth century Gujarat, we find not only the famous Surat rupee, a quality coin for inter-regional commercial transactions, but also the less pure *mahmudi*, produced at mints in neighbouring territories and imported for local use. A non-metallic money medium was also imported for smaller transactions: *badam*, from Persia, of which more later. The *larin* is another example of a coinage produced for a special use: for the growing maritime trade of the Indian Ocean. It was produced by a large number of mints scattered in the littoral states between the Black Sea and Ceylon, and was generally characterized by its purity and reliability, becoming, according to contemporaries, an essential means of payment for longdistance commerce.

Quality differentiation is especially notable in the later eighteenth century. The number of mints supplying coin increases dramatically, and their issues vary in purity and quality of fabrication. We observe this clearly in the Deccan, where the quality *Chandore* rupee is fabricated by a number of different mints (not only at Chandore) for commercial use and is found in markets as far distant as Malwa (and Nagpore) and Bagalkot. *Ankusi*, and other rupees of a similar quality, underpin commercial exchanges and land revenue administration on a more regional scale. In strong contrast, a host of poorer coinages were produced, of both copper and silver, for purely local circulation, and especially for fueling the very widespread advance payments system, whereby large numbers of rural and urban manufacturers were given cash advances, by commercial dealers, creating dependent ties between merchants and producers and enabling the latter to purchase raw materials. In addition, the first stages of land revenue payments, numerous advance-like payments to cultivators (various forms of credit), all transactions in country markets, and the like, were probably also conducted in these two quality issues, and especially copper, a metal used in vast quantities in the later eighteenth century.

An example of such 'shoddy' coinages is the notorious Partabgurh rupee (*Salim Shahi*), low in purity and of shoddy manufacture, and yet produced in a mint run by a group of merchants, of which more later. Lingen and Wiggins' analysis of coinage production in the territories of Central India, ruled by the Sindes (Sindhias) present 23/24 known mints and the likelihood of many other small village mints producing unattributed copper issues. A crude typology of Sinde productions would distinguish quality coinages which followed Mughal models, new, low quality silver productions, and essentially gimcrack copper issues. Later research should introduce much nuance into these distinctions.

Most interesting, in this respect, is the fact that the Northern Deccan was characterized by increasing production of industrial crops, such as raw cotton, financed by merchants and often distant bankers, and ultimately destined for distant markets in Bengal. Much earlier, we can already observe important textile manufacture in a string of towns between Nagpur and Burhanpur.

The numerous 'imitations' of Mughal (and other) coinages by 'successor' regimes in the eighteenth century, can be understood in the light of such a typology. The problem was not that of showing obeisance to an essentially 'paper' imperial authority, as is generally claimed, but of producing coin of recognizable and specific type for particular purposes, coins which merchants, say, could recognize as 'this' or' that' type of coin. It was typical of the eighteenth century that several mints would come to share in the manufacture of a single important coin type, such as the *Ankusi* and *Chandore* rupees, the *Arcot* rupee, and, of course, the *larin*. A provisional study of data for different types of gold *mohur* shows astonishing reliability in the values of different samples of each type, and stability with respect to differences in value between these types over time. In contrast bullion seems to be an unreliable guage for those seeking price data, the purity of the samples being uncertain. In short, we are uncovering a kind of *coin-semantics*, in which the design and message on the faces of the coins, especially of the commercial coinages, were instruments for an elaborate differentiation of monetary issues and commercial practice.

Manufacturing Technology and Production-Bottlenecks

Gimcrack techniques can be related to the problem of supplying a vastly expanding market for monetary media. Although supplies of coinage media from overseas increased from the seventeenth century, and mint output also increased (see below), shortage of cash, as in Europe, continued to be endemic throughout the period. What may also be suggested is that mint production could not even keep up, either with supply of raw materials (bullion or specie brought to the mint by the merchant)' or with demand (in the general sense of economics institutionally organized for a certain level and degree of monetary use). The case of Surat is significant because output can be shown to have increased rapidly in the eighteenth century, and yet loud complaints continued to be made concerning its slow processing of supplies of bullion and specie.

Mughal coining of the sixteenth and early seventeenth centuries still belongs to the age of high quality art-craft production. With the growth of the market for coin, established technology had to adapt itself to faster production techniques. It is highly unlikely that the numbers of craftsmen producing high quality dies, for example, or the skilled artisans required to cut and stamp quality pieces (with accuracy and speed), could be increased sufficiently at short notice under pre-industrial conditions of training and employment.

The answer lay in lowering the quality of manufacture, cutting out or simplifying various stages of the production line, increasing the number of mints and being less fetishstic about purity. The *larin* (a bent piece of silver wire, partly flattened to receive an impression from what seems often to have been merely a coin) is a curious example of a good coinage produced according to quickened production techniques, whilst retaining the reliability required of an international payments medium: pure, but avoiding the skilled craft of cutting, bypassing die production and simplifying the stamping process. Van Laere is quite wrong in his view that the *larin* represents a *stage* of primitive technology, since at the same time that it was minted finely crafted coinages were also factored in Persia and India.

In the eighteenth century we can observe that even quality coinages receive a more utilitarian and simple die impression. Die production is one of the problems hindering rapid increase in output: from European evidence bottleneck we can suggest that good quality steel dies produced little more than 20000–30000 coins (and often much less) merely a day's production in the larger Indian mint. Much fewer coins were produced by the very poor dies used to make gimcrack coinages, or those factored to satisfy a sudden increase in demand (such as a recoinage). The cutting of gimcrack coins is less exacting (corners and tangental surfaces appear on supposedly circular coins), and there is frequent resort to crude rectangles, a notable means of bypassing one of the labour intensive parts of the production process (400 smiths at Chandore and 3 stampers for quality rupee).

In addition, production becomes more localized, the number of mints rapidly increasing in the course of the eighteenth century. For example, there were 8 known mints in Malwa by the 1800s, while in Sinde territories 23/24 have recently been identified. The Maratha Deccan is studded with mints, possibly 3 in Pune, and others in nearby Chakan, Talegaon and Chinchvad. The smaller mints often produced low quality coins for local consumption, even for cash advances. In some regions, coin making may even have penetrated to the level of cottage industry, a proposition that would explain both the qualities of the products and the problem of identifying the mints concerned. A significant exception was Bengal, where mint production was concentrated, but where humble needs were supplied with vast imports of *cauris*.

The remarkable import of *cauris* and *badam* seems to be an especially eighteenth century phenomenon, aimed, I would argue, at bypassing problems of mint supply, the high cost of copper, and copper shortages. *Cauris* satisfied a need for numerous low value transaction. In most part of the sub-continent they were displaced by copper in the eighteenth century, but Bengal, Bihar and Orissa are exceptions, possibly because of low grain prices and thus labour costs. *Badam* also continues in circulation in Surat, according to Stavorinus, together with a copper coinage. Most notable is that these non-metallic media seem to be destined for areas characterized by extensive manufacturing and production of food and industrial crops for distant market: Gujarat, Burhanpur, Agra, Bengal and Andhra. The revolution in mint production enabled coin to replace these non-metallic media elsewhere.

Finally, besides this functional view of coin differentiation, it is probable that a real decline in purities of issues resulted from the increasing silver and copper 'famines' after the end of the eighteenth century, as East India Company imports declined and as Company mints began to meltdown indigenous coinage and dominate supply with their own often poor quality productions.

Who Organized and Controlled the Mints?

High quality coinages were generally contracted out to professional managers but even in late eighteenth century Maharashtra, the regime maintained a degree of supervision over the quality of output, forcing mints to suspend production when issues fell below standard, in certain cases rationalizing a too scattered and random private production of important coin types, and closing older obsolete units in favour of the new more vigorous centres of the later eighteenth century.

But, what is especially remarkable is the role of merchants and bankers in many mints for which evidence is available, and not least those issuing low quality coins. The Pertabgurh mint (see above) is a significant example of merchants producing gimcrack rupees from amint which they in the first place had been responsible for establishing. The Murshidabad mint is another notable example (dominated by the Jagat Seths). A small number of large dealers regularly supplied the raw materials to the mint at Kolhapur, and also to one of the mints at Pune for which documents survive. The various mints of the European companies are further examples producing coinages of all qualities and following Indian models. Many small mints were also in the hands of local nobilities (although we shall need to look beneath the surface to identify who were actually managing them). The political 'decentralization' of the eighteenth century, the development of new relations of private property, extensive monetization and the circulation of coin in small country markets, and the need of local courts to realize *varats* (assignments on their treasuries) and *hundis* (bills of payment), payments of salaries to local garrisons, house servants, craftsmen and shopkeepers, is an essential context for this localized production network. This gives a more positive interpretation to what has generally been viewed negatively: decline in Mughal power being coincident with achange in the character of political order and with a spontaneous upgrowth of local economic activity.

Mint Output

The view that *hand-technologies* were static between the reign of Akbar and the death of Aurangzeb, and that output per mint, in consequence, remained substantially the same over the whole period, is unacceptable. In Europe, machines may well have been introduced to supply an expanding market for coin, as alleged by Spooner (a view to be criticised below), but in India changes in the organization of the production line and in techniques of factoring surely solved an identical problem.

The Surat mint provides a career-profile of rapidly increasing production in the seventeenth century. The pre-mechanized mint is characteristic of industries "before industrialization", in its peculiar mobility (any reasonably secure premises would do, thus often a fort), the ease with which tools and men could be shifted from place to place (Aurangzeb's camp mint, for example). Also typical is the different scales on which production could be organized, from large workshops down to the level of a handful of workers. But it is also one of those unusual cases, like the English brewery and Surat ship building, in which large numbers of craft workers were often concentrated (thus 350 at Chandore).

Elsewhere, mint output could be increased by increasing the number of mints in operation. Production in Malwa, as in the Pune region, for example, should not be interpreted in terms of the output of single mints but in those of regional mint supply. Thus one mint in Malwa might supply 8000–11000 per day, but 7 or 8 mints 70,000–80,000 coins per day.

A number of comparisons between the seventeenth and eighteenth centuries points to this increase. The very important Surat mint produced 30,000 coins per day at its highest quotation in the seventeenth century. At Chandore in the Deccan, one of a number of mints producing the more regionalized *Chandore* rupee in a region of decentralised production, output capacity was quoted at a rate of 20,000 per day, tallying with that of the *Malharshahi* rupee at Bagalkot. The comparison with Surat is surprising, as is also that for regional capacity in Malwa. Seventeenth century Surat is India's Antwerp, with its vigorous international markets; the *Surat* rupee is found dispersed in North Indian hoards. Ahmedabad in the eighteenth century, long past its peak, also seems to have produced 20,000 coins per day, while in Bengal we have more significant evidence: in the late seventeenth century, output is in the order of 10,000, only, at Rajmahal; in the early eighteenth century, at Murshidabad (which has replaced Rajmahal as the principal mint), up to 50,000 may have been produced (an annual figure of over 12 million coins) Once again, the contrast with seventeenth century Surat is significant, Bengal replacing Gujarat as the leading export economy of the eighteenth century.

All these figures concern silver, data for copper being at present unavailable. In my view production of copper is potentially much greater, due to cruder technique and greater tolerance for variations of weight and alloy, In the late eighteenth and early nineteenth centuries, overall production of copper coin must have been very substantial. While many large mints issued copper (Chandore, for example), the question of output runs up against the problem of the scale of most production units; in many cases these were probably very small.

A significant proportion of output figures for silver coin concern actual turnover (not simply capacity), so that there can be little question of the larger mints being closed for large stretches of the year, as is sometimes suggested. Under-utilization of production facilities is hardly a problem, except in such difficult circumstances as affected Pune in the 1800s, (when annual series display an astonishing fluctuation). Evidence of monopolies exercised over access to the mint, of merchant participation in their control, and of a constant inability to satisfy demand, do not suggest under-utilization.

A Comparison between Different Currency Systems

The above observations concern a currency system affected by high degree of merchant participation and spontaneous organization, in which all coinage metals and specie offered to the mints would be minted. Beneath the carapace of political decentralization is an economy which for too long has been *seen* as dependent upon state intervention and political fiat, so that a great deal of its enduring features and activities remains to be researched, Europe's centralized state-run currency systems, frequently manipulated, closely monitored, stand in direct contrast. Official mints decreased in number in several European states from an early date, while coin issues were reduced to one or a small number of types. The contrast is thus between a system which, in India, acted as an admirable commercial instrument for the growing cash needs of peasants and of rural and urban manufacturers, and a system in Europe whose rigidities and vagaries (manipulation, problems stemming from official valuations, poor response to changing condition) made cash payment systems difficult to operate, possibly stimulating the general resort to putting out in Europe.

An interesting confirmation of this thesis is found in the widespread forgery characterizing eighteenth century Europe. Illegal coining activities in the monopolistic systems of Europe took the place of spontaneous mint production in India, responding in the same way to frequently severe local cash shortages, for the growing commercial economy, by production of debased and under weight gold coin, and by shoddy copper productions. A case in point is Yorkshire in the late eighteenth century, at the centre of the domestic worsted and woollen industries, and with numbers of village based mints in which merchant participation is notable. A similar spontaneity, underlying the official system, apparently characterizes the eighteenth century Netherlands and possibly Germany. The infamous black monies of the French and Catalonian peasantries are further possible examples.

The extensive use of advance payments in India implied a greater degree of participation in the monetary economy by humble producers, that would appear to have been the case in those parts of Europe where putting out occurred. However, new research has begun to show that European payment systems were much more complex than has been realized, including some forms of advance payments in cash. The difficulty is that the study of payment systems (so crucial to understanding the development of merchant capitalism, let alone that of the market for minted coin) has been neglected by Europeanists (as also by Indianists), limiting the value of the terms available to us (putting out, advances, etc.). What is more interesting is that the history of putting out seems to have been a late development in India, attempts by English and other East India Companies in the late seventeenth and eighteenth centuries being met with conspicuous failure or accompanied by ruthless, often armed violence, and becoming common only in the early nineteenth century.

It is then that the English East India Company substitutes a currency system of the European type for that of old order India. A new fully mechanized mint (a product of the Industrial Revolution, itself) was imported from England for this purpose, while the numerous currency type's and scattered mints characterizing the earlier system were quickly suppressed. A handful of old order mints continued to operate in the princely states during the nineteenth century (Satara, Indore, for example), apparently supplying gimcrack coin for humble use, thereby supplementing inadequate supplies of East India Company coin in the territories of the latter.

Mechanization in Indian and European Mints

One of the most striking contrasts between Indian and European mints is the gradual mechanization of the latter well before the Industrial Revolution. This leads to the false impression of an India characterized by a static, unresponsive mint organization, in contrast to the dynamism characterizing the European mint. It needs to be emphasized, however, that in both regions at roughly the same time, production methods adapted mere or less successfully to serious new problems, including an unprecedented acceleration in demand. Despite Spooner's claim to the contrary, it is not clear that machinery played an important role in this success in the European case. Machines were introduced gradually and unevenly into the European production line over the course of some two to three centuries. They met with little success up to the mid-seventeenth century, and their introduction remained piece-meal well into the eighteenth. Costs were too high (Spooner cites a case from mid-eighteenth century Holland) products were poor in quality (some early issues having to be reminded by hand), and the motive for introducing them seems to have had more to do with the special organization of the European mint (use of capital intensive equipment to discourage forgery, for example) than with stepping up production. At least, London and Paris were not fully mechanized until the mid-seventeenth century while hand minting continued in some regions into the eighteenth. Figures for output in these European mints compare unfavourably with hand production in India. Once again, reorganization of the production line and decline in quality seem to be major means of stepping up output in this period. Only with the Industrial Revolution was a degree and quality of mechanization provided which revolutionalized productivity, capacity rising from 30,000–50,000 for the larger hand mint, to 30,000 per day for the imported "coin mill" at Calcutta, in the 1820s.

Significantly, before colonial occupation mints established by the various European trading companies utilized hand production methods.

Conclusion

The career of the Indian mint between the seventeenth and eighteenth centuries displayed the flexibility characteristic of industries before industrialization. Premises were convertible to different uses. Production was easily adjusted upwards or downwards by increasing or reducing the numbers of the workforce or the numbers of hours worked. Technology was simple and skills the significant bottleneck factor. Fixed capital was minimal. As in pre-and early-industrial Europe, the rise of the mass market was accompanied by gimcrackery.

Under such conditions as these, the spontaneous character of coin supply is not surprising. The important qualification concerns access to supplies of raw materials (bullion and recoinable specie), and thus merchants able to supply numerous mints dispersed over wide regions on a fairly large scale. Imports into Surat, Bombay and Goa in the eighteenth century were indeed distributed to a surprisingly wide stretch of country, from Rajasthan to Malwa, and the Pune region to Karnataka and beyond.

We know little or nothing of this aspect of money supply, but the existence of monopolies can be seen at various points in the trade, thus at the point of import into Bombay, and at the point of supply to the mint. Monopoly also characterized every stage of production and trade in coinage metals in Europe during this period.

A second point concerns the market for coin. Either we find mints in the hands of those producing coin for their own commercial purposes, or lords and governments concerned with profits of seigneurage and with production of supplies necessary for the functioning of their administrative economies, or mints which in my view were pure and simple business enterprises, producing goods for sale in a market where they were in special demand. The *larin* has this commercial character and so do some of the Maratha coinages.

Superficially, the position in India seems to be in radical contrast to the government dominated, increasingly mechanized mints of Europe. But underneath the carapace of monopoly, and the rigidities resulting from close currency supervision by rulers, a similarly spontaneous, if illegal, supply of coin seems to have occurred in Europe.

Both in India and Europe, spontaneous activity satisfied a great thirst for cash for local commerce, trade and manufacture, not least, in the Indian case, for use in the advance systems characterizing manufacture and market-oriented crop production.

This hypothesis implies that we can take little for granted. We must now begin to research the nuances of *hand-technology*, itself, and especially the organization of skill and production lines, and the changes affecting them over some two or three centuries. We need to know much more about the manner in which different currencies performed varied specialized functions and about mint control. Behind these questions lie a whole set of further enigmas about the workings of the monetary, economy money use amongst ordinary people and the changing character of commercial relationships in a developing international economy.

Surat Mint Output in the seventeenth Century

		Total output per day in no. silver coins	Share of total output by VOC and English EICo	Total output per 250 day year in number. silver coins X 10^6
a	1634	5,000-9,000		1.25–2.25
b	1636	6,000-8,000	V:30,00; E:5,000	1.50–2.00
c	1640		V: 130,00-15,00	
d	1642		V: 10,000	
e	1645	22,000		5.5
f	1647	30,000		7.5
g	1672	30,000		7.5

Output of Coin in Different Indian Mints

Place	Date	Number coins per 10 hour day	Output or capacity	Number coins per 250 day year X 106
Amber (Jaipur)a	1,802/3	(5,000-20,000)	O	1.25-5.00
Bagalkotb	bl,822	20,000	C	5.00
Benares[c]	1,763	11,685	O	2.92
	1,748–76	8,000–12,000	O	2.00-300
	1,762–64	20,000	O	5.00
Indored	b 1,823	11,000	C	2.75
Chandoree	a 1,800	20,000	C	5.00
Saguif	b 1,823	6,800	O	1.70
Rajmahalg	1,676	10,000	O	2.50
Murshidabadh	1,722	48,657	O	12.16

Central India as a Regional Unit of Production

Mint	Number of coins per 10 hour day	Number of coins per 250 day year X 10^6
Indore	11,000	2.75
7 other Central Indian mints	8,000–10,000 each	2.00–2.50
Total capacity of the 8 mints	67000–81000	16.75

Some Comparisons with Hand-Technology in Europe and with Mechanized Production at Different Stages of Development

Place	Production from	Date	Number of coins per 10 hour day	Number of coins per 250 day year X 106
Durham[a]	hammer	a 1,300	6,500 (-9,200)	1.63 (-2.30)
Brugge[b]	hammer	1,468/69	13,333	3.33
Paris[c]	press	1640-2	20000–33320	5.00–8.33
Netherland	horse-drawn press	1733	26640	6.66
Calcutta[e]	factory with 5 steam engines	1824	308000	77.0

Productivity of Hand-Labour in European and Indian Mints

Mint	Date	Number of coins per striker per day	Number of coins per striker per hour
Durhama	a 300	2,200	220
Bagalkotb	b 823	20,000	2,000
Rajmahalc	1,676	10,000	1000

Index